**Karl Shaw** has worked as ~~a~~ marketing. His books include *Royal Babylon: The Alarming History of European Royalty*; *5 People Who Died During Sex: and 100 Other Terribly Tasteless Lists*; *Curing Hiccups With Small Fires: A Delightful Miscellany of Great British Eccentrics*; and *10 Ways to Recycle a Corpse*.

# THE MAMMOTH BOOK OF

# Losers

Karl Shaw

ROBINSON

ROBINSON

First published in Great Britain in 2014 by Robinson,
an imprint of Constable & Robinson Ltd

Reprinted in 2021 by Robinson

3 5 7 9 10 8 6 4 2

A CIP catalogue record for this book
is available from the British Library.

ISBN 978-1-78033-830-9

Printed and bound in Great Britain by Clays Ltd, Elcograf S.p.A.

Papers used by Robinson are from well-managed forests
and other responsible sources

Robinson
An imprint of
Little, Brown Book Group
Carmelite House
50 Victoria Embankment
London EC4Y 0DZ

An Hachette UK Company
www.hachette.co.uk

www.littlebrown.co.uk

*"If at first you don't succeed, try, try again. Then quit. No use being a damn fool about it."*

W. C. Fields

# Contents

## 2 Standing on the Shoulders of Midgets: Scientific Losers

## 3 Who Dares Loses: Business Blunders, Bankrupts and Brand Disasters

## 4 Defeat from the Jaws of Victory: Great Military Losers

## 5 From Bard to Worse: Losers in Art and Entertainment

## 6 Disorder in Court: Criminal Losers

# 7 Quacking Up: Medical Losers

# 8 Slower, Lower, Weaker: Great Sporting Losers

## 9 Close, but No Cigar: a Litany of Losers

# Introduction

In 1682, the French explorer Robert Cavalier La Salle travelled the length of the Mississippi almost entirely by foot all
the way to the Gulf of Mexico; he then returned to France a
hero, claiming the entire valley for King Louis XIV.

La Salle's discovery was a fluke he couldn't repeat. Two
years later, he sailed from France with 280 men, women and
children, plus 200 soldiers and sailors, having promised the
king that he would establish a colony that would rival the New
World riches of Spain. Only this time, when he went back to
find the Mississippi, he landed by mistake on the Texas
coast – 500 miles west of his intended destination. He and his
party tramped thousands of miles on foot looking for the river,
hopelessly lost, meanwhile dying of thirst and attacks by
marauding Indians.

La Salle eventually found his way back to his ship, then
sailed for Canada, only to get lost again, this time finding himself back in the Gulf of Mexico, then ran his ship aground on
a sandbar. He tried to find the Mississippi again on foot but,
by this time, his crew – down to 36 from the original 480 – had
had enough. They terminated La Salle's career as an explorer
with a bullet to his head, stripped him of his clothing and left
him to die where he fell, somewhere in Texas.

History may be written by the winners, but if you manage
to lose in a spectacular or consistent fashion, there's a good
chance you will be remembered, too. Without losers, we
wouldn't have winners. The conquest of Everest wouldn't have

been glorious if someone had skipped to the summit at the first attempt; it was the horribly failed expeditions that came before it that made it special. Many must seek the goal and blow it before the achievement can be called truly heroic.

When it comes down to it, we aren't even too fussed about the actual winning; the important thing is to go down fighting. So the death of Captain Scott, who lost not only the race to the South Pole but also failed to get himself and his team back alive, becomes a brave battle of the underdog against the odds. Why do it efficiently and take huskies like Roald Amundsen did when you can take ponies who will drop dead before you do? The important thing is that, in losing, Scott captured the public imagination. As Jonathan Miller's squadron leader character put it in *Beyond the Fringe*: "I want you to lay down your life, Perkins . . . we need a futile gesture at this stage. It will raise the whole tone of the war."

This book is about those who came close to the pinnacle of their chosen field without quite getting there. The very best, if you will, of the not very good. They are writers who believed in the power of words but spent their entire careers unable to find the right ones; artists and performers who indulged their creative impulse with a passion, if not a sense of the ridiculous, an eye for perspective or the ability to hold down a tune; people who set benchmarks for greatness then failed to follow up; experts who got it spectacularly wrong (take a bow, Lord Kelvin); scientists who had flashes of brilliance only to have them marooned in a vast sea of mediocrity, and others who got painfully close or were just robbed; businessmen who never quite knew when to quit while they were ahead; sportsmen who came close to winning, only for victory to be cruelly snatched away, winning the hearts of the nation along the way for trying very hard, despite being a bit crap.

In these pages, you will find some of history's most spectacularly ill-conceived endeavours and gloriously useless pursuits, tales of black comedy, insane foolhardiness, extraordinary bravery, breathtaking stupidity, dashing incompetence and relentless perseverance in the face of inevitable defeat.

These are the efforts of those who fell short of their goal, the tragically defunct whose lives ended up on the cutting-room floor, forever assigned a second-tier rating in the chronicles of human achievement. We celebrate the men and women who were made of The Wrong Stuff – we salute you for trying.

# 1

## How the West Was Lost: Misadventures in Exploration

*In which some explorers get lost; a man eats his boots and another man eats his crew; an imaginary mountain range is mapped; and a Scottish botanist is crushed to death by a falling bullock.*

### Worst Attempt to Make a Name as a Great Explorer

Timbuktu. For the early nineteenth-century explorer, there was no greater prize. Its location was the most tantalizing geographical riddle of the era. According to legend, the fabled 'lost city', hidden somewhere in Africa's vast uncharted interior, was the seat of great power and learning, home to fabulous palaces and great libraries on which even the roof tiles were made of gold.

Getting there would take a brutal 2,000-mile journey through some of the most hostile territory on Earth. Many had tried and failed. Whoever got there first was guaranteed international fame and a place among history's greatest explorers; at least, so everyone thought. In the event, the man who achieved it was a Scot whose name almost nobody remembers.

Europeans had been vaguely aware of the existence of Timbuktu for hundreds of years but no white man had actually set eyes on it since the Middle Ages. In 1809, an English merchant with a very vivid imagination called James Jackson published a book titled *An Accurate and Interesting Account of Timbuktu, the Great Emporium of Central Africa*. It made extraordinary claims, not only of great wealth but described a city crawling with beautiful, available women. He wrote:

> *The climate of Timbuktu is much extolled as being salutary and extremely invigorating, insomuch that it is impossible for the sexes to exist without intermarriage . . . accordingly it is said that there is no man of the age of eighteen who has not his wives or concubines . . . it is even a disgrace for a man who has reached the age of puberty to be unmarried!*

As it turns out, Jackson's account was so far from the truth that he was possibly suffering from sunstroke when he wrote it, but no one seems to have questioned it at the time and his book became a bestseller, reprinted ten times. Timbuktu was now the dream destination of every red-blooded adventurer.

The great Venetian Egyptologist Giovanni Belzoni was among the first to have a go at finding it, setting off for the African interior from Benin in 1823 in typically flamboyant fashion: "God bless you, my fine fellows, and send you a happy sight of your country and friends!" Having covered only ten miles, Belzoni died of dysentery.

In 1824, the French Geographical Society raised the stakes by offering a generous prize of 10,000 francs for the first person to bring back information about Timbuktu. The race was now on in earnest. The British, of course, were determined to get their man there first. In fact, she had long had her eye on Timbuktu, ever since 1788 when the Association for Promoting the Discovery of the Interior Parts of Africa was founded in London. The African Association, as it was more commonly known, comprised a dozen titled gentlemen from London's upper crust led by the famous botanist and explorer Sir Joseph Banks. Ostensibly, their sole aim was to advance scientific knowledge about the "dark continent". It was a great failing of the so-called Age of Enlightenment, Banks grumbled, that Europeans had sailed all around the world but knew next to nothing about the interior of Africa. And if they just happened to find some gold along the way, all well and good.

Each of the members of the African Association pitched in with five guineas a year to recruit and fund expeditions to Africa. The first explorer they selected to lead an expedition to Timbuktu was an American – John Ledyard. He must have given a good interview because he had never been to Africa and didn't know a single word of Arabic, but his lack of qualifications for this particular trip was apparently outweighed by his "adventurous nature . . . the manliness of his person, the breadth of his chest, the inquietude of his eye". They might have had second thoughts after the Association's Secretary Henry Beauvoir gave Ledyard the good news and asked when he might be ready to travel. Ledyard, showing admirable spirit, if not a complete grasp of what he was getting himself into, replied, "Tomorrow morning". Beauvoir patiently informed him that a little more time would be needed to write up his itinerary.

Ledyard left England on 30 June 1788. Six weeks later, he arrived in Cairo, which is the nearest he ever got to Timbuktu. The African Association was dismayed to learn that, while attempting to self-medicate for a "bilious complaint", Ledyard had died vomiting blood after inadvertently swallowing a fatal overdose of sulphuric acid.

The next to go, an Irishman called Daniel Houghton, got off to a decent start, reaching The Gambia in 1791. There, a fire destroyed most of his supplies and a servant ran off with most of what was left. Then he had a spot of better luck when he was assured by a guide that Timbuktu was just down the road; a man could safely walk there with a stick. Five hundred miles short of his target, Houghton's stick and everything else he had were stolen by bandits, who also beat him up and left him to die.

The legendary Scot Mungo Park tried twice. On his first attempt in 1795, he was robbed, imprisoned and tortured, then gave up and returned home. On this occasion, he set had off with just two companions and returned alone. On his second attempt in 1803, he set off with 46 men to find Timbuktu; not one of them survived. Park himself was drowned.

In 1817, Britain had another go with an expedition led by a 29-year-old Joseph Ritchie, of whom very little is known except that he was a surgeon and a friend of the poet John Keats[1]. More importantly, he had time on his hands and connections in the Colonial Office, under whose auspices these expeditions now fell (the Government had decided that African exploration was too important to leave to the likes of Joseph Banks, who by now was old and quite ill).

Ritchie was either too timid or too stupid to point out that the £2,000 allocated to him to fund the entire expedition was pitifully inadequate. It didn't help either that he had blown all but £75 of the money before he even got to Africa, mostly on useless items. Richie did, however, take the trouble to have himself circumcised, just in case he needed to pass himself off under close inspection as an Arab.

With nothing left to trade with the locals for food apart from firearms and horses, the loss of either of which would have been suicidal, Richie's party went without food for several weeks. Ritchie, so emaciated he could barely walk, looked in the mirror and noticed that his tongue had turned black, but put it down to the fact that he had been drinking black coffee. He was dead within the week.

His starving companions opened a stack of boxes marked "DO NOT OPEN UNTIL TIMBUKTU", hoping to find something useful to sell and found two large chests full of arsenic, one camel-load of corks for pinning insects, two loads of brown paper, hundreds of books and 600 lbs of lead. No one has yet quite figured out what the last item was for.

In 1824, Britain decided to try again. This time it fell to the Secretary of State for Colonial Affairs, Lord Henry Bathurst,

---

1  Keats gave Ritchie a copy of his newly published poem "Endymion", with instructions to place it in his travel pack, read it on his journey and then "throw it into the heart of the Sahara Desert . . . as a gesture of high romance". Keats received a letter from Ritchie in December 1818: "'Endymion' has arrived thus far on his way to the Desert and when you are sitting over your Christmas fire will be jogging (in all probability) on a camel's back o'er those African Sands immeasurable." After that, there was no word.

to find the right man for the job. Bathurst had cultivated some rather odd ideas about how to get to Timbuktu. Nobody actually knew exactly where it was, but the obvious, shortest, most direct and therefore most sensible route into the African interior was to approach it from the west African coast, from where Timbuktu was thought to lie about 500 miles inland.

Bathurst, however, thought you should start from the north. To do that, you had to cross the Sahara, a total distance of about 3,000 miles across some of the most savage terrain in the world. His plan was simple: you would sail to the North African port of Tripoli, hire some camels, then head south across the Sahara, hopping from oasis to oasis, until you got to Timbuktu. He made it sound as easy as a weekend hike for a Duke of Edinburgh's Award.

Experience suggested otherwise. Africa in general and the road to Timbuktu in particular had already established itself as a graveyard for young explorers. The Sahara was one of the most dangerous places on the planet. So you would think that someone would have to be mad, figuratively speaking, to volunteer. Fortunately, Bathurst found someone who was – figuratively and literally.

Alexander Gordon Laing was the son of a Scottish schoolteacher. He joined the Army and was posted to the West Indies, but was forced to return home because of problems with his liver. By 1822, he was serving in the Royal African Colonial Corps in Sierra Leone; he had just turned thirty, and was tall, slim and handsome with wavy hair and luxuriant mutton-chop sideburns. He made a bit of a name for himself in Africa, but not for the right reasons. His fellow officers found him smug and insufferably arrogant. He fancied himself as a poet and had a stint as editor of the local English newspaper, whose pages he liked to fill with doggerel, mostly about himself. As for Laing's army record, his commanding officer wrote, "His military exploits are even worse than his poetry."

Laing, however, was very full of himself and driven by ambition to make his name in Africa, no matter what. He had read adventure tales as a boy and was determined, he later wrote, "to signalize myself by some important discovery". Like most would-be African explorers, he also had his own theory about that other Holy Grail of nineteenth-century exploration, the River Niger, which he had recently published and sent to the Colonial Office.

When Laing found out that Britain wanted to beat the French to Timbuktu, he quickly offered his services. This was his ticket to glory. Not that Laing was particularly well qualified to lead an expedition to Africa or anywhere else. To start with, his general health was described as "delicate". His grasp of African geography was also very hazy and he was quite sure that the Niger flowed into the Gulf of Benin – which it definitely didn't. But Laing was not short of self-confidence and he impressed Bathurst with "his command of the facts, the acuity of his intellect, his courage, and his poise". More to the point, he was also extraordinarily cheap. He offered to find Timbuktu without taking any salary at all from the Colonial Office and with a proposed outlay of only £640 10s. for expedition set-up costs and annual expenses of £173 7s. 6d. His proposal was accepted on the nail.

Laing, who was quite annoyed by the fact that his big idea regarding the course of the Niger had been dismissed as nonsense by the Colonial Office, was now extremely full of himself. He bragged that if he didn't find Timbuktu, no one ever would: "The world will forever remain in ignorance of the place, as I make no vainglorious assertion when I say that it will never be visited by Christian man after me." And he wasn't just going to stop there. After locating Timbuktu, he was going to press on and solve the puzzle of the Niger. "I am so wrapt in the success of this enterprise," he wrote, "that I think of nothing else all day and dream of nothing else all night."

In April 1825, Laing set off for Africa on his cut-price expedition via Malta, where he promptly fell ill again and was bedridden for a month. Eventually, he found his way to Tripoli, where his arrival was awaited by the British Consul Hanmer Warrington, whose job it was to expedite Laing's trip to the African interior. The aristocratic, hard-drinking Warrington was a big man with a forceful personality to match. He had held the position of Consul for eleven years and, during that time, he had seen many young men set off to try to unlock the mysteries of Africa's interior. Most of them never came back.

His initial impression of Laing was favourable; he was, Warrington reported to Bathurst, a "well set-up man ... highly gifted in many ways". When he got to know Laing a little better, he became sceptical, to say the least, about the young Scot's chances of success. To begin with, Laing was obviously still not fully recovered from his recent illness. "The state of his health," Warrington warned the Colonial Office, "will not carry him though his arduous task." When he heard about the ludicrously small budget with which Laing proposed to fund the expedition, he concluded that he must be stark raving mad.

The relationship took an unexpected turn for the worse when Laing promptly fell in love with the second of Warrington's three daughters, Emma. Within a matter of weeks, Laing was down on one knee with a proposal of marriage. Warrington, who was not keen to have a madman as a son-in-law, far less one who was about to set off on a suicide mission, was horrified, especially when the couple announced their intention to tie the knot straight away. He was even more horrified when it dawned on him that, as British Consul, he was the only senior representative of the Church of England in Tripoli and would be expected to perform the marriage service himself.

Warrington did everything he could to put them off and only relented when his daughter tried to kill herself by poisoning. After some furtive and increasingly frenzied correspondence with London while he searched for a loophole, Warrington reluctantly agreed to officiate, on one condition – Laing had to sign an agreement that the marriage would not be consummated until it had been blessed by an Anglican priest. In other words, not until (and if) the groom had successfully returned from his highly dangerous mission. Laing agreed to his terms and, on 14 July 1825, the couple were married.

His mission was now driven by a new, even more manic impetus – frustrated desire for his new virgin (as far as we know) bride Emma. "I shall do more than has ever been done before," he wrote, "and shall show myself to be what I have ever considered myself, a man of enterprise and genius."

Four days after his wedding, Laing set off into the Sahara on his death-or-glory mission with a few camels and a handful of assistants, including a black servant called Jack, two African ship's carpenters (Laing assumed they would come in handy when they reached the Niger) and a couple of camel drivers. Later, they teamed up with a guide called Babani who promised to get them to Timbuktu in ten weeks provided they paid him 4,000 Spanish dollars. Lord Bathurst was horrified when he received the bill, which, at a stroke, had increased the cost of the expedition four-fold.

Laing kept a journal over the coming months, or at least he claimed he did, because as none of the contents were ever divulged, we will never know for sure. More or less everything we know about his expedition is based on a series of letters Laing wrote back to Tripoli. Unfortunately, these revealed much more about his gradually unravelling mental state than they do about the African countryside. Amid the odd poem about himself and the occasional sketch, they were mostly highly emotional, paranoid and disparaging rants about the efforts of rival African explorers, especially Hugh Clapperton, whom Laing clearly despised, although the two men had never actually met.

The Colonial Office, having decided that the discovery of Timbuktu was important enough to risk the lives of one expedition, had now decided that it was worth risking the lives of two. Just before leaving Tripoli, Laing received the unwelcome news that Clapperton had set sail from England with ambitions to reach Timbuktu. To make up lost time, he planned to approach with a shorter, more sensible route from the west African coast. Clapperton, who considered himself with some justification to be the most experienced African explorer of the day, was equally offended to hear that the unknown Laing had been engaged to reach Timbuktu.

Unaware of the resentment they were creating in both camps, the Colonial Office appraised each of the other's progress and, in the spirit of co-operation, asked them to share notes. Clapperton reluctantly went along with the request, possibly just to needle Laing. It did the trick. When Warrington forwarded some advice from his rival, Laing was livid. There were some random and patronizing tips, such as "adopt native costume at all times" and "do not meddle with the females of the country". Laing replied, "I care little for any information that Clapperton could communicate . . . I smile at the idea of his reaching Timbuktu before me."

On the subject of clothing, he revealed that, unlike Clapperton, he had adopted "plain Turkish dress" – except on Sundays when he wore his full military uniform. In all his letters to Warrington, Laing's hatred for Clapperton was never very far from the surface; he was now locked in a bitter personal competition. From now on, getting to Timbuktu first at any cost was more than just a prize for the young Scot: it had become a dangerous obsession.

Laing regularly wrote back to Tripoli begging his father-in-law to send him a miniature portrait of Emma. Without it, he told Warrington a trifle belatedly, "I might go mad". When the miniature finally arrived, Laing was shocked to find that the portrait was not flattering to his beloved; Emma appeared suspiciously pale and wan-looking. Was it just a poor portrait? Or was Emma seriously ill? Half out of his mind with worry, he decided to throw in the towel and dashed off another letter to Warrington informing him that he was returning to Tripoli immediately. Warrington, fearful for his son-in-law's sanity and even more fearful of his early return, tried to reassure him that all was well with Emma and that Laing should press on to Timbuktu.

In the end, Laing was persuaded to continue, not because of any reassurances from Warrington, but by the appearance of a large comet in the sky. "I regard it as a happy omen," he wrote. "It beckons me on and binds me to the termination of the Niger and to Timbuktu." Laing was also cheered by news

that the mission of his arch-rival Clapperton might be close
to failure.

Laing and his small band of followers moved steadily south,
braving midday temperatures of 49°C, suffering "privations
and exposure to a degree of heat which I am inclined to believe
few Europeans' constitutions could stand". He also mentioned
in passing that at one stage he had gone without food for a
whole week.

Five months after leaving Tripoli, they reached the oasis
town of Salah in present-day Algeria. From there, it was a
straight run to Timbuktu across a desert "as flat as a bowling green". The route, however, was notoriously dangerous.
The area was ruled by violent, predatory Tuareg tribesmen
who demanded payment from travellers to secure a safe
passage. Only a madman, local Arab traders told Laing,
would try travel to Timbuktu without paying off the
Tuaregs; better still, they advised, don't try to cross the
desert at all. Laing ignored them; he knew better and didn't
care much for taking advice from foreigners.[2] He had also
overlooked the fact the only other Scot to have passed that
way, Mungo Park, had an unfortunate reputation for shooting any African he thought looked even slightly menacing,
so the presence of one more Scot in the Sahara might not
be very welcome. As for this business of bribing the Tuaregs, Laing would hear none of it.

In January 1826, he and his travelling companions set off
for Timbuktu. Several days later, they were savagely attacked
by Tuaregs who stole all of their possessions and left the expedition leader for dead. Apart from Laing, all that remained was
a wounded camel driver and a couple of camels. The two men
resumed their journey with Laing strapped to the back of one
camel while the injured driver led the way on the other.

We can get an idea of the full horror of what he was going
through from a letter he sent to his father-in-law. Writing with

---

2  Especially Africans. In his memoir, Laing describes them as "depraved,
indolent, avaricious, and so deeply sunk in the debasement of the slave traffic".

great difficulty with the thumb and middle finger of his left hand, Laing recorded his injuries:

> *To begin from the top, I have five sabre cuts on the crown of the head and three on the left temple, all fractures from which much bone has come away; one on my left cheek which fractured the jaw bone and had divided the ear, forming a very unsightly wound; one over the right temple and a dreadful gash on the back of the neck, which slightly grazed the windpipe; a musket ball in the hip, which made its way though my back, slightly grazing the backbone; five sabre cuts on my right arm and hand, three of the fingers broken, the hand cut three-fourths across, and the wrist bones cut through; three cuts on the left arm, the bone of which has been broken but is again uniting; one slight wound on the right leg and two with one dreadful gash on the left, to say nothing of a cut across the fingers of my left hand, now healed up.*

Almost as an afterthought at the end of the letter, Laing mentions that he had caught the plague and was so ill "that it was presumed, expected and hoped that I would die".

Having travelled hundreds of miles of unmapped, hostile desert, with horrific multiple injuries, Laing reached his goal and entered the fabled city of Timbuktu on 13 August 1826. The journey across the Sahara, which Laing had estimated would take a few weeks at most, had in fact taken thirteen months.

His triumphant entry into Timbuktu must have been a disappointment, to put it mildly. Even from a distance it was quite obvious, even to someone as delusional as Laing, that this was not the shining metropolis abounding in wealth and architectural wonders that he and all Europe had imagined. Timbuktu had seen better days, but not since the time of William Shakespeare. Once a bustling centre of commerce and culture, centuries of warfare and decay had reduced it to a dusty relic of its previous self, a bleak, run-down frontier town made of mud brick.

He searched everywhere for the glittering palaces and nubile lovelies he had heard of, but found only stinking hovels full of unwashed people and sick animals. Weirdly, Laing wrote home that "the great capital of central Africa . . . has completely met my expectations". Perhaps he was trying to drum up interest for the publication of his journal; or, just as likely, he was by now completely unhinged.

If reports are to be believed, his behaviour over the next five weeks was extremely odd. He rented a small mud hut on the edge of town, from which he occasionally emerged to strut through the streets in full dress uniform, announcing himself to everyone he met as the King of England's emissary, or by night he rode out on a horse to investigate the surrounding area.[3]

Laing was planning to stay in Timbuktu for about six months, but it soon became evident that he was not wanted. Word had reached the local Sultan of Bello that a strange interloper was wandering around the town; it's not surprising, then, that the Sultan wanted him out. So five weeks after his arrival, fearing for his safety, Laing wrote a final letter home announcing that he was leaving Timbuktu "to return to England with much important geographical information".

The two golden rules of exploration were: (1) discover something worth discovering; and (2) get out alive and find a publisher. Having broken the first rule, Laing was about to break the second.

In his final letter, he recorded his intention to set off southbound towards Sierra Leone. On 22 September 1826, Laing did exactly the opposite and headed north. Three days later, he was set upon and killed by Tuaregs. They throttled him with his own turban, then cut his head off and left him for the vultures. An eye-witness, a servant who survived by feigning death, brought news of the murder to Tripoli in August 1828. Laing was thirty-three.

---

3  The mud hut still stands today. On the wall above the door is a plaque to his memory and, outside, a sign announces that this is "Mission Culturelle, Site No. 2. Gordon Laing".

The missing pieces of Laing's misadventure were eventually put in place by an incredibly brave Frenchman called René Caillée. In 1828, without any government support or financial backing, Caillée walked unassisted into Timbuktu disguised as a Muslim. Compared to Laing's experience, Caillée's journey had been relatively dull, apart from several weeks of illness and a bad fall from a camel. He encountered danger just once when he was forced to hide from the Tuareg under a pile of carpets.

Caillée was able to confirm the few facts about Timbuktu reported back to Tripoli by Laing, visited the mud hut where he had lived, was shown a compass said to have belonged to him, and discovered that Laing's body was buried under a tree to the north of the town. There was, however, no sign of the much-vaunted journal.

Unlike Laing, Caillée lived to tell his tale and returned home to a hero's welcome, publishing the story of his epic trip to Timbuktu two years later. Predictably, the French took great satisfaction in rubbing Britain's nose in it, declaring Caillée the first European to reach Timbuktu – "that which England has not been able to accomplish with the aid of a whole group of travellers and at an expense of more than twenty millions (of francs), a Frenchman has done with his scanty personal resources alone and without putting his country to any expense".

The British Colonial Office retaliated by claiming that Caillée's trip was a hoax and that he had fabricated the whole story from Laing's journal, which had somehow found its way into French hands. In fact, it is just possible that the journal never existed in the first place and had all been a figment of Laing's imagination.

The news of her husband's grisly demise broke Emma Laing's heart and destroyed her health. She remarried and went to live in Italy but appears to have lived out the rest of her brief life in a state of bottomless depression. Just over four years to the day after kissing him goodbye and watching him ride off into the African desert, she died of tuberculosis in October 1829, aged twenty-eight.

## Shortest Space Programme

The first manned rocket flight was attempted in AD 1500 by a Chinese government official called Wan Hu. He built a wheel-chair and attached to the base forty-seven rockets filled with a combustible mixture of charcoal, saltpetre and sulphur. Seated in his wicker chair, grasping a large kite in each hand to keep him airborne, he braced himself and signalled to his assistants to ignite the rockets beneath him. The fuses blazed and the gunpowder ignited in a mighty explosion.

Wan Hu's assistants looked skyward for signs of their master, but in vain. When the billowing clouds of smoke cleared, there was nothing left – no chair, no kites, no Wan Hu. The experiment was presumed a great success. There were, however, no attempts to repeat it.

---

*"Heavier-than-air flying machines are impossible."*
Lord Kelvin, British mathematician and physicist,
president of the British Royal Society, 1895

---

## Least Successful Bonding Exercise

Exploration, it almost goes without saying, is dangerous work. If the pack ice, or the gale-force winds, or brain-boiling heat, or starvation didn't get you, then bandits, or frostbite, or scurvy, or malaria, or dysentery, or some other despicable disease almost certainly could. And yet if you study the historical records, more often than not, the expedition party itself is largely to blame for its own failures. One of the most difficult challenges of expeditionary life was not weathering the elements, it was enduring one's colleagues.

One of the great obsessions of the Victorian era was the search for the River Niger in Africa. The course of the Niger was presumably known to locals, but it was a complete mystery to the outside world. Where did it go? Speculation was rife. Some thought that it flowed west to Gambia or Senegal;

others insisted that the Niger disappeared into a huge swamp called Wangara. There were those who believed it joined the Nile, or that it flowed into the Congo. Another theory had it that it flowed nowhere at all and simply evaporated under the blazing Saharan sun. Dozens of explorers had died trying to find the answer to this, the burning geographic question of the age.

In 1822, Britain had another crack at trying to solve the mystery of the Niger. The task of assembling a team to achieve this fell to Sir John Barrow, second secretary of the British Admiralty. Barrow had the bright idea of using British officers who'd been decommissioned after the defeat of Napoleon. Of course, if you are putting together a team of men that might have to spend months, even years, together, it is really important to get the chemistry right. Two of the three men chosen for the expedition were Scots: Walter Oudney, a naval surgeon from Edinburgh; and the huge, red-bearded, quick-tempered Lieutenant Hugh Clapperton. The third member of their party was an arrogant English army officer called Major Dixon Denham, described by one historian as "the most odious man in the history of exploration". His rude and aggressive behaviour and sense of superiority made him immediately disliked by the Scots. It was a disastrous mix, resulting in a terrible clash of personalities and the most acrimonious and badly planned expedition in the history of African exploration.

The mission was fatally undermined before they even set off by a misunderstanding over who should actually lead the expedition. The two Scots assumed that Oudney was the leader. Denham thought he was the commanding officer because he outranked them both. To add to the confusion, there was no agreement over where they should even be looking. Oudney and Clapperton were under instructions to find Lake Chad, which had been mentioned in an earlier expedition as a possible outlet, while Denham was ordered to look for the Niger to the south.

There was even a huge row over what they should wear on the expedition. The Scots argued that they should "go native" and wear turbans and robes so they would blend in; the Englishman insisted that in the interests of national pride they should wear full dress uniforms to remind the Africans how important Britain was.

The prolonged argument over where they were going and what they should be wearing meant that they set off months later than planned. Meanwhile, the long enforced stay in an unhealthy border town made them ill with fever before they had even started their journey. Eventually, Denham had his own way over the dress code and, in March 1822, they set off across the blazing Sahara in blue frock coats, white waistcoats, breeches and silk stockings. In the event, their choice of clothing actually saved Denham's life; at one point, he was captured by marauding tribesmen who stripped him and started squabbling over his clothes. While his captors were arguing over their catch, he was able to slip away, naked, and dodging snakes and scrambling through thickets was able to scramble, muddied and bleeding, back to camp.

Large portions of their expedition are lost to posterity because, according to their published journal, it was "wholly uninteresting, and is therefore omitted". One of the more illuminating entries in Denham's journal recorded, "Desert as yesterday, high sandhills". The most remarkable thing about their journey across the Sahara was that all the way to Lake Chad, despite braving treacherous sandstorms, bouts of malaria, travelling for days without water, while members of their party dropped dead around them – even the flies and camels were dying from exhaustion – the three men never once stopped squabbling. Clapperton and Oudney were goaded by Denham's habit of constantly giving orders; meanwhile Denham was irritated by Clapperton's mistreatment of his bearers including regular threats to shoot them.

Relations between the three men hit a new low when Denham accused Clapperton of having sex with his native bearers. Casual sex with natives during expeditions into Africa was not unheard of; Denham himself was not averse to the charms of African ladies and it was even alleged the great

David Livingstone fathered a child by an African woman. But these natives were men. Clapperton angrily denied the charge and Oudney backed him up, but from that point onwards even the faintest hope of unity in the camp was abandoned.

As they heartily detested each other, the three men decided that the best way forward was to split into two separate expeditions, Denham going south-east and Clapperton and Oudney going west. Clapperton's journey took him to Sokoto, where he met the local ruler Sultan Bello. When he asked for directions to the mouth of the Niger, the Sultan was only too happy to oblige. Clapperton couldn't believe his luck. It was only much later that he learned that the Sultan had deliberately sent him the wrong way because he feared that the British would steal their country from them if they knew the truth about the course of the river.

In January 1824, Oudney died from tuberculosis aggravated by intermittent bouts of fever. Denham and Clapperton, now reunited, stopped arguing just long enough to agree that it was time to go home. This was only a signal, however, to start another row over which route to take. In the end, they decided to return they the way they had come, and so they bickered and squabbled all the way back to London.

Although they had completely failed to achieve what they set out to do, their return to England on 1 June 1825 caused a sensation and was a day of great national rejoicing.[4] Bizarrely, one newspaper likened the journey to Marco Polo's trip to China.

A couple of years later, during another attempt at finding the mouth of the Niger, Clapperton died from a combination of malaria and a fierce bout of dysentery. In 1826, the only surviving member of the original party, Dixon Denham,

---

4 They returned with a menagerie of animals given to them as presents for King George IV, including a horse, a sheep, a mongoose, four ostriches, three parrots, a monkey, a shark and three slugs. A home was found for the parrots and the monkey but the fate of the others, including the slugs, is not known. According to the records, there was some concern over the fate of the sheep that had become "so much attached to the horse that their separation might be fatal".

published his recollection of the expedition. He took credit for everything and left out almost all mention of his travelling companions.

## Least Successful Hunting Party

The Frenchman Francis Barrallier was a jack of all trades. He was an officer serving in the British Army in Australia's New South Wales Corps, an engineer, surveyor and graphic artist. He was also a significant figure in the history of Australian exploration; he made the first sightings of the koala bear, was the first European to describe the use of the native boomerang, and recorded numerous general observations about botany, geology and the Aborigine people, including their method of hunting kangaroo. His own skills as a kangaroo hunter, however, fell short.

In 1802, Barrallier was sent by the governor of New South Wales to use his surveying skills to lead a detachment of soldiers to try to find a way over the Blue Mountains. Harassed by unfriendly Aborigines and desperately short of supplies, Barrallier's party covered just 130 miles in seven weeks, an average of just one-and-a-half miles a day. Half starved, they stalked kangaroos in vain for several days, before realizing that they might have more success if they first removed their bright red army coats.

*"Airplanes are interesting toys but of no military value."*
Marechal Ferdinand Foch, Professor of Strategy,
Ecole Supérieure de Guerre, 1904

## Least Successful Attempt to Cross Australia

Burke and Wills – in Australian folklore, one name is rarely mentioned without the other. Together, they participated in one of the most miserable failures in the history of exploration.

After 100 years of European settlement, by the mid-nineteenth century the interior of Australia was still a mystery to all but the indigenous Aborigines. The challenge of mapping it had defeated the country's best explorers;[5] fame and fortune awaited the first man who did.

In the 1850s, there was a race to to lay a new Overland Telegraph Line to connect the south coast of the Australian continent via the centre to Darwin in the north. There was fierce competition between colonies because the economic benefits of being at the centre of the Australian telegraph network were huge. In 1860, the Australian Government put up a reward of £2,000 to anyone who succeeded in crossing the continent from south to north, thereby determining a route for the proposed new telegraph line. South Australia and the newly founded state of Victoria each proposed an expedition to try to win the prize. It would be a straight race to the northern coast of Queensland and back, a return journey of about 4,000 miles.

South Australia was ably represented by John McDouall Stuart. He was one of his country's greatest and most successful explorers having already led four expeditions into some of the most hostile territory in the world without loss of one human life. Victoria, with the prestige of its newly founded colony at stake, decided to go with a group of men who hadn't spent a day in the outback between them. Their expedition

---

5  Convinced that he would encounter mighty river systems or even an inland sea, the Scot Thomas Mitchell explored vast tracts of central Australia, dragging two wooden boats over 3,000 miles of arid scrub. Although they never once got wet, he refused to give up on them. He wrote after his third trip with slight understatement: "The boats and their carriage had been of late a great hindrance to us," but added, "I was very unwilling to abandon such useful appendages to an exploring party."

team was put together by a group of armchair experts who called themselves the Exploration Committee of the Royal Society of Victoria. Most of the committee members had never even seen the outback. There were just two members – Ferdinand von Mueller and Wilhelm Blandowski – with any actual experience in exploration, but they were constantly outvoted by the others.

The man they chose by secret ballot to lead the expedition was a forty-year-old Irish career soldier and ex-police officer, Robert O'Hara Burke. He certainly looked the part – a huge, burly man with a wild, bushy beard, a mysterious scar on one cheek and an air of authority. But Burke had no sense of direction, let alone any experience of bushcraft. He regularly got lost on his way home from the pub.

He prepared for his epic journey by lying for hours in a bathtub in his backyard in a pith helmet. Burke was also notoriously wayward in his private life and had racked up a mountain of gambling debts and was prone to terrible rages and impulsive, reckless decision-making.

There was another curious dimension to his leadership – he wasn't motivated by the prize money. He certainly wasn't motivated by the fundamental explorer's trait: curiosity. He simply wanted to impress a young actress named Julia Mathews, a star of the Melbourne stage with whom he had recently become infatuated.

Burke's second-in-command, George Landells, was hired because of his expertise with camels, several of which he had personally imported from India. The committee thought that camels were the ideal beasts of burden for the arid expanses of the Australian hinterland. Landells was accompanied by a young soldier from India, John King, as chief camel-tender, plus four Indian sepoys. Their third-in-command was a young surveyor from Devon – William John Wills. In total, the nineteen-man expedition comprised six Irishmen, five Englishmen, four Indians, three Germans and an American, plus twenty-three horses, six wagons and twenty-six camels.

On 20 August 1860, a crowd of 15,000 turned out in Melbourne's Royal Park to wave them off. Burke promised, "I will cross Australia or perish in the attempt," then wearing his top hat, he mounted his horse Billy and, to the applause of the crowd and the sound of the band playing "Cheer, Boys, Cheer", he set off at the head of a 500-yard-long cavalcade of men and camels carrying twenty tons of supplies and equipment, including a cedar-topped dining table and two chairs, a Chinese gong, twelve dandruff brushes for camels, four enema kits and sixty gallons of rum.

From the outset, progress was painfully slow. The expedition was half a kilometre long and buckling under its own weight, partly due to the committee's insistence on hauling several wagonloads of dried beef instead of travelling with livestock to slaughter along the way. One of the wagons broke before it even left Royal Park. Torrential rain also made their equipment sodden and heavy, but Burke chose to make the journey even more difficult by ignoring the established tracks and travelling cross-country. Meanwhile, Landell's camels got drunk on the rum, given to them in the mistaken belief that it would prevent the animals from getting scurvy.

While Burke rode imperiously at the head of the column, his disgruntled men were left to drag intoxicated camels through slippery mud, or dig out the horses and wagons when they became stuck in sand. They were also less than impressed when, at the end of the first day of travelling, Burke galloped all the way back to Julia Matthews in Melbourne and begged her to marry him. He never did get an answer.

By the time the expedition reached Menindie, the last white settlement on the edge of the Australian desert, the expedition had already taken 56 days to cover 466 miles – the mail coach did the same journey in ten days. To speed things up, Burke decided to lighten the load by dumping some of the supplies, including the lime juice, which they needed to prevent scurvy, and the guns and ammunition. The scientists in the group, to their great annoyance, were ordered to dump most of their equipment and to pitch in and do the same manual work as everyone else.

All the while, Burke was stamping the expedition with his own peculiar style of leadership, sacking and demoting people right, left and centre. Landells had decided by this time that Burke was mad and told him as much. Burke challenged him to a duel. Landells refused and quit, leaving the surveyor, William Wills, as deputy leader. The camel handling went to the small, shy John King. One by one, the men, despairing of Burke's chaotic leadership, deserted and went back to Melbourne. By this time, only two of Burke's original officers remained; fifteen men had been dismissed and another eight hired.

The party was only making about two miles a day, so Burke decided to speed up their progress by splitting the group. One party was sent back to pick up more supplies. Meanwhile, Burke took the strongest horses and seven of the fittest men plus a small amount of equipment, intending to push on quickly to a series of waterholes known as Cooper's Creek, about halfway to the north coast, and then wait for the others to catch up.

In November 1860, Burke and his party reached Cooper's Creek, beyond which no European had ever been before. The most difficult part of their journey lay ahead and they were approaching mid-summer. The sensible thing to do would be to wait for cooler weather, but Burke was impatient to press on. He decided to split the group again and make a dash for the coast. Half the group were told to stay put at Cooper's Creek for three months and wait for the supplies to arrive. On 16 December, Burke, Wills, King and Charles Gray set off for the north coast with six camels, one horse and enough food for just three months.

Burke had fatally underestimated how long the dash to the north coast and back would take. He was counting on covering the 1,900-mile journey in ninety days, but the four men would be walking up to forty miles a day at the height of the Australian summer in temperatures of 50°C. There was another unexpected obstacle – a mountain range. Rather than go around it, Burke decided to take the shortest route straight over the top, forcing the terrified animals to climb up steep slopes and skirt sheer ravines while their feet were badly ripped by the rocks. By the time they made it through, the camels were in a pitiful state.

They were now halfway through their ninety-day journey time, but were still 125 miles away from the north coast. It was clear that if they continued they would not have enough food or water get them back to Cooper's Creek. For Burke, the choice between saving his men's lives and winning the love of Miss Matthews was straightforward – he pressed on. Leaving King, Gray and the injured camels near a creek, Burke and Wills made a final push for the coast. After two months travelling with barely a rest day, they found themselves bogged down in a massive mangrove swamp. Unable to hack their way through the dense undergrowth, they gave up, exhausted, and decided to head back to their colleagues. They were only twelve miles from the coast.

Emaciated, starving and too weak to catch anything to eat, Burke, King, Gray and Wills stumbled back towards Cooper's Creek. They had used up nearly three-quarters of their rations, so each man's share of food and tea was halved. One by one, their beasts of burden, including Burke's horse Billy, were shot and eaten. Gray, who was suffering from dysentery and actually dying of starvation, was caught pilfering an extra ration of porridge. Burke thought Gray was faking illness and gave him a beating. After that, Gray could no longer walk and had to be strapped to a camel. Burke still thought that he was acting. Nine days later, Gray was dead.

On 21 April 1861, Burke, Wills and King staggered into Cooper's Creek camp, expecting to find the support team waiting for them with fresh supplies. It was deserted. The word "DIG" had been carved on a coolibah tree. Underneath the tree, they unearthed a food box with a note that confirmed their worst fears; the support team had left only a few hours earlier, giving them up for dead. Wills wrote in his diary: "Our disappointment at finding the depot deserted may easily be imagined – returning in an exhausted state after four months of the severest travelling and privation, with our legs so paralyzed so that each found it a most trying task to walk just a few yards."

After just a couple of days' rest, Burke made another rash decision. Instead of waiting for the other party to reach the water hole, they would head off south – not back to Minnie by the way they came, but they would go through uncharted desert.

Critically, Burke didn't leave any sign that he and his party had reached the waterhole. As a result, when the original support team finally arrived some days later, ubable to find any evidence that Burke had been there, they went home.

Meanwhile, Burke, Wills and King lay dying only a few miles away, further down Cooper's Creek. They had a stroke of luck when some Aborigines found them and took pity, offering food and water, but when they asked for something in return for their hospitality, Burke fired his gun at them. The Aborigines left them to their fate.

Wills was the first to die, then Burke; King would have died as well had the Aborigines not returned and offered help. King was eventually found by a relief expedition on 15 September 1861. When he was sufficiently recovered, he led his rescuers to Burke's bleached bones, his hand still clutching his pistol.

Seven men had died in the attempt to cross the continent of Australia from Melbourne to the north coast and only one of the four men who failed to reach the north coast, John King, lived to tell the tale. Along the way, they were beset by terrible organization, infighting and disastrous preparation. None of this prevented the Government from proclaiming Burke and Wills national heroes. Their remains were given Australia's first ever State funeral procession, drawing a crowd of up to 100,000 spectators.

John King received a gold watch and a pension of £180 a year from the Royal Society of Victoria but didn't live to enjoy it. His health never recovered and he died of pulmonary tuberculosis aged thirty-three.

South Australia won the construction of the Overland Telegraph Line and John McDouall Stuart was eventually awarded the £2,000 for being the first man to cross the continent and live to tell the story. Victoria's prize for her efforts was just a couple of very famous but very dead explorers.

## Least Successful Expedition by Camel

The name of John Ainsworth Horrocks could have been written large as one of Australia's greatest frontiersmen had his career not been cut tragically short. In 1846, he set out to conquer the hitherto impenetrable hinterland of South Australia with several goats, a bull called Harry and an unnamed camel imported from Tenerife. The addition of the camel to the party was seen as a logistical masterstroke because previous trans-Australian expeditions, equipped with horses and bullocks, had all perished in the fierce heat. The decision turned out to be less of a coup than anticipated when, not long into the journey, the camel attacked their cook, biting a large chunk out of his head, then chewed all of the expedition's flour bags, wasting most of the supplies.

A couple of days later, the recalcitrant camel struck again, lurching into Horrocks just as he was loading his gun, causing him to shoot himself accidentally in the lower jaw, knocking out half of his teeth. Horrocks died in agony from his injuries several days later, the first explorer to be shot dead by his own camel.

---

*"Where a calculator on the ENIAC is equipped with 18,000 vacuum tubes and weighs 30 tons, computers in the future may have only 1,000 vacuum tubes and weigh only 1.5 tons."*
*Popular Mechanics*, March 1949

---

## Most People Lost While Searching
## for a Lost Expedition

Ever since Columbus, explorers have been losing their lives and suffering the agonies of frostbite, scurvy and starvation in search of the Northwest Passage, a shortcut to China and the Indies that was thought to exist somewhere through the ice floes of northern Canada, thereby avoiding the long and treacherous voyage around the Horn of Africa.

As an exercise in futility, it was hard to beat; one long chapter of failure, disaster and tragedy as ships disappeared and explorers failed to return. But there was one name above all forever linked with failed attempts to find the Northwest Passage – that of John Franklin.

Franklin was the ninth of twelve children born to a Lincolnshire shopkeeper. His family had some famous connections – his uncle was the explorer Matthew Flinders, and one of his nieces was married to the poet Alfred Lord Tennyson. His first taste of exploration was on board the ship *Investigator* captained by his uncle Matthew, tasked with a survey of the still largely uncharted coast of Australia. The mission was never completed due to bad planning, scurvy among the crew and the general unseaworthiness of the ship. Franklin found himself shipwrecked on a sandbank for six weeks until he was rescued: a portent for the rest of his career as an explorer.

Franklin was a surprise choice when the British Admiralty asked him to lead an overland surveying party to the Arctic in 1819. He had never taken part in – let alone led – an overland polar expedition before and knew nothing about canoeing or hunting. He was an overweight, unhealthy-looking thirty-three-year-old who suffered from circulation problems in his fingers and toes, even in warm weather. Not exactly most people's idea of the hardy Arctic explorer. But he had impressed the Admiralty with his "dignified and impressive good sense, sound judgement and presence of mind". Presumably, someone also thought that his experience in Australia would come in useful for a trip to the frozen north.

Franklin's first trip to the Arctic set a new benchmark for failed polar exploration. He took insufficient supplies and his men knew nothing about survival techniques. His colleagues found that he was incapable of doing anything without first having a cup of tea and always insisted on sitting down to three square meals a day and even then could never travel overland more than eight miles a day without being carried. He was a very religious man who took with him everywhere a twelve-point checklist entitled "Have I this day walked with God?" He refused to walk anywhere at all on Sundays.

Franklin and his party got completely lost and somehow managed to set fire to his camp three times. As supplies ran low and the crew were weakened by cold and exhaustion, unrest turned to rebellion. Two of his officers fought a duel over a sixteen-year-old Indian girl. Faced with starvation, one of his crew – Midshipman Robert Hood – resorted to cannibalism. He had eaten two of the team and was just preparing a third for the table, with a bullet through the forehead, when he was shot dead by an Indian guide. For his troubles, the guide was executed by Franklin's second-in-command, Dr John Richardson. Franklin, one of the few who made it back, survived by eating lichen, rotting reindeer skins and shoe leather.

The British valued courage rather than talent from their explorers. Despite the fact that eleven out of twenty-three men had died, and having travelled 5,500 miles and only managing to map a tiny portion of coastline that everyone knew existed anyway, Franklin returned to a hero's welcome and earned an unlikely reputation for toughness as "the man who ate his boots".

In 1925, Britain's new hero set off on a second expedition to find the Northwest Passage, this time abandoning his terminally ill wife Eleanor; she died while he was away. Franklin's second expedition was considerably more successful than the first and, although he was forced to turn back by terrible weather conditions and failed in his mission, at least this time no one was eaten.

After this, Franklin took a break from Arctic exploration, married one of his late wife's best friends, received a knighthood, then was posted to Tasmania to serve as lieutenant-governor. His stay in office was controversial and he was recalled when word reached London that most of the decision-making was actually being made by his new wife.

Franklin returned home in 1843 to find that the British Admiralty were launching a fresh attempt to find the Northwest Passage and immediately volunteered his services. His offer was taken up only very reluctantly by British Naval Command; he was settled on as sixth choice after others declined or were rejected as too inexperienced. Franklin received his orders on 5 May 1845, by which time he was pushing sixty and had not taken a ship into the ice for twenty-seven years.

This time, Franklin was equipped with the latest technology – his two ships *Erebus* and *Terror* had steam engines that could make four knots and the ships' bows were reinforced with iron planks to help them break through ice. The cabins were heated by hot water piped through the floor and there were enough provisions to last for five years, including large quantities of china, cut glass and silverware and a library stocked with more than 1,000 books.

Another novel addition to the expedition was canned food, a recent invention. Unfortunately, the tins were not properly sealed, allowing lead to leach into the food. Lead poisoning was thought to be a contributing factor in the deaths of some of the team.[6]

On 19 May 1845, Franklin set sail from London promising once again to deliver on the centuries-long search for the Northwest Passage. The ships stopped for supplies in Disko Bay, Greenland, in early July. They were last spotted by a couple of whalers on 28 July. Some time after that, the whole expedition vanished into the pack ice of Lancaster Sound and not one man was seen alive again.

---

6   Recent research suggests that another potential source for the lead may have been the ships' fresh water systems.

After two years without word from her husband, Lady Franklin pleaded with the Admiralty to send a rescue party. Given that the original expedition was provisioned for five years, the British Government was reluctant to launch a search mission, but they had not bargained for the indomitable Lady Franklin, who put up a prolonged public campaign for a search to continue until her husband was found, meanwhile winning extraordinary sympathy as the loyal, grieving wife of the missing hero. There was even a popular song of the time, "Lord Franklin", to keep the search in the public consciousness.

The government eventually gave way and offered a reward of £10,000 to anyone who could discover the fate of Franklin and his party. This prompted a mad scramble of ships heading northward. Interest in Franklin's fate wasn't only limited to Britain, as the United States also mounted several expeditions, most notably led by Elisha Kent Kane and Charles Francis Hall. A dozen ships were sent out to find Franklin in 1850 alone.

One of the 1850 expeditions found three graves on Beechey Island, dated January and April 1846, and the remnants of a winter camp, including some tattered clothing and a few tins of meat, giving hope that Franklin's party had travelled further west or perhaps north into the Polar Sea and was still largely intact.

By 1854, nine years had passed since Franklin and his crew had set sail and common sense decreed that all 129 of them were surely dead, but yet another expedition went looking for Franklin, led by the explorer John Rae. When he returned home on 29 July, he had some grisly news to report: "During my journey over ice and snow this spring . . . I met with Esquimaux in Pelly Bay, from one of whom I learned that a party of 'white men' (*kabloonas*) had perished from want of food some distance to the westward . . . From the mutilated state of many of the corpses, and the contents of the kettles, it is evident that our wretched countrymen had been driven to the last resource – cannibalism – as a means of prolonging existence."

Rae's sensational report, published in *The Times*, caused a furore in Britain. The suggestion that British explorers had resorted to eating each other in their final days was simply too shocking to be believed (we can only assume that they had very short memories when it came to Franklin's first expedition). Charles Dickens, editor of *Household Words*, asserted, without a shred of supporting evidence, that the dying party had obviously been eaten by the local Inuit. Lady Franklin, meanwhile, was simply furious with Rae for turning back without finding her husband, especially when she found out that Rae had pocketed the £10,000 reward.

In 1857, Lady Franklin sought the advice of a couple of mystics, whose "visions" inspired her to launch yet another search party, this time funded partly by the sale of her jewels and partly by public subscription, despite the fact that the Government had officially pronounced her husband dead three years earlier.

In 1859, Francis McClintock succeeded in reaching King William Island and found the skeleton of a sailor with two letters in his pocket, the only surviving records of what happened to the expedition. The first letter – dated 28 May 1847 – reported that the Franklin expedition had become trapped in ice on 12 September 1846, but on a more cheery note concluded with the words "all well". The second letter – dated 28 April 1848 – confirmed, however, that things had taken a turn for the worse: Franklin had died on board ship on 11 June 1847 while icebound off King William Island. His crews had abandoned their vessels in a futile attempt to trek south to safety.

Over the next four decades, approximately twenty-five more searches helped uncover bits of the story but questions remained unanswered. Why did so many men die in a place where previous expeditions had survived and where Inuit populations would trade goods for supplies? Why didn't they exchange their supplies for food and shelter from the Inuit? The most likely explanation is that a combination of lead poisoning, cold, starvation and disease – including scurvy, pneumonia and tuberculosis – killed the entire expedition. It is likely that the men waited for their colleagues to die before eating them.

Despite the fact that his 1845 expedition had resulted in an impressive 100 per cent fatality rate, the Victorian media portrayed Franklin as a great national hero, thanks largely to Lady Franklin and her many powerful contacts in the government of the day and because the British public preferred the myth that she represented to the horrible reality of cannibalism and failure.

Franklin was rewarded with a memorial in Westminster Abbey which credits him with "The Discovery of the North West Passage". In fact, it was the men who went looking for Franklin who discovered more about the Northwest Passage than Franklin ever did and it was the great Arctic explorer Roald Amundsen who finally proved the uselessness of the Northwest Passage as a major trade route because it is blocked by ice for most of the year.

In all, over forty search missions were launched in the search for Franklin and more men and ships were lost looking for him than on the original expedition itself. It remains to this day the greatest disaster in the annals of exploration.

## Least Successful Transatlantic Crossing by Aeroplane

In the mid-1920s, a New York hotel owner Raymond Orteig offered a prize of $25,000 to the first person to fly non-stop from New York to Paris.

René Fonck, a French aviator and First World War ace,[7] was confident that the prize was his. He persuaded aviation pioneer Igor Sikorksy to build him a new $105,000 S-35 triple-engine

---

7 Fonck claimed he shot down 140 German planes and received credit for 75, falling just short of the Red Baron's 80. His confirmed victories exceed the tallies of any Allied WWII pilot, making him the all-time Allied ace of aces. In his own words, "I put my bullets into the target as if I placed them there by hand."

aeroplane, at the time the most advanced and most expensive aircraft in the world.

For his epic flight, Fonck didn't stint on expense. He asked an interior designer to decorate the inside of the plane with panels of Spanish leather and mahogany walls so that it resembled "a beautifully furnished dining room". With the extra fuel required to cross the Atlantic, the plane was already carrying 4,000 lbs over its maximum weight, but Fonck brushed aside Sikorsky's warnings that the plane should be thoroughly stress-tested. To make matters even worse, the plane was loaded with various gifts from well-wishers, including a bouquet of flowers for the French President's wife and a four-course celebration dinner for six people.

The plane never got off the ground. The landing gear collapsed during take-off and the plane plunged down the runway into a gully where it burst into flames, killing two of the three crew members.

Fonck vowed to try again, but the following spring, on 20 May 1927, twenty-five-year-old Charles Lindbergh flew solo from New York to Paris in a stripped-down, lightweight single-engine plane and won fame and fortune. As for the Frenchman, no one gave much of a Fonck.

---

*"I have travelled the length and breadth of this country and talked with the best people, and I can assure you that data processing is a fad that won't last out the year."*
Editor in charge of business books
for publisher Prentice Hall, 1957

---

### Worst Attempt to Found a Colonial Empire

In the late seventeenth century, everyone who was anyone was busily colonizing the world. France owned most of northern America, from Canada down to the Gulf of Mexico; New

Spain was governed by a viceroy in central America; England was busily building an empire that would become the envy of the world. There was one country, however, missing out on the trade game – Scotland.

It was a desperately unhappy time for the Scots. Years of famine had driven people from their homesteads and choked the cities with homeless vagrants. The country's home-grown industries were dying. Scotland had lost the few overseas colonies that it had, such as Nova Scotia in Canada, and was desperate for new overseas trading partners. A Scot called William Paterson thought he had the answer to his country's problems.

Paterson was a financier and hustler born in Tynwald, Dumfriesshire, in 1658. As a young man, he moved to England and, in 1694, became one of the founding directors of the Bank of England, but he quit his job after a year over a row with his fellow bankers and began organizing a rival bank. When this fell through a year later, he started on an even grander plan. In London, he met a ship's surgeon called Lionel Wafer, who had told him about a wonderful paradise called Darien on the Isthmus of Panama, a thin strip of land between north and south America. It had a sheltered bay, rich, fertile land and a huge forest of hardwood trees.

Paterson immediately saw the potential of Darien as a location for a trading colony. Trade with the lucrative Pacific markets was a hugely expensive business because ships had to make the hazardous trip round Cape Horn on the southern tip of South America. If a Scottish trading post could be established at Darien, goods could be ferried from the Pacific across Panama and loaded on to ships in the Atlantic from there, speeding up Pacific trade and making it much more reliable.

In 1698, Paterson set about selling his dream of building a "New Caledonia" to the Scottish Government. He was a very persuasive salesman. Darien, Paterson promised, would be Scotland's "door of the seas and the key of the universe . . . trade will increase trade and money will beget money". To the Scots, who had watched with envy as their more prosperous neighbour to the south piled up wealth and status from overseas acquisitions, this was very beguiling talk.

On 26 February 1696, the Company of Scotland was set up in Edinburgh to raise capital for Paterson's ambitious venture. The project hit problems from the start when the English Government, who saw it as a threat to the monopoly held by their own East India Company, warned potential English, Dutch and German investors to back off. This left no source of finance but from within Scotland itself. The Scots however were only too eager to invest and they flocked in their thousands, rich and poor, to subscribe to Paterson's plan. It was a massive financial gamble and many were investing their life savings, but within six months £400,000 had been raised to fit out five ships for the expedition.

The next problem was acquiring the ships and, again, the English were unhelpful. The King's Government forbade their shipyards to take commissions from Scottish customers, so the Scots were forced to look abroad to Sweden and Holland. On 4 July 1698, five ships – the *Caledonia*, the *Unicorn*, the *Saint Andrew*, the *Dolphin* and the *Endeavour* – set sail from Leith harbour from the east to avoid detection by British warships, under the command of Captain Robert Pennycook. Of the 1,200 hopeful Scottish colonists, only Pennycook and William Paterson knew their destination, which was outlined in sealed packages to be opened only once the ships were on the open sea. No one, not even Paterson, had ever actually been to Darien to see it for themselves.

Lionel Wafer, who had been promised a huge reward for his information about Darien but had yet to receive a single penny was hugely put out when he found that he wasn't even being offered a place on the expedition. A couple of years later, when he read about the fate of the Scottish settlers, he was very thankful that he hadn't gone with them.

After an arduous and stormy voyage, with many passengers falling ill and dying on the way, the ships made landfall off the coast of Darien on 2 November 1698. Having been fed on stories of long-haired Indians living a life of luxury in a land of milk and honey, the settlers were hopelessly unprepared for the shock which lay ahead. Wafer had neglected to mention that the area was one of the most inhospitable places on the planet, a disease-ridden swathe of impenetrable tropical jungle, swamp and mosquitos.

The new colony was also beset from the start by terrible organization. First they constructed a fort in a place with no fresh water supply; then they tried to grow crops of maize and yams, although none of them knew how. As well as boxes of wigs, heavy Scottish serge cloth and other useless items that the colonists expected to use in their new life, they took with them thousands of combs and mirrors, which they expected to sell to the Indians. But the local Cuna Indians didn't have any money or much in the way of valuables to trade for the Scottish wares. Not that the naked Indians had much use for heavy serge in the heat of the tropics, even if they could afford it. The settlers weren't even able to sell any-thing to any passing traders, which had been the whole point of the exercise. They had no idea how to store food in the heat and humidity of Panama and most of their provisions spoiled. Discipline began to break down among the settlers and thefts and drunkenness were routine. The following spring brought torrential rain and, with it, rampant disease, then slow starvation.

Within a year, all but 300 of the settlers were dead. A sick and broken Paterson returned to Scotland in 1699 to try to stop a second expedition leaving, but by this time it was too late and several more ships and several thousand more settlers had already left for Darien. This time they brought with them a cargo of little blue Scots' bonnets. Unsurprisingly, they couldn't find a market in the jungle for these either. It didn't help matters when three Scottish ministers accompanying the original expedition went mad in the tropical heat and began wandering around the jungle wailing, "We're all doomed!"

There was one other detail Wafer had overlooked. Spain was under the impression that Darien already belonged to them. The settlers faced the constant threat of attack from the Spanish on whose land they were squatting. They couldn't even ask any of the English colonies in the area for help because the English Government had forbidden them to aid the Scots. New Caledonia truly was doomed.

In 1700, Spanish troops surrounded the colony and called on the Scots to surrender. They were allowed to leave with their guns and the colony was abandoned for the last time. Of the sixteen ships that had left for Panama, only one returned to Scotland with just a handful of survivors to face a resentful nation of investors who wanted their money back.

For William Paterson, it was a personal disaster. He had lost his fortune and his wife and his child on the trip and barely escaped with his own life, and the consequences for his country were immense. At least a quarter of Scotland's national wealth had been blown on the project; some estimates put it much higher. The great colonial adventure, instead of making Scotland a major player on the world stage, had ruined their economy and placed it totally at the mercy of its richer neighbour.

England had been trying to push Scotland into a Union for several years and the Scottish Government had always resisted, but this time the English Government was offering compensation to everyone who had lost money on Paterson's scheme as a bribe to accept an Act of Union. Faced with total financial collapse, Scotland had no choice but to accept. In 1707, she joined with England as the junior partner in the United Kingdom of Great Britain. As Robert Burns put it, Scotland had been "bought and sold for English gold".

## Least Successful Arctic Rescue Mission

The American Charles Francis Hall was a veteran of Arctic exploration, having cut his teeth on two failed rescue missions in search of John Franklin's missing 1845 expedition. So when Hall set out for the Arctic again in June 1871, he knew that he might die on the expedition from exposure, scurvy, starvation or all three. He probably wasn't expecting it would be from arsenic poisoning.

Hall was a blacksmith and engraver by trade, earning a living in Cincinnati, Ohio, making seals and metal printing plates. Through his interest in the printing industry, he began a second career as a newspaper proprietor, publishing the *Cincinnati News*. Hall's third career as an Arctic explorer had curious origins: around 1857, he read a newspaper report about Sir John Franklin's lost expedition to find the Northwest Passage. For reasons not entirely clear, the fate of the missing English explorer became Hall's obsession. In 1960, he sold his newspaper, abandoned his pregnant wife and daughter and went looking for the lost expedition himself, despite the fact that he had had no training in cold weather survival, sailing, navigation, hunting, or any other skills that might come in useful as an Arctic explorer. Hall simply believed that God had chosen him to succeed where experienced explorers had failed. And all this despite the fact that it had been fairly well established for at least seven years that Franklin and his crew were all long dead.

Predictably, Hall's first shoestring expedition didn't get far before he was frozen in, but he was rescued by some Inuit who told him about some relics which he interpreted as proof that some members of Franklin's expedition might still be alive.

In 1864, Hall tried again. He got as far as King William Island where he found remains and artefacts from the Franklin expedition, but no clues as to their fate. During this expedition, Hall, who had a hair-trigger temper and was often on the verge of violence, shot dead one of his crew, a young man called Patrick Coleman. Hall claimed that it was an act of self-defence and he was quelling a mutiny, but it seems more likely that he and Coleman had simply quarrelled and Hall had snapped. When he returned home, he had some questions to answer, but the shooting had taken place beyond the borders of Canada, so neither the British nor Canadian authorities would have anything to do with it and the American authorities ignored the matter completely. Hall had killed Patrick Coleman in a legal no-man's land and got away scot-free.

In 1871, having mysteriously talked the US Congress into giving him a grant of $50,000 towards an expedition to the North Pole in the ship *Polaris*, Hall set off to try to discover the fate of Franklin's crew yet again, although by this time even Hall was beginning to concede that they were probably dead.

Hall's crew of twenty-five included the ship's captain Sydney Buddington, navigator George Tyson, and Dr Emil Bessels, German physician and naturalist as chief of the scientific staff. Hall's leadership skills left much to be desired. Despite all his supposed piety, he was a prickly, volatile character and very overbearing in manner and his crew seem to have despised and mistrusted him almost from the start. One day Hall fell ill after drinking a cup of coffee and collapsed in a fit. For the next week, he suffered from vomiting and delirium, then he appeared to make a recovery and accused several of his disgruntled travelling companions, especially the ship's physician Dr Bessels, of having poisoned him. Shortly after that, he fell ill again and died.

The expedition never made it to the North Pole. The ship, now commanded by Buddington, was dramatically abandoned in Greenland on the verge of being crushed by ice floes. The crew dispersed and were finally rescued two years later in what became known as one of the greatest Arctic survival stories ever. In fact, the only member of the *Polaris* not to survive the expedition was Hall himself.

The official investigation that followed ruled that Hall had died from a stroke but, in 1968, tests on tissue samples of bone, fingernails and hair confirmed that Hall had died of poisoning from massive doses of arsenic in the last two weeks of his life. The question of whether or not he was murdered by one of his crew remains unanswered. It is possible that he may have dosed himself with arsenic – a common ingredient of quack medicines of the time, or he may have been overdosed by Dr Emil Bessels. Given the lack of remorse shown by Buddington and Tyson, the culprit could have been any one of three.

Ironically, just as Hall never had to account for his murder of Patrick Coleman, no charges were ever brought.

## Fool's Gold

Some explorers, like John Franklin and his pursuit of the Northwest Passage, gave their lives trying to find something that was widely believed to have existed. Lewis Lasseter was unique because he died trying to find something that was entirely a figment of his own imagination.

Lewis Hubert Lasseter (or Harold Bell Lasseter as he later called himself) was the son of an English labourer who emigrated to Australia in the 1870s. Known to acquaintances as "Possum", he was a short, stocky, swarthy man with a deep scar on his balding scalp. Although self-educated, he was described as literate and very well spoken. The details of his early life, like so much of Lasseter's career, are sketchy, but he claimed that as a teenager he served in the Royal Navy and was discharged in 1901. Some time after that, he travelled to the United States, where he got married and became a Mormon. A few years later, he returned to Australia and, by 1908, was working as a farm hand in New South Wales. During this period, he tried to take out various patents on his own inventions, including a disc plough, a wheat storage system and a device for making pre-cast concrete. None of these ideas ever got off the drawing board and the patents lapsed without the fees being paid.

At the outbreak of the First World War, Lasseter tried to enlist three times but was declared medically unfit. In 1924, he married again, this time to an Australian nurse – Louise Lillywhite – describing himself as "Lewis Harold Bell Lasseter, bachelor", having never actually divorced his first wife. Meanwhile, he was holding down various jobs as a carpenter, including six months spent working on the construction of the new Sydney Harbour Bridge. Later, he wrote to the government of New South Wales, unsuccessfully demanding compensation on the basis that the architect John Bradfield had stolen his design for the bridge.

But Lasseter's capacity for self-delusion hadn't yet peaked. In 1929, he fired off another letter to his government with an

even more extraordinary claim – he had discovered a giant
reef of gold somewhere in central Australia. He claimed he
made his discovery in 1900 while trying to walk alone from
Alice Springs to the west Australian coast. He would have
died had he not been found by a passing camel driver who
took him to the camp of a surveyor named Harding. He and
Harding returned to find the reef but got lost because their
watches were wrong. According to Lasseter, he had spent the
best part of the next three decades trying to raise money for
an expedition to find the reef. The government consulted a
geologist, who dismissed Lasseter as a crank, and decided to
take no action.

Lasseter subsequently retold the story many times and each
time the details varied – according to one version he was only
seventeen when he made the trip. In 1930, he took his story to
the leader of the Australian Worker's Union and part-time
bare-knuckle fighter John Bailey, an extraordinary character
who had literally fought his way upwards in sheep-shearing
sheds. By this time, Lasseter's reef had grown to nine miles
long and had "gold as thick as plums in a pudding". Lasseter,
meanwhile, was presenting himself as "a qualified ship's captain" and said that he had worked for years on coastal boats.
Bailey was sceptical, on account of Lasseter's conflicting and
vague versions of events, but the lure of gold in a time of
economic depression made his pipe dream particularly seduc-
tive. It led to the formation of the Central Australian Gold
Exploration Company, with Bailey as Chairman, to fund an
exploratory expedition to find the reef.

The party set off westward from Alice Springs on 21 July
1930 equipped with a Gypsy Moth aeroplane, a six-wheeled
Thornycroft truck plus a back-up truck. Accompanying Lasseter were expedition leader Fred Blakely; experienced
prospector George Sutherland; engineer and driver Philip
Taylor; driver Fred Colson; pilot Errol Coote; and Captain
Blakeston-Houston, who described himself as "explorer".
There was also a native guide called Mickey, whose job it was
to find water in the desert – a formidable task, as central

Australia was in the middle of a fierce drought and most of the known waterholes had dried up.

Right from the start, Lasseter proved to be a difficult companion and an unreliable guide. His behaviour became increasingly strange; he was morose and uncooperative and spent his time singing Mormon hymns and writing up his diary. His fellow travellers became more sceptical the further into the desert they went. It was becoming more and more obvious from his lack of knowledge of bushcraft that he had never been in that part of central Australia before, let alone discovered a reef studded with gold.

On reaching Mount Marjorie (now Mount Leisler), Lasseter suddenly announced that they were 150 miles too far north of the area they were supposed to be searching. Worse still, they realized that they did not have enough provisions to make the trek to Lasseter's revised location and would have to make a ninety-five-mile diversion back to their base camp to restock.

There was more bad luck when the Gypsy Moth crashed and the pilot Coote was hospitalized. Meanwhile, the trucks were bogged down in sand in temperatures exceeding 50°C. Blakely decided that he'd had enough; he denounced Lasseter as a fraud and quit the expedition. The rest soon followed, leaving Lasseter alone with a twenty-two-year-old dingo-hunter called Paul Johns whom they had met back at base camp. Johns was persuaded to join the party on account of his team of seven camels, which were thought to be more practical than trucks.

Lasseter and Johns set off to find the reef but, once again, Lasseter's erratic behaviour began to create problems and, after a series of petty arguments, relations deteriorated to the point where they were barely speaking. When they reached Malagura Rockhole, Lasseter decided to wander off to look for the reef on his own.

Five days later, he returned to camp with some mineral samples and informed Johns that he had found the gold reef. Johns asked him to reveal the exact location, but Lasseter refused. Johns called Lasseter a liar. A fistfight ensued and Johns quit, leaving just Lasseter and two camels. Shortly afterwards, Lasseter was quite literally caught with his trousers down. Suffering badly from dysentery, he went to defecate but forgot to tether the camels properly. They bolted, taking with them the last of his supplies. Lasseter tried to shoot down the fleeing camels, but missed. The gunshots alerted a nearby Aboriginal hunting party, who took pity on him and led him to a waterhole, but then left him to his fate.

Lasseter spent his final days starving to death in a cave. Self-deluded to the very end, he wrote in his diary: "What good a reef worth millions? I would gladly give it all for a loaf of bread."

A bushman called Bob Buck found his body and his diary, in which Lasseter claimed that he had "rediscovered" his reef and pegged his claim. Modern technology, including satellite imagery, seismic testing and remote sensing, shows that it is geologically impossible for gold ever to have formed in the areas where Lasseter claimed that it was located. But the myth of "Lasseter's Lost Reef" persisted and led to scores of further expeditions.

The expedition leader Fred Blakeley, who also appears to have been a bit of a fantasist, went on to write an account of the expedition – *Dream Millions* – which claimed that Lasseter did not starve to death but somehow made his way to America to avoid being charged with fraud.

### Least Observant Explorer

Louis Antoine de Bougainville was the first Frenchman to sail around the world. In 1767, while sailing through the South Pacific, his passage was blocked by a huge coral reef. He peered through his telescope and could see just beyond the reef a mass of land, but he didn't think it was worth investigating, thereby narrowly failing to discover Australia (and claim it for France) three years before Captain James Cook.

His perceptiveness was also found wanting when it came to his crew. Bougainville set sail with a team of scientists including Philibert Commerson, a French naturalist, accompanied by his faithful assistant Bonnefoy, who lugged his equipment around the South Pacific and shared his cabin. On Tahiti, during an attempted rape by an over-excited local chief, the valet's clothes were ripped off, revealing that Bonnefoy was, in fact, a woman called Jeanne Baret. At first Commerson denied any part in the deception, but he later admitted that they had, in fact, been living together for the previous four years.

Ms Baret is now officially recognized as the first woman to circumnavigate the world; the plant Commerson named after her, however, has now been changed from *Beretta bonnafidia* to *Turrea heterophylla*.

---

*"Radio has no future."*
Lord Kelvin, Scottish mathematician and physicist,
former president of the Royal Society, 1897

---

## Most Inaccurate Discovery of a Mountain Range

In 1824, the Scottish botanist David Douglas set off on an epic plant-hunting expedition in the Rocky Mountains of America, braving whirlpools, grizzly bears, robbery, frostbite and near-starvation to bring 240 new species of plants to Britain, including the ubiquitous Douglas Fir, the staple of the Victorian gentleman's garden.

Douglas suffered from rapidly deteriorating eyesight due to snow blindness, and this impairment led to an epic blunder. On his return home from one of his trips to the Rockies, he announced the discovery of two giant peaks, which he named Mount Hooker and Mount Brown, after two distinguished British botanists. For almost seventy years the mountains were the subject of great excitement and speculation and were listed on every map as the two highest peaks in the Canadian Rocky Mountains. Strangely, however, they continued to elude the best efforts of experienced mountaineers to find either one of them.

The search for Douglas's giant twin peaks was finally brought to a close when someone carefully re-read his original notes and couldn't help noticing that he claimed to have climbed both mountains in a single afternoon. It was also difficult to understand how Douglas, even with his eyesight problems, could have failed to notice that the other mountains nearby were much higher than the ones he had just climbed.

Douglas's short career as a mountaineer ended prematurely. In 1834, while looking for plants in Hawaii, the short-sighted botanist stumbled into a pit that had been dug to trap wild cattle and was crushed to death by a falling bullock.

---

*"It is apparent to me that the possibilities of the aeroplane, which two or three years ago were thought to hold the solution to the [flying machine] problem, have been exhausted, and that we must turn elsewhere."*

Thomas Edison, American inventor, 1895

---

## Most Inaccurate Discovery of a Mountain Range: Runner-Up

In 1818, the Arctic explorer Captain Sir John Ross led two ships, the *Isabella* and the *Alexander*, on the first of a series of attempts to find the Northwest Passage. His plan was to sail around the north-east coast of America and on to the Bering Strait.

When Ross reached Lancaster Sound in Canada, he peered through his telescope and "saw" that his way was blocked by a huge range of mountains, so he turned his ships round and went home. It was all very confusing for his officers because no one else on the ships saw Ross's phantom geographical features and they were urging him to press on.

Back home, Ross stuck to his version of events. He even described the mountains at length in his journal and gave them a name – the Crocker's Hills. A year later, when Ross's former first mate William Edward Parry sailed "through" Croker's Hills, Ross admitted that he might have got it wrong. His detractors suggested they should be renamed "Choker's Hills" instead.

Having embarrassingly mistaken a mirage for a mountain range, and then named it after a secretary of the British Admiralty, Ross was desperate to restore his tarnished reputation. In 1829, he tried again, but this time the Admiralty refused to give him any more ships. Instead, he turned to a friend, Felix Booth, who had made a fortune from Booth's Gin, to underwrite the trip. This, the only significant Arctic expedition ever launched under private sponsorship, resulted in the largest land mass on Earth to take its name from an alcoholic beverage – "Boothia".[8]

Ross sailed away on a tiny, rickety old steam ship called the *Victory* with high hopes but his joy was short-lived. Only a few weeks into the journey, he was so annoyed with the performance of the ship's faulty steam boiler that he had it thrown overboard. He then directed his vessel into an icy cul-de-sac (he named it the "Gulf of Boothia"), one from which his ship, despite years of heroic efforts by her officers and crew, was destined never to return.

Fortified by consumption of gin supplied by his sponsor, in the midst of unspeakable hardship, Ross took time out to run up a flag for the king's birthday, and when a polar bear chewed off a colleague's leg, he ordered the ship's carpenter to knock up a replacement. Long given up for dead, Ross was

---

8 The explorer Robert Peary failed to reach the North Pole, but down to his last two toes from previous attempts, found time to endorse Shredded Wheat and his favourite brand of underpants before naming a remote cape on Ellesmere Island after another of his sponsors, Colgate.

eventually rescued and returned home with a memento from his epic trip – the head of a native Inuit gentleman he had befriended – for phrenological analysis.

Once again, Ross's map-making skills caused controversy. Back in England, using his authority as expedition leader, he named a group of islands he had never actually seen the "Clarence Islands" then added a few fictional islands to the group, just to impress the new king (and former Duke of Clarence) William IV.

## Least Successful Balloon Trip

The history of nineteenth-century Arctic exploration was one of relentless failure. Attempts by sledge and ship had failed; in fact, nobody was even sure wheather the North Pole lay on land or sea. Then in 1896, Salomon August Andrée, Swedish engineer and amateur balloonist, had a bright idea – why not fly to the Pole in a balloon?

Andrée was the son of a wealthy Swedish chemist. He caught the balloon bug when he was twenty-two and on a trip to the United States got to meet the veteran American balloonist John Wise. Andrée was working in the patent offices in Stockholm when he bought his first balloon. He made his maiden flight in 1893 and went on to make another eight.

During these early voyages, his balloon had an unnerving tendency to drift uncontrollably out to sea and drag the basket across the surface of the water. He tinkered with the steering and invented his own system made of drag ropes hanging off the balloon. The friction of the ropes was supposed to slow it down enough to allow small sails to be used to turn the balloon.

Andrée proclaimed his unique steering system a huge success and showed it to the Swedish Ballooning Association. They begged to differ; in theory, Andrée's drag rope system shouldn't work at all. In fact it was a liability because the ropes were likely to break or become entangled with each other, or get stuck to the ground, dragging Andrée's low-flying balloon down with them. They put Andrée's "success" down to wishful thinking and opportune winds. There was also the fact that most of the time he was inside clouds and had no idea where he was or which way he was travelling.

In theory, a balloon could retain sufficient gas for a thirty-day flight, though in practice no one had ever stayed up for more than fifteen days. Andrée was convinced that if a balloon started as close to ninety degrees north as possible, it could sail over the Pole and land on the other side in Alaska.

In 1896, he outlined his reckless plan to reach the North Pole by hydrogen balloon to the Swedish Royal Academy. Despite reservations expressed by the experts, he was a persuasive speaker and his enthusiasm was contagious. When the public got to hear about Andrée's project, there was a huge amount of interest. National pride was at stake; Sweden was anxious to reassert its position in Polar exploration after falling behind Norway. Any anxieties anyone may have had about the validity of Andrée's plan were simply swept away in a tidal wave of patriotic pride.

He figured that it would take about 130,800 krone to fund his expedition – a sum equal to about £1 million today – but once the Swedish Royal Academy were on board, financing proved to be no obstacle. King Oscar II donated 36,000 krone and Alfred Nobel, inventor of dynamite and donor of scientific prizes, pitched in with a considerable sum as well. Other donations quickly followed.

Andree's Polar balloon *Örnen* (the Eagle) was made in Paris and delivered to Danes Island, Spitzerbergen, where he had constructed an enormous hangar. The balloon had three layers of varnished silk, was ninety-seven feet tall and sixty-seven feet in diameter and weighed a ton and a half. For his crew, Andrée selected Nils Ekholm, a meteorological researcher, and Nils Strindberg, a young physics student. Between them, the three-man team covered a broad range of technical and scientific know-how, but they had little experience in large balloons and none in Arctic conditions.

In fact, the whole expedition was based on a series of wildly optimistic assumptions. Andrée believed that the Arctic summer was ideal weather for the expedition because the men could work around the clock in the long daylight conditions. He thought that any snow or ice that might pose a threat by sticking to the balloon, thereby weighing it down, would simply fall off or melt away. He also assumed that the winds would blow more or less in the same direction throughout the expedition. It was all guesswork. Even Ekholm, the Arctic weather researcher, had no idea where the wind was likely to take them because observational data simply did not exist. Fatally, Andrée believed that his navigational system employing drag ropes would ensure the success of the expedition, even though they hadn't really worked on test flights. In fact, there was no proof that *Örnen* would fly at all. It had been shipped directly to Sweden by the manufacturer without ever being tested.

In the summer of 1896, the team assembled at Danes Island to make their first attempt. The launch was covered by journalists from all over the world. For six weeks, the Swedish nation held its breath while the expedition waited at base camp for the right wind and weather. And they waited. It never came.

In August, the captain of the ship they had chartered informed Andrée that he was going home because his iceberg insurance had expired. The balloon was deflated and the expedition crept back to Stockholm; the man who had been labelled a national hero was now an object of international criticism and ridicule, variously denounced as a "fraud" and "publicity seeker" by journalists.

In the spring of 1897, Andrée tried again. This time the winds were favourable and the team was ready to depart. The balloon was heavily loaded. Besides the usual supplies of food, clothing, ammunition and scientific and photographic equipment, they had a collapsible boat, a sledge of Andrée's own design and the materials to construct a darkroom while in flight. In addition, they had an assortment of improbable extras, including Russian and US money in coins, a porcelain bowl, a white shirt in its original wrapping material, a dress tie,

old newspapers and two tickets to the 1897 Stockholm Exhibition. They also had 55 lbs of chocolate, a good supply of
champagne donated by sponsors, and two bottles of port
which had been given to them by the King of Sweden.

There was, however, one dangerous flaw – Andrée's silk
balloon was leaking hydrogen. The worst leakage came from
the stitching holes along the seams – eight million of them.
Strips of silk had been glued on top of them and varnish had
been used to seal the whole balloon, but it wasn't enough. For
every day in the air, the balloon would lose about 150 lbs of lift
force. Ekholm, the only man on the crew with Arctic experience, had warned Andrée about the leaks a year earlier during
the very first trial. By his estimations, at the rate it was losing
hydrogen the balloon could only stay aloft for seventeen days.
But Andrée already knew about the leaks. In fact, he had been
secretly topping up the hydrogen in the balloon to hide the fact
that it was losing gas so rapidly.

At this point just about everyone, including the balloon
maker himself, was advising him to postpone and have the bag
rebuilt. But Andrée remembered the embarrassment of having
to postpone a year before. The sponsors and the media had
followed every delay and reported on every setback and were
clamouring for results. He had become the prisoner of his own
successful funding campaign. Andrée gave the order to set off.

By this time, Ekholm, the only crew member with the sense
to bale out of the project, had been replaced by Knut Fraenkel,
a twenty-seven-year-old civil engineer. The three-man team
made headlines across the globe when, on 11 July 1897, their
ridiculously over-heavy balloon lifted, very, very slowly, into
the Arctic blue, never to be seen again.

Andrée's plan was to communicate with the outside world
via homing pigeons, bred in Norway in the hope that they
might fly back there. The pigeons were to carry messages written in Norwegian, with instructions to deliver them to Sweden.
He released at least four pigeons, but only one was ever
retrieved, by a Norwegian steamer, on which the pigeon had
landed only to be promptly shot.

The fate of the *Örnen* remained a mystery until thirty-three years later, when a boat carrying geologists and seal hunters landed on uninhabited White Island, now called Kvitoya. Amid the ruins of a camp they found a skull, bleached by the Sun and diaries and tins of film that picked up the story.

Within minutes of the launch, the mission was in trouble. The drag ropes pulled the balloon down so far that the basket actually dragged on the water, no matter how much cargo they ditched over the side. At the same time, the ropes became tangled and pulled free from their holds. In all, 1,630 lbs of weight was lost. With the loss of weight, the balloon soared 2,300 feet into the air and the lower air pressure made the hydrogen leak even faster. With no steering and having drifted hopelessly off course, after ten-and-a-half hours the balloon crashed for the first time, then bumped along the surface for another forty-one hours before finally coming to rest.

The crew started to walk south towards Spitzbergen but the ice floe took them east. After three months in the Arctic, the team found themselves on Kvitoya Island. All three men were dead within a couple of weeks, cause unknown. This in itself was unusual because they had packed enough provisions to keep them going for much longer.

One possible cause of death was carbon monoxide poisoning from a faulty stove. It has also been speculated that they had committed suicide. Among their unlikely cargo was a large stash of opium, certainly enough to do the trick. According to another theory, they perished from a combination of exposure and severe food poisoning after dining on undercooked polar bear.

## Least Successful Surveyor

Unlike his contemporary American explorers Lewis and Clark, the name of Zebulon Montgomery Pike is relatively unsung, save for its use on a mountain he never actually climbed.

Pike first came to public attention in 1805 when he was sent by the US Army commander General James Wilkinson to explore the recently acquired lands from France under the Louisiana Purchase. Pike's job was to find the source of the Mississippi River – which he failed to do – but when he returned to base he incorrectly identified it as Cass Lake.

Although it was obvious Pike couldn't explore his way out of a paper bag, in 1806 Wilkinson mysteriously chose him to lead another expedition, this time to find the northern boundary of Spanish possessions in the American south-west. Pike set off from St Louis and, after travelling around in circles for weeks, he ended up in Colorado where he discovered the mountain today bearing his name – Pike's Peak. He attempted to climb it, but gave up. Irked by his inability to judge the height of a mountain at distance, he wrote in his journal, "No man will ever climb Pike's Peak."

He and his group turned south and set up camp on what he thought was the Red River, which was on US territory. At this point, a troop of Spanish cavalry arrived and assured him that he was actually camping on the Rio Grande. Pike was arrested for unwittingly invading Spanish territory and escorted to Santa Fe. He was eventually released when his captors realized that he genuinely had had no idea where he was.

Back home, Pike's meandering expedition aroused suspicions. Surely no one could be that clueless; there had to be some shadowy plan. There was speculation that he had been sent on a secret mission to provoke a war with Spain. Either way, he failed.

Instead of returning as a heroic explorer, the luckless Pike was forced to clear his name. He got the opportunity to repair his tarnished reputation when war was declared on Great Britain in 1812. He led an attack at the Battle of York but was fatally wounded when a powder magazine exploded and a flying rock hit him on the head.

## Most Futile Attempt to Find a Lost Tribe

According to Welsh legend, the discovery of the New World was accomplished not by Christopher Columbus or Amerigo Vespucci, but by Madoc, the son of a twelfth-century Welsh prince called Owen Gwynedd. The story goes that Madoc sailed from Wales for America in 1170 with 300 men and landed in Mobile, Alabama. These plucky pioneers were never heard of again but, according to the legend, they settled and became the progenitors of a tribe of pale-skinned Welsh-speaking Indians.

The origin of the legend of Madoc is obscure. Owen Gwynedd certainly had several sons but none called Madoc, although a seafarer named Madoc, unrelated and possibly mythical, crops up in medieval Welsh literature; one story has him colonizing an unspecified island paradise.

In 1580, a Welshman – John Dee – revived the legend of Madoc in an attempt to trump Spanish claims on the New World. Dee claimed that, as a Briton had landed in America long before Columbus, Elizabeth, not the King of Spain, had ownership of all American territories.

The story of the lost tribe of Welsh-speaking Indians grew down the years, as reports of Madogwys (Madoc's people) were brought back to Britain from travellers all over America. All told there were sightings of at least twenty tribes of Welsh-speaking Indians ranging from Peru to Canada, nearly always in areas inaccessible to white settlers.

John Thomas Evans was born in 1770, the son of a Methodist preacher from Waunfawr, a village near Caernarvon in north Wales. He had grown up with the legend of Madoc and came to believe that he had been chosen by God to find the Welsh Indians. When he was twenty-one, he went to London and met a group of Welsh nationalists, including an eccentric poet and laudanum addict called Iolo Morganwg. While on one his drug-induced highs, Morganwg announced he was off to America to find the Madogwys and settle the issue once and for all.

Evans couldn't believe his luck and immediately volunteered to go with him. Morganwg, who everyone knew as a fantasist (not to mention a criminal forger), soon forgot about the whole thing, but Evans decided to go it alone. In 1792, at the age of twenty-two, he set sail for Baltimore to begin his quest, taking with him a Welsh Bible so that he could pray with his long-lost kinsmen in their ancestral language.

He also carried letters of introduction to several worthy Welshmen in Philadelphia and elsewhere, including a Dr Samuel Jones. He received little encouragement from the Welsh settlers, who urged him to go home. The American settlers had been warring with native Americans for years and, if you were white and valued your scalp, it wasn't a great idea to go wandering off into the American wilderness. But Evans, propelled by his sense of destiny, marched westwards alone.

Informed opinion had it that the wilds of North Dakota would be a good place for Evans to start looking. It was rumoured that the local Indian tribe, the Mandan people, had very pale skin and spoke a language that sounded very much like Welsh. Mandan women were also very talkative even in bed – conclusive evidence of Welshness, apparently – although there was no word as to whether the Mandan menfolk played rugby or had a choir.

In March 1793, shortly after St David's Day, Evans set out for North Dakota, through the Allegheny Mountains and then by boat up the Mississippi to the small frontier town St Louis. Although most people in the area spoke French, Louisiana was under the flag of Spain and King Charles IV, who was very hostile to the British. Instead of recognizing Evans as a harmless crank, he arrested him as a spy and threw him in jail. Evans of course protested that he was not in fact an agent of the British Government, he was simply on a mission to find some lost Welsh Indians, but for some reason the Spanish didn't believe him.

After a couple of years in prison, Evans was able to persuade his captors that he was a crank after all, but he just might be useful to them. At the time, Spain was looking find a route across the Rocky Mountains to its territories on the Pacific coast. The route was thought to be infested with extremely hostile natives, but it would also take Evans close to the Mandan settlement about 1,800 miles from St Louis. Evans was released, on condition that he agreed to assist a Scot called John Mackay to lead a Spanish expedition to find a route through the Rocky Mountains to California.

Evans had no idea what dangers lay ahead and his grasp of the local geography was sketchy. He thought that the area was populated with woolly mammoths and had mountains made of salt. In July 1795, he and Mackay set off accompanied by thirty Spanish soldiers and four large boats loaded with blankets and tobacco for trading. A Methodist preacher, working for a Scot in the service of Roman Catholic Spain, was now looking for Welsh-speaking Indians on the edge of the known world.

About halfway to the Rockies, the party was frozen in for the winter at Fort Charles in Nebraska. In February, Evans set out with a few men to find the Mandan settlement. Mackay gave him instructions to claim all of the lands he passed through for the king of Spain and to make notes of everything they saw. In particular, he was to keep special watch for a one-eyed monster said to live in the area. After about 300 miles, the party was attacked by marauding Sioux and they fled back to camp.

Undaunted, Evans tried again in June and this time actually reached the Mandan village in North Dakota – his great moment of triumph. He had crossed a continent, braving sub-zero temperatures, bears, snakes and dangerous Sioux Indians, and survived. The legend of Madoc was about to be proved as fact. Evans was going to be a hero.

The Mandans, Evans was immensely relieved to find, were not at all like the Sioux and received their guest very warmly.[9]

---

9  It turned out that Evans wasn't even the first European to pass this way that year. A few weeks earlier, a Canadian fur trader called René Jusseaume had arrived via a different route, established a small trading post, raised a Union Jack, and then left. Little wonder the Mandans were so relaxed about Evans' arrival.

He got to know their chiefs, Big White Man and Black Cat, quite well, living with them in their large beehive-shaped dwelling through the bitterest of winters. He made himself at home, learning all about their culture, now and then entertaining them by playing his little flute. He spent a total of seven months in their village, but in all that time Evans heard not a word of Welsh.

With a heavy heart, Evans said *hwyl* to his hosts and returned to civilization after a two-year absence. In 1797, he reported the bad news back to his friends, saying, "I am able to inform you there is no such people as the Welsh Indians."

His spirit crushed, Evans drank himself to death in a St Louis bar two years later, aged twenty-eight.

As for the Mandan tribe, the story was similarly bleak. Contact with Europeans, and smallpox, wiped most of them out a couple of generations later.

## Least Convincing Denial over Eating One's Crew

The Greely Expedition of 1881 was commissioned by the US Government to collect meteorological data from the North Pole and was billed as the most ambitious scientific research mission ever sent into the Arctic.

The omens were not good from the start – Polar exploration was usually the province of naval personnel or other seafarers. Adolphus W. Greely was a Civil War veteran whose seafaring experience was limited to a two-way crossing of the Atlantic and the passage up from New York to St John's. On the very morning after departure, Greely was so seasick that he hid in his cabin and failed to appear on deck until that afternoon. Of his expedition team, mainly ex-Civil War soldiers, not one could sail a boat and few even knew how to row. But Greely, notorious as a strict disciplinarian, kept order on ship with an iron fist. One morning, he sacked his second-in-command, Frederick Kislingbury, because he was late for breakfast.[10]

Greely and his party made it further north than any preceding expedition. But during the severe winter of 1882, relief parties carrying provisions twice failed to reach him. The following year, Greely's ship hit an iceberg and sank. With no food, he and his crew began to starve.

Thanks to the persistence of Greely's wife Henrietta, the search was never abandoned. Three years later, of the original party of twenty-five, Greely and six emaciated colleagues were found still alive. The rest had perished from starvation, drowning, hypothermia, suicide, and in one case, gunshot wounds from an execution ordered by Greely for stealing food.

According to the dramatic authorized narrative of events, when Greely's rescuers found him he gasped, heroically, "Yes, seven of us left, here we are, dying like men. Did what I came to do – beat the best record!"

Other members of the party recalled the meeting differently. One reported that Greely told his rescuers, "If we've got to starve, we can starve without your help ... we were dying peacefully until you came." Another remembered Greely's words as "Give us something to eat!"

When he returned home with the surviving crew in 1884, Greely became a celebrity. But then more grim details of the Greely party's denouement began to emerge, including the crew member who hacked off his own feet to avoid gangrene. There was also one, big, nagging question about the surprisingly healthy state of the survivors. Given the length of time they had spent on the frozen barren ice without any food, just how, exactly, had they stayed alive?

Shockingly, it all pointed to one conclusion – cannibalism. The survivors denied the charge, but what about the

---

10  Kislingbury, although discharged from the expedition for insubordination, missed his boat home and had no choice but to hang around. He died of starvation on 1 June 1884.

half-eaten remains of the deceased crew members, they were asked? Greely explained that they had been used as "bait" for capturing shrimp.

## Worst Survival Skills

The English botanist Thomas Nuttall is remembered eponymously in Nuttall's woodpecker, Nuttall's blister beetle, Nuttall's sunflower, Nuttall's evening primrose and *Pica nuttalli,* the yellow-billed magpie.

In 1811, he joined an expedition with John Jacob Astor's Pacific Fur Company, travelling 1,500 miles along the Missouri River to study the local flora and fauna. Nuttall's lack of skills as a frontiersman made him a legend among his fellow French-Canadian travellers. He couldn't hunt, shoot, swim, light a fire or cook and had little sense of direction. They christened him le *fou,* the madman, after an encounter with some Sioux Indians. While checking their guns, they discovered that Nuttall's rifle was completely plugged with mud. He had been using it to dig up plants and thought the mud in the barrel was a handy place to store seeds.

Nuttall spent most of his time completely lost. He kept wandering away from his group while collecting plants and couldn't find his way back. One night when he failed to return, a search party was sent out to look for him. Nuttall saw them approach him in the dark and, mistaking them for Indians, ran off into the bush. The annoyed rescuers chased him for three days without success, until he accidentally wandered back into the camp unassisted.

In North Dakota, Nuttall somehow managed to stray 100 miles away from his group. Lost and exhausted, he collapsed and lost consciousness. A passing Indian took pity on him and carried him three miles to the river and paddled him home in a canoe. Amazingly, Nuttall somehow found his way back to England where he spent the next few years studying the hundreds of plant specimens he had brought home with him at the British Museum of Natural History and came to be regarded as the world's leading authority on the flora and fauna of north-west America.

As Nuttall rarely knew where he was at any given moment, his notes on the locations of some of his discoveries have since been found to be less than trustworthy. For example, he claims to have encountered the Willamette daisy in the "Rocky Mountains toward Oregon"; however, it is now known that he must have found the plant in the Willamette Valley since it has never been known to grow anywhere else.

## Most Predictable Outcome of Plucky British Amateurism

Robert Falcon Scott had the key characteristic that was expected of any British hero – he was capable of extraordinary fortitude in the face of insurmountable adversity. He was the quintessential British loser, the enigmatic underdog who strove against hopeless odds but whose efforts resulted in valiant, but ultimately tragic, failure. A less generous historian, however, would point out that his 1911 race with Roald Amundsen to the South Pole was not so much heroic as just plain dumb.

Unlike his great rival, Robert Falcon Scott didn't set out to be an explorer; the driving force in his life was money. When he was young, his brewery-owning father went broke, then died, leaving the family in financial crisis and their fate on Scott's shoulders. He joined the Royal Navy and rose through the ranks to become an officer. As Britain was between wars and the opportunities for a young naval officer to advance himself were limited, he thought he could skip a few rungs of the promotion ladder by reinventing himself as an explorer.

In 1901, at the age of thirty-one, he was given command of the ship *Discovery* for an expedition to the Antarctic. The highlight of the expedition was a three-month march across the polar ice by Scott and two shipmates including Ernest Shackleton. They travelled further south than anyone had ever done before and Scott returned home a national hero.

Having caught the exploring bug, he immediately began planning a new expedition. This time he was reaching for the most coveted prize in the modern age of exploration – the South Pole. Scott spent years struggling to raise funds for the trip, before finally departing on the whaling ship *Terra Nova* from Cardiff, Wales, in June 1910. In typically amateurish fashion, at this point not even all the money required to fund the expedition had been raised. The remainder was to be appealed for by means of a whip-round in ports of call along the way. Scott was stunned to find a telegram waiting for him in Melbourne: "Beg leave to inform. *Fram*[11] heading south. Amundsen." Scott now had a new challenge he hadn't bargained for – he was in a race to the Pole.

The Norwegian Roald Amundsen was already a highly experienced Arctic explorer, having been the first to travel the Northwest Passage in his ship *Gjoa* in 1903–06. He was trying for the North Pole in 1809 when rival American explorers, Robert Peary and Frederick Cook, announced within weeks of each other that they had beaten him to it. Robbed of the North Pole, Amundsen simply decided to go for the South Pole instead.

Scott's expedition should have taken precedence, but Amundsen wasn't going to be trumped again. He sailed from Oslo on 3 June 1910 with the professed intent of sticking to his old plan to sail the *Fram* round Cape Horn and back north to Alaska and the easier route to the North Pole. It was only when he reached Madeira, while Scott was on his way to Australia, that Amundsen revealed his true intentions.

Amundsen planned his expedition down to the very last detail. For his team, he hand-picked accomplished skiers and taught them tips and techniques learned from the Inuit. He took sledges and 100 well-trained dogs to pull them. By using the dogs instead of men to haul the sleds, Amundsen's team could rest and regain their strength without risking the rations. He spent endless amounts of time fine-tuning his equipment. He invented and

---

11  Amundsen's ship.

tested special boots, and used a type of Inuit clothing to keep warm and dry instead of the usual heavy winter clothing. He took seal meat to ward off scurvy and used innovations such as the thermos flask so that they didn't have to stop and set up camp just to prepare something to eat. Cleverly (or deviously, depending on you choose to look at it), Amundsen had also concealed his plans until the last minute to wrong-foot Scott.

The Norwegians sledged to the South Pole in double-quick time, reaching it on 15 December 1911, a month before Scott, before returning safely to their base camp, eating their dogs as they went. Amundsen's attention to detail had been so great that they made his expedition seem no more dangerous than an extended field trip. It was efficient, well prepared and focused solely on the goal of getting to his destination and back.

But this was not the British way of doing things. Although Scott was already an Antarctic veteran, he ignored some of the basic lessons of polar exploration. His first mistake was not taking enough food because he thought he and his party could survive 'indefinitely' on seals and penguins. He discovered too late that seals disappeared as soon as bad weather set in and penguins were summer visitors. As a result, his men had a deficit of 3,000 calories a day and each man had lost 25 kg of body weight by the time they reached the North Pole.

He was also unprepared for extreme temperatures, dressing his team in the best Jaeger wool. This was fine for underwear but completely useless as an outer covering because it allowed the wind to penetrate and gathered snow. His team had faulty goggles or no goggles at all and suffered from painful snow-blindness – actual burning of their corneas.

Just as important as having the right clothing is knowing where you are going. Instead of the lightweight sextant that Amundsen used, Scott took a heavy, cumbersome theodolite, and only one navigator, having dismissed an offer to have the man trained to read latitudes.

Whereas the Norwegian had banked entirely on sleds hauled by huskies, Scott decided on a complex strategy that involved horses, motor sleds and man-hauling, clanking along with a fully tooled-up scientific expedition, taking with him all sorts of heavy equipment, including three particularly useless motorized sledges. The sledges had been invented for the trip, but Scott decided to leave the man who had built and designed them behind at the last-minute. One fell through the ice and the other two stopped working in the cold.

Scott's decision to rely largely on ponies instead of dogs was arguably his biggest single mistake. The dogs wanted to eat the ponies, while the ponies kept falling through the ice and had to be put down; the man Scott put in charge of the ponies mistrusted the horse-snowshoes that had been specially made for them so he left them at base camp. The few dogs Scott did take were fed dried fish, which made them ill and difficult to handle. He hadn't learned how to drive them properly and ran his sledges too fast, making it hard for his team to keep up. Ten out of a team of thirteen dogs plunged into a crevasse and, although they were eventually saved, the incident convinced Scott that dogs would never make it to the Pole, so he sent them back to base camp.

He also packed his sledges badly, forcing the men to pack and unpack them every single day to pitch camp, and failed to seal the fuel canisters properly, despite knowing from previous expeditions that the seams would fail in the sub-zero temperatures. Half the fuel, required for heating men and food, leaked out.

Scott took men who barely knew how to ski. One of the men he hand-picked to take with him – Lawrence Oates – had one leg an inch shorter than the other due to a bullet wound sustained in the Boer War. As a result, Oates actually limped the 860-mile route taken by Scott's party to the Pole and part of the way back. Compounding Scott's difficulties, he and his team were hauling an extra 30 lbs of rock samples, although they could have easily left the samples at one of the cairns along the way to be picked up later.[12]

---

12 Although Scott never made it back himself, a lot of his samples did, plus the Edwardian version of *Frozen Planet* – the first movie film of Antarctic creatures ever recorded. Film of Weddell seals and killer whales was truly groundbreaking. There were also the Emperor Penguin eggs he found. Not a total disaster then.

His final misjudgement was taking five people with him on his final push to the Pole, when his supplies had been based on a team of four, effectively condemning his team to death.

Scott's five-man crew reached the South Pole on 17 January 1912 and were horrified that the Norwegians had already been and gone. Most gallingly, among the detritus of the abandoned Norwegian camp – flags, sleeping bags, broken instruments – was a letter to King Haakon VII of Norway, together with a request that Scott be kind enough to deliver it when he got back.

Scott and his party didn't hang around to dwell on their defeat. The temperature had dropped to -30°C, eight degrees lower than it had been when the Norwegians arrived. They took a few pictures and trudged back towards camp. With 400 miles still to travel, the party's prospects steadily worsened with the deteriorating weather. One by one, they died of exhaustion, frostbite and starvation. Edgar Evans, the team's fittest member, was the first to die, weakened by a blow to the head after falling into a crevasse a few days earlier. Laurence Oates was next. Lame from severe frostbite and fearing that he was slowing his companions down, he walked out into the blizzard to his death with the words, "I am just going outside and may be some time."[13] He was carrying thirty opium pills but didn't take them because to have done so would have been a coward's way out.

By 22 March, the three remaining men had two days' food left, but were three days short of their next depot. Then a blizzard struck and stopped them moving on. Despite his deteriorating condition, Scott continued to record their fate in grim detail right to the bitter end. At one point, he seems to have been genuinely puzzled when the blackish, "rotten-looking" nose of one of his colleagues seemed likely to drop off. Scott noted, "To my surprise, he shows signs of losing heart over it."

---

13   These were Laurence Oates' last words according to Scott's account. Some historians have suggested that Scott made them up.

Scott, Wilson and Bowers died in their tent out on the Ross Ice Shelf from a combination of scurvy, exposure and starvation. It was another ten months before the tragic news was cabled to London that not only had Scott been beaten to the South Pole by Amundsen, but this man who carried a nation's hopes on his shoulders had tragically frozen to death in his tent a mere ten miles from safety.

But nobody puts a gloss on disaster quite like the British (see also The Charge of The Light Brigade). There were tributes in the House of Commons and *The Times* described their deaths as "'the noblest tragedy in history". King George V led a memorial service for Scott and his men and thousands stood outside St Paul's Cathedral – far more than had turned out for the *Titanic* dead the year before. For the next fifty years, Britons erected monuments to his name across the country and over £1 million was raised for the dependents of the expedition, and although you can't be knighted posthumously, his wife was granted the rank of knight widow.

Poor Amundsen, meanwhile, who not only won the race to the Pole but returned without losing a single man, was largely forgotten. Worse still, he was somehow regarded as a cheat. Indeed, such was the British disdain at Amundsen's professionalism that Lord Curzon, President of the Royal Geographic Society, sarcastically toasted the Norwegian success with "three cheers for the dogs". Amundsen resigned from the Society in disgust, noting, "Victory awaits those who have everything in order; people call this luck. Defeat awaits those who fail to make the necessary precautions; this is known as bad luck."

Of course, Scott couldn't respond to this taunt; he and his crew were long dead.

## Most People Lost While Looking for a Lost City

Travelling without a map in strange lands with unfathomable natural hazards, unknown diseases and possibly murderous indigenous peoples takes suicidal courage and infinite resourcefulness. It also helps if you're mad. Fortunately,

Colonel Percy Harrison Fawcett had all three of these qualities in abundance.

Fawcett was born in Torquay in 1867, the son of Captain Edward Boyd Fawcett, renowned Sussex county cricketer, member of the Royal Geographical Society and equerry to the future Edward VII. Fawcett Jnr was known to all as "PHF", although his wife called him "Puggy".[14] When he was nineteen, he joined the Royal Artillery where he learned the basics of surveying in the hope that it might involve lots of travel, and he subsequently spent several years in Sri Lanka. During this time, he became interested in the Spiritualist movement and may have become a Buddhist.

Fawcett's ticket to adventure arrived in 1906 when the Royal Geographical Society invited him to undertake a survey of Bolivia's frontier with Brazil. The territory between the two countries was rubber-rich, but no one could agree where the exact boundary lay. Fawcett was only too happy to sign up, commencing his lifelong love affair with the Amazon jungle.

By 1915, Fawcett was back in uniform and was posted to France where he spent eighteen months in the trenches. In 1916, he took up a new post as an artillery corps counter-battery colonel, detailed to suppress German heavy guns. Fawcett's subordinates were surprised to learn that their new leader was not in the least bit interested in the innovative work being done on the detection of German guns by flash-spotting and sound ranging, He could detect German targets, he informed them, on his Ouija board.

After the war, Fawcett returned to the uncharted and dangerous Amazon basin several times, surviving in the jungle for years at a time, without contact with the outside world, armed with little more than a machete, a rifle and a compass, often living for days on a handful of nuts, singing "Onward Christian Soldiers" and "A Bicycle Built for Two" as he tramped through the mosquito-infested hinterland.

---

14   Because he was pugnacious, not because he resembled a Pug.

Fawcett wrote up accounts of his journeys in a series of popular books. One of his discoveries, Tabletop Mountain near the Verde River, inspired his friend and fellow loony, the writer Arthur Conan Doyle, to use his field reports as the basis for his book, *The Lost World*.

No one could fault Fawcett's bravery, but his stories, describing attacks by cannibals on the Amazon and encounters with vampire bats, giant snakes and a killer spider the size of a dinner plate in a hotel bedroom, raised a few eyebrows back home. This description of the shooting of a monstrous anaconda in Bolivia is typical:

> *I sprang for my rifle as the creature began to make its way up the bank and, hardly waiting to aim, smashed a .44 soft-nosed bullet into its spine, ten feet below the wicked head. At once there was a flurry of foam, and several heavy thumps against the boat's keel, shaking us as though we had run on a snag. We stepped ashore and approached the creature with caution. As far as it was possible to measure, a length of 45 feet lay out of the water and 17 feet lay in the water, making it a total length of 62 feet.*

Fawcett may have trained as surveyor but his measuring skills were suspect; his monstrous snake was at least double the maximum length of any anaconda yet discovered. There were more strange zoological encounters, including the discovery of a breed of dog with two noses.

All the while he was pestering the Foreign Office and the Royal Geographical Society for money to fund his trips. In 1920, an irritated John Keltie, secretary of the RGS, noted: "Fawcett has a reputation of being difficult to get on with, and has a queer manner in many ways, being a mystic and a spiritualist, but all the same he has an extraordinary power of getting through difficulties that would deter anybody else."

Despite his growing reputation as a crackpot, Fawcett was now recognized as the world's foremost authority on South America and became a recipient of the Gold Medal, the honor bestowed on an explorer by the Royal Geographical Society.

During Fawcett's travels in Amazonia, he became fascinated with the possibility of finding a mythical lost city called "Z". Rumours of a fabulously wealthy South American lost city had abounded in European folklore for centuries. Fawcett had studied ancient legends and historical records, in particular a fragmentary, anonymous document, known as Manuscript 512, written by an early Portuguese explorer, which spoke of a magnificent inland city. Although Fawcett had great admiration for the South American natives, he was an Englishman of his time and endemically racist. He refused to believe that the Amazonian Indians themselves could have created this great city. Fawcett came to the conclusion that "Z" must have been built by people of European ancestry, perhaps the Celts. He was also convinced, based on a combination of serious research, intensive fieldwork, wishful thinking and clairvoyance, that the lost city existed somewhere in the Mato Grosso region. Fawcett approached the Foreign Office again for money to mount an expedition and was again rebuffed. He would have to fund it alone.

His first attempt was in 1921. He set off from Cuiabá and got as far as the Xingu River, but it ended in failure when he was forced to turn back with an injured leg. Later that year, Fawcett tried again, this time completely alone, travelling west from Bahia in Brazil for three months, but once again he returned in failure.

In 1925, at the age of fifty-eight, he made his third and final attempt, this time accompanied by his eldest son Jack and his son's friend Raleigh Rimmell, plus two hired Brazilian porters, two horses, eight mules and two dogs. The last anyone ever heard of the group was as they crossed the Upper Xingu, a south-eastern tributary of the Amazon. Fawcett's last telegraph, sent on 29 May 1925, assured his wife Nina: "You need have no fear of failure". The party then simply vanished without trace.

Before he set off, Fawcett left strict instructions that in the event of his failure to return there should be no risky attempts to follow in his footsteps. To date, over one hundred people have died ignoring his advice. George Miller Dyott, a member of the Royal Geographical Society, was the first to try in 1928, with a mission either to rescue Fawcett or at least find his earthly remains. Months later, Dyott and his men returned from the jungle sick, emaciated and mosquito-bitten. He claimed he had evidence that Aloique, chief of the Nahukwá, had murdered Fawcett, but this proof amounted to nothing more than Aloique's unreliable testimony. Dyott wrote about his exploits in the book, *Man Hunting in the Jungle.*

One of the most famous of at least a dozen separate failed expeditions to discover what happened to Fawcett was told in the book *Brazilian Adventure* by the journalist Peter Fleming in 1932. The expedition, commanded by an eccentric American colonel called Pringle, was so badly organized that no one had bothered to learn Portuguese or read the news, otherwise they would have known that Brazil was in the middle of a revolution. The group ended up wandering aimlessly and panic-stricken around the Brazilian hinterland, blazing away with their guns at anything that moved. In the same year, Stefan Rattin, a Swiss trapper, emerged from the jungle to claim that the elderly Fawcett was being held captive by Indians. Although his story attracted a great deal of attention from the world's press, Fawcett's surviving son Brian was not inclined to believe that his father, who had been bald for some time, was now the old man with long white hair described by Rattin.

Hopes were raised then dashed again when some human bones discovered in the jungle in 1951 proved on examination not to belong to Fawcett. In 1996, a wealthy banker, James Lynch, and his sixteen-year-old son James Jr, retraced Fawcett's journey to Fawcett's last known position, where they were kidnapped by the Kalapalos Indians, whose punishment for trespassing was either death by piranhas or stinging bees. The Indians didn't release Lynch and his son until after he gave them all his supplies and equipment worth an estimated $30,000.

In 2005, American journalist David Grann visited the Kala-palo tribe and discovered that there was a local oral history about Fawcett and his party, the first white men the tribe had ever seen. The Kalapolos claimed that Fawcett stayed at their village and then left heading eastward. He was warned not to go that way because they would almost certainly be killed by the "fierce Indians" who occupied that territory – but Fawcett insisted on going anyway. Grann also believed that Fawcett deliberately falsified the coordinates of his route plan, and that previous expeditions had therefore been looking in the wrong place.

In 2004, previously unreleased private papers revealed another more outlandish explanation for Fawcett's post-war vanishing act. The explorer, according to letters he sent to friends, had no intention of returning to Torquay. He was, in fact, lured by a beautiful native "she-god", an erotic siren who draws white men into the jungle. There, he planned to set up a com-mune based on a cult involving the worship of his son, Jack.

Had Fawcett been eaten by jaguars, or had he lived alone as a native, or starved or been murdered by fierce natives, or had he settled down in the jungle with a native she-god, retelling tales of unnaturally large serpents to fellow members of a theosophical commune? The question is unlikely ever to be answered.

## Cosmic Martyrs

When explorers die it is usually down to bad planning, bad luck or unaccounted for physical or biological hazards. Some explorers were never intended to return alive in the first place.

In October 1956, the Soviet Union blazed a trail into space by launching Sputnik, the first satellite in orbit. It was a cause of huge national rejoicing, but it was still not enough for Premier Nikita Kruschev. Within days, he was commanding his space programme to come up with something even more spectacular for 7 November, the fortieth anniversary of the Bolshevik Revolution. No pressure then.

Someone suggested sending a dog into space. Great idea, everyone agreed. The trouble was there was barely enough time to design a spacecraft, let alone a re-entry craft. Sputnik 2 was not designed to come back.

A stray mongrel bitch – probably part-Siberian husky – called Laika ("Barker") was plucked from the streets of Moscow and designated for international stardom. She was apparently chosen from ten standby dogs because of her photogenic good looks – "lucky" Laika's face would soon be printed in newspapers around the world.

On 31 October 1957, she was placed inside a padded, pressurized cabin within Sputnik 2. There was enough room for her to lie down or stand but she was chained to prevent her turning around. An air regeneration system provided oxygen, and food was dispensed in a jelly form. Laika was fitted with a harness, a bag to collect waste and electrodes to monitor vital signs.

The early signals before take-off indicated that the dog was agitated but eating her food. During the launch, her pulse rate rose to three times normal, an indication of stress. It was reported that she died when her oxygen ran out on day six, or as the Soviet Government initially claimed, she was humanely put down prior to oxygen depletion.

In fact, Laika was dead within hours after launch, roasted alive when Soviet ground engineers failed to notice a problem with the cooling system. Her coffin lapped the Earth another 2,570 times until it burned up in the atmosphere in April 1958. Few people openly questioned the ethics of sending a dog into space. The true cause and time of her death were not admitted publicly until 2002.

After Laika's début, at least thirteen Russian canine cosmonauts followed her into orbit between 1957 and 1961, of whom five died in flight. A variety of large and small animals have since been flown to space for scientific experiments in orbit. In 1958, the USA launched their first animal into space, a squirrel monkey named Gordo, aboard a Jupiter AM-13 booster on a suborbital flight. Gordo completed the flight and returned safely, but during his recovery a flotation device in the rocket's nose cone failed and Gordo drowned.

Six months later, the USA tried again with a female rhesus named Able aboard a Jupiter AM-18 rocket. The monkey flew to an altitude of 300 miles at speeds over 10,000 mph and was weightless for nine minutes. Able returned safely to Earth, but afterwards sensors that had been used to transmit her vital signs were removed in surgery; Able died from the anesthetic during the operation.

## Worst Attempt to Climb Mount Everest (or the Most Successful Attempt to Climb Mount Everest by a Transvestite)

On 2 June 1953, the front page of *The Times* carried the headline: "EVEREST CONQUERED: HILARY AND TENSING REACH THE SUMMIT" . News had reached Britain late the previous evening that a UK expedition led by John Hunt had finally become the first to reach the summit of Chomlungma or "Mother of the World" to the Tibetans, Sagasmatha or "Goddess of the sky" to the Nepalese, or Peak XV to the British, until William Lambton's Great Trigonometrical Survey of 1806 when they renamed it Mount Everest after the Surveyor-General of India, Sir George Everest.

Before 1953, ten expeditions at the cost of at least sixteen lives had set out to confront the physical and logistical challenges posed by the world's highest mountain.[15] Apart from the odd Swiss and Canadian, it had been mostly Britons who had died trying to reach the roof of the world. The most famous failed attempt was by the legendary George Mallory, whose response when asked by a journalist, "Why do you want

---

15  The first Everest casualty was Scottish mountaineer Dr A. M. Kellas, who didn't actually make it to within 100 miles of the mountain, having died on his approach. The rest of his party gave up at 23,000 ft – a vertical mile below the summit – and went home pronouncing their mission "a total success". Expedition leader W. H. Murray explained, "It was thought that the mountain could indubitably be climbed were it 5,000 feet smaller."

to climb Everest?" produced the reply which has since slipped into common usage when offering a reason for taking on a formidable challenge: "Because it is there."

The strangest attempt was by thirty-three-year-old Yorkshireman Maurice Wilson, a mill worker's son from Bradford, who was an unlikely mountaineer. He had been shot twice during the First World War leaving his left arm immobile and, since the war, had wandered aimlessly and struggled to hold down a job for long. Eventually, he left Yorkshire for New Zealand where he became the manager of a women's clothes shop. A couple of years before his climb, he was struck down by tuberculosis and suffered a nervous breakdown. It was during this time that he began to dabble in mysticism and faith healing. Wilson later claimed he was able to conquer both illnesses by undergoing a treatment of thirty-five days of intensive prayer and complete fasting, a technique he had apparently learned from a mysterious man he met in London who had cured himself and over 100 other people of various "incurable diseases". Wilson declined to reveal the man's name, nor did he ever offer any proof that he really existed, but from then on he become a fanatical believer in the power of prayer and fasting and spreading the word of these powers was his new vocation in life.

In 1931, while recuperating from his illnesses, he came across a newspaper article about the ill-fated Mallory, who had vanished somewhere near the summit of Everest in 1924. Wilson was intrigued and wanted to know more, so he dug deeper into the life of Mallory. Within six months, he had made his mind up to become the first man to climb the world's highest peak. What better way to spread the word about his newfound faith than by climbing Mount Everest?

It goes without saying that the challenges involved in climbing Everest, even for an experienced mountaineer, were enormous. Apart from the hostile climate and the sheer scale of the mountain itself, there were many other obstacles to consider. Some were political – the Chinese forbade anyone to climb the mountain via Tibet. That left only the route via

Nepal. The Nepalese authorities didn't want to encourage random foreign climbers to wind up dead on their territory either, so access to the mountain was carefully restricted. Other challenges were more practical – it took, for example, about thirty porters just to carry the cash required to pay your way because paper money was not acceptable in that part of the world.

But Maurice Wilson had a bold plan that would circumvent all of these obstacles. He would achieve the first solo ascent of Everest by simply flying halfway round the world, crash landing the plane on the slopes at altitude – then walk to the summit.

There were a couple of flaws in his plan – he didn't own a plane and had never flown one before, nor did he have any experience of mountain climbing. Unperturbed by these minor considerations, he bought a used 1925 Gypsy Moth – the type with an open-cabin biplane – and renamed it *Ever-Wrest*, then booked himself a few flying lessons at the London Aeroplane Club. He was a poor student and it took him twice the average time to get his pilot's licence. His instructor warned him he would never reach India. Wilson replied that he would get to Everest, or die trying.

His preparation for the mountaineering challenge that lay ahead was even more rudimentary. He didn't buy any specialist kit, such an ice axe or crampons, and spent just five weeks walking around Snowdonia before declaring himself ready to set off on his great adventure. Fasting and prayer would enable him to succeed where George Mallory and others had failed. He was quite literally on a wing and a prayer.

Wilson planned his departure for Tibet in April 1933 but was delayed when he crashed *Ever-Wrest* in a field near Bradford. He escaped unscathed but the plane's fuselage was buckled and took three weeks to repair. Wilson was now front-page news and *The Times* alone followed his quest with 150 news stories, but it also attracted the attention of the Air Ministry, who promptly banned him from flying to Nepal because it violated a British Government treaty with the Nepalese authorities.

The mountaineering establishment was similarly unimpressed by Wilson's endeavour. Every previous British expedition to conquer the mountain had been under close supervision by the Alpine Club and the Royal Geographic Society and neither looked kindly on the efforts of dilettante madmen to upstage them. But despite the best efforts of the authorities to thwart Wilson's apparently suicidal attempt, on 21 May 1933 he slipped out of the country and set off for India, just after tearing up a telegram from the British Government threatening action if he went ahead with the flight.

A solo flight halfway across the world would have tested the best aviators of the day, but Wilson was planning to do it with basic maps. His destination was 5,000 miles away but his plane had only a 620-mile fuel range. His route meandered from London to Freiburg, Freiburg to Passau, followed by a failed attempt to cross the Alps, then back to Passau and Freiburg, then over the Alps again to Rome. At one point, he was flying blind through total cloud cover – a challenge for a professional pilot, let alone a novice – but somehow he managed to pull it off. A few days later, he set off again for Cairo, then Baghdad. The Persian authorities refused him a permit to fly over their territory and he was forced to turn south and fly along the Arabian Peninsula, an area for which he had no maps at all. He bought himself a children's atlas and then set off on the 620-mile stretch from Baghdad to the next airfield in Bahrain. Flying in the brain-boiling summer heat, he managed to land just before running out of fuel.

In Bahrain, the implications of flying without British Government backing finally caught up with him. The local police informed him the air space ahead was "closed to civilian air traffic" and he was to turn back immediately or face arrest. Wilson promptly took off, pretending to fly back to Iraq, but then turned his plane and headed straight for India. Just a few hundred miles short of the Indian border with Nepal, his primitive plane stalled and Wilson was forced to perform an emergency landing at Gwadar. The police promptly impounded his plane and placed him under surveillance.

Having been forced to abandon his plane, Wilson decided to complete the rest of his ascent on foot. He sold the Gypsy Moth and went to Darjeeling where he hoped to get a climbing permit from the Tibetan side. The local authorities were still determined to stop him; there would be no permit granted for Wilson to ascend Everest by any means. One morning in March 1934, he slipped away disguised as a Tibetan priest and, accompanied by three Sherpas, hiked overland through Tibet and ten days later arrived at the foot of Mount Everest.

After four days of slow progress and camping on exposed ledges, they were confronted by an impassable forty-foot ice wall. Wilson was still convinced that he could surmount any obstacle via a combination of fasting[16] and prayer. His Sherpas begged to differ and returned to base camp, after imploring him to go with them. Wilson climbed on alone.

Whether he genuinely believed at this point that he could still conquer Everest alone, without extra oxygen or proper climbing gear, or whether he continued because he preferred death to the humiliation of returning to England in defeat, is open to debate. He was last seen alive setting out alone up a glacier equipped with a tent, three loaves, two tins of oatmeal, a camera, a Union Jack and a shaving mirror. The latter was to be used to signal monks at the Rongbuk Monastery fifteen miles away by flashing sunlight down to them that he had reached the summit. The signal never came.

A year later, a British party found his frozen, emaciated corpse wrapped in his tent. There was women's clothing in his rucksack and he was wearing women's underwear. Beside his body was his diary. Wilson's final entry for 31 May, read: "Off again, gorgeous day."

---

16    He seems to have lapsed with his fasting, though – in Wilson's diary, he admits to eating large amounts of anything he could get his hands on.

# 2

## Standing on the Shoulders of Midgets: Scientific Losers

*In which Mr Scheele tastes the periodic table; the world's greatest astronomer dies of good table manners; Mr Newton loses his marbles; Mr Wallace lets someone else get the credit for discovering evolutionary theory; and Mr Midgley lowers the world's IQ.*

### Least Accurate Scientific Textbook

The first-century Roman scholar Pliny the Elder wrote a forty-seven-volume book *Historia Naturalis,* which was to become the foremost authority on scientific matters right up to the Middle Ages.

Pliny didn't take the trouble to verify most of what he wrote about. His book contained detailed descriptions of monstrous races in far-off lands, including evil-eyed Illyrians, one-legged Monocoli and animal-human hybrids, and assured readers that the hippopotamus walks backwards to confuse anyone trying to track it.

Pliny's fact-checking on medical matters was similarly lax. He recommended treating a scorpion bite by drinking the insect's ashes in a glass of wine, advised that toothache was caused by malevolent worms living inside teeth and was preventable by eating mice twice a month, and prescribed green frogs, toads and worms as a cure for halitosis. *Encyclopaedia Britannica* describes Pliny's book as "a work of uneven accuracy".

*Historia Naturalis* was so influential that by the time anyone got around to seriously challenging his teachings, Pliny the

Elder had been dead for over a thousand years, having discovered during the eruption of Vesuvius in AD 79 that there was no cure for standing next to a volcano to get a better look.

> *"I cannot conceive of any vital disaster happening to this vessel. Modern ship building has gone beyond that."*
> Edward J. Smith, captain of the RMS *Titanic*, 1912

## Least Accurate Attempt to Date the Earth

In the summer of 1650, an Irish priest from Armagh, James Ussher, published a monumental book called *The Annals of the Old Testament*. The project, which occupied 2,000 pages in Latin, was a formidable piece of academic research that took up twenty years of Ussher's life and caused him to go half-blind in the process, but the most important piece of information in the whole book appeared in the very first paragraph of the very first page.

By adding together the life spans of all the descendants of Adam, Ussher worked out that God created the Earth on the evening of Saturday, 22 October 4004 BC – at nightfall, around 6p.m., if you want to be more precise. What happened before that, at 5.30 p.m. for example, Ussher didn't say, or rather couldn't. According to Christian doctrine, before 6p.m. on 22 October 4004 BC, time itself did not exist. God did nothing all.

Ussher was congratulated by almost everyone for his stunning piece of historical scholarship. It confirmed something Christians had assumed to be correct for centuries: that the world and mankind were as old as each other – that is, not very old at all. In 1675, a London bookseller called Thomas Guy started publishing Bibles with Ussher's date printed in the margin of the work. It was a great bit of business and Guy's Bible became immensely popular, although this might have had more to do with his engravings of bare-breasted biblical women than the inclusion of Ussher's chronology. A few years later, the Church of England also began printing Ussher's date in its official Bible and, before long, the date was appearing in Bibles so often that it was practically accepted as the word of God.

Of course, there was the odd sceptic, and not just about Ussher's dating system. A Frenchman called Isaac La Peyrère politely pointed to some discrepancies in the Old Testament itself. If there were no other people in the world before Adam and Eve, where did their son Cain find himself a wife? And why did God have to mark Cain so that people knew who he was? Surely, if the only people around were Cain's parents and his sibling, they would know who he was anyway?

When La Peyrère wrote up his concerns in a book called *Men Before Adam*, he was hauled before the Pope and forced to apologize. Long afterwards and at a safe distance from the Vatican, La Peyrère insisted that, actually, he had only mumbled his apology and had not, in fact, retracted a single word, and for the rest of his life he was quietly convinced that the book of Genesis had got it all wrong.

La Peyrère was very lucky. The Catholic establishment was not known for being reasonable with people who entertained doubts about the literal accuracy of the Bible. In 1600, Giordano Bruno was burned to death for questioning Christ's divinity and suggesting that the universe was infinite. The Inquisition cut out the tongue, strangled, then burned a doctor called Giulio Vanini who suggested that there might be a logical explanation for the biblical miracles. Little wonder then that Ussher's date for the age of the Earth continued to hold sway, largely unchallenged, for the next 200 years or so. In fact, it was still being printed in the margin of Bibles right into the twentieth century.

La Peyrère's hypothesis, however, had opened people's minds to the possibility that the Earth might just be longer in the tooth than the Church said it was. In 1770, the French scientist Jean-Baptiste-Claude Delisle de Sales challenged the age given by Ussher. He claimed that, based on astronomical data, the Earth was around 140,000 years old and had taken at least 40,000 years to cool down since its formation. For his pains, de Sales was jailed and most of his books were burned.

In the 1860s, Ussher's date was once again challenged by science; in particular, a cheeky new arrival called geology suggested that the Earth was at the very least twenty million years old.[1] Thanks to radiometric age dating, we know now that the Earth is about 4.55 billion years old. So Ussher was only out by 454,994,346 years . . . give or take.

## "Hard Luck" Scheele

Despite having had no formal scientific education, the eighteenth-century Swedish pharmacist Carl Wilhelm Scheele made remarkable contributions to chemistry.

He discovered oxygen three years before Joseph Priestley, but didn't get around to publishing his findings until 1777, by which time Priestley had already taken all the credit. He went on to discover several more elements – such as barium, chlorine, manganese, molybdenum and tungsten – as well as compounds including citric acid, lactic acid, glycerol and hydrogen cyanide. He also discovered a process similar to pasteurization and a means of mass-producing phosphorus, which led Sweden to become one of the world's leading producers of matches. But in every case, someone else took the credit.

Scheele might have gone on making great discoveries if it hadn't been for his habit of sniffing and tasting every chemical he worked with, including such lethal substances as mercury and hydrocyanic acid – a chemical so deadly that even inhalation or contact with the skin could lead to a horrific, painful death. Any one of these could have accounted for his sudden and premature death at his laboratory workbench at the age of forty-three.

---

1   See "Least Comprehensible Scientific Paper".

> *"Beef cattle the size of dogs will be grazed in the average man's backyard, eating specially thick grass and producing specially tender steaks."*
> Science Digest *article "Your Life in 1985", 1955*

## Most Accident-Prone Astronomer

The history of proper astronomical research began with a Dane called Tycho Brahe. Before Brahe, astronomers made the odd observation of their own, then added their findings to whatever else had been handed down to them from the great stargazers of antiquity. Brahe was the first person to see that a proper understanding of the movements of the planets required a long series of painstaking observations of their motions relative to the fixed stars. But Brahe is remembered today not so much for his brilliant scientific career as for being prone to bizarre mishaps.

He was born in 1546 to a noble Danish family in Knud-strup, now in Sweden but then part of Denmark. His father Otto served the King of Denmark as Privy Counsellor. Brahe was groomed for a career in law, but wanted to become an astronomer, very much against his family's wishes, after witnessing a partial eclipse of the Sun when he was a teenager. His big break, however, came not as an astronomer, but as an astrologer.

On 28 October 1566, there was an eclipse of the Moon and, on the basis of a horoscope he had cast, Brahe announced that the eclipse foretold the death of the Ottoman Sultan, Sulemain "the Magnificent". At the time, it was not difficult with a little imagination to read astrological significance into just about anything observable in the sky; the religious wars of the Reformation were in full swing and Europe was in turmoil. Brahe's prediction, however, was very popular because Sulemain, as a Muslim, was hated by Catholics and Protestants alike. When news broke that the Sultan had indeed expired, Brahe's reputation as a man of learning was sealed. Some of the gloss was taken off the prediction by the fact that Sulemain was already eighty years old and it later emerged that he had, in fact, been dead for several weeks before the eclipse, but no one seems to have made too much of it. Brahe was now internationally famous and able to hob-nob with the crowned heads of Europe. One of his biggest fans was King James VI of Scotland, the future King James I of England.

Brahe was planning to move to Basel in Switzerland where he could be closer to the southern European centres of culture, but in 1576 the Danish King Frederick II, basking in the reflected glory of his new home-grown hero and desperate not to lose him permanently, made him an offer he couldn't refuse. Frederick gifted his celebrity astronomer the island of Hveen, along with substantial treasury funds, to set up a permanent observatory.

Brahe set about constructing a fantastic castle observatory, which he called Uraniborg, equipped with a range of instruments of remarkable size and precision, the like of which the world had never seen. It cost the equivalent of 30 per cent of the annual revenues of the Danish crown, about $5 billion in today's currency, but in scientific terms it was money well spent. Although he didn't even have the benefit of a telescope, armed with his naked eye and a quadrant Brahe made a vast number of astonishingly accurate astronomical measurements, including a comprehensive study of the solar system, pinpointing the positions of hundreds of stars.

As well as his scientific duties, he was also obliged to provide annual astrological predictions for the royal court, although by now Brahe wasn't entirely convinced of its usefulness. This didn't stop him from drawing up a list of days in the year called "Tycho Days" when it was considered advantageous to stay in bed, because unfortunate events were bound to occur. Even today in parts of Scandinavia, a day when everything goes wrong is called a "Tycho Day".

Brahe's future seemed secure, but not everyone was enamoured of the King's favourite. In between mapping the skies, the astronomer ruled his island kingdom in a grand style and with a thoroughly autocratic hand. It was home to a huge retinue of servants and scientific assistants and, as well as his observatory, he built a chemical laboratory, a paper mill, a printing press and a dungeon for imprisoning recalcitrant tenants.

The Danish astronomer royal was not the sort of man you would want to get into an argument with. Arrogant and hot-tempered, he fought duels, scandalously kept a mistress who bore him eight children, employed a dwarf as a jester, dabbled in alchemy and generally tyrannized the local peasantry. Then there was some unfortunate business concerning Brahe's pet elk, which apparently got drunk during the night, fell down some stairs, broke a leg and had to be shot. What it was doing upstairs drunk in the first place is of course nobody's business but Brahe's.

There was something else that set Brahe apart. As a twenty-year-old student at Rostock, he got into a quarrel at a party with fellow academic Manderup Parsbjerg over who was the better mathematician. They decided to take it outside in the form of a duel, conducted in pitch darkness, with rapiers. Brahe escaped with his life but not his nose. He concealed the loss of face as best he could with an artificial bridge made of gold, silver and copper. He carried a small pot of glue with him at all times to keep his precious metal proboscis firmly in place.

Brahe's bad behaviour was tolerated so long as his friend King Frederick was alive. His son King Christian, however, was less forgiving of the high-maintenance celebrity astronomer and promptly cut off Brahe's pension. Brahe left Denmark in a huff and went to Prague seeking employment with the Holy Roman Emperor Rudolf II. He and Brahe got along famously: the Emperor had a number of odd interests, including a pet tiger, and was thought to be insane. Brahe was appointed Imperial Mathematician, although the job description also required him to keep the Emperor up to speed on any other general insights he had about the mysteries of the universe and he was also expected to cast the odd horoscope.

It was probably drink that did for Brahe in the end. In October 1601, he was invited to a banquet at the Prague palace of the nobleman Peter Vok Ursinus Rozmberk. He enjoyed the copious amount of food and drink on offer but, being a nobleman and well versed in table manners, etiquette prevented him from leaving his seat to empty his full bladder before his host left. By the time he got home, his bladder had swollen so much that he was unable to sleep or urinate. Intestinal fever and delirium followed and he died in agony eleven days later. His final words were: "Let me not seem to have lived in vain."

For many years, it was assumed that Brahe had died either from uremia, or from a burst bladder, but the unusual circumstances of his death has since led to suspicions that it was not accidental. Brahe employed an assistant, Jahannes Keppler. The two did not enjoy a particularly amicable working relationship because Brahe always jealously guarded his astronomical data and didn't allow Keppler to see it. Brahe's children were not acknowledged as his legitimate heirs and, when he died, there was a great deal of confusion as to who was in line to inherit his research. Keppler took advantage of the situation and stole the data, using it to further his own research into the underlying laws that govern the orbits of planets. On the back of Brahe's data, Keppler became much more famous than his luckless former employer.

A forensic analysis of Brahe's hair in 1991 showed a sudden spike in the amount of mercury in his body shortly before his death, leading many to believe that he had been poisoned by Keppler. Perhaps Brahe's final misfortune was to have been killed in the name of science by an ambitious rival.

## Least Successful Horoscope

The sixteenth-century Italian polymath Girolamo Cardano wrote on a wide variety of subjects including medicine, astronomy and philosophy. His addiction to gambling led to his pioneering studies of probability and chance. His reputation as a mathematician was so great that he was consulted by Leonardo da Vinci on questions of geometry.

As a sideline, Cardano also earned international fame as the most successful astrologer of his day and he was hired to cast horoscopes for the crowned heads of Europe, including England's young King Edward Vl. He once cast a horoscope for Jesus Christ and was briefly imprisoned for blasphemy. He even predicted his own death, down to the very hour, at the age of seventy-five. When the time arrived (21 September 1576) and Cardano found himself in robust good health, he committed suicide rather than admit he was wrong.

> *"Housewives in fifty years may wash dirty dishes right down the drain. Cheap plastic will melt in hot water."*
> *Popular Mechanics,* 1950

## Least Comprehensible Scientific Paper

The idea that the world has existed for a very long time indeed – or, at least, much longer than the Bible claimed it did – came from a Scot called James Hutton. Born in the Scottish borders in 1726, Hutton trained as a doctor and enjoyed a successful career as a chemist, then retired in his early forties to become a farmer. He was also a member of the Oyster Club in Edinburgh, a posh talking shop where enlightened men of independent means – lawyers, writers, philosophers, doctors and artists – could share ideas over claret, salt haddock and oysters. Membership included the economist Adam Smith, the philosopher David Hume and the chemist Joseph Black. Hutton took an interest in everything from canal building and heredity to fossil collecting, but his chief interest was in rock formations.

It occurred to Hutton that by tracing back the origin of the various rocks and minerals on his farm, he might arrive at some clear understanding of the history of the Earth. He spent over thirty years of travel and field observation building up a vast knowledge of rocks and their distribution throughout the British Isles. One thing that baffled Hutton, something that had puzzled people for ages, was that shells and other marine fossils could be found on top of mountains. Some people thought they had the answer: they had been deposited by mighty floods – the biblical Flood, perhaps. Hutton had another idea; what if the fossils had risen along with the mountains themselves?

Hutton gave his theory its first public airing in 1785 in front of the new Royal Society of Edinburgh. He said that the planet was in a state of continuous change. Continents were being eroded and renewed by processes at work at that time, had always been at work and would be repeated in the future. Soil was washed down to the sea, formed into rock and then uplifted under the tremendous force of subterranean heat. These cycles of decay and renewal occurred in indefinite time, "so that, with respect to human observation, this world has neither a beginning nor an end". Hutton's insight was simply quite brilliant – it opened the door for scientific theories from the biological evolution of Darwin to atomic theory and the Big Bang.

Unfortunately, hardly anyone at all took any notice. For all of his intellectual brilliance, a gifted communicator James Hutton was not. He was incapable of writing plain English even if his life depended upon it. When he got around to publishing his theory, it ran to two volumes and nearly a thousand pages of the most unreadable prose ever written. It was a rambling, grammar-free mess, crammed with the sort of jargon that even fellow geologists found impossible to follow. And that was the easy bit. Half of the book consisted of quotations from French sources, still in the original French. In a very crowded canon, it was the mother of unreadable scientific books. Even the experts thought that life was too short to spend reading Hutton's book about time.

And so it was that that Hutton very nearly became, at best, a footnote in the history of geological discovery. Fortunately, however, there was someone who had not only taken the trouble to read Hutton's book, but could actually understand all of it – his friend John Playfair, who was a professor of mathematics at Edinburgh University. Five years after Hutton's death in 1802, Playfair published a heavily edited version of Hutton's principles, called *Illustrations of the Huttonian Theory of the Earth*. For anyone who took an interest in geology, it was revelatory.

But buried somewhere in his original, unfathomable 2,000-page manuscript was an even more extraordinary insight. Hutton had also written a chapter on the origin of species, in which he noted:

> *If an organized body is not in the situation and circumstances best adapted to its sustenance and propagation, then, in conceiving an indefinite variety among the individuals of that species, we must be assured, that, on the one hand, those which depart most from the best adapted constitution, will be most liable to perish, while, on the other hand, those organized bodies, which most approach to the best constitution for the present circumstances, will be best adapted to continue, in preserving themselves and multiplying the individuals of their race.*

No one, not even John Playfair had a clue what this meant. In fact, what this obscure paragraph shows, and which absolutely no one at the time had spotted, was that Hutton had anticipated Charles Darwin's theory of natural selection by more than half a century. But Playfair only wrote up Hutton's geological hypotheses; had he also made the effort to translate his friend's speculations about evolution, it might have been Hutton, not Darwin, who became known as the "father of evolution". To be fair, though, given the violent Establishment reaction against Hutton's revolutionary ideas about the age of the Earth, he might not have lived long enough to enjoy it.

## The Wrong Chemistry

The eccentric Russian chemist Dmitri Mendeleev was distinguished by his long white beard and shaggy mane of white hair, which he cut once a year, a task performed every spring by a local shepherd with a pair of sheep shears.

Mendeleev was born in Tobolsk in western Siberia in 1834, the youngest of either fourteen or seventeen children – the family was so big that no one could keep track of it. Although he fared badly at school, he showed a deep interest in science and, in 1855, he qualified as a chemistry teacher. He had an astonishing capacity for sustained spells of hard work; when he realized that there was no such thing as a Russian textbook in organic chemistry, he sat down and wrote one himself – all 500 pages of it – in just sixty days.

His notoriously short fuse and foul temper made Mendeleev a difficult man to work with and he spent a large part of his life falling out with colleagues and storming out of laboratories. It cost him the Nobel Prize.

Mendeleev did for chemistry what Newton did for physics and Darwin for biology. His greatest contribution – the Periodic Table of Elements – in which the elements are arranged in order of their atomic weight, came to him in a dream after he had fallen asleep during a game of patience. It was a miraculous piece of organization on which all of modern chemistry is based. Mendeleev's table was such a brilliant piece of work, in fact, that it predicted the existence of elements that hadn't yet been discovered.

In 1906, the Nobel committee selected Mendeleev to win the Nobel Prize for Chemistry, but the Royal Swedish Academy of Sciences stepped in and overturned the decision. The man behind the intervention was the Swedish chemist Svante Arrhenius, who'd won the chemistry prize in 1903 for his theory of electrolytic dissociation. Mendeleev had been an outspoken critic of the theory and Arrhenius seized the opportunity to get his own back.

Posthumous recognition of sorts came for Mendeleev in

1955 when the element 101 was named mendelevium in his honour. Aptly, it is a highly unstable element.

## Most Failed Attempts to be Named in a Scientific Textbook

You may have come across the name Robert Hooke in your school Physics lessons. Hooke's law of elasticity states: "The power of any spring is in the same proportion with the tension thereof". Or you may have encountered him in connection with Boyle's invention, the air pump. He was also the first person to describe a cell in biology; his book *Micrographia*, published in 1665, amazed the academic world by illustrating and commenting on findings made with a microscope. He had a hand in Huygens' theory of the isochronous clock and Harrison's longitude timekeeper. In fact, there wasn't any subject that Hooke wasn't prepared to delve into. He became involved in everything from anatomical dissections to map-making and scientific instrument-making and offered new explanations for all sorts of natural phenomena, from the life story of the mosquito to the origin of lunar craters. His ideas about the origins of the Earth, the formation of rocks and the development of species anticipated the works of great geologists like James Hutton and Charles Lyell and the naturalist Charles Darwin. In short, he mastered more branches of science than any other man could hope to achieve. And yet, unless you have a special interest in the history of science, the chances are you may never have heard of him at all.

The world of English science in the mid-seventeenth century was run by gentlemen of independent means who had the time and money to dabble in "natural philosophy" as it was then called. In 1660, a group of twelve of these free-thinking amateurs got together at Gresham College in Bishopsgate, London, to form themselves into an association. There were no entry qualifications, only an admission fee of ten shillings' membership plus one shilling per week subscription. A couple of years later, the newly restored King Charles II granted them a royal charter and they became The Royal Society of London for the Improvement of Natural Knowledge, known simply as The Royal Society.

The Royal Society's labyrinth of separate committees and subcommittees covered the gamut of scientific knowledge from anatomy to zoology. Members debated such wide-ranging subjects as the birth of a dog with no mouth, the remedial properties of cow's urine and the penis of a possum. Mesmerism was taken as seriously as mathematics or the properties of a unicorn's horn. At any given time, you could find them attempting to grow moss on a dead man's skull (the new cure for epilepsy) or blowing bellows into the chest cavity of a live dog to find out how lungs worked, or grafting a cock's spur and feathers on to its head. Blissfully unaware of the importance of blood type compatibility, they once gathered to witness the transfusion of twelve ounces of sheep's blood into the unfortunate Arthur Coga. (Samuel Pepys recorded in his diary: "The patient speaks well, saying that he finds himself much better, as a new man . . . but he is cracked a little in his head.") You could listen to lectures on the existence of water on the Moon, devices for walking on ice, or how to make thunder and lightning effects for the stage, or you could learn about wombs in plants.[2]

The Royal Society and the bizarre experiments that took place within its walls were the butt of many jokes. Jonathan Swift satirized it in *Gulliver's Travels* when he described an academy on the island of Lepta where scientists performed all manner of pointless experiments, such as attempting to extract sunlight from cucumbers. Charles Dickens parodied The Royal Society as "The Mudfog Association for the Advancement of Everything".

In the very eye of this hurricane of scientific activity was Robert Hooke. In 1662, he was appointed as their first full-time Curator of Experiments, which basically made him the

---

2  They are impregnated by insects, allegedly.

first ever fully professional scientist. His job was to provide a minimum of three experiments for each Society meeting. The demands on his time were huge, but Hooke had unlimited intellectual curiosity and great stamina. The variety of his work and his capacity for original research was astonishing. At any given moment, he could be working on air pumps or barometers or microscopes, or making astronomical instruments, or timepieces for mariners.

Although unquestionably brilliant and almost superhumanly industrious, Hooke was certainly a difficult man to get along with and he had a talent for making enemies. He was also morbidly secretive, terrified that other scientists would try to steal the credit for his work. Secrecy wasn't unusual among scientists, but for Hooke it was an obsession. Hooke dabbled widely and extensively but it never occurred to him that there might be other talented scientists working on projects similar to his own. He also never quite learned that in science you earned recognition, not by inventing theories, but by proving them. For example, he claimed he invented a pocket watch accurate enough to be used by navigators, but somehow neglected to produce a single working prototype to back it up. This was the recurring pattern of Hooke's career, keeping his own ideas secret, then responding to the discoveries of other scientists by claiming that he had known about them for years. It led to a series of bitter, very personal and embarrassing clashes with fellow scientists over priority.

His biggest mistake was when he fell out with the most powerful and the most vindictive man in the history of science – Isaac Newton. The most famous spat in the history of physics began with a bet. In 1683, Hooke was sitting in a London coffee house with his friends, the great astronomer Edmond Halley (of comet fame) and Sir Christopher Wren. The latter was Professor of Astronomy at Gresham College – an astronomer first, it is now largely forgotten, and an architect second.[3]

---

3 This was the age of the polymath. In his spare time, Wren experimented on the effects of injecting various liquids into the bloodstream of dogs and once

The conversation in the coffee house turned to the solar system. All three men knew that the planets orbited in an ellipse, but no one had ever been able to explain exactly why. Wren generously offered a prize of forty shillings to the first man who could provide the answer. Hooke claimed that he had already solved the problem; he just wasn't going to tell anyone what it was – not yet, anyway. It was up to the others to find that out for themselves. Hooke would "conceal it for some time, that the others might have to value it". No doubt this raised a couple of knowing smiles from his companions. He had also recently claimed he had discovered the secret of manned flight, another accomplishment Hooke chose to keep to himself.

Halley immediately took up Wren's challenge and decided to enlist some help from an expert. Where better to start than with Cambridge University's Professor of Mathematics, Isaac Newton? When Edmond Halley tracked Newton down to his rooms at Cambridge and told him his problem, it did not take Newton long to produce a solution. At the heart of the explanation was a mathematical equation called the "Inverse Square Law of Gravitational Attraction". In fact, Newton already had it all worked out on paper; he just couldn't remember where he put it. Now this may seem truly astonishing[4] but it would not have surprised anyone who knew Newton well. As a student he invented calculus, but then forgot to tell anyone about it for twenty-seven years. It was the same with his work in optics – extraordinary insights into the understanding of light, not shared with anyone for three decades.

Halley urged Newton to write up his calculation again and produce a paper. But Newton did much more. After a couple of years' hard slog, he produced *Principia Mathematica*, the

---

wrote to Hooke boasting that had cured his wife's thrush by hanging a bag of live boglice around her neck. The Wrens also had a confusing family tradition of naming sons after their fathers. In Christopher Wren's case, it was even more confusing because he was actually the second son of Christopher Wren senior; he had an older brother, also called Christopher.

4  Bill Bryson notes in *A Short History of Everything* that this was like saying you've found a cure for cancer but had forgotten where you put the formula.

great landmark mathematical work that outlined Newton's laws of motion.

When Robert Hooke heard about *Principia* – in particular, Newton's Inverse Square Law of Gravitational Attraction – he made an extraordinary claim. He was sure that Newton had stolen the idea from a letter he had sent to him years earlier. The inspiration had been his and Newton's calculations had merely confirmed it. Hooke demanded a formal acknowledgement.

Newton, the touchiest of scientists, was livid. He and Hooke had form; they had already clashed a couple of times before. The first was a dispute over light waves. In January 1672, just over a week after he had been elected a Fellow of the Royal Society, Newton presented a paper called *Theory of Light and Colour*. He promised that it was "the oddest if not the most considerable detection which has been made in the operations of nature". This was quite a bold claim for a twenty-nine-year-old scientific novice, but when Newton's paper was read out to the Royal Society, it did not disappoint. His revolutionary understanding of light was received with great enthusiasm. The only person not impressed was Robert Hooke. He wrote a note faintly praising the "niceness and curiosity" of Newton's experiments, then proceeded to dismiss them as very inferior to his own "wave" theory of light. Any other young scientist might have taken this critique by a much more established colleague on the chin, but not Newton. Notoriously sensitive to criticism, he reacted like a petulant child and threatened to resign from the Royal Society.

Newton finally ended his sulk eighteen months later. He wrote to Hooke, who was by now the Royal Society's full-time secretary, to inform him that he was building a new telescope to study the path of heavy bodies falling to Earth. Instead of taking the olive branch, Hooke was at his patronizing best. He re-read Newton's letter and found a tiny mistake (Newton was only human after all). Instead of keeping it to himself, Hooke delighted in sharing his rival's error with his colleagues. Newton was furious.

Now it seemed that Hooke was trying to take the credit for his discovery of gravity. This was the last straw for Newton, who threatened to stop the publication of his work completely, then thought better of it, but went through the manuscript and struck out every reference to Hooke, even the bits where Hooke was due at least some credit. Hooke's albeit modest part in the greatest discovery in science was simply written out of history.

Robert Hooke continued to press his charge of plagiarism against Newton for years, but he never received the acknowledgement he believed he was due. The rest of Hooke's career, and his life, were overshadowed by his row with Newton. His public reputation also suffered, a pointed reminder of which he received in May 1676 when he went to the theatre to see playwright Thomas Shadwell's newest work *The Virtuoso*. The play's central character, Sir Nicholas Gimcrack, had spent £2,000 on microscopes to learn about the nature of eels in vinegar. He had transfused sheep's blood into a madman who then bleated like a lamb, observed military campaigns on the Moon and read his Bible by the light of a rotting leg of pork (a reference to the recent discovery of bioluminescence). There was no doubt that Shadwell's play was a satire on Hooke and London's seventeenth-century gentleman scientists. Hooke didn't get the joke; in fact, he was furious. "Damned dogs," he wrote in his diary, "people almost pointed."

Hooke's reputation wasn't helped by his scandalous private life. He and Newton were the oddest of bachelors. Newton was solitary, obsessive and possibly gay; Robert Hooke's single status, however, was not really out of choice. No authenticated portrait of him survives, so we have to rely on pen-portraits of people who knew him well. Take this account by his friend Richard Waller: "As to his Person, he was but despicable, being very crooked . . . he was always very pale and lean, and latterly nothing but Skin and Bone, with a Meager Aspect, his Eyes grey and full, with a sharp ingenious Look whilst younger; his nose but thin, of a moderate height and length; his Mouth meanly wide, and upper lip thin; his Chin sharp, and Forehead large; his Head of a middle size. He wore his own Hair of a dark Brown colour, very long and hanging neglected over his Face uncut and lank."

In other words, even in his best periwig, Hooke was not attractive to women. Other unflattering descriptions of Hooke call him "dwarfish" and mention a "twistedness which grew worse with age", a reference to his pronounced stoop, which he blamed on long hours spent at a workbench lathe, but is more likely to have been caused by a congenital condition. Hooke was certainly someone to be stared at. He was so odd-looking that people avoided him in the street or openly laughed at him. Newton's barb – directed in a letter to Hooke sent on 5 February 1676, observing, "If I have seen further, it is by standing on the shoulders of giants . . ." – was a cleverly disguised insult. Newton wasn't just mocking Hooke's intellectual pretensions, he was also laughing at his disability.

But Robert Hooke had a sex life, although not with the plentiful supply of London prostitutes available at the time. Given his reputation as a miser, he probably hated the idea of paying for sex. Like Samuel Pepys, Hooke was a candid diarist and, like Pepys, could not keep his hands off his servants. In Hooke's sex diary, he used a symbol to signify an orgasm, usually next to the names of housemaids, especially Nell Young and her successors Doll Lord and Bette Orchard. Taking sexual advantage of your female employees was one thing; having sex with your niece almost a third your age was another.

Robert Hooke had a brother, John, who was a grocer on the Isle of Wight. In 1672, John sent his ten-year-old daughter Grace up to London to live with her Uncle Robert. At some point in the early 1670s, John Hooke, via Robert, arranged for her to become engaged to the son of Thomas Bloodworth, a wealthy merchant who had been both a Sheriff and a Lord Mayor of London. There was some sort of pre-nuptial legal contract that bound the two to marry at a later date. Robert Hooke acted as an intermediary between his brother and Bloodworth. For reasons unknown, at some point the Bloodworths decided to break off the contract.

In 1678, John Hooke hanged himself, possibly because he was struggling with mounting debts. Robert Hooke then became his niece's guardian, but it is clear from his diary that he was also sexually obsessed with her. In effect, Hooke groomed her. He paid for her education, bought her gifts and clothes and, when she reached sixteen, began sleeping with her. He even flaunted the relationship and took her out on the town. When the tiny, twisted little hunchback scientist was seen out and about with a pretty young girl on his arm, even though the age difference wasn't particularly gross by the standards of the day, they would have certainly turned heads. The relationship continued until her premature death from pneumonia in 1687, at the age of twenty-seven. Hooke was devastated by his niece's death and never fully recovered from it.

Hooke was also a raging hypochondriac and took various alarming self-medications, which he listed meticulously in his diary. There were purgatives, emetics, mercury, tobacco, spirit of wormwood (unfermented absinthe) and laudanum (opium in liquid form), even steel filings. One particularly toxic substance he favoured was sal ammoniac – ammonium chloride. He became addicted to a variety of painkillers and, as the side-effects of the drugs worsened, took even more dubious pharmaceutical remedies to dull the pain. In 1689, he delivered a lecture at the Royal Society on a new substance he had discovered, "a certain plant which grows very common in India" – cannabis. Hooke said he appreciated its aphrodisiac qualities.

Hooke's self-medication took its toll and he became a feeble, emaciated wreck, increasingly plagued by bouts of depression and severe dizzy spells, which he attributed to wearing a heavy wig, and was prone to anxiety attacks, especially when he suspected that someone was trying to steal one of his ideas. He also took a small pinch of silver filings every now and then to improve his memory, but he never forgot about any of the perceived injustices he had suffered at the hand of Newton and others.

As his health and productivity declined, Hooke was fast declining into an aggressive, paranoid and miserly old crank. His relationships with other scientists deteriorated into bitter acrimony over more petty priority disputes – in the case of Christian Huygens, over the invention of the balance-spring watch. His conviction that he had been overlooked and deprived due recognition for a whole range of scientific discoveries – some justified, others wishful thinking – were a serious embarrassment to his colleagues at the Royal Society.

In spite of ill health, bitter resentment towards Newton and others and his anger over the way he had been treated during his long career, he kept working, even though by now he had acquired a reputation as an inventor of useless and impractical gadgets and ideas – he suggested that the day should be divided into twenty-nine hours, for example, or that cancer might be cured by smoking tobacco. In one of his final lectures to the Royal Society, he announced that there were people living on the Moon.

Hooke's final years were a long and ungraceful decline. According to his friend Waller, he was "much over-run with scurvy". He also became extremely miserly and never changed his clothes or washed and refused to spend money on soap. It was widely rumoured that he had actually starved to death his live-in maidservant. The forgotten man of science spent the final year of his life blind and bedridden, before dying alone and broke, or so it was assumed, believing to the last that he, not Newton, had discovered gravity. He was buried at St Helen, Bishopsgate, in an unmarked grave. After his death, his executors discovered a treasure chest hidden in his cellar stuffed with money and expensive jewellery.

You might think that having triumphed in his priority dispute with Hooke that Isaac Newton would have let the matter lie, but he was determined to obliterate Hooke's name from scientific history. Thanks to Newton, there isn't even a single known surviving portrait of Hooke to commemorate his extraordinary life. In 1703, the year of Hooke's death, the Royal Society relocated to new headquarters and the move was personally overseen by Newton. One of the many items to be relocated, hanging in Newton's old office, was Robert Hooke's portrait, the only one of him that was ever known to have been painted, but during the move it mysteriously disappeared. There is little doubt that Newton had it destroyed.

Today, the only achievement you will find Robert Hooke's name next to in science textbooks as being his alone is an obscure piece of relatively worthless information about the tension in a spring – not much for a man now regarded as one of the great intellectual giants of his age.

## Least Convincing Attempt to Prove God's Work in All Its Glory

The Victorian naturalist Philip Gosse was the author of a number of successful books on zoology and marine biology, but is mostly remembered for his strangest – *Omphales* – published in 1884.

As a devout Christian, Gosse was preoccupied with the knotty problem of whether or not the biblical Adam possessed a belly button. It goes without saying that, strictly speaking, Adam didn't need an umbilical cord, having never spent time in a womb. But as the prototype for all men, was he equipped with all the working parts? Gosse's conclusion in his book *Omphales* (Greek for navel) was that Adam did indeed have a belly button. God had created Adam's navel – and the fossil record – to create the impression that the world was very old. It was an almighty hoax to tempt humankind and test their faith.

Gosse thought his explanation was a work of genius and sat back to enjoy the plaudits, but to his astonishment they didn't come. Scientists simply sniggered, while fellow Christians really didn't like the implication that God was a practical joker.

When thousands of copies of *Omphales* remained unsold, Gosse was genuinely mystified. Convinced that the title of the book was the problem, he reissued it with the more accessible title of *Creation*. This didn't help. Crushed by overwhelmingly indifference, he gave up science and took up watercolour painting instead.

---

> *"The horse is here to stay but the automobile is only a novelty, a fad."*
> President of the Michigan Savings Bank advising Henry Ford's lawyer not to invest in the Ford Motor Co., 1903

---

## Most Pointless Lines of Research by Someone Who Should Have Known Better

*"Two things are infinite: the universe and human stupidity, and I'm not sure about the universe."*

Albert Einstein

As any scientist will tell you, progress is achieved through trial and error – but mainly error. Scientists are, after all, much more human than we ever give them credit for. And even the greatest of them all could get it horribly wrong.

It is impossible to overstate Sir Isaac Newton's contributions to science. He had arguably the sharpest scientific mind the world has ever known. What he produced in just a few short years (his *anni mirables* – years of wonder, as they became known) became the cornerstone for maths and physics as we know them today. In 1999, the *Sunday Times* named him Man of the Millennium. In 2002, BBC viewers voted him the sixth-greatest Briton of all time, ahead of Shakespeare and Darwin. His friend and fellow scientist Edmond Halley said of him, "No closer to the gods can any mortal rise." What a shame, then, that the bulk of his life's work was just a complete waste of time.

Newton was more than a little bit odd. Neurotic, humourless and solitary, he pursued his science like a hermit. He got into ugly disputes with other scientists, including Robert Hooke and the German mathematician Gottfried Wilhelm Leibniz. He took part in bizarre self-experimentation. He once stuck a large, blunt needle into the back of his eye socket between his eyeball and the bone and jiggled it about, nearly blinding himself in the process, then stared directly into the Sun with one eye for as long as he possibly could just to see what would happen. Although he escaped any permanent damage, he had to lie down in a darkened room for days before his eyesight recovered. He had no interest in any kind of social activity and made few friends, apart from one strange and stormy relationship with a young Swiss student called Nicholas Fatio de Duillier.[5] It was said that Newton laughed only once in his entire life, when someone asked him what use he saw in Euclid.[6]

He went properly "mad" for a while in 1692 when he was fifty. He experienced a breakdown followed by a period of mental instability that lasted for the best part of eighteen months. A Cambridge colleague described the episode as "a distemper that much seized his head"; it may have been triggered by depression or overwork. Whatever the cause of his illness, those closest to him were convinced that he had lost his mind. He became deeply paranoid, accusing colleagues of conspiring against him. He sent a very strange letter, written in a shaky hand, to the philosopher John Locke, accusing Locke of trying to "embroil him with women and other means".

Newton recovered from his "black year", wrote a few letters of apology to various people and was soon back at work. His breakdown, however, had a longer-lasting effect. Although he had emerged from his period of psychosis with his faculties apparently intact, his work took off in a new and very, very weird direction.

---

5  It has been claimed that Duillier was Newton's gay lover, but there is really no evidence to prove it one way or the other.
6  Winner of the Edinburgh Fringe Best Joke 1873.

In 1936, the economist John Maynard Keynes bought a trunkload of Newton's papers at auction. He was expecting to find loads of notes relating to calculus or optics. What he actually found astonished Keynes and everyone else. By the time he was famous, Newton had more or less given up proper science. He was now obsessed with the study of alchemy.

Alchemy first became fashionable in Europe in the twelfth century. Its exponents hunted for the most sought-after object of the day, the Philosopher's Stone, a mythical, magical article said to possess not only the ability to change base metals into gold but capable also, if mixed properly with wine, of producing the Elixir of Life, a cure for all illnesses. In 1404, the English parliament passed the Act of Multipliers which prohibited anyone from practising alchemy (despite the fact that no one had ever succeeded at it). It was still legal in Scotland, where one of its most famous advocates was the Italian John Damien de Falcuis, alchemist to King James IV of Scotland. Having repeatedly failed to deliver on his promise to turn base metal into gold, in September 1507 Damien tried to impress his employer by "flying" to France by launching himself off the walls of Stirling Castle, which was perched high on top of a cliff. The alchemist only made it as far as a dunghill directly beneath the castle walls.[7] Despite these repeated setbacks in his experiments, King James was still very generous to Damien and gave him a pension of 200 ducats when he finally retired from the court in 1513, but alchemical research was never quite the same again.

Newton had dabbled in it on and off for years, but when he was in his forties and at the peak of his powers it become an obsession. He was anxious to prove that a substance known as "child of Satan" (antimony) gave off magnetic rays that would attract the life force of the world. Newton believed that it contained "God's signature". He spent a fortune on alchemical

---

7   Damien, with his freshly broken leg, explained to the king that the hen feathers in his winged contraption had apparently been so strongly attracted to the dung below that it had caused him to crash.

books and equipment and built a small furnace in his garden. Hidden away in his laboratory with his assistant Humphrey Newton (no relation), Newton slogged for up to nineteen hours a day, spending sleepless nights poring over ancient texts, hunched over bubbling retorts of mercury, lead, antimony and sulphur, trying to cook up the legendary Philosopher's Stone. His work on alchemy was so all-consuming that he often forgot to eat and sometimes went to bed at five or six in the morning. It was all very baffling for his assistant, who noted simply, "What his aim might be I am unable to penetrate it." It has often been suggested, although never proven, that Newton's breakdown may have been caused by his exposure to these heavy metals.

In all, the greatest mind in science spent over thirty of the most productive years of his life trying to change base metals into gold and wrote over a million words on the subject – an exercise in futility and wishful thinking that amounted to so much waste paper.[8]

At a stretch, you could forgive Newton for his alchemy. At the time, there was a very dim understanding of the laws of science and nature and the idea of turning lead into gold was no more remarkable than manned space flight or splitting the atom. But alchemy wasn't Newton's only line of pointless research. He was a deeply religious man (he once broke off all relations with his best friend because he told him a crude joke about a nun) and to outward appearances was a respectable, orthodox member of the Church of England, but he was secretly a member of an obscure heretical sect called Arianism. It was named after the fourth-century Libyan Arius who was excommunicated for his views in AD 321. Followers of Arianism rejected the doctrine of the Holy Trinity – that is, that Christ and God were as one. Newton kept very quiet about his religious beliefs. By this time he was, ironically, a master of Trinity College and, if his

---

8  Which is a pity because it might have come in useful later for his job as Master of the Mint.

employees had found out about it, he would have lost his job, or worse.

There was, however, an even more curious aspect to Newton's faith. After completing his monumental *Philosophiae Naturalis Principia Mathematica*, he began to devote more and more of his time searching for hidden codes in the Bible, which he believed contained God's secret laws for the universe. He claimed that the mathematical formulae in *Principia* were first revealed by God to a group of mystics at the dawn of civilization, a tradition to which Newton was chosen as heir. He believed that the Old Testament King Solomon, son of David, was "the greatest philosopher of the world". Newton was convinced that Solomon had secretly incorporated the pattern of the universe into the design of his temple.

He taught himself Hebrew and spent long hours poring over floor plans of Solomon's temple hoping to find mathematical clues to the Second Coming of Christ. Newton predicted that the world would end in 2060, a calculation he made by studying the Book of Daniel and the date of the foundation of the Holy Roman Empire. The Second Coming of Christ, according to Newton, would follow plagues and war and would precede a 1,000-year reign by the saints on Earth – of which he would be one.

Newton spent more time and energy writing about biblical history than he did on any of his great scientific works. During the last thirty years of his life, he wrote over a million words attempting to establish a new chronology for the Old Testament. But whatever his skills as a scientist, Newton was a terrible historian. For example, as his starting point for his timeline, he took as fact the legend of Jason and the Argonauts, including the winged harpies and multi-headed serpents. He re-wrote his *Chronology of Ancient Kingdoms* at least sixteen times before he was happy with it. When it was finally published, a year after his death, even his most dedicated admirers were left scratching their heads as to why the great man had devoted his unique talent to such a bizarre project. When the full range of his oddball religious beliefs became apparent, years after his death, Newtonian scholars quietly swept the details under the carpet.

At the age of thirty-five, Newton had turned his back on proper science completely,[9] but he had two new careers. The first was as a very reticent MP for Cambridge University – he spoke in Parliament only once, to ask an usher to close a window to stop a draught. His other job was Master of the Mint, the institution that controlled the production of coins for the whole country. One of his duties was to prosecute counterfeiters. A successful prosecution usually meant the death sentence. Newton personally pursued counterfeiters to the gallows with chilling efficiency – the same ruthless streak he showed when seeing off his scientific rivals.

You can't help wondering what might have been if only Newton had stuck to science.

## Second-Most Pointless Lines of Research by People Who Should Have Known Better

In terms of scientific importance, Edmond Halley (1656–1742) ranks a distant third behind his two contemporaries Newton and Robert Hooke, but he managed to cram more into his career than either of them.

Halley was an outstanding polymath, publishing on such diverse subjects as mortality rates, how to determine the positions of the tropics, how the length of the shortest day varies with latitude, how deformed fingers are inherited within families, how crabs and lobsters re-grow amputated claws and the age of the Earth. He predicted that Venus would transit the face of the Sun in 1769 and explained how accurate timings of the event from widely spread locations could greatly aid navigation, allowing Britannia to rule the

---

9 He did not officially relinquish his position as Lucasian Professor of Mathematics at Trinity College, Cambridge until 1701, but by then he had long stopped giving lectures and rarely even visited the university, although he continued to draw the very substantial salary of £1,500 per annum.

waves. He was a naval captain, the leader of the first ever scientific expedition made by the Royal Navy, a diplomat and, it seems highly likely, even a spy working for the British Government.[10]

Halley was a precocious student with a keen interest in astronomy. He was making observations at sixteen and wrote his first scientific paper while still an undergraduate at Oxford. He even played a very important role in persuading a reluctant Isaac Newton to share with the world his ideas about gravity. If it hadn't been for Halley, Newton's *Principia Mathematical*, arguably the most important book in science, might never have been published in the first place.

When the first part of Newton's *Principia* was delivered to the Royal Society in April 1846, they didn't want to publish it because their one previous effort at publishing a book, Francis Willoughby's *History of Fishes*, had been an embarrassing sales disaster. There were so many unsold copies of it lying around that the Royal Society tried to fob Halley off with fifty books instead of the £50 they owed him in wages.

Halley felt honour bound to pay for the publication of *Principia* out of his own pocket. Fortunately, there was a happy ending: *Principia* was a modest commercial success (it was a difficult read and written in Latin – Newton didn't want it accessible to any old riff-raff) and Halley was able to make a small profit out of it. He went on to use Newton's new theory to correctly predict the return of a certain meteor. When Halley's Comet returned bang on schedule – on Christmas Day 1758 – it was an outstanding moment in scientific discovery and confirmed Edmond Halley as one of the greatest astronomers of all time.

So much for the sensible stuff. It might be significant that Halley once wrote a paper on the benefits of taking opium, because he was also responsible for one of the weirdest theories ever proposed by a respected scientist.

---

10    And he would have been very surprised to find that he is largely remembered for giving his mispronounced surname to a fat American rock 'n' roll singer.

On 25 November 1691, Halley read a paper to the Royal Society entitled "An Account of the Cause of the Change of the Variation of the Magnetical Needle with an Hypothesis of the Structure of the Internal Parts of the Earth". Halley's paper set out to prove that the Earth's core comprised three concentric spheres, stacked inside one another like giant Russian dolls. The two larger shells, he explained, were roughly the same size as Mars and Venus, while the solid inner sphere was about the size of the planet Mercury.

What Halley proposed next was slightly more surreal. The interior of the Earth, the great astronomer explained to his audience, was inhabited. He never got around to specifying what sort of creatures these underground species might be, but Halley went on to explain that God in his infinite wisdom had simply provided extra living space by maximizing the interior surfaces of the Earth, plus an atmosphere and a special source of light to support life. This light source would occasionally burst out through fissures in the North Pole, spreading through the atmosphere as the aurora borealis display. Halley gave an example to back up his theory. "We ourselves live in cities where we are pressed for room, commonly build many stories over the other, and thereby accommodate a much greater multitude of inhabitants." He finished off his lecture by challenging his audience to think of "a less absurd" hypothesis. We don't know what Halley's fellow scientists made of all this elaborate subterranean speculation because, perhaps wisely, he never mentioned it again in public.

Although he was the first scientist of major repute to endorse it, to be fair Halley was not the first – or the last – respected scientist to seriously consider hollow-earth theory. Fifty years earlier in 1641, the great German renaissance man and pioneer of microscopy Athanasius Kircher, grappling with an understanding of plate tectonics, suggested that giants made of fire lived beneath the Earth's crust. Relatively speaking, Kircher's theory wasn't all that odd given that he also believed that the plague was caused by rotting mermaids.

Halley's exciting version of hollow-earth theory encouraged others to take it up, occasionally adding their own modifications. For the devoutly Christian, it was the ideal place for sinners to repent before the Last Judgment. A mathematician, the Scot Sir John Leslie proposed that the Earth, in fact, had two interior suns, which he named Pluto and Proserpine. The famous Swiss mathematician Leonhard Euler replaced Halley's multiple spheres theory with a single hollow sphere which contained a sun 600 miles wide that provided heat and light for the flourishing civilization that lived within. Euler lost his eyesight, literally, after staring at the Sun for too long.

Perhaps hollow-earth theory was not completely mad, given that Halley lived in an age when even the most educated minds were still getting to grips with the nature of the universe. It was entirely sensible to speculate about what might lie beneath our feet. Altogether odder, however, was the theory put forward by Sir William Herschel, one of the most distinguished astronomers of all time.

Born Friedrich Wilhelm Herschel in Germany in 1738, he was actually a professional musician and an obsessive amateur astronomer. The word "obsessive" barely does his hobby justice. Nothing could keep Herschel from his telescope, not even when it was so cold his ink froze. His energy was inexhaustible; working regular shifts of sixteen hours, rubbing his hands and face with raw onion to keep himself awake, he completed four detailed surveys of the northern sky and catalogued 2,500 nebulae, more or less inventing stellar astronomy along the way. He still found time to discover infrared radiation, make more than 400 mirrors and sell over sixty complete telescopes to other astronomers. He also discovered the first new planet in recorded history. In the tradition of royal brown-nosing, he wanted to name it *Georgium Sidius* in honour of his patron King George III. You can imagine his face when he found out it was actually going to be called Uranus. Herschel refused to call it anything other than *Georgium Sidius* for the rest of his life.

Unfortunately, Herschel didn't confine himself to the collection and publication of vast quantities of observational data and the manufacture of sundry astronomical requisites – he also liked to theorize. Herschel knew that the surface of the Sun was hot – too hot to support life – but he also believed that beneath the Sun's surface lay a more temperate land where intelligent beings lived. These beings, Herschel revealed, lived in a society very much like our own. He found at least a couple of scientists who agreed with him, including the famous French physicist Dominique Arago. As recently as 1952, the German Godfried Buren reprised Herchel's argument, hypothesizing that inside our hollow Sun lurked a cool region with a lush vegetation. Buren was so pleased with himself that he offered a huge cash prize to anyone who could disprove his theory. When the German astronomical society did precisely that, Buren refused to pay up, until they took him to court and won.

Another unorthodox theory in Herschel's day concerned the planet Venus. As the features of Venus are permanently obscured by dense cloud, for many years it was assumed that it rained a lot – a bit like Manchester only nearer the Sun. Another puzzling feature of Venus is that, like the Moon, it is sometimes observed as a crescent, but with the dark area slightly illuminated. The German Franz von Paula Gruithuisen, professor of astronomy at Munich University, found the cause of this phenomenon. It was not, as most people now believe, the result of refraction in the planet's atmosphere; it was due to the Venusian custom of setting the forests ablaze to celebrate the succession of their new emperor. Gruithuisen went on to argue energetically in favour of advanced life on the Moon and on the insides of various hollow planets and wrote various papers on the subject including "Discovery of Many Distinct Traces of Lunar Inhabitants, Especially of One of Their Colossal Buildings" in which he claimed that he had seen roads, cities and a star-shaped temple on the Moon. Still, he got to have a small lunar crater named after him.

Gruithuisen was not alone in being sympathetic to the idea of civilized races on our near neighbours in the solar system. Christian Huygens, the Dutch mathematician, astronomer and physicist who beat Robert Hooke to patenting the first balance-spring clock, speculated that the planet Jupiter was blessed with large supplies of hemp. How did he know this? The clues lay in Jupiter's moons. According to a fashionable theory of the day, the Earth's Moon was provided by God as a navigational guide for seafarers. As Jupiter had four moons, it followed that the planet had four times as many sailors. And where there were lots of sailors, Huygens reasoned, there were lots of boats. Lots of boats implied lots of sails and ropes to work the sails. And rope required loads of hemp . . . QED.

More recently, the twentieth-century American astronomer Perceval Lowell, who endowed the famous observatory that bears his name, studied Mars for fifteen years, mapping the "canals" he could see on the surface. His books *Mars and the Canals* and *Mars as the Abode of Life*, now serious embarrassments for Lowell's heirs, were hugely influential on astronomers and scientists alike, including Nikola Tesla and Guglielmo Marconi, who both claimed they had received radio signals from Martians.

A more recent controversial addition to the debate about extra-terrestrial beings was contributed by an argumentative Yorkshireman called Fred Hoyle. It was he who coined the expression "big bang" to describe the theory that the universe was created by a huge explosion.[11] Hoyle was a world-renowned astronomer and one of the most important cosmologists of the twentieth century. He made major contributions to several branches of astrophysics, including the origin of the solar system, the evolution of stars, the origin of cosmic rays, the mystery of dust in interstellar space, the formation of the Milky Way, radio sources, pulsars and quasars.

---

11  Hoyle believed that the "big bang" theory was complete nonsense and was ready to argue with anyone who said otherwise. When he first came up with "big bang" during a radio talk on the BBC, it was a flippant remark intended to mock the theory; he clung stubbornly to his belief that the universe had always been there to his death. Unfortunately for Hoyle, he had created such a memorable sound bite that everyone thought he created the original theory himself – to Hoyle's eternal annoyance.

Unfortunately, as his obituary in the journal *Nature* pointed out, he also "put his name to much rubbish".

Hoyle was never far from controversy. During a radio broadcast in the early 1950s, at a time when Australia was dominating England at cricket, listeners were puzzled to hear Hoyle remark that somewhere in the Milky Way there was a cricket team who could beat the Australians. He also raised a few hackles when he claimed, without any evidence, that the famous *Archaeopteryx* fossil in the Natural History Museum was a fake and had been created by pressing bird feathers into a tub of cement. Palaeontologists were outraged by Hoyle's claim; even less impressed were the museum staff who had to spend days fielding phone calls from the world's press.

In his later years, Hoyle's reputation was further eclipsed when he said that life on Earth evolved from microbes falling from cometary tails about four billion years ago. According to Hoyle, the AIDS virus arrived from space in the mid-1970s and was originally passed to humans from rainwater via cuts on their feet. Hoyle went on claim that humans had evolved protruding noses with downward pointing nostrils to stop alien pandemic from falling into them from the sky.

## The Man Who Discovered the N-Ray

The French professor René Blondlot, head of the physics department at the University of Nancy and member the Academy of Sciences, was one of the most brilliant scientists of the early 1900s. He discovered that electricity moved through a wire at almost the speed of light and devised experiments to examine polarization and velocity of radio waves and X-rays.

It was X-rays that really excited Blondlot. Wilhelm Rontgen had discovered them in 1895, but no one knew much about them, let alone had any inkling of what the long-term effects of exposure to them might be. Radiation was touted as a cure-all for every imaginable disease – you could buy radioactive toothpaste for whiter teeth and better digestion, radioactive face creams to lighten the skin and radium-laced chocolate bars. A brisk trade in radioactive patent medicines thrived well into the 1930s. One of the most popular preparations, radium water, promoted in the USA as a general tonic and known as "liquid sunshine", was responsible for the deaths of several thousand people.

Scientists were not even quite sure what X-rays were. Were they a stream of particles, like gamma rays, or did they travel in waves, like light and radio? In 1903, Blondlot was determined to find out. He fired X-rays through a cathode tube into a charged electrical field and placed a detector near the path of the X-rays. If the electrical field polarized them, deflecting their path and sending them through the detector, causing a spark across a gap to grow brighter, this would prove that they were waves, not particles. They did, exactly as Blondlot had predicted. In doing so, he had correctly proved that X-rays are waves.

It was just then that Blondlot stumbled across a strange phenomenon. He noticed that radiation leaking from the apparatus also seemed to make the spark grow brighter. It couldn't be the X-rays; it had to be something else. On further investigation, he found that this radiation caused a screen coated with calcium sulphide to glow. He suddenly realized that he had discovered a new form of radiation. He called them N-rays, after his home town of Nancy.

Blondlot filled his university laboratory with a vast array of testing apparatus and he and assistants spent the next twelve months setting up experiments. Before long, Blondlot was detecting N-rays everywhere. Not only that – they had amazing potential; they had an ability to intensify flames and sparks, so they offered the prospect of enhanced vision in dim lighting.

He found that the Sun emits N-rays – although not many on a cloudy day. Various other types of light source also gave out N-rays, including electric lamps, but not Bunsen burners. Ordinary objects warmed in sunlight also gave out N-rays. He wrote: "Pebbles picked up at about 4pm, in a yard where they had been exposed to the Sun, spontaneously emitted N-rays; bringing them near a small mass of phosphorescent sulphide was sufficient to increase its luminosity. Fragments of calcareous stone, brick etc., picked up in the same yard, produced analogous results."

You could also store N-rays in salt water. This meant that the entire planet, which is mostly covered in salt water, was in effect a giant N-ray battery, storing the Sun's N-rays and radiating them back. In theory.

N-rays also had some very curious properties. A prism-shaped piece of aluminium could bend N-rays, just as a glass prism bent visible light. They seemed to emit from just about everything, except green wood and certain treated metals; or, for reasons unknown, bricks wrapped in black paper. Another puzzling thing was that loud noises appeared to make N-rays go away.

But the most curious thing about N-rays was this: the effects of N-rays were not immediately obvious to the human eye. To see the effects of N-rays, on a phosphorescent screen for example, required a certain amount of practice. You had to sit in a darkened room for at least half an hour beforehand to acclimatize your pupils. Then – here was the really important bit – you had to look slightly away from the screen and view it with peripheral vision. Even then, Blondlot warned, not everyone would be able to see the effects. Some scientists, Blondlot explained, were naturally equipped with better N-ray vision than others.

Blondlot announced his discovery to the world on 23 March 1903 in the Academy of Sciences newsletter and it provoked worldwide interest. This was all highly frustrating for the likes of elderly distinguished scientists such as Lord Kelvin, who apparently was not equipped with N-ray perception. In fact, quite a few scientists struggled to replicate Blondlot's experiments. No matter how many darkened rooms they sat and squinted in they just couldn't catch a glimpse of his N-rays. Even then, they kept an open mind. No one was prepared to suggest openly that someone as eminent as Monsieur Blondlot might have made a mistake.

But a lot of scientists as it turned out did have the requisite N-ray vision (most of them French) and, before long, the science journals were being filled with the results of N-ray experiments. In 1904, the French physics professor Augustin Charpentier revealed that the human body emits N-rays – or, at least, some body parts do, especially the biceps and the brain. His results were confirmed by the esteemed medical journal *The Lancet*, who wrote in 1904, "There would no longer appear to be any doubt that N-rays are given off by active muscles and nerves."

Meanwhile, Blondlot was busy investigating the effects of N-rays on the human body, using himself as a guinea pig. One day he sat in a completely blacked-out laboratory waiting for his eyes to acclimatize. It was so dark that he couldn't see his hand in front of his face, let alone the clock on the lab wall opposite. After exposing his eyes to a chunk of N-radioactive material, he realized that he could not only clearly see the clock, he could even tell the time from it. This was truly amazing.

When Blondlot published his results, other scientists rushed to copy the experiment. Not only did exposure to N-rays improve eyesight, it sharpened the other senses as well. Professor Charpentier bombarded the heads of some dogs with N-rays and found that it improved their hearing and sense of smell.

In France, any doubts that may have lingered about N-rays were dispelled when Blondlot was awarded the prestigious Lecomte Prize with a purse of 50,000 francs for his discoveries. He was now officially France's greatest living physicist. All that was left for him to win was the Nobel Prize for Physics. Surely, it was only a matter of time.

Across the Channel, the reaction to news of Blondlot's award was decidedly mixed. To date, not a single British scientist had been able to replicate his results. Perhaps it was time to settle the matter once and for all. The British Association for the Advancement of Science arranged for a sceptical US physicist Robert W. Wood to visit Blondlot in his lab for a private demonstration.

Blondlot was very happy to go along with it. His lab was hundreds of miles from Paris and he didn't get many visitors;

he was always keen to show his N-ray results. Wood didn't speak much French so he and Blondlot conversed in German. But he knew just enough French to make out the odd confidential exchange between Blondlot and his assistant. Blondlot immediately set up a test by painting some luminescent circles on a card. Then he turned the lab lights down, and with the circles faintly glowing in the dark, he "bombarded" the card with N-rays.

"Did you see the change in luminosity?" enquired Blondlot.

"No," replied Wood.

Wood suggested another test. Sitting in the dark lab, he took a lead screen and passed it in and out of the path of the N-rays, while Blondlot reported fluctuations in the luminosity. Blondlot got it wrong every time. He even called out fluctuations when Wood did not move the screen. Wood asked for another test.

This time, the key was Blondlot's aluminium prism. One of the curious properties of N-rays, you will remember, was that an aluminium prism could bend N-rays, just as a glass prism bent visible light. As Wood looked on, Blondlot used the prism to record a series of N-ray wavelengths. Of course, as Wood couldn't see the wavelength lines himself, he had to take Blondlot's word for it.

So he asked Blondlot to repeat the measurements. Only this time, Wood took advantage of the dark and quietly removed the prism. In spite of this, Blondlot and his assistant still "saw" the N-ray measurements. Wood quietly replaced the prism.

Wood had seen enough and was ready to call it a night, but Blondlot's assistant smelled a rat. He suspected, correctly, that Wood had removed the prism. The assistant called for one more test. The lights were turned down again. This time, Wood made a move towards the prism and *pretended* to remove it, but left the apparatus intact. The assistant, thinking that he had outwitted Wood, reported to Blondlot in German, "I see nothing . . . there is no spectrum. I think the American has removed it."

The evidence was overwhelming and damning. Wood's report destroyed Blondlot, and N-rays vanished from the realms of science just as quickly as they had appeared.[12] Poor, humiliated Blondlot continued to work as a university professor in Nancy until his early retirement in 1910, enduring whispers among colleagues that he had lost his mind.

He continued to "see" his phantom rays until his death in 1930, refusing to admit that it had all been in his head. N-rays did not go down in history as a hoax; instead, they were a cautionary tale of how deluded researchers can see whatever they want to see. A real life emperor's new clothes story.

## Least Successful Weatherman

Robert FitzRoy couldn't have had a better start in life. Born into the English aristocracy, he had impressive bloodlines on both sides of the family. He was a direct descendant of King Charles II and his grandfather, the third Duke of Grafton, was a prime minister; his uncle was foreign secretary. He was a brilliant student and, at the age of fourteen, graduated with distinction from the Royal Naval College in Portsmouth. By 1824, at the age of nineteen he was a lieutenant in the Royal Navy having passed the examination with "full numbers" (100 per cent), a result never before achieved.

An early test of his impressive seamanship took place during one of his very first postings on HMS *Beagle*, under the command of Captain Pringle Stokes, who was charting the South American coastline. While off Tierra del Fuego, Stokes shot himself in the head while suffering from depression. It took twelve days for him to die. FitzRoy steered the ship back to Rio, where he assumed full-time command of the *Beagle* at the age of twenty-three. By now FitzRoy was widely regarded as the most brilliant seaman of his generation.

Three years later, he and his survey ship *Beagle* were assigned to carry out a three-year survey of coastal South

12   Except in France, where Blondlot's discredited science refuses to go away. The idea persists that a glowing "biofield" surrounds the human body and French clinics will offer you a healthier life through N-rays.

America. Having had already spent a couple of years on a similar survey with the unfortunate Captain Stokes, FitzRoy was very wary of the loneliness that such a command could bring. He was also uncomfortably aware that there was a history of depression and suicide in his own family. His uncle Lord Castlereagh slit his throat when FitzRoy was fifteen, leaving a lasting impression on the boy. The solution, FitzRoy decided, was to take with him some "gentleman company", someone who could share the captain's table and engage him in intellectual discourse. The young naturalist Charles Darwin fitted the bill. Only four years apart in age (Darwin was twenty-two, FitzRoy twenty-six), both had a yearning for adventure and an interest in "natural philosophy".

At their first meeting, however, FitzRoy had doubts, on account of Darwin's nose. FitzRoy's studies of physiognomy told him that "people with a broad, squat nose like his don't have the character". Not that Darwin was particularly qualified either for a journey halfway round the world; the longest field trip he had been on up until then was three weeks spent in North Wales collecting insects.

FitzRoy's initial reservations about nose shape, however, were outweighed by the fact that the young amateur naturalist had also studied divinity. FitzRoy was deeply religious and a fervent believer in the literal truth of the biblical account of Creation. Darwin, FitzRoy thought, would be useful in helping him find data that would reveal God's work. Seldom in history has an appointment misfired so spectacularly.

FitzRoy had another motive for wanting to go back to South America. On his previous trip to Tierra del Fuego, straying some way beyond his Admiralty brief, he had 'kidnapped' four natives and taken them back to England. His plan was to introduce them to the "benefit of our habits and language", before returning them to Tierra del Fuego as missionaries. FitzRoy pursued his mad scheme with evangelical zeal. Of the four Fuegians, one died of a smallpox vaccination; two males – York Minster, aged twenty-seven, and Jemmy Button, fourteen – and Fuegia Basket, a twelve-year-old girl, were sent to school in Walthamstow where they were taught English, arithmetic and "the basic truths of Christianity".

FitzRoy's great social experiment was cut short when York Minster was caught raping Fuegia Basket. Using his powerful family connections, FitzRoy hurriedly persuaded the Admiralty to let him return his Fuegians to their native land, along with a few items he thought necessary to recreate a piece of England on the wild coast of South America, including chamber pots, tea trays, crockery, beaver hats and white linen.

The *Beagle* was a ten-gun brig of the type known in the Royal Navy as a "coffin" because they tended to capsize in heavy weather. Fortunately, FitzRoy was a brilliant navigator. Despite negotiating some of the most dangerous waters of the world, surviving storms, earthquakes and disease, and encounters with hostile natives, the aristocratic young sea captain returned home with his ship and most of its crew intact.

Darwin, meanwhile, suffered dreadfully from seasickness, but this was the least of his problems. He quickly discovered that the man he had to share his meals with three times a day in a tiny cabin had a short fuse and was highly opinionated. The two men had lively exchanges of views, later described by Darwin as quarrels "bordering on insanity". FitzRoy also suffered from bouts of deep depression. At one point, he stopped eating and shut himself away for several weeks. He eventually emerged, thin and haggard, and offered his resignation. He told the crew he feared he was going to go the same way as his uncle and his predecessor, Captain Stokes. At this point, it seemed that the voyage would have to be cut short.

Luckily for science, FitzRoy's loyal second-in-command, Lieutenant Wickham, was able to talk his captain round and continue the mission by crossing the Pacific and returning to England at the conclusion of the circumnavigation they had set out to achieve.

FitzRoy was both very odd and completely unknowable. In spite of their differences, he had been won over by Darwin's easy charm and they became friends and remained in contact subsequently for many years. Darwin was most surprised therefore, shortly after they got back, at the news that FitzRoy was about to marry a woman to whom he had been engaged for several years. Weirdly, FitzRoy had never once spoken a word about his engagement, or his intended bride, Mary, throughout the five-year voyage.

The *Beagle* voyage, of course, turned out to be the defining experience of Darwin's life, providing him with the evidence for his book *On the Origin of Species* that would forever change our view of the world and our place in it. But following the *Beagle*'s return, it was the ship's captain, not Darwin, who won the initial plaudits. Robert FitzRoy wrote up his account of this voyage, including masses of detailed weather observations, and was awarded a gold medal by the Royal Geographical Society.

There was also a change in career direction. FitzRoy entered Parliament, serving for two years as Tory MP for Durham. His unpredictable temper got the better of him and almost resulted in a duel with another Tory candidate – in the end, they settled for a fist fight in The Mall.

In 1843, FitzRoy's life took another unexpected turn when he accepted the position of Governor of New Zealand. His time as governor was an unhappy one; his rigid discipline and unbending sense of religious duty made him deeply unpopular, especially when he upset the apple cart with his principled defence of the local Maori against unscrupulous immigrant settlers. The Colonial Office swiftly recalled him less than two years later without offering him the customary knighthood.

He returned to his naval duties as captain of the frigate HMS *Arrogant*, but a morbid depression, one of many, forced him into retirement in 1850. And there he would have remained, snubbed by the Establishment and forgotten, if the Admiralty had not turned to him for help in 1854.

There had been systematic attempts to understand weather patterns ever since the Crimean War, when the British had suffered disastrous losses during a storm at Balaclava Bay. The urgent need for a system for predicting storms at sea was tragically underlined when the passenger ship *Royal Charter* was destroyed by a violent gale off the coast of Anglesey with the loss of 450 lives.

The Admiralty sent for FitzRoy and asked him to investigate the effect of the weather on the British fleet. He immediately set about making weather maps on which he plotted wind, barometric pressure and temperature using symbols to denote clouds, rain and snow. He made the first use of conical storm symbols – the standard gale warning still in use today.

He also began what he called (and what everyone still calls) the weather forecast. Before FitzRoy the weather had only ever been presented retrospectively. *The Times*, for example, would print a report of how the weather had been across Great Britain for the period of 8 a.m. to 9 a.m. the previous day. Thanks to FitzRoy's weather maps, on 1 August 1861 *Times* readers could actually read what the weather was going to do over the next two days. Queen Victoria soon got into the habit of consulting FitzRoy as to when she should make the short boat trip across the Solent to her residence on the Isle of Wight.

In FitzRoy's mind, however, storm clouds were gathering. His new wife Mary was an even more uncompromisingly devout Christian than he was and marriage had marked a radicalization of his own religious beliefs. He had continued to visit his old friend Darwin at his home, Down House, but all that changed in 1859 with the publication of *On the Origin of Species*. FitzRoy, the ardent creationist, became a rabid opponent of Darwin and wrote letters to *The Times* explaining that giant animals such as the Mastodon had not survived the biblical flood because they were too big to get into Noah's Ark. He was convinced that Charles Darwin was going to hell.

Seven months after the publication of Darwin's book, science and religion finally went head-to-head on Saturday, 30 June 1860 when Darwin's theory was debated at a famous meeting of the British Association for the Advancement of Science at Oxford. Darwin didn't join in the debate, leaving the fighting to his more combative friends Joseph Hooker and T. H. Huxley, dubbed "Darwin's Bulldog" for his staunch defence of the theory, in much the same way as Richard Dawkins is dubbed "Darwin's Rottweiler" by some today.

More than a thousand people crowded into the chamber to hear stinging attacks from both sides. According to reports, in the ensuing commotion Lady Brewster fainted and had to be carried out. Meanwhile, Robert FitzRoy, who was attending the meeting to present his own paper on weather patterns, walked around the hall brandishing a huge copy of the Bible above his head, shouting, "The truth is in here!" He was shouted down and escorted from the building.

To the end of his days, FitzRoy blamed himself for allowing Darwin to be his personal guest aboard the *Beagle* and consequently for the blasphemy of evolutionary theory. His misery was compounded by the fact that the world was also unappreciative of his pioneering work in meteorology. Almost as soon as his first weather forecasts appeared, people began complaining that they were wrong. He faced pressure on all sides, not only from people who were angry with inaccurate reports, but those simply irritated that he was predicting bad weather at all – in particular, fishing fleet owners who were upset about losing business when their fishermen refused to head out to sea in the wake of an unfavourable FitzRoy prediction.

There was also criticism from an unexpected quarter – for many of his fellow scientists, the very idea of weather prediction was flawed. FitzRoy and his forecasts, which were notoriously imprecise,[13] had "undermined the processes of legitimate scientific work". Scientists, they complained, should stick to the establishment of certainties, not risk their reputation on unknowable outcomes. Even FitzRoy's successor at the Meteorological Office went out of his way to promise "facts, not prophecies", much to the relief of his fellow meteorologists.

There was also much public mockery. Cartoons published in *Punch* poked fun at the uselessness of official weather reporting with a series of badly drawn synoptic charts

---

13   His first weather forecast which was printed in *The Times* on 1 August 1861, noted: "General weather probable during the next two days."

populated by a flurry of made-up symbols. Even *The Times*, which ran his forecasts, took to printing disclaimers, effectively disowning their author. "During the last week, Nature seems to have taken special pleasure in confounding the conjectures of science." The piece continued that this was not the fault of the laws of nature, but that "accurate interpretation is the real deficiency". There were even questions asked in Parliament.

A perfectionist and workaholic, the thin-skinned FitzRoy took the criticisms personally. Whether it was his apparent failure as a weatherman that cost him his life, or torment over his decision to take Darwin on board the *Beagle*, we will never know for sure. On the morning of 30 April 1865, the world's first weatherman got up early without waking his wife, kissed his daughter, then locked himself in his dressing room and slashed his throat with a razor.

The ultimate irony was that FitzRoy had only taken Charles Darwin on board in the first place as a companion to prevent him from killing himself. When he heard about FitzRoy's death, his counterpart – the Dutch meteorologist Christoph Buys Ballot – warned gravely, "We must remember that anyone who has to forecast the weather, if he does it earnestly and conscientiously, is in great danger of going off his head through nervous excitement."

## The Nearly Man of Computing

The West Country mathematician Charles Babbage is recognized today by a handful of people in the know as one of the major figures in the development of one of humanity's greatest technological achievements. But his ideas were mocked and derided in his own lifetime and he was largely forgotten for a long time after his death.

The story of the computer is littered with false starts. It is generally reckoned to have begun in the early 1600s with a German, William Shickard. He created a machine he called a "calculating clock" to help his friend, the great astronomer

Johannes Keppler, predict the movements of the Sun, the Moon and the planets. Unfortunately, we have no idea if the machine worked or not; Shickard's machine and his blueprints were completely destroyed when French soldiers set fire to his house during the Thirty Years War, so instead of going down in history as the man responsible for the most important technological step forward since the horse-drawn plough, Shickard is remembered as a minor expert in Hebrew grammar.

Coincidentally, 1623 – the year Shickard is thought to have invented his calculating clock – also saw the birth of the man responsible for the next significant advance in digital computing, the French mathematician Blaise Pascal. He was the son of a royal tax collector. According to legend, Pascal wanted to help his father with his book-keeping so he devised a machine that could add and subtract figures up to eight digits. It had a complex series of wheels connected to rods with toothed cogs and gears and was beset with technical problems, stretching seventeenth-century technology to the limit. Pascal went on to build more than fifty versions of his machine, a few of which still survive today in full working order.

Throughout his life, Pascal suffered from ill health and took to wearing stockings soaked in brandy to keep his feet warm; curiously, this does not appear to have harmed his reputation as a philanderer. At the age of thirty-one, however, he was involved in a near-fatal coach crash, and underwent a cathartic religious experience, which caused him to suddenly renounce sex. He spent the last years of his life a sexually frustrated religious zealot, trying to prove the mathematical certainty of God's existence.

In 1673, the great German scientist Gottfried Leibniz saw one of Pascal's amazing machines in Paris and decided to have a go at building one himself, possibly just to annoy his rival Isaac Newton. Leibniz's prototype version was much more sophisticated than Pascal's. It could add, subtract, multiply, divide, even calculate square roots. When he showed it to the Royal Society in London, however, his fellow scientists greeted it with stony-faced indifference, so Leibniz gave up on his project and wrote a fifteen-volume history of the royal House of Hanover instead.

The next big advance in computing came in the early nineteenth century from an unlikely source – a technician in the French weaving industry, Joseph Marie Jacquard, who made an innovative loom that could be programmed to weave a pattern by using punched cards. Jacquard's idea provoked a riot and redundant loom workers stormed the factory and destroyed his machines, but his card-punching method survived. More importantly, one of the key elements of computing, the idea of programming, had now been invented. It would take an English mathematical genius, however, to work out what to do with it.

Charles Babbage (1791–1871) was born in the early years of the Industrial Revolution to a wealthy banker from Devon. He was a sickly child and was mostly tutored at home. He dazzled at mathematics at an early age and, in 1810, he entered Trinity College, Cambridge, where he ran rings around his maths tutors, although he still managed to leave without a first-class honours degree after a fallout with the university authorities. This pattern of clashing with the Establishment would haunt him later in life. After leaving Cambridge, he wrote a couple of major papers on functional equations and, in 1816, at the astonishingly early age of twenty-four, he was elected a fellow of the Royal Society of London.

Babbage dabbled in half a dozen sciences and published widely on a range of topics from chess and deciphering weather patterns to tree rings, railway tunnels and stomach pumps. He was also a prolific inventor; he was the brains behind black box recorders for railways, railway cowcatchers and skeleton keys. There were countless other Babbage inventions that never made it off the drawing board, including a seismograph for detecting earthquakes, an altimeter for measuring height above sea level, a flat-bottomed boat that would aquaplane on water, a system of tin tubes for long distance telephony (he calculated it would take seventeen minutes for words spoken in London to reach Liverpool) and a system for sending messages enclosed in small cylinders along wires suspended from church steeples. He also invented a pair of shoes for walking on water, but when he tried out his miracle footwear on – or more accurately, in – the River Dart in Devon, he almost drowned and only just about made it back to the riverbank.

Above all else, Babbage was obsessed with facts, data and statistics. He thought that every scrap of information he came across, no matter how trivial, was worth storing because "the preservation of any fact might ultimately be useful". Babbage wanted to quantify everything from the heartbeat of a pig (to be listed in his "Table of Constants of the Class Mammalia") to the breath of a calf. He took daily records of food consumed by zoo animals and the "proportion of sexes amongst our poultry". He suggested tables to calibrate the amount of wood (elm or oak) a man could saw in ten hours, or how much an ox or camel could plough or mow in a day. He once walked around a factory counting the number of broken window-panes he saw then wrote a study called a "Table of the Relative Frequency of the Causes of Breakage of Plate Glass Windows". Using his powers of deduction, Babbage concluded that fourteen were broken by "drunken men, women or boys". He hoped the table might induce others to furnish more extensive collections of similar and related facts.

In "Conjectures on the Conditions of the Surface of the Moon", we find him describing experiments on lunar cooking – "very respectable stew of meat and vegetables in blackened boxes (with window glass) buried in the earth". He once had himself lowered into Mt Vesuvius so he could closely observe volcanic activity. On another occasion, he allowed himself to be baked in an oven at 265°F for "five or six minutes without any great discomfort", meanwhile taking notes on his pulse and the quantity of his perspiration.

Babbage had spent years studying death rates, and was very irritated when he read these lines from Alfred Tennyson's poem "The Vision of Sin": "Every moment dies a man, Every moment one is born." Babbage took exception to the verse because it implied that the population of the world was stable, when in fact it was increasing. He wrote to Tennyson with a suggestion:

> *Sir,*
>
> *In your otherwise beautiful poem "The Vision of Sin" there is a verse which reads – "Every moment dies a man, Every moment one is born." It must be manifest that if this were true, the population of the world would be at a standstill. In truth, the rate of birth is slightly in excess of that of death. I would suggest that in the next edition of your poem you have it read – "Every moment dies a man, Every moment 11/16 is born." The actual figure is so long I cannot get it on to a line, but I believe the figure 11/16 will be sufficiently accurate for poetry.*
>
> *I am, Sir, yours, etc., Charles Babbage*

Another of his odder enterprises was working out the statistical probability of the biblical miracles. He calculated that the chances of a man rising from the dead were 1 in $10^{12}$ – a figure he arrived at by dividing the estimated total number of people who had ever lived by the number of witnessed accounts of someone being brought back from the dead – i.e. one. Even the more broadminded within the scientific community came to regard him as a crank.

In spite of Babbage's eccentricities, however, no one doubted that he was determined, visionary and quite brilliant. And, in spite of the odd commercial failure, he was also very wealthy. Or, at least, he was until he sank his personal fortune into his dream of building a giant calculating machine.

On 12 January 1820, Babbage was one of a handful of diners present at the Freeman's Tavern in Lincoln's Inn Fields when the Astronomical Society was formed, along with his friend John Herschel, son of the famous astronomer William Herschel. Babbage and Herschel soon found themselves working on a series of mathematical tables for the Society, the accuracy of which was particularly important for navigators; one mistake could mean life or death for a seafarer.

It would be an understatement to say that mathematical tables were something of a Babbage obsession. He was a connoisseur and collector of tables. He owned a private collection of tables running to more than 300 volumes. He even studied the ergonomics of table reading. His idea of a quiet evening in was to draw up tables with various different coloured papers and inks to find out which combination caused the least stress to the reader; just to make sure he had every option covered, he tested green ink on several different shades of green paper. Babbage was incensed by the discovery that the existing tables of computations included far too many errors. Mathematical errors were the scourge of the nineteenth-century scientist. The first edition of the *Nautical Ephemeris for finding Latitude and Longitude at Sea*, to give one example, was found to contain over a thousand table errors. The textbooks of the day came with errata sheets appended by more errata sheets. The source of error was clear – human fallibility. Suddenly, a thought struck Babbage – what if someone could create an all-purpose, infallible calculating machine, one that could achieve "absolute integrity of results"? The Industrial Revolution was making everything else by steam; why not mathematical calculations and perfect tables?

In July 1822, Babbage wrote a letter to the president of the Royal Astronomical Society, describing his plan for a calculating machine. He called it the Difference Engine. In 1822, he demonstrated a small working model of his device. It was an ungainly piece of hardware with a bewildering array of brass wheels and cogs and shafts, but the Society were impressed and awarded him their first Gold Medal. A year later, Babbage persuaded the Government to give him a grant to build his invention. The triumphal birth of Babbage's enterprise, however, would also prove to be the high point of his career. He never got anywhere near completing his giant mechanical calculator, his efforts confounded by a self-destructive streak that would result in a lifetime of personal conflict, political confrontations and silly vendettas.

To begin with, he had completely underestimated the costs involved. The apparatus he envisaged was a fantastically ambitious undertaking with about 20,000 moving parts, well beyond the limit of nineteenth-century skill and machinery. Most of the precision machine tools needed to shape the wheels, gears and cranks of his engine did not exist and Babbage and his craftsmen would have to make them. In fact, as no minutes were ever made of his initial meeting with the government, no one could agree how much it was supposed to cost in the first place. With no agreed budget and no delivery date, work on the machine wore on and on.

Meanwhile, there were plenty of other distractions to keep Babbage from finishing his grand calculating machine. There was little he wasn't prepared to put his mind to. Once, while bored at the ballet, it occurred to him that he might be able to enliven proceedings with some experimental lighting. He devised "the Rainbow Dance", a ballet in which sixty female dancers, representing fireflies, each dressed in pure white, would take on the colour of any light projected on them. The light came from a huge battery of oxy-hydrogen blowlamps fitted with coloured filters. Although there was a rehearsal with two fire engines standing by, the ballet was never shown to the public because the theatre manager was terrified the building would burn down mid-performance and kill everyone in it.

More successfully, he published the first ever treatise on actuarial theory, in the process more or less creating the insurance industry. When he applied his new methods to a study of wasteful practices in the printing trade, his publishers were so offended that they refused to print any more of his books. He had better luck when he tried his method out in an analysis of the Victorian postal system. He was able to prove that the cost of assigning a value to every piece of mail according to the distance it had to travel was more expensive than the cost of transporting it. The British Post Office adopted his findings and began to charge a flat rate, independent of the distance each piece had to travel. The "penny post" system still exists around the world to this day.

The strain of years of hard work on his calculating machine without reward or recognition, plus the sudden deaths inside a year of four members of his immediate family, including his wife, took their toll on the scientist. The once affable young man turned into a prematurely aged, bad-tempered crank. He got involved in a number of pointless public feuds and spent his spare time firing off abusive letters written in green ink on yellow paper at various targets, including publishers of mathematical tables, lambasting them for obscure inaccuracies he had uncovered.

The scientific Establishment was a favourite subject for his abuse. Babbage thought that the Royal Society was run by incompetents and idiots, a point he made in a series of highly personal broadsides against leading Society members, including one accusing the great Sir Humphrey Davy of fraud. Apart from anything else, this was a shocking breach of scientific etiquette, but in doing so he had also managed to offend the very scientific body who had on three occasions recommended Government support for his Engine.

They were not the only important people to feel the rough edge of Babbage's tongue. He was hoping for financial support from a government whose membership, for the most part, was still drawn from the aristocracy. So he decided to publish a pamphlet called *A Word to the Wise*, a savage attack on the hereditary system of privilege titles, denouncing the British aristocracy as wholly corrupt. As career moves go, it was not the best.

In 1827, he was appointed Lucusian professor of mathematics at Cambridge, a highly prestigious post once held by Isaac Newton. The new position came with a generous income and even more generous terms and conditions. There were absolutely no regular tutoring responsibilities: the sole requirement of the job was to deliver one course of lectures a year. Babbage abused even that simple condition. He held the post for eleven years until 1839, but never gave a single lecture, much to the disgust of the other dons, because he said he was too busy developing his mechanical computer.

Babbage twice tried his hand at politics, as a Whig candidate to Parliament for the Borough of Finsbury in the general election of 1832 and again in the by-election two years later. He was a terrible politician. During both campaigns he was heckled with questions about the financing of his Engine project – a touchy subject bound to set him off on a purple-faced rant. His public speeches were almost totally incoherent. After predictable defeats in both campaigns, he surrendered all further political ambition.

Meanwhile, work on Babbage's calculating machine wore on. Each stage of construction posed a new set of technical problems, each requiring a succession of brilliant innovations in mechanical engineering. His original plan was enlarged into a machine of around 25,000 parts. Ten years after the project was first announced, all he had to show for it, however, was one small working section. The Prime Minister Robert Peel noted sarcastically, "How about setting the machine to calculate what time it will be of use?"

As the question of the government's exact financial obligation to Babbage's Difference Engine remained unresolved, he was having to pay for the project out of his own pocket. He fell out regularly with his engineer, Joseph Clement, who by all accounts could match Babbage for stubbornness. In March 1833, Clement submitted a bill and Babbage refused to pay; he told him to send it to the Treasury instead. When the Treasury rejected it as "unreasonable and inadmissible", Clement downed tools. Work on the Difference Engine stopped, never to resume again. By this time, costs had spiralled to an astonishing £17,500 – enough to build a couple of battleships. By comparison, Robert Stephenson's recently built steam locomotive *John Bull*, commissioned by the United States, had been constructed at a total cost of £785.

One of Babbage's biggest mistakes was that he had never bothered to try to explain to the public, or for that matter his financial backers, what the benefits of his invention were in terms anyone could understand, so no one knew what the fuss was about in the first place. He was to receive some unexpected publicity, however, when a lengthy article appeared in the *Edinburgh Review* by Professor Dionysius Lardner of University College, London, which gave a lengthy, glowing write-up of Babbage and his marvellous Engine. This was exactly the shot in the arm his project needed, or so you might have thought. Lardner was certainly a scientific writer of some repute. The trouble was, it wasn't the sort of reputation you would necessarily want to be associated with (see Worst Scientific Pundit).

Babbage couldn't stop tinkering with his design. Every time it looked as if one means of constructing his device might actually work, he thought of a new and better way of doing it. Almost every room in his house was filled with abandoned models of his engine. By the 1830s, he was already committed to an even more ambitious project, the Analytical Engine, a quicker, more advanced machine that could be programmed with punch cards to do computations and store data. He had come up with the essential features, no less, of the modern computer.

Babbage wanted to tell the Government all about his exciting Analytical Engine, but they didn't want to hear about an expensive new project; they had had enough of the old one. It would be cheaper to build a new navy from scratch. It didn't help matters either that he was in the habit of pestering the Prime Minister Robert Peel and his Treasury with terse letters on the subject of money he thought was owed to him, without giving a moment's thought to some of the problems that may have been preoccupying Britain's leader. This was the "hungry forties" when some feared the country was actually teetering on the brink of revolution. Probably the last thing on Peel's mind was the solvency of some mad scientist with a plan for producing steam-driven maths tables.

Peel finally agreed to meet Babbage in November 1842. Babbage was warned in advance not to push his luck: the Prime Minister was under a lot of pressure and in no mood to be lectured. Once again, Babbage couldn't resist pushing the self-destruct button. He harangued Peel about his own financial problems and the government's responsibility for his project. Peel gave him short shrift; the meeting ended abruptly with Babbage storming out in a huff.

Finally, in November 1842, the government, weary of delays and of Babbage's crankiness, gave up on his project officially when the Chancellor of the Exchequer sought the opinion of an expert, Sir George Airy, on the usefulness of the machine and was told it was "worthless". Peel offered Babbage a knighthood by way of compensation. Babbage turned him down. Anyone could get a knighthood, he believed; he told the authorities that the most important scientific figure of the age would only settle for a life peerage. It was never granted.

As his calculating machine schemes ran into the sand, Babbage embarked on increasingly desperate money-making schemes to revive them. He was assisted by Ada, Lady Lovelace, daughter of the poet Lord Byron and now recognized as one of the ablest mathematicians of the era. She encouraged him to come up with a method for mathematically predicting the outcome of handicapped horse races. Although he received hundreds of letters from race-goers who wanted to know more, Babbage turned out to be a disastrous tipster and Ada Lovelace was almost ruined by gambling debts.

Another abortive moneymaking scheme was his attempt to build the first automatic gaming machine, an automaton that could play noughts and crosses. He reminisced in his 1864 autobiography, "I imagined that the machine might consist of the figures of two children playing against each other, accompanied by a lamb and a cock. That the child who won the game might clap his hands whilst the cock was crowing, after which, that the child who was beaten might cry and wring his hands whilst the lamb began bleating." He soon discovered that the mid-Victorian public were not interested in noughts and crosses. The market for travelling novelties that year, Babbage noted with disgust, was completely sewn up by P. T. Barnum's midget, General Tom Thumb.

Although Babbage's game-playing machines were commercial failures, his theoretical work created a foundation for the future science of game theory, pre-dating even that twentieth-century genius John von Neumann by about a hundred years.

There were other discoveries for which Babbage never received his due. For years, he had worked on cracking ciphers – techniques for encoding messages so that only someone with a key could understand them. Ciphers would allow British intelligence to enjoy a major advantage over the Russians in the Crimean War, but Babbage's important part in this was never acknowledged. In 1847, he invented an ophthalmoscope – a device for examining the inside of the eye. He took it to London's top eye specialist Thomas Wharton-Jones, who saw no use for it. Four years later, the slightly less short-sighted Hermann von Helmoltz created an almost identical instrument and was credited with its invention. The luckless Babbage had lost out again.

Babbage's last hope was that he could at least salvage some pride from his abandoned project and that the unfinished Difference Engine would be carefully preserved in a prime location in the British Museum. To his disgust, it was put behind glass in an obscure corner of King's College London alongside a collection of eighteenth-century scientific instruments made for George III. Babbage and his engine were completely overlooked for the Great Exhibition of 1851, the largest industrial manufacturing spectacular ever staged. For Babbage, who liked to think of himself as the elder statesman of the industrial movement, this was the ultimate insult.

The Engine was dusted off and briefly brought out for the London International Exhibition of 1862 but was put, again to Babbage's horror, in a dark corner where hardly anyone could find it. When he complained, he was told that the extra space was needed for a display of children's toys. Once again, Babbage reflected bitterly (and very tactlessly) that the ignorant British public had shown themselves to be more interested in entertainment than intelligent engineering.

Mocked by his critics, Babbage became a reclusive and very bitter old man, but he carried on working. He spent his final years mulling over ways to prevent bank note forgery. In 1864, his autobiography *Passages from the Life of a Philosopher* was published. This was largely a rant about his pet hates, especially street buskers. Babbage's wife, Georgina, is not mentioned at all and there is just a single oblique reference to 1827, the year four members of his immediate family died. Alone and suffering from severe headaches and hallucinations, he reflected that he could not remember a single happy day in his life. Babbage's biographer Bowden recorded: "He spoke as if he hated mankind in general, Englishmen in particular, and the English Government and organ grinders most of all."

He died in 1871, two months before his eightieth birthday, his groundbreaking work on computers hidden under a dust-sheet in King's College.

## The Evolutionist Who Wasn't Darwin

In the world of scientific priority, timing is everything. Consider the case of Charles Darwin and Alfred Russel Wallace – two men, from very different backgrounds, working on opposite sides of the Earth, independently putting forward the same idea at the same time. But for only one would posterity bedeck the laurels as the inventor of the theory of evolution. As for the other, his name would virtually vanish.

Alfred Russel Wallace had none of the privileges accorded to university-educated Charles Darwin, whose father was a prosperous doctor. He was born in 1823 in Llanbadoc, Wales, the second-youngest of nine children. He was forced to leave school at fourteen to take up an apprenticeship as a builder because his family had fallen on hard times. He had an early interest in natural history but was almost entirely self-taught, attending scientific lectures in his free time and reading extensively in public libraries. One of the books he enjoyed was Darwin's journal from the voyage of the *Beagle,* a lively travel book that gave almost no hint at all of the evolutionary ideas of its author.

Wallace worked as a surveyor for several years before setting out for the Amazon to search the rainforests looking for

exotic insect specimens to sell to European buyers. At this
point, he was officially more of a commercial collector than a
scientist but he spent four years exploring remote headwater
regions, making observations, gathering specimens, taking
notes and drawing sketches. His four-year trek in South America was at times horrific. One day, he disturbed a swarm of
wasps and was badly stung. Then he caught yellow fever (and
watched his brother die from the disease) followed by several
bouts of malaria.

More calamities lay in store. He was heading up the River
Negro when a gun carried by one his colleagues went off
accidentally, shooting Wallace in the hand. Having suffered
countless injuries, including the loss of a chunk of his hand, he
was finally looking forward to going home to England, but
Wallace was blighted by bad luck again. His great specimen-
gathering expedition to the Amazon ended in disaster when
the ship returning him to Britain caught fire and sank, taking
with it thousands of specimens and his hopes of an assured
income. Then the ship that rescued him, an old tub called the
*Jordeson*, ran into a terrible storm and almost sank as well.
Wallace survived with only a couple of notebooks and an
indignant parrot.

Wallace vowed never to sail again, but he needed to make a
living and, within days of limping ashore, he was planning his
next trip. This time, he was heading east to the Malay
Archipelago.

Wallace spent the next eight years wandering the islands,
sleeping rough, eating whatever the natives ate and paddling himself around in a canoe. His feet became infected
several times and he suffered multiple bouts of malaria. He
was very particular about what he collected – usually at
least six specimens for every species. He noted how many
different species adapted specifically to their environment
and wondered what might cause one species to transform
into a new species with new physical traits. Wallace sur-
mised that the fittest of a species survived and that the traits
which enabled them to survive were then passed down to

future generations, eventually creating a new species, or multiple species.

In 1855, Wallace published a paper entitled "On the Law Which Has Regulated the Introduction of New Species" in a prestigious natural history journal, *Annals and Magazine of Natural History*. His paper was read by many people, including Darwin, but almost no one recognized that this unknown young naturalist was making a big step towards a theory of evolutionary origins. Instead of the positive feedback Wallace had hoped for, he got a curt message from one scientist noting that he should stop theorizing and stick to gathering facts.

Wallace was struck down with malaria again on the island Ternate in the Malay Archipelago and was bedridden for several days. While lying weak in a quinine-induced haze, he had a flash of insight on how species change. The result was a new scientific paper "On the Tendency of Varieties to Depart Indefinitely from the Original Type". Although he didn't actually use the term "natural selection", he argued the same thing.

Wallace had long been in the habit of writing to fellow scientists to share ideas. Instead of sending his paper directly to a publisher, on 9 March 1858 Wallace sent the manuscript to the person he thought might appreciate it the most – Charles Darwin. Wallace's short essay covered all the basic ideas of evolution by natural selection and came with a covering letter, in which he said that he hoped the idea would be as new to Darwin as it was to him.

Of course, it wasn't new to Darwin at all. He had been working on the same idea for more than twenty years and thought it was all his own; he just hadn't got around to publishing it. After two decades of procrastination, he had nothing to prove ownership apart from 230 pages of notes outlining his theory lying in storage under a stairway in his home in a securely sealed packet, labelled "Only to be opened in the event of my death". He had put off publishing it because he was terrified of the implications. He knew that his theory was likely to cause deep offence,[14] not least to his own wife Emma, who was deeply religious, as were many of their closest friends.

When he eventually plucked up the courage to sound out a few close associates, like the geologist Charles Lyell, to gauge their reaction, they urged him to make his views public, but Darwin was too scared to publish. He told the Kew Gardens botanist Joseph Hooker that believing in evolution "felt like confessing a murder". Darwin had already been warned by a couple of friends who had seen Wallace's 1855 paper that the young man might be on to something, but he hadn't taken their warnings very seriously. When he saw Wallace's paper, he was devastated. Now he was about to be scooped by a young upstart.

Darwin faced a dilemma – he could have quietly binned Wallace's essay and no one would have been the wiser. After all, it had taken months to arrive and the international mail in the mid-nineteenth century was hardly reliable. After a great deal of agonizing on Darwin's part, a couple of his powerful scientific friends arranged to have Wallace's paper and Darwin's various notes on the subject read at the same Linnean Society meeting, in London on 1 July 1858.

It was customary at the Linnean Society for double contributions to be read in alphabetical order. And so in Darwin's absence (he was burying his youngest child that day), his detailed notes were read out at length, and then, almost as an afterthought, came Wallace's essay. Not that Wallace had any say in the matter; while Darwin was getting all the publicity, Wallace was still roughing it on the other side of the world.

---

14 Even in Darwin's day, evolutionary theory was not entirely new. The idea that species can adapt and change over the course of time had been put forward by several people before – including Darwin's own grandfather Erasmus. Seventy years before Darwin finally got around to writing *On the Origin of Species*, an aristocratic Scot, James Burnett, Lord Monboddo, published a six-volume treatise called *Of the Origin and Progress of Language*, the first work to suggest that mankind is descended from apes. He believed that the human tailbone was a vestige of our ape ancestry and spent his life convinced that babies were born with tails and that there was a universal conspiracy of silence among midwives who cut them off at birth.

Some historians have argued that that Darwin received Wallace's manuscript earlier than he admitted and stole some of his ideas to bolster his own theory. A study of 1858 postal connections, published at the end of 2011, retraced the 77-day journey of Wallace's packet to Darwin, from Ternate to Down House, via a Dutch mail steamer and a brief trip on the back of a camel between Suez and Alexandria.

In 1972, a researcher found another letter from Wallace to a friend named Bates that was also sent on the March 1858 steamer from the island of Ternate. The letter still bore postmarks from Singapore and London which confirmed that it arrived in London on 3 June 1858, two weeks before Darwin said he received the essay from Wallace.

Thus began the mystery. How could Wallace have sent two letters two letters on the same day, travelling along the same mail route back to London, and yet one arrived two weeks later than the other? Did Darwin collude with his friends, Lyell and Huxley, to hide the truth that Wallace had been swindled?

But we also have Darwin's word that he received the letter exactly when he said he did. Everything we know about him suggests that he was a man of honour and incapable of behaving so unethically. All the same, we know that Darwin was mortified when he realised that someone else had got there first: he certainly had the means and motives to cheat his reval.

To be fair, the humble Wallace was very generous about receiving less credit and seemed content with his role of almost total anonymity. He said he was flattered even to have had a part in prompting Darwin to publish his own theory. In fact, he and Darwin became good friends and Darwin, in turn, campaigned to secure Wallace a government pension.

Wallace went on to publish dozens of books and papers and built a reputation as one of the greatest field biologists of the nineteenth century, but his fame faded quickly after his death and, for a long time, he was a relatively obscure figure in the history of science. Darwin, on the other hand, remains venerated to this day, his features appearing on the current £10 note.

The suspicion remains that Wallace got a raw deal. It is undeniably remarkable that two people should have independently reached such a strikingly similar theory at the same time. There is also the uncomfortable fact that Darwin submitted Wallace's paper, along with his own, to be read out at the Linnean Society without seeking Wallace's permission, which if not a crime, was certainly a breach of ethics. What would have happened if Wallace had sent his paper to a publisher instead of Darwin? The history of science would have been very different. The term "Darwinism" would be unknown, and we would most likely speak of "Wallacism" today when talking about natural selection.[15]

## Worst Science Pundit

In the 1830s, Dionysius Lardner was a popular scientific lecturer and writer whose talks on a wide range of subjects from steam engines to magnetism drew huge audiences and made him a celebrity.

He also had a knack for getting it spectacularly wrong. In 1838, Lardner warned that "steam intercourse" between the continents of Europe and America was impossible because coal-fired ships would require so much fuel there would be no room for passengers. "As to the project announced in the newspapers of making the voyage from New York to Liverpool," Lardner snorted, "they might as well talk of making a voyage to the moon."

Brunel's *Great Western* made the crossing very soon afterwards. Twelve months later, Lardner predicted that rail travel above 40 mph would be lethal for passengers, who would die of asphyxiation.

His private life was similarly gaffe-prone.[16] In 1840, Lardner

---

15  It was neither Darwin nor Wallace who were the first to coin the phrase "survival of the fittest". It was first used by the English biologist Herbert Spencer, who was, ironically, a raging hypochondriac.

16  He left his wife Cecila in Dublin in 1820 and began a relationship with a married woman, Anne Boursiquot, who had a child rumoured to be Lardner's. Just in case anyone was in any doubt, she named her son Dionysius Lardner Boursiquot.

hit the headlines again when he eloped to France with the wife of a cavalry captain, who tracked the couple down to a Paris hotel bedroom, where he gave Lardner a sound flogging. The scandal, widely reported in the press, ended with Lardner fleeing to America with his lover to begin another career as an expert in science and technology.

He was hired by a firm of locomotive builders to investigate a fatal accident where a boiler had exploded on a new train. Lardner confidently pronounced that the accident had been caused by lightning, which meant that the company was not personally liable for the accident as it was an "act of God". It was pointed out at the coroner's inquest that there was no lightning present at the time, that the pumps had been faulty, the water indicator was badly designed and the bridge-bands had been made of cast iron rather than wrought iron.

## Most Convincing Surrender to Newton's Law of Gravity

In 1912, an Austrian-born French tailor, Franz Reichelt, invented a fashion accessory for aviators to help them survive a fall from their new-fangled aircraft: the "coat parachute". He tested his device by dropping dummies from the fifth floor of his apartment building.

Far from satisfied with the limited range of results, he applied for permission to jump from the Eiffel Tower in Paris. The tower owners reluctantly gave way, provided that Reichelt obtained police authorization and signed a waiver absolving them of all responsibility. Incredibly, the police allowed him to get on with it. It had not occurred to them that he was planning to test the parachute by wearing it himself.

At 7 a.m. on a cold February morning Reichelt, accompanied by a handful of well-wishers and press photographers, climbed to the level of the first platform, stepped over the edge and plunged to a painful and messy death.

Today, Reichelt's contribution to the invention of the

modern parachute is largely ignored. But he is the mainstay of dozens of books and websites about stupid deaths.

---

*"He's passé. Nobody cares about Mickey anymore . . .*
*I think we should phase him out."*
Roy Disney on his brother Walt's creation Mickey Mouse, 1937

---

## The Forgotten Man of Forensics

The Victorian polymath Francis Galton could fill a chapter on his own as a prolific author of useless research. He wrote down, logged, cross-referenced and quantified anything and everything he came across – the length of a man's nose, the strength of his hand grip, or the number of brush strokes on a painting (the results of which he reported in his article entitled "Number of Strokes of the Brush in a Picture". He once wrote a scientific paper on male facial hair.

In 1897, he published a paper on the precise length of rope required by a hangman to break a criminal's neck without decapitation, in which he triumphantly revealed an error in previously used calculations that did not take into account the bigger neck muscles in fat men. A select bibliography of some of Galton's more esoteric works might include: "Arithmetic by Smell" (*Psychological Review*, 1884); "Intelligible Signals Between Neighbouring Stars" (*Fortnightly Review*, 1896); "Gregariousness in Cattle and in Men" (*Macmillan's Magazine*, 1861); "Note on Fitting Normal Curves to Distribution of Speeds of Old Homing Pigeons" (*Homing News and Pigeon Fanciers Journal*, 1894); not forgetting his seminal "Cutting a Round Cake on Scientific Principles" (*Nature*, 1906). In his spare time, he also developed a complex formula for determining the best way to make a cup of tea.

Statistically, Galton's work was bound to hit on something eventually that was actually useful. And to be fair it did, although it turns out that he probably stole the idea from someone else.

Galton spent several years pestering his acquaintances for their thumbprints, which he recorded with a little inky pad and roller he kept in his pocket. Galton's primary interest in fingerprints was as an aid in determining heredity and racial background. He was disappointed to find that fingerprints offered no firm clues as to an individual's intelligence or genetic history but, after studying 2,500 sets of prints, he suddenly realized that they were all different and that fingerprints do not change over the course of a lifetime. In 1892, he published a 200-page essay simply titled "Fingerprints", in which he established the individuality and permanence of fingerprints and wrote up a classification system for them. Galton took full credit for inventing fingerprint identification but his "discovery" was, to say the least, highly controversial.

Fourteen years before the publication of "Fingerprints", a Scot called Henry Faulds was working in Japan as Surgeon-Superintendent of Tsukiji Hospital in Tokyo. Faulds was another of those eccentric gentlemen of science who dabbled in a bit of everything, but his background was very much unlike that of Galton, who enjoyed all the advantages of wealth and class.

Faulds had been born into great austerity in the small town of Beith, Ayrshire. At thirteen, he was forced to leave school and went to Glasgow to work as a clerk to help support his family. He later studied medicine at Glasgow University.

Faulds also was deeply religious and, in 1874, he was sent by the Presbyterian Church of Scotland to set up a medical mission in Japan. He became fluent in Japanese, taught at the local university and was responsible for founding the Tokyo Institute for the Blind.

In 1878, he visited an archaeological dig and noticed that shards of ancient pottery had the fingerprints of those who had made them embedded in their work. Moreover, the finger-ridge patterns were unique to each individual. A piece of pottery could be matched to a particular potter by the ridge markings left in the clay. Faulds hit upon the idea of solving crime by fingerprinting. He got the chance to put his theory into practice when a bottle of surgical alcohol was stolen from his hospital. He was able to trace the culprit through a set of ten greasy prints on the bottle to one of his employees. Later, he was able to show the local police that a sooty palm print left on a hospital wall by a suspected burglar could not have been left by the person accused of the burglary. It was the first time in recorded history that both innocence and guilt were proven by the use of fingerprints.

In 1880, Faulds wrote up his findings and sent them to Charles Darwin. He hoped a word or two from the great Darwin might help him find backers to fund his research. The elderly Darwin pleaded illness and forwarded the letter to his cousin, Francis Galton, with a note: "My Dear Galton, the enclosed letter may perhaps interest you, as it relates to a queer subject." But Galton was apparently too busy to read it so he, in turn, forwarded it to the Royal Anthropological Society, who took no notice at all.

A few weeks later, Faulds sent a paper to the scientific journal *Nature* titled "On the Skin-Furrows of the Hand", in which he described how to take impressions using printer's ink and mentioned the use of prints in forensic identification of criminals. Crucially, he also mentioned in closing the "forever-unchangeable finger-furrows of important criminals". It seems that no one took the Faulds article very seriously because his claims were not supported by data, although in the very next issue of *Nature* there was an indignant letter from William Herschel, grandson of the famous astronomer, that he had been using fingerprints as a means of identification while working as a civil servant in India since 1860.[17]

What Faulds did with his research after that is unclear, although we know that in 1888 he took his discovery to

---

17   Later Herschel sent another letter to *Nature* giving full credit to Faulds for his original discovery, but this disclaimer went largely unnoticed and, by this time, Galton had already usurped Faulds' place in history.

Scotland Yard, who dismissed him as a crank, possibly on account of his aggressive and generally weird behaviour. He followed up with letters to police forces all around the world, to no avail. The scientific study of fingerprints seems to have sunk without a trace, until Galton revived it four years later.

When Faulds read Galton's "Fingerprints" and realized that it contained no mention of his own contribution, he was furious. He was convinced that he had been cheated out of his claim as the true inventor of fingerprinting by a conspiracy hatched between Herschel and Galton. He spent years badgering government departments, demanding official recognition. When he heard that Galton had received a knighthood, he even petitioned the Liberal Home Secretary Winston Churchill for one of his own.

Meanwhile, his professional life fell apart. Faulds returned to Britain after quarrelling with the missionary society which ran his hospital in Japan. He worked as police surgeon at first in London and then in North Staffordshire. He died in 1930 aged 86 in Wolstanton, embittered, unrecognized and financially destitute.

In 1938, a Scottish judge George Wilton published a book entitled *Fingerprints: History Law and Romance*, in which he tried to correct the injustice that had been done to the memory of Dr Faulds. In fact, right up to his death at the age of 101, Wilton gave lectures and wrote letters on the subject.

Belated recognition for Faulds finally came in Japan where a memorial tablet was erected in 1951 at the site of his old hospital in Tsukiji, giving him credit as the true discoverer of fingerprinting.

## Most Successful Attempt to Destroy a Reputation as a Great Scientist

On 18 June 1952 the front page of the *Los Angeles Times* carried the headline: "BRILLIANT SCIENTIST KILLED IN EXPLOSION". The victim, thirty-seven-year-old Jack Parsons, was the unsung hero of the space race, recognized as the one of the world's foremost authorities on rocket propulsion. Parsons invented a range of solid and liquid fuels whose later forms were eventually to help drive Apollo 11 to the Moon. Werner von Braun acknowledged Parsons as the "true father of the American space programme". His innovations also led to a range of first-generation American missiles, including the solid-fuelled submarine-launched Polaris. His work was so highly regarded that French scientists a generation later named a crater on the dark side of the Moon after him. But Parsons' contribution to science was almost completely overshadowed by a very colourful private life.

Jack Parsons' death in his backyard laboratory was initially reported as a terrible accident – he was the victim of mishandled chemicals. And that is how the press might have let the matter lie, had it not been for the fact that four hours after Parsons' death, his mother Ruth killed herself with a fatal overdose of Nembutal.

The press began to dig deeper. A couple of days later, the police let slip that Parsons had been investigated by them before – more than once. America's foremost rocket scientist was living a curious double life. There was talk of drugs, of black magic and "deviant" sexual activities. It went from a straightforward story about the tragic death of much respected member of the scientific community to one of sensational and lurid speculation.

Before Jack Parsons, rocket science was the stuff of sci-fi and B-movies. The first serious attempt to advance the science of rocketry was by an American – Robert Goddard – who began experimenting with rocket propulsion in the early 1900s. In 1920, he speculated how a rocket might reach the moon. When the press picked up on it, Goddard was portrayed as a madman. When he launched an eleven-foot missile in 1929, his local paper covered the story beneath the cynical headline: "MOON ROCKET MISSES TARGET BY 238,799½ MILES" . In 1940, he was mocked in the House of Congress as "a crackpot with mental delusions that we can travel to the Moon" and the entire House fell about laughing.

Jack Parsons' pioneering work, however, would soon help turn rocket science into reality. He was born in Los Angeles in 1914, the son of a wealthy and well-connected family living in a sprawling mansion on Pasadena's Millionaire Row. His father deserted the family early on and Parsons had a lonely childhood, spoilt by his mother. Bullied at school, he buried himself in science-fiction magazines. It was through sci-fi mags that Parsons discovered his passion in life (or one of them, at least) – explosives. Juvenile experiments with homemade rockets shattered the peace of leafy Pasadena and he was expelled from high school after blowing up the school toilets.

Although Parsons had little formal education beyond high school, his self-taught knowledge of combustible chemicals got him a job at Halifax Explosives Co. Photographs of him around this time show a tall, slim, handsome youth with a fondness for ripped jeans and T-shirts; he is sometimes referred to as the "James Dean of American rocketry", although, in fact, he looked much more like a younger version of the man he would one day work for – Howard Hughes.

At twenty-one, in spite of what he described in his own words in his diary as a "dangerous attachment" to his mother, Parsons met a girl called Helen at a church dance and, after a brief courtship, they were married. His fascination for rocketry, meanwhile, was noticed by Robert Goddard and, at the age of twenty-two, Parsons was invited to become a member of the three-man California Institute of Technology's rocket research group. They were known as "The Suicide Squad" because of the alarming explosions they caused on campus. When the USA joined the Second World War, the military called upon Parsons and his crew to see if their rockets could propel planes into the air in places without adequate runways. Their successes went far beyond the original brief, developing a fuel source that would burn long enough and with sufficient thrust to reach outer space.

After the war, Parsons and his friends from the Suicide Squad founded Aerojet Corp., now the world's largest rocket producer and manufacturer of solid-fuel boosters for space shuttles. Their chief consultant was Caltech's colourful professor of astronomy, Fritz Zwicky.

A star in the field of cosmology, Zwicky was one of the twentieth century's most brilliant astronomers. He coined the term "supernova" to describe exploding stars whose cores collapsed to form small, ultra-dense neutron stars. More controversially, he also noticed that galaxies were spinning so rapidly that logically they should fly apart. Something was keeping them together, but what? It was nothing that the eye could see. Zwicky reasoned that there must be some invisible matter that was providing just enough gravity to hold it all together. And so the concept of dark matter was born. The cosmological world thought that Zwicky had lost his marbles. It wasn't until the 1970s, when astronomers returned to the idea to explain the same phenomenon they were observing in other galaxies, that he turned out to be right.

Zwicky fell out with just about everyone he ever worked with. He once threatened to kill his closest collaborator Walter Baade and accused him of being a Nazi – which Baade never was. In the end, Baade was so scared of Zwicky that he refused to be left alone in the same room as him. Zwicky's aggressive behaviour and explosive temper were legendary. A fitness fanatic, he was in the habit of dropping to the floor mid-conversation to demonstrate his one-arm push-up. He was known to accost unfamiliar students in the astronomy building at Caltech and ask, "Who the hell are you?"[18]

Clearly, Zwicky was not a man to be crossed, but Jack Parsons did it anyway. When Zwicky ordered a batch of chemicals Parsons had not personally recommended, he retaliated by simply blowing the batch up, almost taking half the company with it. Zwicky was, in any case, deeply unimpressed by

---

18  In another career-limiting move he referred to his fellow astronomers at Mount Wilson and Paloma as "spherical bastards". Why spherical, he was asked? "Because they are bastards any way you look at them." Some of his work methods didn't do much to varnish his reputation either, including the time Zwicky persuaded the night assistant at the observatory to fire a cannon out of the dome slit in the direction the telescope was pointing to see if that improved the viewing.

Parsons and his "Buck Rogers"-style rocket propulsion, believing he was wasting his time on a scientifically invalid subject. Rockets, Zwicky said, could never, ever operate in deep space because they required an atmosphere to push against to provide thrust. As evidence to the contrary mounted, the mighty Zwicky was forced to recant.

Parsons was described as "slightly crazy" by his colleagues, a slight understatement as it turned out. Before each rocket test, he routinely invoked Pan, the horned god of fertility, although his eccentricities extended far beyond the odd pagan chant. While busy inventing the rocket fuel that made the space age possible and almost killing his work colleagues in the process, he was enjoying a bohemian double life. His home, a vast mansion in Pasadena, was regularly full of assorted lodgers and hangers-on. He had placed local adverts offering accommodation, specifying that only musicians, artists, atheists and anarchists need apply. There were rumours of strange goings-on, including black magic and orgies. One visitor wrote that "two women in diaphanous gowns would dance around a pot of fire surrounded by coffins topped with candles . . ."

One night in 1942, police called investigating reports that a pregnant woman was jumping naked through a fire in the back yard. Parsons, at his charming best, convinced the officers of his position as a respectable scientist and the matter was dropped. Soon afterwards, a sixteen-year-old boy reported Parsons to the police claiming the scientist's followers had forcibly sodomized him during a "Black Mass". The police didn't believe him. Parsons' "cult", they reported back, was merely "an organization dedicated to religious and philosophical speculation, with respectable members such as a Pasadena bank president, doctors, lawyers and Hollywood actors".

In fact, Parsons had long since immersed himself in the philosophy of the infamous British occultist Aleister Crowley. "The Beast", as Crowley was known to his mother, was born into a wealthy brewing family and spent his early years combating boredom by dabbling in his two favourite activities

– mysticism and sex. He later combined the two when he discovered "mystic sodomy", one of the many dubious practices Crowley advocated for self-improvement. In 1941, Parsons joined the California branch of the Crowley cult. They were quick to latch on to the wealthy young scientist as a potential saviour for their movement and invited him to become their leader. He accepted and, styling himself "The Antichrist", began donating most of his salary to the upkeep of his lodge brethren.

By this time, Parsons had left his wife Helen and was having an affair with her eighteen-year-old sister Betty. Visitors to Parsons' home, meanwhile, included the young sci-fi pulp writer and fellow Crowley enthusiast L. Ron Hubbard, for whom the Scientology movement was still just a twinkle in his eye. Parsons was mesmerized by Hubbard, especially by his extensive knowledge of Crowley's writings. Hubbard moved in with Parsons and the two became close.

While pursuing some more material scientific pursuits, Parsons at this time was apparently trying to create a "Moon Child", a magic being conjured via mystic ritual who would usher in a new age of liberty and signal the end of the Christian era. This involved something called "magical masturbation", apparently carried out in front of Hubbard.

Unfortunately, Parsons was rather useless as a magus. After a couple more failed attempts to communicate with the whore of Babylon, he and Hubbard decided to embark on a more business-based venture – Allied Enterprises – buying boats on the East Coast for resale in California. Parsons went off the idea when Hubbard took off for Florida with his girlfriend Betty and most of his money, supposedly to buy some boats. It was the last Parsons saw of Betty or his money,[19] although he remained mysteriously devoted to Hubbard. A month later, Betty and Hubbard were married. When the *Sunday Times* published an article in 1969 exposing the connection between

---

19  Hubbard used the money he defrauded from Parsons to publish his book *Dianetics*, the basis for the Scientology movement.

Hubbard, Parsons and the bisexual drug addict Crowley, the Church of Scientology was keen to explain a "misunderstanding". Their founder, they explained, had, in fact, been sent by US Naval Intelligence to infiltrate Parsons' evil black magic cult and "rescue" a girl.

Not surprisingly, Parsons' professional reputation suffered; nor did he escape the attentions of one J. Edgar Hoover. From the early 1940s, he was watched by the FBI, initially because of suspected communist affiliations. It was only much later that they got wind of his occultist activities. You can imagine how much shelf space an FBI file on a communist occultist alone would occupy, but yet another FBI file on Parsons was opened in 1951, this time for alleged espionage. He was caught stealing classified documents from his then employer Hughes Aircraft and passing them to the newfound state of Israel. In fact, Parsons was probably only looking for a new job, but the implication was that he was part of a covert effort to help Israel build a nuclear weapon. He was lucky to escape prosecution for treason and was stripped of his security clearance. Flat broke, the scientist who once dreamed of blasting Man into outer space was reduced to working as a petrol pump attendant, supplemented by stints on Hollywood B-movies as a special-effects expert.

Parsons didn't live to see his fuel invention take Man to the Moon. While working at home in his backyard laboratory, he accidentally blew himself up. The police found the residue of the highly combustible explosive fulminate of mercury in a litter bin, together with shards of a tin can. Parsons had been mixing the chemical in a coffee tin when he accidentally dropped it in the bin. From the blast marks on his body, it looked as though he'd tried to catch the tin before it made impact with a hard surface. The resulting small explosion ignited other chemicals in the laboratory causing a devastating blast. His distraught mother Ruth took her own life a few hours later.

According to Parsons' biographer John Carter in *Sex and Rockets, the Occult World of Jack Parsons*, there was another interesting item found by police investigators on the Parsons property after his death – a small black box. It contained a film, showing Jack Parsons having sex with his dog and his mother.

## Most Prolific Inventor of Things that Should Never Have Got Off the Drawing Board

Thomas Midgley Jnr was a born inventor who, over the course of his career, came to hold more than 100 patents. But the world would have been a safer place if Thomas Midgley Jnr hadn't been born at all.

He had an uncanny knack for developing solutions that seemed all right at the time. Take leaded petrol, for example; that was one of his. In 1916, he was hired to work in the laboratory of the Dayton Engineering Laboratories Company on automotive research. One of his first assignments was to find a solution to engine "knock", a destructive phenomenon that occurred in internal combustion engines, characterized by an annoying "ping" sound, accompanied by overheating, jerky motion and sluggish response. Leaded petrol had many benefits – increased engine horsepower, greater safety, reliability and speed. Unfortunately, leaded petrol also turned out to be a major air pollutant. By the 1970s, millions of city dwellers had greatly elevated levels of highly toxic lead in their blood. Thanks to Midgley, children all over the world had lower IQs because their brains were poisoned by lead.

But that wasn't the half of it. A decade later, the well-meaning Midgley had another bright idea. Refrigeration at that time was often an appallingly risky business. Fridges used dangerous gases that were flammable, unstable and could leak. In 1929, a leaky refrigerator at a hospital in Ohio killed more than a hundred people. Midgley discovered that chlorofluorocarbons (CFCs) were an almost perfect substance for refrigerators, air-conditioners and aerosols. In 1931, he demonstrated just how safe CFCs were by filling his lungs with the vapour and exhaling it to extinguish a candle. He was lauded as a genius. It was only much later that CFCs were found to destroy the ozone layer. The chlorofluorocarbons that had cooled the world and chilled its food were also destroying its protection against the Sun's rays.

Midgley never knew how much havoc he had wreaked with leaded petrol and CFCs because he died long before anyone else realized it. There was at least poetic justice in his death. In 1940, he contracted polio which left him wheel-chair-bound. Finally – and fatally – he devised a contraption comprising ropes and pulleys that allowed him to hoist himself out of bed without assistance. On the morning of 2 November 1944, his wife found him lifeless, having strangled himself with his final invention.

# 3

## Who Dares Loses: Business Blunders, Bankrupts and Brand Disasters

*In which Mr Edison invents a concrete piano; a man tries to grow tea in Sweden; Mr Ratner's punchline fails; fear of masturbation shapes the modern breakfast table; and Mr Goodyear gets into a spot of bother with his rubber vest.*

### Most Flawed Get-Rich-Quick Scheme

For reasons unknown, in 1669 a Hamburg merchant called Hennig Brand became convinced that he could turn human urine into gold. He collected a small lake of the stuff – between fifty and sixty bucketfuls in all – each bucket taking at least a fortnight to fill. He then allowed the urine to stand and putrefy until, in his own words, it "bred worms". Ignoring the protests of his wife, he then boiled it down into a waxy residue, and left it in his cellar for several months until it had fermented and turned black. Brand then heated the black fermented urine and distilled it into a large beaker.

What remained, Brand was disappointed to discover, was not gold. His golden shower, however, did have some very peculiar properties – it glowed in the dark and was highly combustible. Purely by chance, he had discovered the chemical element phosphorous.

Notwithstanding the fact that half the neighbourhood must by now have been aware of Brand and his malodorous lake of ancient piss, he demonstrated his new discovery to a handful of friends, proudly heralding it as one of the best kept secrets of seventeenth-century science. But finding something useful to do with this stinking by-product was another matter, something that completely eluded Brand to his death. The other problem was that he had had to boil nearly 5,500 litres of urine in order to produce only 120 grams of phosphorus.

Eventually, Brand sold his "secret" to a German chemist called Krafft who exhibited phosphorus throughout Europe. Unfortunately, word got out that the substance was made from urine, which was all anyone needed to work out their own means of purifying phosphorus.

In the 1750s, a Swedish chemist worked out how to make phosphorus in bulk without the smell of urine. One of the first uses of the new substance was in the manufacture of matches, resulting in "phossy jaw", one of the most horrific occupational diseases known to mankind, in which the victims' jawbones would literally rot and glow in the dark and was only treatable by surgical removal of the jawbone, an agonizing and disfiguring operation.

## Worst Follow-Up to a Great Idea

The American Thomas Alva Edison (1847–1931) was one of the most prolific inventors the world has ever seen. In his eighty-four years, he had 1,093 patents to his name, including the electric light bulb, the gramophone and the motion picture camera, to name but a few. The automotive genius Henry Ford said, "To find a man who has not benefited by Edison and who is not in debt to him it would be necessary to go deep into the jungle." In 1922, readers of the *New York Times* voted Edison "the greatest living American".

For all his creative successes and his prodigious production-line of inventions, Edison was no stranger to complete commercial failure. Or, for that matter, coming up with ideas that were just completely barking mad. Edison's greatest achievements were all made before he reached the age of forty, but he continued inventing right up until his death at the age of eighty-five at a rate of one invention every ten days.

He never knew when to quit – or to resist the temptation of trying to rescue a bad idea with an even worse idea. For example, he first saw the phonograph as a device not for music and entertainment, but for dictation, documenting oral histories, preserving dying languages, teaching elocution, recording speech and telling time for the blind. In May 1928, he said, "Americans require a restful quiet in the moving picture theatre and, for them, talking from the lips of the figures on the screen destroys the illusion . . . the idea is not practical. The stage is the place for the spoken word." The following year, the first talkie, *The Jazz Singer*, appeared and was a massive success.

In 1887, he tried to rescue his faltering phonograph works by entering the toy business. It led to one of his greatest flops, the mechanical talking doll – actually, a doll with an Edison phonograph stuffed inside. Despite several years of experimentation and development, the Edison Talking Doll was a disaster and was removed from the shelves after a few short weeks in early 1890.

His worst idea ever, in fact one of the most colossal flops in the history of innovation, came in the late 1880s. Edison proposed a new process for refining low-grade iron ore using magnets and massive crushing rollers. He might have left it at that, but his idea was ridiculed in the press; one newspaper dismissed it as "Edison's Folly".

The irked inventor was determined to prove them wrong. He built a huge plant with a separator that could extract iron from unusable, low-grade ores and a town to go with it. In order to finance his project he had to sell all his stock in General Electric. The enterprise cost him more than a decade of wasted effort and several million dollars. Instead of selling the equipment for scrap and calling it a day, Edison decided to use the huge rollers to manufacture high-grade cement, but the cement plant soon become another, even deeper, financial black hole.

If no one wanted Edison's cement, he would just have to create his own demand with yet another invention – the

Edison concrete home. His new concrete houses, he promised, would revolutionize the American way of life. Fireproof, bombproof, insect-proof and easy to clean, the walls could be supplied in attractive concrete tints and need never be repainted. In fact, every fixture and fitting could be pre-cast as a single slab of concrete in a process that took just a few hours. If you needed more living space, you could simply pour another floor. And at only $1,200 apiece, they were cheap enough for anyone to afford.

Edison's early prototypes were a disaster. Marketed as "in the style of François I", they looked more like oversized portable toilets. Clearly, Edison was no architect, as his critics were quick to point out; one noted cruelly, "It is not cheapness that is wanted so much as relief from ugliness, and Mr. Edison's houses do not achieve that relief."

Instead of simple moulds, Edison's pre-fabricated houses also required nickel-plated iron forms containing more than two thousand parts and weighing nearly half a million pounds. Prospective builders were required to invest in at least $175,000 of plant and machinery before they could pour a single house. But there was another problem Edison had not foreseen. No one was keen to live in a house the great man himself had dubbed "the salvation of the slum dweller".

In spite of these seemingly insurmountable setbacks, Edison wasn't going to let it go. In 1911, he tried again. This time he had discovered a product line for which he thought concrete was ideally suited – home furnishings. He wanted to make everything from concrete phonograph cabinets and concrete pianos to concrete bedroom sets – "more durable and beautiful than those in the most palatial residence in Paris or along the Rhine" according to his marketing blurb. The *New York Times* observed drily, "As to concrete dogs to stand warningly in the front yard and concrete cats to purr stonily under a concrete kitchen range, he made no announcement."

In the face of much ridicule in the press, Edison shipped a pair of concrete phonograph consoles to a much-hyped New York trade show in crates marked "Please Drop and Abuse

This package." The hauliers took him at his word and the indestructible cabinets made it to their destination in several pieces. Edison refused to discuss the subject of concrete furniture ever again. The Edison Portland Cement Company went bankrupt twice, closed for good after its founder's death, and was the subject of a book with the title *The Romance of Cement*.

Edison saved his most bizarre pet project yet for last. From the 1920s until his death in 1931, he was busy developing a Spirit Phone that would allow him to communicate with the dead.[1] But the well-known workaholic didn't let death slow him down. He continued his work post mortem and had a breakthrough via his spirit communicator in 1967 – or at least that was what was claimed by a medium called Sigrum Seuterman.

## Best Get-Poor-Quick Scheme

Charles Ponzi was fourteen years old when he emigrated to the USA from his native Italy in 1896. By the age of eighteen, he was declared a "financial wizard" after offering a staggering 50 per cent return on investment in forty-five days and 100 per cent return in ninety days. He did it by using "profits" from new investors to pay interest to old ones (taking an estimated $200,000 a day at his peak) from an ever-growing pool of more than 40,000 investors in his Securities Exchange Company in Boston, which claimed to leverage exchange rates through an international postage stamp reply coupon trading system. It became known as a Ponzi or "pyramid" scheme.

As pyramid schemes require an exponential increase in members to keep going, like a nuclear chain reaction, inevitably they end in disaster. Ponzi's activities were finally curtailed and he was deported back to Italy. After embezzling more funds from the Italian financial sector, Ponzi fled to Brazil, where he died, penniless, in a charity hospital, half-blind and partially paralysed.

---

1   Edison's dying breath was preserved in a sealed test tube by his friend Henry Ford.

Long after his death, Charles Ponzi's scheme continues to ruin lives. In 1997, up to 90 per cent of the population of Albania lost their life savings when multiple, large-scale pyramid investment schemes collapsed. It led to uncontained rioting, the government fell and the country descended into anarchy and a near civil war in which some 2,000 people were killed.

> *"Sensible and responsible women do not want to vote."*
> Grover Cleveland, US President, 1905

## Most Expensive Failure to Spot a Lemon

Launched on "E Day" – 4 September 1957 – the Ford Edsel was the most hyped car of its era. Ford had just spent more than $400 million developing it and its launch came on the back of an expensive and finely honed marketing campaign that had everybody talking about it. Months before the car appeared in showrooms, adverts had begun to appear simply showing the teaser slogan: "The Edsel is Coming".

Ford went to great lengths to keep the car's features and appearance a secret. Dealers were told to store their Edsels undercover and risked a fine or loss of their franchise if they showed the cars before the release date. It even had its own TV special – *The Edsel Show* – on 13 October, featuring Frank Sinatra and Bing Crosby. With unprecedented fanfare and hype, it was no surprise that consumers were eager to see what all the fuss was about.

At first the pre-publicity seemed to work. When the big day arrived, car showrooms were packed with curious visitors seeking their first glance of the car – almost three million in the first week alone. For a couple of days, Ford executives were rubbing their hands together with glee, anticipating sales of at least 200,000 cars in the first year. It was an ambitious target – about 5 per cent of the entire US car market.

But it soon became clear that looking was all the visitors were doing. The car sold just 64,000 units in its first year. In the next year, sales fell to 44,891, and 2,846 the year after that. The awkward Edsel was finally put out of its misery on 19 November 1959, a little over two years after its launch, having sold far less than half of the units Ford projected it needed to sell to break even, losing a reported $1.55 billion.[2] From that day on, the Edsel would be known as "the *Titanic* of the auto industry", the classic brand failure of all time.

Why did it fail so spectacularly? Some blamed the timing. After a boom period for the US car industry during the mid-1950s, the Edsel was being launched at the start of a recession, just as almost all car models were seeing a drop in sales, some by as much as 50 per cent. Ford had taken a decision to highlight the Edsel's powerful engine. But the Edsel was fuel thirsty and people were looking for cheaper, more fuel-efficient cars. The Edsel's high price may have been acceptable if it had been worth paying, but the car quickly gained a reputation for mechanical problems. Edsel now stood for Every Day Something Else Leaks.

Then there was the hype. For months, Ford had been encouraging people to expect something radically new when, in fact, the Edsel shared its engineering with other Ford models.

As well as the disappointing technology and over-hyped advertising, the car also had a stupid name. The company had undergone extensive market surveys, and had even polled their own workforce for suggestions. Eventually, they had a pool of 10,000 names to choose from. It was too many for the company chairman, Ernest Breech, as he scanned through the list. "Why don't we just call it Edsel?" he suggested. Henry Ford II, the grandson of Henry Ford, agreed; Edsel was the name of his father and the Ford founder's only son. It could have been a lot worse: at one point, Ford hired the poet Marianne Moore and asked her to find a name

---

2   Adjusted for inflation.

which would signify a "visceral feeling of elegance, fleetness, advanced features and design". Her suggestions included Mongoose Civique, Resilient Bullet, Utopian Turtletop and the Varsity Stroke.[3]

But mostly, people blamed the styling. There was no escaping it – the Edson was ugly. The motor journals variously described it as "an Oldsmobile sucking a lemon" and "a Pontiac pushing a toilet seat". One reviewer said the grille looked like "a vagina with teeth".

## Least Successful Celebrity Endorsement

When the designers of an iconic Victorian coffee brand needed a poster boy to promote their new product in 1885 they could think of no one more fitting than the man of the hour Major-General Hector Macdonald.

Born a Scottish crofter's son, the legendary "Fighting Mac" rose through the ranks to become one of Britain's greatest Victorian heroes. His military career was the stuff of legend; while serving in Afghanistan in 1879, he was offered either the Victoria Cross or an officer's commission. He turned down the VC with the words, "I'll win the medal later."

He got his nickname in the first Boer War for hand-to-hand fighting. Having been disarmed by the enemy in the field of battle, he refused to surrender and resorted to fisticuffs until he was again overpowered. He saved the British Army from destruction at the Battle of Omdurman, ending the rule of the mighty Mahdi in the Sudan and the lives of an estimated 14,000 Muslim warriors – the brave "fuzzy wuzzies" of Kipling's poem.

In 1902, while in command of British troops in Ceylon, Macdonald, scourge of Afghans, Boers and Whirling Dervishes, was accused of a "habitual crime of misdemeanour"

---

3   In the spirit of bad car names, there was also the Probe, which some women drivers referred to as the "Speculum"; and the Nova, which in Spanish-speaking countries translates as "won't go".

with four schoolboys in a railway carriage. It followed more accusations of indecency including an alleged relationship with a Boer prisoner of war and another with a Belgian soldier.

Under Victorian military law, homosexuals could be shot. In spite of a personal appeal to King Edward VII, the War Office ordered Macdonald to return to Britain to face a court martial. On his way back to Ceylon, he stopped off in Paris at the Hotel Regina. The following morning, he came down for breakfast and picked up a copy of the *Daily Express* from the hotel concierge and saw his name in a story under the headline "GRAVE CHARGE". He went back upstairs to his room, sat on his bed, put a pistol to his head and blew his brains out.

Today, the coffee bottle still bears the likeness of the doughty Victorian Gordon Highlander soldier sitting outside his tent in a far-flung corner of the British empire drinking a cup of coffee. The only difference today, in the interests of political correctness, is that he is no longer being brought his drink by a Sikh manservant; the new label for the old beverage shows the Sikh soldier sitting beside his former boss with a cup and saucer of his own. The brand? Camp.

## Least Successful Celebrity Endorsement: Runner-Up

In 1987, the US meat industry was concerned about the growing menace of vegetarianism, so the Beef Industry Council decided to hit back with an advertising campaign. First, they turned to the actress Cybil Shepherd, best known for her role starring alongside Bruce Willis in the TV drama *Moonlighting*. She signed up to an alleged $1 million deal to become the spokeswoman for American beef with the slogan "Real food for real people".[4] She tried to sex up the hamburger by calling it "something hot and juicy and so utterly simple you can eat

---

4   A less-than-impressed Texas rancher complained to the *New York Times*: "For a million bucks she ought to walk around with a hamburger in her mouth all the time."

it with your hands. I mean, I know some people who don't eat burgers. But I'm not sure I trust them."

The campaign was only weeks old when she told a magazine, "I've cut down on fatty foods and am trying to stay away from red meat." Ms Shepherd was dropped from the campaign.

Next, they tried the actor James Garner, star of *Maverick* and *The Rockford Files*. Surely Maverick wasn't a secret vegetarian? Of course he wasn't; Garner loved a steak as much as the next man. He was shown carving his way through mountains of roasts and grills – which was fine, until they had to rush him to the cardiac unit for emergency quadruple by-pass surgery. A less-than-ideal representative for their artery-clogging product, as it turned out.

At this point, the BIC abandoned their search for a celebrity figurehead and decided to go for a poster campaign instead. Their advertising agency accordingly produced an eye-catching poster of an all-American boy holding the Stars and Stripes. This was surely the image they were looking for ... which it was, until someone pointed out the poster was almost identical to an old Nazi recruiting poster from the Second World War. After distributing the posters to hundreds of supermarkets across the country, a BIC spokesman said the striking resemblance was just a coincidence, adding, "We're not trying to send out any subliminal Nazi messages."

## Least Credible Economic Growth Plan

When you think of Sweden, a model welfare state may come to mind, but not necessarily paddy fields and tea plantations. In the eighteenth century, however, Swedish priorities were slightly different.

The Swede Carl Linnaeus, a doctor specializing in cures for syphilis, was the great organizer of life. Before Linnaeus, taxonomy – the science of identifying and naming species and putting them into systems of classification – was a shambles. There were few agreed upon names even for the most common plants and no basic principles of classification or description.

Plants were given long names, always in Latin. Plant naming got completely out of hand as botanists vied to outdo each other by adding more and more detailed descriptions. Names could go on to ridiculous lengths; the humble tomato, for example, was *Solanum caule inermi herbaceo, foliis pinnatis incise*s – "the solanum with the smooth stem which is herbaceous and has incised pinnate leaves". The world's flora and fauna was crying out for someone to make sense of it all.

Carl Linnaeus hit upon the idea of a single, universally applicable scientific language whereby plants were given a family name, shared by all the other members of the group. His *Systema Naturae* was largely based on the sexual behaviour of plants. Not only do plants have sex, Linnaeus said, they also enjoy it. He gave one species of clam the names "ovula", "labia", "pubes", "anus" and "hymen". There was no escaping the link between Linnaean botany and sex. And just in case anyone had missed it, he named a whole class of flowers *Clitoria*.

The plant-nookie references were all too much for the British scientific community, who dismissed his botanical classification system as "too smutty for English ears" and "unspeakably vulgar". Worried translators hunted feverishly for less offensive English terms to replace the sexually explicit Linnaean language. William Withering, an English physician who made a name for himself by treating heart problems with extract of foxglove (digitalis), took it upon himself to translate Linnaeus's sexually explicit terminology into harmless English equivalents. Thanks to his expurgated version, women could now discuss flower arrangements safely without fear of embarrassment. A few Linnaean names however remained; the slipper limpet still answers to the name *Crepidula fornicata*: It was also all a bit too much for the Pope, of course, who completely banned Linnaeus's works.

For all his brilliance, Linnaeus was not a likeable man. Arrogant and overbearing, he liked to style himself "Prince of Botanists". As a rule, it was never wise to question his authority; those who did found they had weeds named after them.

There was also much that the godfather of plant and animal classification got wildly wrong. Linnaeus thought there might be around 40,000 species all told: estimates today range from 10 million to 100 million. His system incorporated mythical beasts and "monstrous humans", including the "wild man" *Homo ferus*, who walked on all fours, and *Homo caudatus* – "man with a tail". He thought that all existing species had survived Noah's flood by clinging to the slopes of Mount Ararat. He also believed that epilepsy could be caused by washing hair, that leprosy could be cured by eating herring worms and that swallows wintered at the bottom of lakes. One of his more hopeless ventures was a clock based on the opening and closing times of various flowers.

Linnaeus's most catastrophic error was his attempt to turn Sweden into a giant market garden. He thought that by transplanting the world's best crops in Sweden he could transform his country's economy and make it less dependent on foreign imported food. He sent his best students out all over the world on botanical pilgrimages to collect exotic plants and bring them home, confidently anticipating the day when the Swedish countryside would be covered with coffee plantations and paddy fields. Unfortunately, his plan had not taken into account one rather formidable obstacle – the Swedish weather. Linnaeus was untroubled by this minor technicality, saying that he would start off by growing the plants in the warmest, southernmost part of Sweden, then very gradually move them north, small distances at a time, thereby "tricking" them into becoming acclimatized. When some of his brighter students pointed out that his plan was a crock of poo,[5] Linnaeus reminded them that there were more than a hundred dissertations supporting his theory. Of course there were – Linnaeus had written them himself.

Sadly, Sweden did not become a major producer of silk, tea, coffee nor rice. Most of the plant samples never survived the rough sea passage north. A large number of the unfortunate

---

5   Swedish for "scientifically invalid".

students sent out to collect them also perished, mostly as a result of tropical diseases or drownings at sea. The few plants that did survive the journey rarely lasted long. One that did make it, the potato, was a golden opportunity missed. Potatoes, Linnaeus asserted, were related to the deadly nightshade plant and were therefore highly poisonous. They came in useful, however, for making wig powder.

## Biggest Business Boob

In 1914, a nineteen-year-old New York socialite, Mary Phelps Jacob, was getting herself ready for a débutante ball when she noticed that the stiff boned corset she was expected to wear was far too bulky for the new, sheer evening gown she had bought especially for the occasion. She got her maid to take two silk handkerchiefs and some pink ribbon and together they knocked together the very first brassière. Family and friends were impressed and asked Jacob to make brassières for them as well. She realized that she was on to something big when she got a letter from a complete stranger offering her $1 for one of her contraptions.

Mary Phelps Jacob set up her own bra business, but with no commercial experience, her venture quickly collapsed, so she sold the patent rights to the Warner Corset Company for a one-off payment of $1,500 – roughly equivalent to $21,000 today.

Over the next thirty years alone, Warner's made $15 million from the patent.

---

*"Man will not fly for fifty years."*
Wilbur Wright, American aviation pioneer, to brother Orville, two years before their first successful flight in 1903.

## Least Credible Self-Improvement Guide

In March 2004, the American business magnate Donald Trump published a book titled *How to Get Rich*. It was a crowded market; among competing titles on the bookshelf that year were *Stay Home and Get Rich* by Stewart Kime; *How to Get Rich While You Sleep* by J. David Huskin; *How to Be a Male Go-Go Dancer and Get Rich* by Ray Costa; and *How to Get Filthy, Stinking Rich and Still Have Time for Great Sex! An Entrepreneur's Guide to Wealth and Happiness* by Lee Milteer.

Just five months later, Trump's publicly-traded development company Trump Hotels & Casino Resorts filed for bankruptcy for the second time in twelve years.

---

*"I am tired of all this sort of thing called science here . . .*
*We have spent millions in that sort of thing for the*
*last few years, and it is time it should be stopped."*

Simon Cameron, US Senator,
on the Smithsonian Institute, 1901

---

## Worst Business Brain Behind
## a Global Brand Name

In 1894, a health food fanatic John Harvey Kellogg, superintendent of a sanatorium in Battle Creek, Michigan, was working on a new kind of wheat meal for his patients when he made an accidental discovery. Rolling out wheat dough that had been forgotten overnight, he found that instead of loaves of bread he got thin flakes. Kellogg's patients liked the new food – corn flakes.

The free-thinking Mr Kellogg, whose dietary advice to his patients was concerned with reducing "sexual stimulation", was delighted. His creation was the ideal aid to controlling masturbation,[6] which, Kellogg taught his patients, led to leprosy, tuberculosis, heart disease, epilepsy, dimness of vision, insanity, idiocy and death.

Kellogg's younger brother Will, who was obviously the business brain in the family, saw a different route for John's invention. On February 1906, the Battle Creek Toasted Corn Flake was set up. Will ran the venture and was happy to have his initials on every box. John, the inventor, took a different view. "It is exceedingly distasteful to have my name associated with the food business or with anything commercial. But we sometimes have to swallow bitter pills against our will." In fact, thanks to John's reluctance to make money, by the time they had set up their company they had already allowed others to exploit their product and at that time there were forty-two other companies making corn flakes in Battle Creek alone.

Eventually, a feud caused the brothers to split. Will went off to market the cereals and make a fortune, marketing his products as the W. K. Kellogg Company. John Harvey Kellogg's claim to fame, meanwhile, would rest on his fifty-odd books written to advance his theories about sex and bowel movements. On his wedding night with the lucky Mrs Kellogg, née Ella Eaton, he spent all evening writing a 644-page treatise on the evils of sexual intercourse entitled "Plain Facts for Old and Young".

John Harvey Kellogg may not have had much of a business brain, but at least he practised what he preached. His marriage with Ella Eaton was never consummated.

## Worst Business Brain Behind a Global Brand Name: Runner-Up

In the early 1830s, natural rubber was touted as a new "miracle" product, but not for long. The problem was that gum elastic, as it was known, was not very elastic. It had an

---

6  Perhaps he was on to something after all; it is almost impossible to eat cornflakes and masturbate at the same time.

unfortunate habit of melting in hot weather and cracking in cold weather.

Charles Goodyear, a thirty-one-year-old from Springfield, Massachusetts, decided to develop an improved, more stable form of rubber. Working doggedly for the best part of a decade, he tried mixing rubber with everything from witch hazel to cream cheese. He even gave up his day job in pursuit of his cause, plunging himself and his wife and children into poverty. Undeterred by pleas from friends and relatives to get a proper job and complaints from neighbours about the stink of burning rubber emanating from the Goodyear household, he stubbornly continued in his quest, meanwhile reduced to begging for food and pawning family possessions to finance his experiments. After five futile years, Goodyear had nothing to show for his efforts except mounting debts. He was at rock bottom.

Then one day in 1839, he spilled a drop of rubber and sulphur on his brother's burning stove and inadvertently discovered that the sample had turned tough and strong – the "vulcanized" rubber which is commonplace today. The rest is history . . . or so it might appear.

Goodyear knew he had made a major breakthrough. He knew now that heat and sulphur miraculously changed rubber, but he didn't know how much heat, or for how long. He worked feverishly for several more years to try to replicate the formula.

He eventually did find the recipe, but despite his genius for innovation, he was a terrible businessman. Instead of sticking to basic manufacturing interests which might have made him a millionaire, he started experimenting again. He wanted to make everything out of rubber; banknotes, musical instruments, flags, jewellery, ships' sails, even rubber ships. He had his portrait painted on rubber, had his calling cards engraved on it, his autobiography printed on and bound in it. He even wore rubber hats, vests and ties.

Meanwhile, Goodyear had problems with "patent pirates" and had to pay the cost of fighting thirty-two patents all the way to the Supreme Court. He was particularly slow in filing foreign patent applications. He sent samples of his heat-and-sulphur-treated gum to British rubber companies without revealing any details. But the English rubber pioneer Thomas Hancock, who had been trying for twenty years to make weatherproof rubber, worked out how it was made. By the time Goodyear applied for an English patent, he found that Hancock had "reinvented" vulcanized rubber and had filed the patent a few weeks earlier.

At the Paris World's Fair in 1855, Goodyear installed a great pavilion built entirely of rubber, but his French patent was cancelled on a technicality and his French royalties stopped before he could pay his bills. He was seized by gendarmes. When Emperor Napoleon III awarded Goodyear the cross of the Legion of Honour, it had to be delivered to him in the debtor's prison.

Most people naturally assume that Goodyear founded the Goodyear Tire & Rubber Company, but in fact it was named in the inventor's honour nearly forty years after his death by Frank and Charles Sabering in 1898. He failed to make any money from his invention and, when he died aged fifty-nine, he was $200,000 in debt.

Ironically, Charles Goodyear never even dreamed of seeing his name on a set of tyres. He died decades before the automobile was invented.

## Least Successful Trade Minister

In 1973, Juan Pablo Pérez Alfonso, the minister in charge of Venezuela's growing oil boom and founder member of OPEC, announced, "Ten years from now, twenty years from now, you will see . . . oil will bring us ruin. Oil is the devil's excrement."

Four decades later, despite having the biggest oil reserves in the Americas, 30 per cent of Venezuelans live on less than £1.25 a day and Caracas is the world's most violent capital. On the upside, Venezuela's tally of eleven Miss Worlds and Miss Universes is unsurpassed. Although, perhaps in the spirit of señor Alfonso, Venezuela's President Chávez tried to put an end to that. In 2011, he announced that "monstrous breasts" did not square with his revolutionary policies.

> *"The Americans are good about making fancy cars and refrigerators, but that doesn't mean they are any good at making aircraft. They are bluffing. They are excellent at bluffing."*
> Hermann Goering, Commander-in-Chief
> of the Luftwaffe, 1942

## The Real Thing

On 8 May 1886, Coca-Cola went on sale for the first time at Jacob's Pharmacy in Atlanta, Georgia, as a headache and hangover remedy. By the 1940s, it was the world's favourite beverage. By the late 1950s, Coke was outselling its nearest rival, the emerging upstart Pepsi, by a ratio of more than five to one. *Time* magazine celebrated Coke's "peaceful near-conquest of the world".

In the 1960s, however, Coke's chief rival repositioned itself as a youth brand and managed to narrow the gap. In the 1970s, Pepsi raised the stakes even further by introducing the Pepsi Challenge – testing consumers blind on the difference between its own brand and "the real thing". To the horror of Coca-Cola's company president, Robert Woodruff, most of those who participated preferred Pepsi's sweeter formula. Coke's number-one status was starting to look vulnerable. By the mid-1980s, the market share had slipped to an all-time low of just under 24 per cent. Something had to be done.

In April 1985, after four years in development, Coca-Cola executives stepped up to a podium and told the world that the 99-year-old Coke formula was being shelved in favour of something called "New Coke". As the ads said, you were gonna love it. Company Chairman Roberto C. Goizueta said New Coke was "smoother, rounder yet bolder", as though it was a fine wine.

Customer reaction was immediate, but not one Goizueta was looking for. The company received over 46,000 complaints a day. New Coke was variously described as "sewer water" and tasting like "furniture polish" and, harshly, "two-day-old Pepsi".

In fact, Pepsi was the first to rub their noses in it. Within weeks of the launch, it ran a TV ad with an old man sitting on a park bench, staring at the can in his hand. "They changed my Coke," he said, clearly distressed. "I can't believe it."

Soon people were hoarding cases of the old stuff. In June 1985, *Newsweek* reported that black marketeers sold old Coke for $30 a case. A Hollywood producer, giving an old vintage its proper respect, reportedly rented a wine cellar to hold 100 cases of the old Coke.

Staggered by the backlash, within a matter of weeks New Coke was yanked from the store shelves, replaced by old Coke – rebranded "classic" Coke – so everyone knew they were getting the real thing.

Coke could have saved themselves a lot of bother. Pepsi-Cola, bankrupted three times, had been offered for sale to the Coca-Cola Company in 1932; Coke turned down the offer.

## Quickest Route to Financial Suicide

During the 1980s, the Ratner name was a fixture on British high streets. Gerald Ratner had built his eponymous business into the world's biggest brand of cut-price jewellery through a series of well-timed publicity stunts and takeover deals. He destroyed his brand in one sentence.

On 23 April 1991, Ratner was speaking at a business dinner at the Institute of Directors in London and thought he would share a few humorous words among friends: "We also do cut-glass sherry decanters complete with six glasses on a silver-plated tray that your butler can serve you drinks on, all for £4.95. People say, 'How can you sell this for such a low price?' I say, 'Because it's total crap.'" He went on to reveal that his store's earrings were "cheaper than an M&S prawn sandwich but probably wouldn't last as long".

His speech got a laugh but Ratner's investors and customers didn't see the funny side. His company's share price plummeted from £2 to less than 8p; consumer confidence sank without trace, wiping an estimated £500 million from the value of the company. Gerald Ratner and his famous brand were forced to exit the jewellery trade.

He noted later, ruefully, "Someone said he had met comedians who wanted to be millionaires, but I must have been the only millionaire who wanted to be a comedian."

---

*"With over fifteen types of foreign cars already on sale here, the Japanese auto industry isn't likely to carve out a big share of the market for itself."*
*Business Week,* 2 August 1968

---

## Least Consumer-Friendly Product

In the Middle Ages, the emperor Charlemagne was thought by some to possess magical powers. He convinced a group of hostile warlords of these powers one day when he pulled a tablecloth from his table, threw it into the fire and then pulled it out, unburned. The cloth was woven from asbestos.

The Ancient Greeks and the Romans also knew all about the flame-proof qualities of asbestos and they even wore clothes made of it – even though they had noticed that people who wore them had a worrying tendency to develop sickness of the lungs and fall prematurely dead. They were quite literally dressed to kill.

But when the industrial age came around, so great was the demand for an indestructible substance that could be spun, woven or turned into a building material, such worries were overlooked. By the 1850s, the rise of the versatile material was unstoppable. Firemen were sporting asbestos helmets and jackets and it was turning up in everything from lagging to gaskets. European factories began making asbestos boards and, in 1896, Ferodo, an English company, began using a mixture of asbestos and resin in brake linings.

Nobody seemed very much bothered when a physician from Vienna pointed out that inhalation of asbestos dust caused terrible lung problems. In the 1939 movie *The Wizard of Oz*, the Wicked Witch of the West was equipped with an asbestos broom. During the Second World War, combatants on both sides were using the flame-proof material. By the time health concerns began to re-emerge in the 1960s, schools and hospitals were already packed with the stuff.

Today, we know that the microscopic asbestos fibres, light enough to be carried in the air, remain embedded in the lungs causing mesothelioma, lung cancer and asbestosis, three potentially fatal diseases. The first symptoms may not show up for as long as forty years after the victim's exposure to asbestos.

By 1999, Britain had banned the import and use of all asbestos, but it is still killing around 3,500 people each year. Ironically, there is today a new thriving asbestos industry . . . safe removal and disposal of this deadly mineral.

## Least Successful Branding: the Main Contenders

### Black and Tan

Just in time for St Patrick's Day 2012, Nike unveiled its new trainer after Ireland's great export, Guinness. The £57 limited-edition, beer-themed shoe had a black leather and tan upper, a creamy Nike swoosh and an image of a pint of beer on the insole.

Someone should have told Nike that naming the trainer after a violent British paramilitary unit that terrorized the Irish wasn't such a good move. The Black and Tans conjure bitter memories for the Irish, it being the nickname of a notorious British paramilitary unit, the Royal Irish Constabulary Reserve Force, after their distinctive army tunics, who conducted a brutal and often murderous crackdown against the Roman Catholic civilian population in the early 1920s. It was, according to the *Los Angeles Times*, akin to launching a shoe called "the Al-Qaeda".

## Incubus / Zyklon

At least Nike wasn't alone in putting its foot in it. In 1995, Reebok named their new women's running shoe "Incubus", after a mythical demon that, in mediaeval times, raped young ladies while they were sleeping.

In 2002, Umbro launched a trainer called Zyklon, sharing its name with the lethal cyanide-based gas used in the Nazi extermination camps during the Holocaust.

## Ayds

Despite finding that their range of slimming products shared a name with a modern-day plague, the manufacturer of Ayds decided to tough it out. They didn't even consider altering their unintentionally unfortunate strap line: "Ayds helps you take off weight and helps you keep it off." It was only when their sales shrank by over 50 per cent that they had a rethink, and came up with the new name "Diet Ayds". The company went out of business soon afterwards.

## i.Beat.blaxx

In 2007, the German electronics manufacturer TrekStor tried to climb on the bandwagon created by the Apple iPod phenomenon with their own MP3 player. So sticking an "i" in front of their product name was a no-brainer, and "beat" was a word that music lovers could understand in any language. The MP3 player was black, so they called it i.Beat.blaxx. Taken by surprise by the ensuing furore, a TrekStor spokesperson explained that "beat" is "not meant as a verb, but refers to the beats of the music you are listening to".

## Retardex

This is a British brand of toothpaste so you can't even blame the translation. Recommended by dentists, presumably in a more innocent time when the word "retard" didn't have such a negative connotation.

---

*"What use would this company make of an electric toy?"*
Western Union President Carl Orton, turning
down Alexander Graham Bell's offer to sell him the
complete rights to the telephone for $100,000.

---

## You're Never Alone in a Cancer Ward

The tobacco industry has spent much of the past half century denying a link between smoking and disease. Paradoxically, it has also dedicated a significant amount of time and money to developing a "safe" cigarette.

In August 1988, in reply to a mounting outcry against smoking in general and second-hand smoke in particular, the US tobacco company R. J. Reynolds threw a gala party to launch their new "smokeless" cigarette called Premier. After years of work and a bill of more than $1 billion, it was one of the most expensive consumer product developments in history, promising "a whole new era of smoking enjoyment". Unfortunately, problems with the new smoke became immediately apparent.

To begin with, there was the difficulty of actually using the product. Although it looked like a conventional cigarette, special instructions were required to teach smokers how to light it. One smoker noted, 'Inhaling the Premier required vacuum-powered lungs ... lighting it virtually required a blowtorch." Once successfully lit, there was an odour issue. "Smells like burning lettuce ..." was one of the kinder comments. Others described it as "like burning sneaker" and "as if you just opened a grave on a warm day".

Then there was the taste. One person who "smoked" Premier complained that it "tasted like shit"; and he was R. J. Reynolds' chief executive. To cap it all, there was a damaging rumour that the smokeless cigarette could be used as a delivery device for crack cocaine. Hardly the kind of brand association R. J. Reynolds had hoped to create. The brand was discontinued within weeks of the launch.

The most infamous British commercial cock-up of all time was the promotion of Strand cigarettes. Unlike Premier, it didn't taste like shit and you could light it with a match without inducing a hernia. It was launched in 1960 with a massive marketing campaign behind the slogan "You're never alone with a Strand . . . The cigarette of the Moment". The TV advertisement depicted a dark, wet, deserted street scene in which a solitary, rain-coated character, played by the actor Terence Brook, puffed reflectively, with just his cigarettes for company. It was accompanied by a catchy jingle known as "The Lonely Man Theme" that made the UK singles charts. The cigarettes, however, stayed on the shelf.

The public had got the message – if you smoked Strand cigarettes, no one would want to know you. The brand was withdrawn just eighteen months later. It was literally the cigarette of the moment.

## Least Convincing Tourist Campaigns

*Singapore*

Once described as "Disneyland with the death penalty", Singapore has some of the world's most punitive laws against chewing gum (fine £500), jaywalking (£500), dropping litter (£500), failing to flush the toilet (£75) and drugs (death).

In 2006, the Singapore Government launched an advertising campaign designed to improve the country's image – especially the welcome given to foreign visitors – which they called Four Million Smiles. The country's biggest newspaper, the *Straits Times*, accordingly ran a feature giving their readers the low-down on smiling etiquette. It also provided a list of helpful tips where smiling might not be appropriate – at the scene of a car crash, for example. Even more helpfully, the *Straits Times* also featured a recruitment call by escort agencies for young, athletic girls between eighteen and twenty to offer themselves for a possible spike in demand for escort services.

## Gloucester

In 1994, the world's media descended on Gloucester, England, following the discovery of several bodies in a "garden of death" belonging to Britain's then-biggest serial killers, Frederick and Rosemary West. Gloucester city fathers, upset by the negative publicity generated by the murders, decide to launch an advertising campaign to improve their city's image. The Touchpaper agency emerged with the winning slogan: "Gloucester – easy to get to, hard to leave."

## Hong Kong

SARS (severe acute respiratory syndrome) was a deadly new strain of pneumonia that started in southern China and quickly moved to Hong Kong before spreading around the world. In 2003, just as the burgeoning SARS epidemic was spreading fear among travellers worldwide, the Hong Kong tourist board commissioned a series of magazine ads telling readers that a visit to the city will "take your breath away". Unfortunately, shortness of breath is one of the main symptoms of SARS.

> *"Ours has been the first and doubtless to be the last,*
> *to visit this profitless locality."*
> Lt Joseph Ives, after visiting the Grand Canyon in 1861.

## Most Expensive Typo

It is known in the trade as "fat finger syndrome" – the occasional tendency of stressed traders working in fast-moving electronic financial markets to press the wrong button on their keyboard and, in the process, lose their employer a mint.

In 1994, Juan Pablo Davila was working for the Chilean state-owned copper company Codelco, trading commodities, when he accidentally hit the key for "buy" instead of "sell". After realizing his mistake, he went into a frenzy of buying and selling, but only dug himself into a bigger hole, ultimately losing $206.8 million, or approximately 0.5 per cent of his country's gross national product.

In Chile, his name has became a verb – "*davilar*", meaning "to screw up royally".

It was not the last embarrassing Chilean typo blunder. In 2010, the general manager of the Chilean mint, Gregorio Iniguez, was dismissed after thousands of coins were issued with the name of the country spelt wrongly. Instead of C-H-I-L-E, the coins had C-H-I-I-E stamped on them. The 50-peso coins – worth about 6p (10 cents) – were issued in 2008 but no one noticed the mistake until two years later.

> *"Good enough for our transatlantic friends . . . but unworthy of the attention of practical or scientific men."*
> British Parliamentary Committee,
> on Thomas Edison's lightbulb, 1878

## Most Failed Attempts to Turn a Great Idea into a Profitable Business

Nikola Tesla was a legend of nineteenth-century electrical engineering. By rights, he should be at least as well known as his contemporaries Edison and Marconi. He made astonishing contributions to science; he was one of the pioneers of radio, built the first AC power system, took some of the first X-ray photographs and constructed the first radio-controlled robots. His scientific abilities were so great, his work rate so phenomenal and the range of his research so astounding that some people questioned whether he was actually of this world. But Tesla's name today is usually only associated with pseudo-science, bizarre cults and conspiracy theories. And while the ideas he put forward made others a fortune, he died almost penniless, alone and forgotten.

Tesla was born a Serb in 1856 in a mountain village in Croatia. His first invention, not long after he had learned to talk, was a device for catching frogs. At the age of four, he jumped from the roof of the family barn clutching an umbrella to see if he could fly, a line of research that was abandoned after he spent six weeks in traction. At five, he was working on the design for a tiny windmill powered by beetles, until a friend ate his entire fuel supply, a sight that caused the young inventor to throw up.

Like most prolific inventors, Tesla was an obsessive. This first revealed itself when as a student in Prague he decided to read the complete works of Voltaire. He had no idea at this point that Voltaire's back catalogue spanned 100 volumes of small, dense print. Although it almost resulted in complete mental breakdown, Tesla refused to quit until he had finished reading the lot.

His childhood was plagued by ill health. He contracted cholera shortly after graduating from high school and was bedridden for nine months and, at one point, his parents thought he would die. He recovered, but claimed from then on that he experienced visions – literally blinding flashes of inspiration that came to him as though he had been struck by a bolt of lightning.

One of these "visions" came to him during an afternoon stroll through a Budapest park with a friend in January 1881. At the time, he was studying to be an engineer at the Graz Polytechnic Institute. Tesla suddenly stopped dead in his tracks, grabbed a stick and began to sketch a diagram in the dirt; it was an induction motor. When Tesla put his design on paper and showed it to several European electrical engineers, they dismissed it as nonsense, so in 1884 he joined the tide of emigration to the United States to look for work at the Edison Machine Works.

According to Tesla's autobiography, along the way he was robbed of all his luggage and most of his money. He arrived in New York with 4c. in his pocket, a book of his own poems and his latest plans for a flying machine. He also had a personal letter of introduction to the great Thomas Edison himself from a former work colleague in Paris. It read, "I know two great men and you are one of them – the other is this young man."

As well as being an extraordinarily talented scientist, Tesla was a showman, an attention-seeker with a compulsion for spinning tall tales. Like his blinding "visions", no one knows for sure whether his story about being robbed on the way to New York was true or not, but he knew the value of a good yarn and that his rags-to-riches story would strike a chord with the great American public. It was all part of the Tesla mythology. He always understood the value of publicity but he lacked the business sense to turn his unlimited scientific curiosity into commercially viable inventions. He was very soon, however, to get his first taste of the harsh realities of commerce from the most ruthless of them all.

Thomas Edison was an inventor of mythic proportions, but his greatest talent was claiming other people's work as his own, including Joseph Swan's lightbulb, George Bartlett Prescott's quadruplex telegraph and Edward Muybridge's kinetoscope. Like the great Isaac Newton, Edison had a sinister, vindictive side to his personality – a killer instinct. Newton did it by standing on the shoulders of giants, but Edison simply thieved, as Tesla was soon to find out.

It quickly became apparent that Edison and Tesla didn't see eye to eye about the merits of alternating current (AC). Edison thought it was just a pipe dream. Besides which, he'd already invested millions of dollars in designing and promoting a direct current (DC) system. But he was impressed with Tesla's amazing workrate so he agreed to hire him to make improvements in his DC generation plants. He gave him a two-month deadline and promised a $50,000 bonus if Tesla succeeded.

Working long hours with little sleep, Tesla made twenty-four design improvements to Edison's original concepts. Edison was delighted with the results, but when Tesla asked him for his bonus money, he told the young Serb that the offer of $50,000 was just a joke. "You don't understand our American sense of humour," Edison told him. Tesla resigned in disgust. He and Edison would remain bitter rivals to the grave.

Soon afterwards, Tesla was approached by a group of investors who were interested in a method of arc lighting he had invented. He agreed to go into partnership with them and the group provided him with finance to start the Tesla Electric Light Company. He immediately set to work on creating a beautifully designed, highly efficient new arc lamp. The arc lights sold well and Tesla hoped to make enough money to develop his AC system, but it turned out to be the first of a series of catastrophic business decisions that were to plague his career. Although it earned a lot of money for the investors, he found out that his 50 per cent share did not entitle him to a 50 per cent voting share and he was voted out of his own company. All he was left with was a stack of worthless stock certificates. The destitute Tesla was reduced to digging ditches for $1 a day.

His luck, however, was about to change. The Western Union Company agreed to invest in Tesla's idea for an AC motor. In a small laboratory only a short distance from Edison's office, Tesla was able to develop all the components for the system of AC power generation and transmission that is used universally throughout the world today. In 1887, in the space of two months, Tesla filed for seven US patents for AC motors and power transmission. They would turn out to be the most valuable patents since the telephone.

A Pittsburgh industrialist named George Westinghouse heard about Tesla's AC system and made him an offer. He purchased the patents for just $60,000, plus a generous royalty for every horsepower of electrical capacity sold. Tesla later tore up the contract which would have made him incredibly wealthy and said he was just grateful to Westinghouse for believing in his invention. He still had a lot to learn as a businessman.

The advantages of Tesla's AC over Edison's DC were obvious – high-voltage AC carries power with very little electric current. That means that there is very little power loss in the wires, so the power can be sent for long distances using long wires. DC, on the other hand, is not only weaker; it can only be transported for short distances and would require huge electric generating plants in every neighbourhood.

Edison, however, wasn't going to give up without a fight; and he was always prepared to fight dirty. He launched a smear campaign to frighten the public into believing that AC was highly dangerous. At first, he used his contacts in the press to place wildly exaggerated stories about the hazards and unpredictability of AC power. When that failed to make an impression, he sponsored an electrical engineer called Harold Brown to travel the country electrocuting small animals. Brown gave children a nickel a head to bring him stray dogs and cats, then invited reporters to demonstrations where the animals were placed on metal sheets and electrocuted with 1,000 volts of AC.

The animal-killing campaign reached a new low in 1903. At Coney Island's Luna Park, an elephant named Topsy was to be put to death for killing three people. One of the three was Topsy's severely abusive handler. Edison set up a public execution of the animal wherein 6,600 volts of alternating current were slammed through the elephant's body, killing it in seconds. Edison personally supervised the filming of the event and released it later that year as *Electrocuting an Elephant.* "Is this what your wife should be cooking with?" he asked.

For Edison, even the barbaric electrocution of an elephant wasn't quite enough. This time, his PR offensive required the death of a human being. In 1890, the first ever state execution by electric chair, of William Kemmler, convicted of the murder of his lover Tillie Ziegler with an axe, was scheduled to take place in Auburn, New York. Edison saw an opportunity to damage the credibility of AC power permanently. If the public saw that AC could kill a human being, they would always associate it with danger.

Without his knowledge or consent, Edison persuaded the authorities to use Westinghouse's apparatus in the fatal electrocution of Kemmler. Edison told them that AC was so deadly that it would kill instantly, making it the ideal method of execution. Edison even volunteered his services as technical adviser.

On 6 August 1890, Kemmler was strapped into the chair. His execution was a horrifically slow, drawn-out affair. After eight minutes, smoke was coming off his body and a second burst of power was required to finish him off. The stench of burning flesh was so overpowering that several spectators unsuccessfully tried to leave the room. The *New York Times* reported that the victim "was literally roasted to death". It was, they reported, "an awful spectacle, far worse than hanging".

The death of Kemmler, a pawn in a vicious battle between two players to control the future of electric generation, backfired spectacularly for Edison. Despite his devious attempts at subterfuge, Westinghouse's more efficient AC prevailed and it continues to power our lives today. Ironically, Edison's direct current is now considered to be more dangerous than alternating current since it allows electricity to be stored even after the power has been turned off.

In 1891, at the age of thirty-five, Tesla became a US citizen and established a laboratory in South Fifth Avenue, New York. He was at the peak of his creative powers. In rapid succession, he developed new types of generators and transformers, radar, robotics, early models for wireless radio, fluorescent lights and a new type of steam turbine. One of his strangest enterprises was a vibrating platform that had a strong laxative effect. Tesla's friend Mark Twain once saw the scientist make a desperate dash for the toilet after staying on the platform too long.

There were other more hazardous bouts of self-experimentation. Tesla began to work with X-rays, a recent discovery by Wilhelm von Roentgen. Blissfully unaware of the dangers, he took part in horrific experiments on himself and on his laboratory assistants. He repeatedly exposed his head to X-rays "to stimulate the brain". He wrote, "An outline of the skull is easily obtained with an exposure of 30-40 minutes. In one instance, an exposure of 40 minutes gave clearly not only the outline but also the cavity of the eye, the lower jaw and connections to the upper one, the vertebral column and connections to the skull, the flesh and even the hair . . . in a severe case the skin gets deeply coloured and blackened in places and ugly, ill-foreboding blisters form; thick layers come off, exposing the raw flesh. Burning pain, feverishness and such symptoms are natural accompaniments."

In 1880, Tesla's interest turned to radio waves. There had been faltering attempts at using electro-magnetic waves as a means of communication before, most notably by the Scot James Clerk Maxwell. In 1888, Heinrich Hertz, a student of Maxwell, invented the first spark gap transmitter and receiver, thus becoming the first person to successfully utilize radio waves. Tesla made a major modification to Hertz's system with the invention of the Tesla coil – an integral part of every TV and radio. He also hit upon the idea of using radio waves to transmit power to lightbulbs – the first remote control.

Tesla patented his radio apparatus in 1893 but, two years later, on the eve of an experiment to demonstrate radio on a boat on the Hudson River, a fire all but destroyed his New York laboratory. It would take him another two years to build a new facility, during which time others stole a march on his radio work. In 1895, an enterprising young researcher called Guglielmo Marconi demonstrated a device in London which could transmit radio waves over a mile-and-a-quarter. His system was almost identical to Tesla's, but Marconi insisted that he had not read any of Tesla's papers, even though an Italian translation had been freely available for some time.

By 1897, Tesla had built a new laboratory and had patented a radio communication device, but he refused to involve potential investors in his system until he was absolutely sure it would work. By this time, he had set off in a completely new direction, investing his time and his own money in developing a radio-controlled boat designed to carry six torpedoes and no crew. Tesla demonstrated a model in a water tank at Madison Square Garden in New York. Although the trial was impressive, he scared off potential investors by claiming that he was controlling the boat with his mind.

Meanwhile, Marconi was busily attracting investors to his Marconi Wireless Telegraph Company. In 1901, Marconi sent his first transatlantic radio signal. When informed of this development, Tesla simply replied, "Marconi is a fine fellow . . . let him continue. He is using seventeen of my patents." Unfortunately, it would take Tesla years of litigation to prove it and, by the time he did, he was already dead.

Tesla's greatest interest was, as it had always been, electricity. He was the electrical showman of the age, dazzling audiences with brilliant light displays. His flamboyant lectures and demonstrations in high-frequency currents made him internationally famous and, for several years, he was hardly ever out of the public eye. He made extraordinary headline-grabbing claims for electrical power; it could be used as an anaesthetic or as stimulant for lethargic schoolchildren (wire them to their desks!) or as an energizer for actors by running electrical surges through their bodies before performances, or even as a cure for tuberculosis.

In the late nineteenth century, electricity was often seen as something closer to magic than science and when Tesla gave his amazing light shows he appeared to take on an otherworldly quality. One of his most famous photos, faked by double exposure, shows him sitting inside a metal cage with millions of volts passing through him.[7] At the Chicago World Fair in 1893, Tesla ran 200,000 volts through his body. According to newspaper reports, his clothing and body continued to glow for some time after the current was switched off (he told his

---

7   According to legend, this photo inspired the Universal Studios remake of *Frankenstein* starring Boris Karloff.

audience that a similar surge of power could keep a naked man warm at the North Pole). One of his light shows caused so much alarm that it panicked the audience into a stampede for the exit.

Tesla revelled in his role as showman. Strikingly tall and slim, he was very obsessive about his personal grooming and ridiculously overdressed even for his regular laboratory work, always wearing a starched collar and tie with a silk handkerchief in his suit pocket. When he "dressed up" for public lectures he looked more like a concert pianist than a scientist in white tie and tails, and on his large hands he wore grey suede gloves, which were discarded after he had worn them a couple of times because of his morbid fear of germs.

He began to build a very large fan base of followers who adored him with a reverence bordering on the unhinged, including a cult following of science groupies who believed he was a superior being from another planet and had travelled to Earth on a flying saucer to advance the human race. A biography published as late as 1959 by Margaret Storm, written entirely in green ink, claims that Tesla was from the planet Venus.

The great pioneer of radio and electricity was not short on sexual magnetism either, and he attracted droves of female admirers. But he never married, nor did he ever have intimate relations with women or, for that matter, men. Tesla was a lifelong celibate, apparently believing that sex was a drain on creativity. When a newspaper reporter presumed to ask him why he was still single, Tesla challenged him to name more than a couple of inventions made by married men. His bachelor status was the subject of great media speculation, an issue made even cloudier when he expounded on the topic of women in an interview for *Collier's* magazine, mysteriously noting that women were probably better students than men and that fully trained women might bring about an efficient society resembling that of bees.

It didn't help that Tesla had a couple of well-documented phobias that made dating difficult, including a revulsion for women's jewellery, especially earrings and pearls. Once, at a dinner party, he found he had been strategically seated next to Anne Morgan, the beautiful unmarried daughter of the industrialist J. P. Morgan. Tesla spotted her pearl earrings and sat throughout the meal in silent anguish, gnashing his teeth. He hated any form of physical contact and said he could never bring himself to touch anyone else's hair, "except perhaps at the point of a revolver". He found fat people, especially fat women, particularly repellent. He fired his female secretary because she was overweight, although she begged him to let her keep her job.

In the early 1890s, Tesla moved his experiments to Knob Hill, near Colorado Springs, in a huge laboratory with a roll-back roof where he could play with his new giant transformers. The first time he tested one at full power, the roar was heard more than ten miles away and blew the town's entire electricity supply, causing a blackout. The local power company refused to supply him any more until he paid for the repairs in full, which he did out of his own pocket. His time in Colorado gained him a huge amount of media attention but very little of any use came out of it and he found it increasingly difficult to find any backers for his work. In 1899, he abandoned his work in Colorado and moved back to New York.

As Tesla grew older his schemes became more surreal and only served to tarnish his reputation. He built a powerful radio receiver in his lab and claimed that he was receiving messages from Mars. The much respected but now very elderly British physicist Lord Kelvin was the first to congratulate him on his remarkable discovery. (Kelvin went on to explain to colleagues that the Martians had obviously chosen to reveal themselves to New York, as opposed to London, because New York was well lit and the only place visible from Mars.) Most of the scientific community, however, ridiculed Tesla's claim and demanded proof of his discovery, but Tesla declined to offer any. Similar scepticism was reserved for his claim that he could split the Earth like an apple, that he could modify the weather and that he had invented a death ray capable of destroying 10,000 aeroplanes at a distance of 250 miles.

Tesla's eccentricities, meanwhile, became more pronounced. He claimed that his hearing had become hypersensitive and informed disbelieving associates that he could hear a clock ticking three rooms away and the whistle of a steam engine twenty miles distant. He said he could hear the landing of a fly on a nearby table as a loud thump and that he had to put rubber castors under the legs of his bed to eliminate nocturnal vibrations. He also claimed that he could detect, in complete darkness, the presence of an object at a distance of twelve feet.

Tesla's alleged bat-like powers were the least of his problems. He suffered from obsessive-compulsive disorder, which turned his daily life into a series of bizarre rituals. He spent his entire adult life holed up in expensive New York hotels where his behaviour constantly tried the patience of the staff. Everything he did had to be done in multiples of three: he always walked around the block before entering his hotel three times, counting his steps to make sure the total number was divisible by three. He chose room numbers that were also divisible by three – a favourite was room 207 at the Alta Vista Hotel. He phoned the hotel kitchen with detailed advance instructions for preparations for his meals. He insisted on calculating the cubic volume of any food or drink that he consumed. Napkins, crockery and cutlery also had to be provided in multiples of three. Before eating, he inspected each of his eighteen napkins in turn, then discarded them in a pile in the middle of the table. He refused to touch anything bearing the slightest hint of dirt or to touch anything round, which posed some quite obvious hurdles for an engineer.

He was disarmingly candid about his undiagnosed disorder. In 1919, he informed readers of *Electrical Experimenter* magazine, "I get a fever looking at a peach and, if a piece of camphor was anywhere in the house, it causes me the keenest discomfort."

Although Tesla struggled to form relationships with people, he was an obsessive pigeon fancier. Almost every day and night for several years, he could be seen in Bryant Park, a small green square behind New York's public library, carrying a brown paper bag full of breadcrumbs and covered in a carpet of pigeons. Surprisingly for someone suffering from severe mysophobia, he kept a flock of sick and wounded pigeons in his hotel room where he nursed them back to health. Tesla took pigeon fancying to a new level when he fell in love with a favourite white pigeon with brown-tipped wings. "I loved her as a man loves a woman and she loved me," he wrote in his autobiography. "When that pigeon died, something went out of my life . . . I knew my life's work was finished."

By the 1890s, Tesla had blown most of his money on a series of increasingly expensive scientific white elephants. As the hotel bills mounted and the years wore on, his circumstances grew ever less salubrious. Still the showman in him craved publicity and, in his final years, he took to giving interviews to various journalists from his hotel room. Although his days as a serious scientist were long gone, he was still guaranteed to give good copy. At the age of seventy-five, he gave a press conference announcing that he could disprove Einstein's general theory of relativity; he would tell the world about his own idea when he was ready. He recommended that the USA should surround itself with an invisible force-field made of rays that could melt a squadron of aeroplanes 250 miles away; he only needed the government to give him $2 million and he would have the force-field ready within three months.

He seemed to revel in the caricature he had been reduced to in the popular press and took to signing his name "GI" – Great Inventor.[8] He was a regular but moderate drinker and believed that alcohol had life-enhancing qualities and was so upset when the USA established Prohibition in 1919 that he withdrew his long-standing prediction that he would live to 140. Over the years, he eliminated red meat from his diet, then fish and, by the 1930s, he had just about given up on solid foods altogether. His final years were spent holed up in his

---

8  The very first *Superman* comic in September 1941 featured the superhero battling a mad scientist called Tesla who was threatening New York City with a death ray.

hotel room surrounded by pigeon excrement – he had become a fragile, almost ghostly figure, living on a diet of warm milk and crackers.

Tesla's light finally went out on 7 January 1943. A maid ignored the "Do Not Disturb" sign on his hotel door and discovered the emaciated corpse of the scientist on his bed, dead from heart failure, aged eighty-six. At the time, he held more than 700 patents; there were probably a couple of hundred more innovations he dismissed as "small-time stuff" and didn't bother to patent, letting others pirate his work. Nine months after he died, the US Supreme Court eventually pronounced on the validity of Marconi's wireless radio patents and decided that Tesla was the true "father of radio".

As with so much of Tesla's work, he had finally been vindicated, but never lived to see a penny in compensation.

# 4

## Defeat from the Jaws of Victory: Great Military Losers

*In which King Harold falls for rope-a-dope; Lord Cardigan leads a suicide charge; a ship torpedoes itself; a general fails to frighten the enemy away by playing "God Save the Queen"; spies fail to kill Hitler with a set of deadly false teeth; and Mr Jenkins says, "Pardon?"*

### Most Underachieving Invasion Force

The Jutes.

Who?

Quite.

In the middle of the fifth century, three Germanic tribes – the Angles, the Saxons and the Jutes – sailed across the North Sea, landed on the coast of Britain and conquered the indigenous Celts. We know this because a monk called the Venerable Bede says so in his book *The Ecclesiastical History of the English People.* He wrote: "They [the invaders] came from among the three most powerful Germanic tribes, those of the Saxons, the Angles and the Jutes."

The Angles gave their name to East Anglia and moved inland to create the kingdom of Mercia in the Midlands. The Saxons established kingdoms in the south – Sussex, Essex, Middlesex and Wessex.

Meanwhile, the Jutes arrived in Kent ... and the Isle of Wight.

The Angles and the Saxons combined to create a powerful kingdom that became England (Angle-land) and dominated the country for the next 600 years. Their rule ended in 1066 after the Norman Conquest, but the influence of the Anglo-Saxons continues to this day. They created most of England's county boundaries and many English customs. Most importantly, they also gave their name to the language which was spoken and written by their descendants and went on to form the basics of modern English. Today, the English language is spoken in one form or another by a quarter of the world's population. It reigns supreme as the language of international business, diplomacy, science, technology and of the Internet. That's quite a legacy for a couple of small tribes from northern Europe; they were certainly punching above their weight.

As for the Jutes – what have they been up to since the Dark Ages? Not much, frankly. The impact of the Jutes on England was so negligible that you'll struggle to find any evidence that they invaded at all. One theory is that the Jutes, who were mostly farmers, were "ethnically cleansed" by the more warrior-like Saxons, although there is no real evidence for this. Some historians began to wonder if Bede hadn't just made the bit about the Jutes up. He said, for example, that the Jutes (or *lutae*) came from Jutland in modern Denmark, which sounds logical enough, except that language experts point out that the two names come from completely different roots. So later historians with a different perspective of the foundation of the English nation started to write the Jutes out of the history books.

More recent archaeological evidence, however, shows that Bede was right all along. The Jutes did come from Scandinavia, they did conquer Kent and they did occupy and rule the Isle of Wight. Then they opened a couple of farm shops.

## The (War) Elephant in the Room

In war, there are winners and losers, but sometimes even the winners are losers. Pyrrhus, the Greek king of Epirus from 318–272 BC, was widely regarded in the Ancient World as one of the great military commanders. Plutarch and Hannibal rated him as the greatest the world ever saw. History only remembers him as a footnote for the phrase "pyrrhic victory" – a technical victory but won at ruinous cost.

Over a period of five years, Pyrrhus fought and won a series of battles against the Romans in Italy. But each battle got a little bit harder. In the first, at Heraclea, the Greeks faced a Roman Army of around 50,000 men; Pyrrhus had only half that number, but he also had a secret weapon – twenty war elephants. At first, the elephants were a tactical triumph. Few Europeans had ever seen one before and they caused widespread panic in the troops as they stampeded the Roman cavalry horses. Pyrrhus was able to defeat the much larger Roman Army, but at a price. Up to 13,000 of his men were killed in action.

After Heraclea, Pyrrhus marched north, hoping that many Italians, unhappy with Roman domination, would rebel and join his cause. But he had badly misjudged the situation. The Italians had grown used to Roman protection from enemies and only a handful rose up to join Pyrrhus.

Pyrrhus fought the Romans again, but this time the shock value of the elephants had gone. The Romans had learned that if they simply stood aside, the elephants would charge harmlessly past. As they went by they jabbed them in their sides and trunks with short throwing spears, which panicked the elephants, causing them to go on the rampage trampling all over their own troops.

Another innovative Roman counter-attack was their use of flaming pigs. Supposedly, the Romans tarred pigs with pitch, set them alight, and sent them in the general direction of the elephants, causing them to stampede.

Pyrrhus won the battle, but again lost many of his best men.[1] In fact, he had lost two-thirds of his Army during the fighting and had little to show for his efforts.

His career as a general came to an end two years later when he was storming the city of Argos and a woman dropped a roof tile on to his head.

---

1 Pyrrhus was recorded to have said reflectively, "One more victory like that and we're totally fucked." Or words to that effect.

If Pyrrhus had done his homework, he would have known that the use of war elephants was a two-edged sword. In 162 BC, Eleazar Maccabeus was fighting at the Battle of Beth-Sechariah in a battle between the Jewish Maccabeans and Greek forces when he dashed underneath an elephant and speared the beast in the stomach in an attempt to bring it to its knees to dislodge the rider. He killed the animal instantly, but it promptly fell on him and crushed him to death.

## Bravest Attempt to Defeat an Enemy with a Tin of Biscuits

Brigadier-General Sir Charles MacCarthy inherited a tricky situation when he was appointed Governor of Africa's Gold Coast in 1821. Two local rivals – the Fante and Ashanti tribes – were at each other's throats in a territorial dispute. Matters got completely out of hand when the Ashanti executed a Fante serving in a British garrison for insulting the Ashanti king, Osai Tutu Kwadwo. MacCarthy responded with a British declaration of war against the Ashanti Empire.

MacCarthy, described by a military historian as "a decent, proud, but stupid man" had fatally underestimated the power of the Ashanti. Starting with a force of 6,000 men, he divided it into four columns. The plan was for the four groups to converge and then surprise the enemy with overwhelming force. It fell apart when MacCarthy's own force, numbering 500, found themselves up against 10,000 Ashanti while the other columns were ten miles away.

MacCarthy had a brainwave: he instructed his men to stand to attention while his band struck up "God Save the Queen" in the belief that this would scare the Ashanti into running away. It didn't.

A ferocious battle ensued, MacCarthy's thin line of troops bravely holding their own until their ammunition ran out. He called on his stores manager Charles Brandon to break open the reserve ammunition. As the Ashanti warriors closed in,

Brandon unscrewed the ammunition boxes only to find they were full of biscuits, not bullets.

The Ashanti overran and massacred the British force. The wounded MacCarthy shot himself rather than face capture and torture. They cut off his head, ate his heart, then converted his skull into a drinking cup and used his jawbones as drumsticks. It took another fifty years of intermittent warfare to subdue the Ashanti.

## King Harold: Runner-Up at Hastings

When Halley's Comet appeared in 1066, the Anglo-Saxons saw it as a portent of doom. They weren't wrong. Before the year was out, there were two dead kings, two invasions and three major battles, including the most important military defeat in English history.

The Battle of Hastings was one of those rare armed conflicts that decided the fate of nations, wiping out overnight an Anglo-Saxon civilization unique in Dark Age Europe for its wealth, art, literature and its longevity. But it could just have easily have gone the other way. The English lost not because they were outfought by a superior enemy but because of a series of poor decisions and a run of very bad luck.

The English crown, the oldest in the world, was forged in the tenth century when the kingdom of Wessex was gradually transformed by conquest into a kingdom of England. From the start, the new nation was beset by constant feuds over power and territory. The king was usually chosen by a *witan*, or great council. They selected someone who commanded respect and was not necessarily of royal lineage. In effect, they chose the best man for the job, although that usually meant a close relative of the deceased king. The *witan*, however, didn't always agree, which meant that the succession was easily wide open to deadly dispute. From 828 when Egbert, former King of Wessex, was recognized as the first king of all England until 1066, England had twenty-one kings, each with an average reign of just over eleven years. Violent death in office reduced the mean age of death to thirty-seven, only a year longer than that of the average serf.

In January 1066, Harold Godwinson, the new King Harold II, inherited the English crown in highly controversial circumstances. The old king Edward the Confessor had died childless. The non-royal Harold, related to Edward only by marriage to his sister, was chosen by the *witan* to succeed because it was apparently Edward's dying wish that he should do so, but there were no witnesses.

Harold was only one of several legitimate contenders. The most dangerous of these was William "the Bastard", Duke of Normandy, a distant blood relative of Edward "the Confessor" and the illegitimate son of Robert I of Normandy and a tanner's daughter. He was descended from a much-feared Viking warrior called Hrolf Ganger, better known to history as Rollo, a goliath of a man who was said to be so huge that there wasn't a horse strong enough to take his weight. William had inherited Rollo's Viking temperament and then some. His idea of fun was skinning his enemies alive then chopping their hands off.[2]

William of Normandy was also a dangerous Viking with a grudge. According to William's chroniclers, in 1064 Harold was sailing down the English Channel (for reasons not known to modern historians) when his ship blew off course and he was forced to land in Normandy. William took Harold prisoner and persuaded him – or possibly tricked him – into swearing support for William's claim to the English throne. Harold did as he was told, the story goes, but then forgot all about it when he got back home and, when the old king Edward died, had himself crowned King of England.

If the story about Harold swearing an oath was true (not everyone agrees that it was) then William had some justification for his attack. All the same, the oath was given under

---

2   During one siege, William's foes mocked him by hanging tanned hides from the battlements. Unwisely, as it turned out, because once he had captured the place, he chopped off the hands and feet of every member of the garrison.

duress and there were several others who had a much closer blood claim to the throne than William of Normandy. The dying King Edward either didn't know about the oath or did not regard it as binding because he named Harold as his rightful successor – an event that even the Normans acknowledge to have occurred.

When William heard about Harold's accession, he was furious, and decided to press his claims by force of arms. His noblemen, however, were reluctant to embark on a foreign invasion, so he took his cause to the Pope, citing the broken oath and stories about how Harold was defiling churches. Once he had the Pope's blessing, the noblemen flocked to William's banner. He raised an Army, built a fleet and prepared to set sail for England.

Harold steeled himself for an invasion. He sent at least one spy to keep an eye on developments in Normandy but the man was captured and brought before William. Instead of brutally killing the spy, as one might expect of a renowned psychopath, William released him back to England with instructions to tell Harold, "If he has not seen me in one year, he may rest secure for the remainder of his reign."

Harold's Army sat on the coast all summer waiting for William to attack, but luck seemed to be on this side. Wind direction prevented William from sailing and Harold knew that he was unlikely to gamble on a winter invasion. By September, Harold was ready to pack up and go home. Then news came that his treacherous half-brother Tostig had allied with the King of Norway, Harald Hardrada, and had landed an Army in the north of England. Harold had to leave the south coast undefended and race north to fend off another invasion.

The English and the Viking armies clashed at Stamford Bridge near York. It was a crushing victory for Harold, but at a price. The fighting had considerably weakened his forces and his men were tired. Meanwhile, William's luck had changed. The wind that had kept his impressive fleet at berth had turned. With the bulk of the English Army at the other end of the country, William was able to land unopposed on the beach near Hastings on 28 September. Unluckily for Harold, in anticipation of William's attack, he had left a garrison to guard the more obvious landing berths at Romney and Dover.

After the battle of Stamford Bridge, Harold rested for just two days, then he and his remaining troops had to slog some 200 miles south again, pausing only at Waltham Abbey to pray for victory. This was his second big mistake. He was hoping to surprise the Normans by returning quickly, but he had taken heavy losses and the bulk of his Army was exhausted. By choosing not to rest before he travelled back down to Hastings, or to give his warriors a chance to divide up the spoils of their recent victory, he alienated some of his supporters and there were many desertions.

Harold's brother, Gyrth, urged him to stop off in London and wait for reinforcements, and in the meantime burn all the land between William's Army and the capital. This would effectively keep William penned in at the coast because he would not be able to bring an Army and their horses through a wasteland. Gyrth also tried to persuade Harold to allow either himself or their brother Leofwine to lead the Army at Hastings while Harold held a second Army in reserve to defend London.

But Harold wouldn't listen; flushed with victory from Stamford Bridge, he wanted to attack quickly. Overruling his brother's plan for a second front meant that in the event of an English defeat at Hastings, London would be undefended and at the mercy of the Norman Army.

At this point, William had the tactical advantage. Most sources agree that Harold's Army was slightly bigger but the Normans were far better equipped militarily. Harold had predominantly foot soldiers at his disposal armed with old-style Anglo-Saxon battleaxes. William had infantry and archers, but he also had chain-mailed mounted knights charging with couched lances. Harold also made the mistake of choosing to engage the enemy close to their own supply lines. By the time his troops got to Hastings, they were already exhausted. William, meanwhile, had time to consolidate his position, stealing crops and razing the area to feed his troops. It was in his best interests to fight a tired Harold as soon as possible.

Facing such difficulties, Harold had little choice but to fight a defensive battle. He took up a position at the top of Senlac Hill, relying on the much-vaunted English shield-wall, behind which his infantry could stand and let the Norman cavalry break themselves.[3]

At first, Harold's tactic was a great success. Wave after wave of Normans charged up the hill, hurling themselves against the well-defended ranks of soldiers hiding behind their shields, only to be repelled. Meanwhile, the English rained down a barrage of stones, javelins and maces, inflicting heavy casualties among the Norman ranks. At one point, the Normans looked like fleeing the battlefield on rumours of William's death, until he rallied them by raising his visor and showing his face.

Against all the odds, it looked as though Harold would win after all. He now held all the tactical aces. After nine hours of fighting, the two sides had battled almost to a standstill. Sunset was approaching, at which point they would have had to call a halt for the night. In the morning Harold would be able to call on reinforcements and a defensive victory would have been all but assured the next day. All he had to do was keep his discipline and hold his position.

It is at this point that the history of the battle becomes murkier. According to tradition, the Normans charged up the hill again, but this time they feigned a retreat. The Saxons, thinking that the enemy was finally on the run, charged after them. It was only when they were off the hill that they realized they had been tricked. William's cavalry appeared in a swift-counter attack. Harold's foot soldiers, their advantage lost, were soon massacred. According to the Bayeux Tapestry, Harold was killed by an arrow through his eye but a

---

3  The first casualty was William's jester Taillefer who rode out ahead, singing the "Song of Roland" while juggling a sword. He was promptly killed by an English warrior. The Normans probably omitted this detail from the Bayeux Tapestry out of embarrassment.

contemporary report says that he was brutally dismembered by Norman broadswords.

This is what happened according to the Bishop of Amiens: "The first Norman knight split Harold's chest, driving the point of his sword through the king's shield. The gushing torrent of blood drenched the Earth. The second knight struck off his head below the helmet and the third stabbed the inside of his belly with a lance. The fourth cut off his leg and carried it away."

By the time they had finished with Harold, even his wife couldn't recognize him and they had to get his mistress, Edith Swan-neck, to identify him by some intimate marks on his body.

The orthodox version of the battle – with William winning through a series of clever, staged retreats which lured the Saxons down from their vantage point and on to flat ground, where the Norman cavalry would have a clear advantage – is very much open to doubt. The Battle of Hastings was more fully documented than almost any other battle that took place in western Europe in the Dark Ages because it was recognized even at that time that it was an event of huge historical importance. The problem for historians is that, almost without exception, the accounts were all written by the winning side and were highly flattering to William, congratulating him on his tactical abilities.

In fact, far from being a battlefield genius, he was strategically inept because despite having been berthed for over a month before the battle, he failed to secure the high ground. For William to have organized staged retreats on a mass scale with an entire Army would have been difficult if not impossible, and would have required mass coordination and superb timing. It is more likely that some Normans fled and others recovered the situation. But still the Saxon line should have held. As the tide turned against them, the survivors drew together, thereby exposing their flanks. The deciding factor was Harold's death, which broke morale.

So Harold's defeat was far from inevitable. Of course, he had no way of knowing that he would be subject to two invasions within a few weeks of each other and so could not have known that he would need to modify his strategy accordingly. If the wind had not blown in the wrong direction at the wrong time, he would not have had to face two invasions at all. His troops would not have been exhausted or depleted and he probably would have been able to repel the Normans and gone on to live a long and peaceful reign.

But Harold was still the bookies' favourite to win. The odds were always against the invader of a country, especially when the invasion is by sea and the defender is prepared for it. The English had the high ground, a larger force and were fighting in an area they were familiar with. The Battle of Hastings was lost by Harold's inability to hang on to an insurmountable tactical advantage, with incalculable consequences for history.[4]

As for William, he was just a lucky bastard.

## Worst Military Decision

The Black Death was the most deadly pandemic in recorded history. It came from Asia and reached Europe in the spring of 1348. By the time it played itself out three years later, up to twenty-five million people had fallen victim to it. The symptoms came on rapidly – swellings under the armpits and in the groin oozed blood and pus and the body became covered in dark blotches. This was accompanied by intense headaches, high temperatures and projectile vomiting. The infected were usually dead within the week.

The first outbreak in England was reported in Dorset in August 1348 and the disease quickly spread through Devon and Somerset, then reaching Bristol, Oxford and followed by

---

4 William marched on London unopposed and was crowned King of England on Christmas Day in Westminster Abbey. A cheer went up in English and French as the crown was placed on his head. The Norman guards outside, thinking that something had gone horribly wrong, attacked the crowd outside slaying many innocent bystanders and setting fire to several buildings. Sales of commemorative tea towels were very slow.

London by November. By 1349, it had reached the north of England and had killed at least one-third of the population.

When the Scots heard that their neighbours were being ravaged by a highly infectious disease, they were delighted. Having suffered a series of humiliating defeats at the hands of King Edward III, anything that undermined the English was worth celebrating. They also assumed that the Scots were naturally immune. Surely the disease was "the revenging hand of God" against the much-hated English. Then someone had a bright idea. Wouldn't this be the perfect time to invade England?

In the autumn of 1349, Scottish troops raided Durham. No one seems to have spotted the obvious flaw in their bold invasion plan until the Scottish troops started to drop like flies in their thousands. At this point, they decided it was time to retreat, taking the disease home with them. Within a year, more than a quarter of the population of Scotland was dead.

---

*"Too far-fetched to be considered."*
Editor of *Scientific American* in a letter to Robert Goddard about his idea of a rocket-accelerated aeroplane bomb, 1940. German V2 missiles rained down on London three years later.

---

## Least Intimidating Declaration of War

In August 1914, most of Europe was caught up in the Great War. Andorra, a tiny and usually neutral little mountain principality wedged between France and Spain in the Pyrenees mountains, came off the fence and declared war on Kaiser Wilhelm II's Germany.

The Kaiser was not unduly worried; in fact, he couldn't actually locate Andorra on a map. His enemy's Army, meanwhile, comprised ten part-time soldiers, and with no military budget, and the only ammunition they had were ceremonial blank cartridges. Fortunately for Andorra, no actual fighting ever took place.

Embarrassingly, when the conflict was formally concluded at the 1919 Versailles Peace Treaty negotiations, nobody remembered Andorra. And since no peace treaty was enacted, Andorra remained technically in a state of war with Germany for the next twenty-five years. The oversight was discovered in 1939 when a separate peace treaty was concluded, formally ending Andorra's state of war against Germany and ending its involvement in the First World War.

The government of Andorra sensibly decided to sit out the Second World War.

## Most Underperforming Battleship

"Second to God, the welfare of the kingdom depends on its navy."

So said the Swedish King Gustavus Adolphus, famed as "the Lion of the North". Accordingly, in 1628 he ordered construction of the biggest warship the world had ever seen – the mighty *Vasa*. The king designed it personally, with the shipbuilders at Stockholm instructed to follow his blueprint to the letter. A thousand oaks went into building her hull; her masts would be fifty metres high and she would be adorned with five hundred sculptures decorated with gold leaf – to impress foreigners. Even more impressively, she would carry sixty-four massive guns to blow away any unfortunate foreign ship she came across.

As it turns out, trusting your king to design a ship instead of the people whose job it is to make ships is not such a great idea. The shipbuilders realized immediately that the *Vasa* would be top-heavy. Worse still, it was so narrow across her bottom that no amount of ballast could rectify the problem.

Before her first sailing, a stability test was carried out. With the ship tied up, thirty of the crew were ordered to run backwards and forwards across her deck. The *Vasa* swayed so alarmingly that after just three runs the test was halted before she keeled over. Admiral Klas Fleming, who ordered the test, is reported to have said, "If only His Majesty were at home." Unfortunately, the king was not at home – he was away leading his Army in Prussia and was keen to see his very big ship join the Baltic fleet. And nobody, not even an admiral, was about to disappoint him.

On 10 August 1628, the magnificent *Vasa* set sail on her maiden voyage. It was a beautiful summer's day and most of Stockholm came down to the city harbour to watch. All around the *Vasa* was a small flotilla of sailing boats bedecked with flags and full of well-wishers, including civic dignitaries and wives and children of the crew.

The *Vasa* sailed for just one nautical mile, then the whole thing tipped over and majestically sank. The biggest and most expensive battleship ever built couldn't cope with a modest gust of wind. The portholes for the cannons were so close to the waterline that, as the ship swayed, the ocean flowed freely into its underbelly. Within minutes, the Vasa and between thirty and fifty crew were on the seabed.[5]

An inquiry was organized by the Swedish privy council to find out who was responsible for the disaster. Unsurprisingly, since King Gustavus Adolphus had personally approved all measurements and armaments, in the end no one was punished for the fiasco and it was put down to an "act of God".

Despite the chastening experience of the *Vasa*, in the 1700s warships continued to get bigger and bigger, until Spain decided to build the largest of all, the *Santísima Trinidad*. It carried a massive 140 cannons and was so heavy it could only move at a crawl, giving rise to its nickname *el Ponderoso* – The Ponderous. So many men were needed to man it that its supplies ran out very quickly unless it was near a friendly port. The *Santísima Trinidad* served at the Battle of Trafalgar but was too slow to make an impact and it eventually surrendered

---

5  Where they would remain until 1961 when a salvage team brought the ship to the surface and dragged it off to a museum.

to the British fleet. The day after the battle it capsized in a storm due to its high centre of gravity.

## Worst Military Aircraft

Most people know about the classic aircraft designs of the Second World War – the Spitfire, the Mustang, the Lancaster. But there were hundreds of aircraft types used on both sides and many were failures. One stands above the rest as the most remarkable failure of all.

Benito Mussolini's most difficult job during the Second World War was getting Italians to fight, a problem he attributed to eating too much pasta.[6] But *Il Duce* had a secret weapon – the Lynx ground-attack aircraft was his pride and joy. It had a sleek, streamlined design and retractable undercarriage, both of which were highly advanced for the time. When it made its début in 1937, it set two world speed records, scoring a great propaganda victory. The military potential of the Lynx was obvious; it was a fast, had good range, and would have made a perfect reconnaissance plane. But Mussolini decided it should carry bombs.

As soon as it took on the extra weight of weapons, armour plating and equipment, the effect on its performance and handling was disastrous. This quickly became apparent when it was first used against French airfields in Corsica and was found to have all the speed and agility of a flying hippo, but it was the only heavy fighter available to the Italian Air Force so sixty-four were sent to North Africa. The addition of sand filters robbed the aircraft of what little power it had left, to a point where it became useless. In 1940, an attack on a British airfield had to be aborted when the fully laden Lynx failed to reach operational height or maintain formation.

---

6 The Roman legions, Il Duce reasoned, had survived on a diet of stodgy barley porridge and conquered the known world, while his own soldiers struggled even to defeat Albania on a diet of spaghetti. According to the fascist leader, flaccid tagliatelle was symbolic of the Italian male's lost virility.

Far from being a world record-setter, the Lynx could now only just about reach half its claimed speed and even then had to set off in the direction of its destination because it lacked the power to make a banking turn. The operational career of the Lynx was aborted.

In a final ignominy, the remaining aircraft were parked up and used as decoys for attacking Allied aircraft. Others were sent to the scrap yard straight from the factory, thus completing the career of the most embarrassingly awful aircraft ever to see combat.

## Most Literal Taste of Defeat

General Marcus Licinius Crassus was one of the most respected and honoured elder statesmen of the Roman republic. He was known as "the richest man in Rome" and was possibly one of the wealthiest men in all history.[7]

Despite his great riches, Crassus wasn't satisfied. More than anything he craved recognition for his military achievements. He wanted to be remembered as Rome's greatest general, more celebrated even than his peers Julius Caesar and Pompey, whom he believed had stolen all the glory for his defeat of the Spartans.

In 54 BC, at the age of sixty, Crassus decided to have one last shot at the title, leaving his idyllic, powerful, wealthy lifestyle to lead an Army on a 1,500-mile trek across the Adriatic, over Asia Minor and into the wastelands of Mesopotamia to fight the Parthians.

Nobody else in Rome, certainly not the Senate, wanted a war with Parthia. It was no great threat to Rome and, in fact, there was a peace treaty signed between the two countries. But Crassus hated being in the shadow of Pompey and Caesar and decided to attack anyway.

On paper, Crassus's Army should easily have been able to overwhelm the Parthians. He had at his disposal 20,000 of

---

7   His net worth today has been estimated at £160 billion.

arguably the best infantry in the world, plus around 4,000 horsemen armed with spears and another 6,000 horsemen under his ally Artabazus, the king of Armenia. The total force was four times that of the Parthian force, which was entirely made up of archers on horseback.

The sensible and most obvious route for Crassus would be to take his infantry into Parthia through a chain of Armenian mountains where the Parthian cavalry would be at a disadvantage. But Crassus was impatient for a quick victory and was determined to take the faster route across some flat valleys – ideal terrain for cavalry and the worst possible place for his infantry to meet the Parthian horsemen head on. He also entrusted himself to a local "guide" who led him straight into a Parthian trap.

Although outnumbered by four to one, the Parthians were fine horsemen and world-class archers. They could ride and fire at the same time and were able to shoot as well backwards as they could forwards. They rode in circles around the Romans, firing volley after volley of arrows. Bewildered by this style of combat, Crassus sent wave after wave of his foot soldiers, all wearing heavy armour and carrying swords and spears, to chase after the Parthian horsemen. The Parthians would get within shooting range, rain a barrage of arrows down upon Crassus's troops, turn, fall back and charge with another attack.

In the ensuing bloodbath, Crassus was killed along with his son and about 20,000 Romans. One legend has it that the Parthians captured him alive and poured molten gold down his throat to cure his thirst for gold. Many of his generals committed suicide rather than fight on hopelessly. A further 10,000 were taken alive and sold into slavery. Parthian losses came out to about 100.

Crassus lost the standards of his seven legions to the enemy. It took an embarrassing twenty-seven years to negotiate their return. Having pursued an unnecessary war, the greedy Crassus earned for himself a place in history as the most disastrous general Rome had ever produced.

## Least Convincing Excuse for a War

In 1325, rivalry between the Italian city states of Modena and Bologna got out of control when a band of Modena soldiers thought it would be really amusing if they raided Bologna (about thirty miles away) and stole their civic wooden bucket.

Bologna, hoping to restore both its bucket and its pride, promptly declared war on Modena. The so-called War of the Bucket raged on for 12 years and an estimated 2,000 people lost their lives, but Bologna never did get its bucket back. The war was a decisive Modenese victory and the bucket remains to this day in their town hall.

Barring bouts of Italian stupidity, the silliest pretext for an armed conflict was the War of Jenkins Ear. In 1739, relations between Britain and Spain were on a knife edge. Hostility between the countries had been bubbling up for decades, each accusing the other of stealing their trade routes and wanting to steal their colonies. But despite the odd minor skirmish, the British Prime Minister, Robert Walpole, defied public opinion and kept Britain out of a war.

Then a man called Robert Jenkins presented himself before Parliament. He had a severed and very shrivelled left ear in his pocket and a tale to tell. Some eight years earlier he had been the captain of a commercial trading ship, the *Rebecca*, sailing off the coast of Cuba. On 9 April 1731, some Spanish coast guards, suspecting that the *Rebecca* was carrying smuggled goods, boarded the vessel and demanded to inspect the ship's cargo and its manifest. When they found contraband aboard the ship, the Spanish captain drew his sword and cut off Captain Jenkins' ear. According to Jenkins, the Spaniard said, "Were the King of England here . . . I would do the same for him!"

It's not entirely clear why Jenkins waited eight years before he made his complaint or, for that matter, why he had the ear pickled and carried it around with him. What is clear is that his aural mishap was simply the last straw. Parliament was outraged and Walpole was obliged to declare war on Spain.

The War of Jenkins' Ear lasted three years from 1739–41 and, as wars go, didn't amount to much. But because Europe was a mesh of alliances and political intrigue, the War of Jenkins' Ear erupted into the War of Austrian Succession, which in turn erupted into a truly global conflict called the Seven Years War.

Three wars and two million dead . . . over an ear. There's even some doubt about whether Jenkins had really lost his ear in the way he'd said he had in the first place.

## Most Futile Display of Bravery

*"This is a story about the English and the French and why the English hate the French. Which is because they eat frogs, they smell bad, and they're twenty-five miles away."*

William Ellis

In the early fourteenth century, armoured knights on horse-back reigned supreme on the battlefield. They were the ultimate killing machine, the medieval equivalent of a battle tank. At the battle of Crécy, however, they were about to receive a very rude shock.

In 1346, England was at war with France – again – this time under the reign of King Edward III. Edward became king aged just fifteen but he didn't let his youth and inexperience hold him back. In 1333, while still a teenager, he won a great victory over the Scots. This was mightily impressive, but beating the Welsh and the Scots was one thing; if you really wanted to be remembered as a truly great English king, you had to inflict a crushing and humiliating defeat on the French. Against all odds, that's exactly what Edward III was able to do and then some.

Edward was spoiling for a scrap with the French and thought he would stir things up a bit in 1337 by declaring himself King of France, a claim based on the fact that his mother was the sister of the old king, whereas the new King Philip VI of France was merely the former king's cousin. To Edward's annoyance, Philip didn't take the bait. In 1340, however, Edward found the excuse he needed to invade France to protect England's wool trade in Flanders.

Taking on the kingdom of France was a formidable challenge. It was much bigger and more prosperous than England with a population five times as great. France could also count on the support of a number of smaller allies who were prepared to provide troops in time of war.

In the early fourteenth century, the armoured knight was thought be close to invincible. The knights of France were the greatest of all, both in number and splendour. The best a well-disciplined infantry could hope for was to kill or frighten his horse then surround the de-horsed knight and pick at him until they got a dagger between his armour. His only other vulnerability lay in attacks from bowmen, but a line of bowmen was thought to be no match for a charge of knights on horseback protected by plate armour, visored helmets and shields armed with lances, two-handed swords, battle-axes and maces.

But Edward had acquired a secret weapon from his recent wars against the Welsh – their deadly longbows. Made of yew and 6-foot long they could fire iron-tipped, armour-piercing arrows 250 yards with murderous accuracy at a rate of twelve arrows a minute. It was crucial to Edward's war effort and he needed all the longbowmen he could get, but they were difficult weapons to master and it took years of practice to be able to fire one properly. Accordingly, he banned all sports except archery on pain of death. It is actually possible to identify the skeletons of longbowmen from their bone spurs and over-developed left arms.

He finally got to try his longbows out for real on several thousand French knights at Crécy in 1346. Edward had an Army of around 8,500 fighting men of whom 5,000 were bowmen. The French Army, led by King Philip VI, had 12,000 French, German, Bohemian and Spanish knights. Riding with Philip were three kings – Charles, King of the Romans; Jaime II of Mallorca; and John of Bohemia. It was the largest assembly of knighthood ever seen on a medieval battlefield and the cream of European nobility.

There were so many competing egos on the field that Philip wasn't completely in control. The battle kicked off when 4,000 Genoese mercenaries with crossbows opened fire on the English line of attack. No one knows for sure if Philip ordered the attack, or if the Genoese just decided to wade in.

The Genoese crossbow was also a formidable weapon, but it was cumbersome to use, slow to load and didn't have the range of a longbow. Much to the amusement of Edward, the Genoese crossbow volley fell short and the English returned fire with their longbows. The Genoese had never experienced anything like it. Crossbowmen were trained to slaughter infantry, not exchange fire with people who could actually shoot *back*. They retreated in panic, many cutting their bowstrings and throwing down their weapons. The sight of this angered Philip so much he called out to his mounted knights, "Quick now, kill all that rabble! They are only getting in our way!" So Philip's knights waded into the struggling Genoese archers, hacking their way through them as they went.

Meanwhile, into the middle of this Edward's longbowmen continued to rain a hailstorm of arrows so dense, according to a French chronicler, that it blotted out the Sun. An estimated 60,000 arrows were hitting Philip's knights every minute. But the rules of chivalry dictated that knights should only fight their equals on the battlefield, so instead of attacking the people who were doing all the damage, Philip's knights largely ignored the longbowmen and went for the English knights.

By the end of the day, Edward had won a stunning victory. A small and completely outnumbered English Army had devastated not just the French Army, but the French aristocracy. Less than 300 Englishmen were killed while the French death toll exceeded 30,000, including 11 princes, an archbishop and 1,200 knights and noblemen.

There were two more battles – at Poitiers in 1356, and Agincourt in 1415 – where French knights lost heavily to English longbowmen, but Crécy is credited as being the point in history where the concept of chivalry in warfare and the dominance of the knight on horseback ended for ever. But the age of chivalry went down fighting, because Crécy is also famous for one final, spectacularly futile act of bravery.

King John "The Blind" of Bohemia, an ally of the French King Philip, had lost his eyesight a decade earlier to an eye infection while fighting in Lithuania, but he didn't want to miss out on the action. He ordered his men to strap him into his saddle and point him in the direction of the enemy. He rode into the fray and somehow made it to the top of the slope, then, unsurprisingly, he was very quickly killed along with the fifteen knights who escorted him. Before he set off, he was reported to have said, "Let it never be the case that a Bohemian king runs from a fight."

His gesture was not entirely in vain. According to tradition, the King of England's son, the 'Black Prince', was so impressed by this display of lunacy that he decided to adopt[8] King John's personal crest of three white ostrich feathers and his motto "Ich Dien" (I serve) as his own. It is the Prince of Wales's motto to this day.

## Least Successful Espionage Mission

The Tower of London has seen off many an illustrious traitor – the German spy Josef Jakobs wasn't among them. Jakobs was parachuted into a field in Huntingdonshire, England, on 31 January 1941, but was spotted in his descent by the local Home Guard who raced to his landing point to detain him. They could have taken their time, because Jakobs had broken his ankle upon landing and was immobile. Still wearing his German flying suit, he was carrying forged papers, a radio and a German sausage. That was the end of his espionage mission.

Found guilty of spying and sentenced to death, ten days later Jakobs was taken to the Tower rifle range, strapped into a chair and executed by firing squad.

---

8   i.e. "steal".

At least Jakobs, who was an otherwise rather inept spy, made his mark in history as the only person to have been shot at the Tower of London and the last to be executed at the site. All future executions of Second World War spies took place by hanging at Pentonville or Wandsworth Prisons.

---

*"I'm just glad it'll be Clark Gable who's falling on his face and not Gary Cooper."*

Actor Gary Cooper, on his decision not to take the leading role in *Gone with the Wind*.

---

## Worst Expeditionary Force

King Charles I had certain set beliefs. One was that, as King, he was always right about everything. So when he decided to launch a futile attack on Spain in 1625, he wasn't going to shift or modify his beliefs regardless of what arguments were put before him.

The only person Charles was prepared to take advice from on foreign policy was his friend and favourite, the unpopular and incompetent Lord Admiral, Duke of Buckingham. When Buckingham suggested placing Sir Edward Cecil at the head of the invasion fleet, Charles agreed. Unfortunately, although Cecil was a battle-hardened soldier, he couldn't navigate a rubber duck in a bathtub.

Buckingham and Cecil's bold plan was to ambush several Spanish treasure ships coming back from the Americas loaded with valuables and then attack the Spanish mainland. It got off to a bad start when Cecil realized too late that his ships had been provisioned with mouldy food and infected water. Then stormy weather hit the fleet, rendering many of his ships barely seaworthy, causing major delays. They were so late that they completely missed the Spanish treasure fleet they were supposed to be attacking.

As a consolation prize, Cecil decided to attack the Spanish city of Cédiz. Meanwhile, several Spanish vessels that might have been captured were allowed to escape to the safety of Port Royal because everyone was waiting for orders from Cecil, but none came.

After landing his forces, instead of immediately attacking Cádiz he decided to attack and capture what he identified as the strategically important nearby Fort Puntel. The attack on Puntel was a complete waste of time and resources because the fort didn't need to be captured.

After capturing Puntel, Cecil landed his troops further up the coast from where he planned to march his Army into Cádiz. The troops were ill-disciplined, poorly trained and desperately short of provisions. He allowed them to set up camp in a field next to some deserted buildings, which housed gallons and gallons of wine. Before long, Cecil's thirsty Army was completely drunk, with men shooting each other and threatening any officer who tried to keep order.

Realizing that he had a potential mutiny on his hands, Cecil ordered his men back to their ships. When the Spanish Army arrived, they found over 1,000 English soldiers still drunk; they were put to the sword by the Spanish without a single shot fired in retaliation.

After the Cádiz fiasco, Cecil decided to try to intercept another fleet of Spanish ships that was bringing gold back from the Americas, but this failed as well because the Spanish were tipped off and easily avoided the planned ambush without any trouble from Cecil or his fleet.

With disease and sickness sweeping through the ranks and his ships in a terrible state, Cecil decided he had seen enough and his fleet limped home empty-handed, having cost the English an estimated £250,000. There was widespread outrage over the embarrassing Cádiz Expedition but King Charles, us usual, refused to explain or defend any of his decisions and even gave Cecil a promotion.

In 1627, Charles put Buckingham in charge of yet another military failure, this time in the siege of the French fortress city of Saint-Martin on the isle of Ré near La Rochelle. The English siege engineer drowned during the landing and the siege ladders turned out to be too short to scale the walls. Eventually, Buckingham gave up and sounded the retreat but was harassed by pursuing French troops, and lost about 5,000 men out of a force of 7,000.

Despite the ignominious failure of two expeditions against Spain and France, the King was determined to send Buckingham with another force to La Rochelle but, in 1628, Buckingham spared his nation any further embarrassment by getting himself stabbed to death in a public house in Portsmouth by a sailor with a grudge. Parliament was even less forgiving with the King: two ignominious military defeats started the process that led to Charles finishing his reign eight inches shorter than he was when he started it.

## Unluckiest Invasion Fleet

Armies are usually defeated because they face a bigger and more powerful opponent, or they lose because they are outwitted by a cunning adversary. Just occasionally they lose because of some bizarre set of circumstances no one could have foreseen.

By the late thirteenth century, the Mongol Empire stretched from Korea to Hungary in eastern Europe, making it the largest contiguous empire the world has ever seen. The Mongols were also the only people in history ever to have successfully pulled off a winter invasion of Russia. So when it came time to invading tiny Japan, victory was assumed to be a formality.

Just to make sure there were no slip-ups, Kublai Khan's counsellors advised him to bide his time until he had built an invincible armada of war ships, so he commissioned the construction of the greatest fleet in history and filled it with a conscripted Army of some 40,000 men.

Japan, meanwhile, could muster only about 10,000 fighting men from the ranks of the often-squabbling samurai clans. Japan's warriors were seriously and hopelessly outmatched. Only one thing could stop a Mongol victory – a typhoon. So to make absolutely sure that the weather couldn't wreck their plans, the Mongols planned their attack well after typhoon season.

In November 1274, Kublai Khan sent his mighty fleet of about 600 ships across the narrow strait between Korea and Japan, only to see it smashed by a typhoon. Dismayed but not defeated, Kublai Khan spent the next seven years regrouping for a bigger, even stronger attack.

In August 1281, the Mongols sent an estimated 900 ships across the narrow strait again – only to see their fleet destroyed by a second, even bigger typhoon of the type that is estimated to occur only once every few hundred years. Almost all of the invaders drowned in the storm; the few who made it to shore were hunted and killed without mercy by the samurai.

Convinced of a divine intervention, the Japanese called the two storms "*kamikaze*", or divine winds. For once, Kublai Khan wasn't arguing. The Mongols never attempted to invade Japan again.

## Least Successful Tactical Withdrawal

There are not very many examples in history where an entire well-trained and well-equipped Army surrenders without a fight, even though they massively outnumber the forces they're fighting against. The British Army's retreat from Kabul in 1842 was called "the most disgraceful and humiliating episode in our history of war . . . up to that time."[9]

It all began in the 1830s when Britain was preoccupied with protecting India and its role as "The Jewel in the Crown". In 1838, the British Governor-General of India, Lord Auckland, decided to take down India's troublesome Afghan neighbour the Emir of Kabul by force. British troops subsequently invaded Afghanistan with the intention of deposing the Emir and installing an unpopular former ruler, Shah Shuja. The first round of the conflict was an easy win for Britain as they routed

---

9   According to Field Marshall Sir Gerald Templar (1898-1979), British soldier and military historian.

the Emir and captured Kabul, but the British soon learned that
beating the Afghans was not quite the same as controlling
them.[10] Enter Major-General William Elphinstone, the only
general to have lost an entire British Army.

In 1841, Elphinstone took command of the British garrison
in Kabul, numbering around 16,000 troops and support staff.
Lord Auckland thought Elphinstone was the right man for the
job because "he was of good repute, gentlemanly manners,
and aristocratic connections". His Lordship overlooked the
fact that Elphinstone's previous active service had been at
Waterloo, twenty-five years earlier, and he was now a flatulent,
incontinent sixty-year-old, so stricken with gout, rheumatoid
arthritis and heart disease that he could barely move.

Even Elphinstone recognized that he was too old for the job
and was reluctant to go, but Lord Auckland would hear none of
it; after all, the average age of your British general was such that
you were considered fit for active service if you could remember your own name (see also Most Pointless Cavalry Charge).

When Elphinstone got to Kabul, he was told by the outgo-
ing General Cotton, "You will have nothing to do here . . . all is
peace." But no sooner had he arrived that things started to go
very badly indeed. Communications with India were severed
by Afghans in the hills and he found himself besieged in Kabul.
The predicament became a great deal worse when the nearest
British fort fell to the rebels.

The Kabul garrison was built with little consideration for
defence. It was located in a low, swampy area surrounded by
hills and the stores were placed some 400 metres away outside its perimeter. It was an open invitation to the enemy to
seize their supplies and starve the population inside, which is
exactly what happened. Before long, bandits were looting the
British stores and freely killing any Britons who strayed out
of camp.

As autumn turned to winter and fighting intensified, the
British camp came under daily attack from snipers on the

---

10   This may sound familiar – Ed.

heights above them, an area Elphinstone had failed to secure. When the British formed squares to repel Afghan light cavalry, their sharpshooters found the obligingly bright red uniforms impossible to miss, even at a distance.

At this point, Elphinstone was permanently bedridden and had to be carried everywhere on a litter. He was also fatally indecisive. Completely ignorant of Afghanistan or its people, he was inclined to consult widely with men of all ranks then agree with whoever he spoke with last – everyone, that is, except his second-in-command, Brigadier Shelton, whom he hated and refused to include in any discussions. Shelton, meanwhile, didn't even attempt to disguise his contempt for Elphinstone and took his bed roll into meetings with his superior and pretended to fall asleep.

With supplies gone and casualties mounting, Elphinstone continued to vaccilate. The British envoy in Kabul, Sir William McNaughton, unable to stand Elphinstone's dithering any longer, took it on himself to try to negotiate some kind of truce and arranged a meeting with the Afghan leader outside the British camp. McNaughton was promptly cut to pieces within sight of the camp; his hands, feet and torso were paraded victoriously through the streets of Kabul while his head was placed in a horse's nosebag and displayed in the bazaar. Elphinstone, who had no stomach for a fight, refused to order reprisals, much to the disgust of his junior officers.

The farce descended further when Elphinstone got himself shot in the buttocks. This seems to have spurred him to make a decision, even though it turned out to be the worst of his life. He cut a deal with the Afghans. In exchange for handing over all of his gunpowder reserves, his newest muskets and most of his cannon to the Afghan rebels, the British troops and civilians were promised a safe passage to India, through the infamous Khyber Pass.

After abandoning a fortified position in Kabul, Elphinstone was now attempting to march his 4,500 men to the garrison of Jalalabad, ninety miles away, in winter, with

12,000 civilians in tow. To reach their destination, Elphinstone's column of 16,500 men, women and children would have to cross Afghan mountain passes, marching through snow a foot deep in terrible wather conditions and with little food. Most knew from the outset the crossing would be deadly.

Despite assurances of protection, as Elphinstone's Army staggered through the mountains, their numbers were very quickly whittled down by disease and freezing weather. Their passage through the snow was also marked by a trail of the blood of slaughtered stragglers, picked off by Afghan raiders. After three days, around 3,000 had died, frozen to death or shot, or in some cases having committed suicide.[11]

On the fifth day, the Afghans attacked in force near Gandamak and the rest of the party were massacred, many with their throats cut as they lay defenceless in the snow. Only a handful survived, including one regular soldier, albeit with part of his skull missing, but the Afghans took a dozen high-ranking prisoners including Elphinstone and Shelton, who had agreed to become hostages. It was the most cowardly act in British military history – a commanding officer and his senior aide surrendering to save their lives while their soldiers died around them.

The loss of 16,500 people was a shocking and humiliating defeat for Britain and India. Upon hearing the news, Lord Auckland, Governor-General of India, had a stroke. Major-General William Elphinstone did not survive to face the furious indignation of Victorian Britain. Wounded and suffering from dysentery, he avoided a court martial by dying in captivity a few months later.

Elphinstone was later depicted by George MacDonald Fraser in his book *Flashman*: "Only he could have permitted the First Afghan War and let it develop to such a ruinous defeat. It was not easy – he started with a good Army, a secure

---

11  The sick and injured, who had been left behind as arranged, were massacred within minutes of the last British soldier leaving Kabul.

position, some excellent officers, a disorganized enemy, and repeated opportunities to save the situation. But Elphy, with a touch of true genius, swept aside these obstacles with unerring precision, and out of order wrought complete chaos. We shall not, with luck, look upon his like again."

## Quickest Surrender

On 27 August 1896, Britain and Zanzibar fought the shortest war in history. The catalyst for the conflict was the sudden death by poisoning of Zanzibar's Sultan Hamad bin Thuwaini at the hand of his twenty-nine-year-old nephew, Khalid bin Bargash, who declared himself successor. The move displeased the local British consul, from whom Bargash had neglected to seek approval for his action, which he was obliged to do in accordance with a treaty signed ten years earlier. Moreover, the old sultan was basically a loyal figurehead for a British-run government, unlike Bargash who was a supporter of the Germans who were trying to establish colonies and build rival trading stations in Africa.

The consul fired off a telegram to Prime Minister Lord Salisbury asking for clarification of their position. Meanwhile, the Royal Navy lined up five warships in the harbour in front of Bargash's palace. The reply from Salisbury came: "You are authorized to adopt whatever measures you may consider necessary, and will be supported in your action by Her Majesty's Government. Do not, however, attempt to take any action which you are not certain of being able to accomplish successfully."

In other words, attack . . . but if it doesn't work out, you're on your own.

At 8 a.m., Britain delivered an ultimatum through a loud-hailer ordering Bargash to vacate the palace within one hour or else. Bargash refused, defying the Royal Navy, the most powerful maritime power the world had ever seen, to defeat Zanzibar, whose entire military arsenal comprised a single medieval cannon and an armed luxury yacht, the *Glasgow*.

British ships opened fire on the palace at 9.02 a.m. The shelling stopped thirty-eight minutes later – the time it took Zanzibar to run up the white flag of surrender.[12]

About 500 Zanzibaris were dead or wounded while just one British sailor was reported injured. As a final act of humiliation, Britain forced the Zanzibar Government to pay for the 500 shells and 5,000 rounds of machine-gun ammunition fired on their country.

## Most Pointless Cavalry Charge

*"English is full of battle-poems, but it is worth noticing that the ones that have won for themselves a kind of popularity are always a tale of disasters and retreats. The most stirring battle-poem in English is about a brigade of cavalry which charged in the wrong direction."*

George Orwell

The Battle of Balaclava was a relatively minor military engagement with a predictable outcome. The number of dead was not even exceptional. But thanks to a solitary newspaper reporter, it has become the ultimate tale of senseless slaughter, military incompetence, blind obedience and hopeless heroism.

In 1853, Britain's ongoing power struggle with Russia erupted into war in the Crimea, a small peninsula in the Black Sea. It was a fiasco from the outset. The British Army had changed little since the Napoleonic Wars forty years earlier and was badly in need of reform. The tactics they were using were basically still the same used by Wellington at Waterloo and hadn't kept pace with the new and much greater firepower available to both infantry and cavalry.

The supply line was also fatally flawed. The Crimean campaign got off on the wrong foot, literally, when the Army was sent 5,000 left boots. The Britain had arrogantly presumed that the war would be over by Christmas so they weren't

---

12   Some accounts say forty-five minutes. Whatever, it was quick.

equipped with adequate clothing for the Russian winter. British soldiers tried to keep warm by pulling woollen socks over their heads and cutting eye holes in them. When news reached Britain that their troops were freezing to death, a large quantity of warm clothing was shipped out to the Crimea, but the ship carrying the consignment, the *Prince*, sank without trace, taking 40,000 greatcoats and pairs of new boots down with it. By the end of November, another 12,000 greatcoats had safely arrived at Balaclava to replace the lost consignment, but more than 9,000 remained locked in store because there was an army regulation that said that soldiers couldn't be issued more than one new greatcoat every three years. Men were dying of exposure because of red tape.

There was even a shortage of good maps. One officer wrote home to his mother: "Will you also be kind enough to send me a map of the Crimea with the forts etc., well marked out in Sebastopol. You can chose which you think best and send it by post."

Then there was the diet. While the officers sat in their heated tents (or in Lord Cardigan's case, on his private luxury yacht in the harbour) dining on chicken and champagne, the ordinary soldiers lived on half rations or no food at all. Their rations – salt beef and biscuits – were largely inedible, didn't supply nearly enough nutritional value and increased the risk of scurvy. Most of the soldiers found they couldn't eat the salt beef because it gave them diarrhoea, so they threw it away and got by on a diet of rum and biscuits instead. In November 1854, 150 tons of vegetables were shipped to the Crimea on board the *Harbinger*. But the ship arrived without the correct papers and the captain couldn't get anyone to unload his cargo. While officials argued over procedure, the food rotted and eventually had to be thrown overboard.

It was the issue of green coffee that caused the most aggravation. Coffee beans for the troops were sent to the Crimea unroasted, because there was less chance of the beans becoming damp or mouldy. But without any means of grinding or roasting the beans, the soldiers had to drink a concoction that was not only foul-tasting but was also harmful to their health.[13]

Not a single vegetable reached the British troops at the front. It was much the same with the issue of lime juice. It was a well-established fact by the time of the Crimean War that lime juice could prevent scurvy. A ship carrying 278 cases and 20,000 lbs of limes had been dispatched to the Crimea for general issue to the British troops. For three months, it sat untouched in Balaclava harbour. Everyone knew it was there, but no one knew whose job it was to tell the Army it had arrived. Meanwhile, the British camp was ravaged with scurvy.

Amid this chaos, there was also some fighting to be done, and this was where the British Army faced its biggest problem – lack of leadership. The British way of becoming an officer in the armed forces was to either buy a commission or, for some of the top positions, via appointment by politicians, who often selected their friends. Hence the highest ranks of the British Army were filled by elderly aristocrats vying to outdo each other to see who could achieve the most incompetence. Of Britain's five infantry divisions in the Crimea, only one of the officers chosen to lead them was under sixty and he had never seen action before.[14]

In 1854, the combined British and French forces were advancing towards the Russian port of Sebastopol when they met the defending Russian Army near Balaclava. The Army was commanded by Fitzroy James Henry Somerset, Lord Raglan. The elderly Raglan hadn't seen combat since losing an arm at Waterloo more than forty years earlier and had never commanded an Army in the field before.[15] He was appointed

---

13  The real killers in the Crimean War were typhoid and cholera – 20,000 deaths to disease as against 3,400 in actual warfare.

14  Not that the British had a monopoly on useless generals. François Canrobert of the French Army was nicknamed "Robert Can't" for his indecisiveness in the Crimea.

15  While they sawed Raglan's arm off, without anaesthetic, he remained stoically silent. The only comment he made was when they threw his severed limb into a basket. "You there, bring my arm back, there's a ring my wife gave me on the finger."

because it was his turn and nobody objected. It didn't help that he kept referring to the French as "the enemy". His senior officers had to keep reminding him that this time the French were on his side – the Russians were the enemy. The fate of the Light Brigade would hinge on Raglan's ability to articulate a clear order.

The British had a large amount of cavalry at Balaclava but the Russians countered with an impressive array of guns and artillery. The defenders also had control of the valley. The one-armed Raglan peered across the landscape from his high vantage point on a hill and could see Russians in the distance trying to drag away some captured British cannons. Raglan sent down an order to his Lieutenant-General, George Charles Bingham, the third Earl of Lucan, to recover them. Lord Lucan had just returned after seventeen years in retirement. Famously dim, he was much more concerned with the appearance of his cavalry than the actual business of waging war. He spent more on uniforms than the actual wage bill for the men who wore them.

The order to attack was given to Captain Lewis Edward Nolan for delivery. Nolan was chosen because he was one of the best horsemen in the cavalry and would be able take a speedy, more direct route down to Lucan. He was a "merit" officer with barely disguised contempt for his elderly aristocratic superiors. He had also written a book about cavalry tactics and wanted everybody to know it. The order handed to Nolan read: "Lord Raglan wishes the Cavalry to advance rapidly to the front, follow the enemy, and try to prevent the enemy carrying away the guns. Troop Horse Artillery may accompany. French Cavalry is on your left. Immediate."

Now, the order made perfect sense if you were on top of the hill and could see everything that was going on, but Lucan was in a position 600 feet lower than Raglan and didn't have the same view. When he read the order from Nolan, he was baffled. Which guns was he supposed to attack? He asked Nolan for clarification. Like Lord Raglan, Nolan had seen the location of the guns that were obscured from Lucan's view, but

instead of pointing directly to where they were, he simply ges-
tured in the general direction of the Russians and said; "There,
my Lord, is your enemy. There are your guns." Nolan repeated
that the order was to attack immediately then trotted off.
Lucan, who didn't see eye to eye with the arrogant Nolan,
didn't bother to ask for further clarification.

The only guns Lucan could actually see were at the far end
of the valley, where masses of Russian cavalry were concentrated. He assumed that these were the guns he was supposed
to attack. Lucan rode over to James Burdened, the seventh
Earl of Cardigan,[16] the commander of the Light Brigade –
"light" because they were lightly armed, as opposed to the
"heavy brigade".

Cardigan was thought by some to be actually mad, possibly
the result of a near-fatal blow on the head in a childhood riding
accident – "His progression through the Army was marked by
many episodes of extraordinary incompetence" is just one of
many references to him. He was, even by the standards of the
English aristocracy, highly eccentric. He was subject to flights
of terrible rage and was a famous stickler for "proper form".
In 1840, Cardigan was embroiled in an extraordinary Victorian
officers' mess dispute known as "The Black Bottle Affair" – a
difference of opinion over the correct receptacle for decanting
wine. Cardigan had a fellow officer arrested because he had
placed a black bottle of moselle on a table instead of a decanter.
When an account of the incident was leaked to the *Morning
Chronicle*, Cardigan challenged its author, Captain Harvey
Tuckett, to a duel on Wimbledon Common. Tuckett was
injured and the Earl was tried in the House of Lords, but
acquitted for lack of evidence. Tuckett conveniently failed to
appear and, it was generally assumed, had been bought off.

Lucan and Cardigan despised each other. Cardigan was
married to Lucan's youngest sister but they were now sepa-
rated. The animosity between the two men was well
documented; they often came close to trading blows in front of

---

16  You may have noticed the emerging knitwear theme.

their own troops. So there was no small-talk or discussion about tactics; Lucan simply pointed down the valley and ordered Cardigan to attack. When Cardigan mentioned the obvious flaw in Lucan's plan – i.e. that the valley was heavily defended by Russian guns – Lucan merely told Cardigan to ride at moderate speed so as not to exhaust the horses. Lucan would follow up with the Heavy Brigade. Lucan and Cardigan both knew that the order was suicidal, but neither wanted to lose face. So instead of ignoring an absurd order to attack from their elderly and incompetent commander-in-chief, both men just got on with it.

Leading the charge, Cardigan followed his orders with his customary parade-ground formality and discipline. He was taking his 673 men into a narrow valley a mile-and-a-quarter long. Russian gunners were at the end and on both sides, forming a 'valley of death'.

Nolan was the first to die as he charged to the front when a shell burst nearby and a chunk of shrapnel hit him squarely in the chest. He may have been trying to ride forward to warn Cardigan he was heading in the wrong direction, although some historians dispute this.[17]

To the Russians, the manoeuvre appeared to be of such unfathomable stupidity that they assumed the British were all drunk. In fact, some of Cardigan's men did manage to get through to the guns, but were then surrounded by the Russian troops. When they turned to retreat, they were easy targets. The slaughter took about twenty minutes and cost about a third of the attacking force. The commander of the French cavalry, General Bosquet, summed up the unfolding disaster most accurately. *"C'est magnifique, mais ce n'est pas la guerre . . ."* – "It is magnificent, but it is not war."

The first the British public knew about all this was two days later when they read about it over breakfast in *The Times*. It wasn't even the headline story. The paper's war correspondent

---

17  After the battle, Cardigan said his first emotion was anger at Nolan's attempt to upstage him by riding to the front, not the loss of his men.

William Howard Russell, who had wired news of the event home by telegraph, buried it in a general piece about the war, but it was still hard not to notice that, of the 673 men who had charged down the valley at Balaclava, only 195 had returned alive and 500 horses had been killed. It was a good thing, of course, that for the first time these aristocratic blunders were not going unreported. Unfortunately, Russell's uncensored reports were also being read by the Russians who got everything they needed to know about British troop movements by reading the morning paper.

In the post mortem that followed, everyone vigorously tried to smear each other. Raglan blamed Lucan for losing the Light Brigade; almost everyone else blamed Lord Cardigan because he had led the actual charge straight into the cannon battery; Cardigan blamed Lucan, who, in turn, blamed the dead Nolan for the vagueness of delivery of the orders. The one thing everyone agreed on is that the charge was an unmitigated disaster. Nearly 500 British soldiers died because their arrogant and incompetent commanders were no longer on speaking terms. But Balaclava was soon being subtly rewritten as a story of British heroism against all odds. This was what the British public wanted to hear – a symbol of heroic failure, self-sacrifice and great devotion to duty. Alfred Lord Tennyson confirmed this new slant on the story with his poem *The Charge of the Light Brigade*, which quickly became famous throughout the world as a story of great heroism against the odds. Sixty years later, the poets of the First World War would look upon this kind of tactical blunder very differently.

Miraculously, Lord Cardigan returned home almost unscathed from the Crimea as a hero and an unlikely fashion icon.[18] Ironically, he died fourteen years later after falling off his horse while taking his regular morning ride.

---

18 Although his men were freezing to death, Cardigan had his little knitted waistcoat made especially for the cold Russian weather and it became a popular item of clothing.

## Longest War Without Anyone Getting Hurt

On 29 September 1883, the Spanish King, Alfonso XII, was riding through Paris on a State visit when he was rudely abused and stoned by the Parisian mob.[19] When reports of the royal snub reached Lijar, a small town in southern Spain, the mayor, Don Miguel Garcia Saez, was outraged. He was so angry that, on 14 October, he and the whole of Lijar (population 300) declared war on France.

During the ensuing hostilities, not a single shot was fired and no casualties were sustained on either side. In 1981, a full ninety-eight years later, Lijar decided it was time to let bygones be bygones and agree a ceasefire with France. "We have forgiven them now," said the Mayor, Diego Sanchez, "making this the first time in two centuries that France fought a war and didn't lose."

---

*"So many centuries after the Creation it is unlikely that anyone could find hitherto unknown lands of any value."*
Committee advising King Ferdinand and Queen Isabella of Spain regarding a proposal by Christopher Columbus, 1486

---

## Most Clueless US Commander

The American Civil War was not short of amusingly incompetent characters on both sides. The Union Army commander-in-chief, Winfield Scott, was too fat to mount a horse or even climb into a train, so he effectively handed command to Robert E. Lee, who repaid his faith by quickly resigning and joining the enemy. Scott planned to starve the

---

19 King Alfonso's decision to arrive on a state visit to France wearing a Prussian military uniform, twelve years after the people of Paris had suffered horribly in a siege during the Franco-Prussian War, was straight from *The Duke of Edinburgh Book of Tact*.

South into submission by blocking all of their ports, despite the fact that he didn't have enough ships to mount and sustain a blockade of the Confederate's 3,000-mile coastline.

The US Confederate, General Thomas J. Jackson, had several nicknames before he earned his new handle "Stonewall" at the first battle of Bull Run by sitting astride his horse "like a stone wall" while bullets flew around him. When he was a junior officer, he wore his thick army greatcoat throughout a long and very hot summer because he had not received an order to do otherwise. He was also a strict Presbyterian, hence the nickname "Deacon Jackson". His deep religious convictions also meant that he refused to fight on Sundays. During the thick of the battle of Mechanicsville in 1862, Jackson spent the day praying alone on a nearby hill, refusing to speak to anyone, while his troops took heavy casualties. He was accidentally shot by his own men during the battle of Chancellorsville and died from complications a week later.

The Union general, Ambrose Everett Burnside, was famous for two things: the most ridiculous-looking facial hair [20] and the most awesome incompetence on either side in the war. It was said that no numerical or tactical advantage was so great that he could not throw it away.

In September 1862, Burnside sent his men across the Antietam Creek using a thirty-eight-metre-long narrow stone bridge; it was just wide enough for two soldiers to walk side by side. The crossing was slow, making them easy targets for Confederate sharpshooters, who lined up on a nearby ridge and shot them for fun. Most of Burnside's men were killed. If he had been slightly better prepared, he would have known that that river he was trying to cross was only waist deep.

A month later, Burnside was rewarded for his failure with a promotion, although he had turned down two earlier offers of

---

20 If the aim of the war was to grow impressive amounts of facial hair, then Burnside was the US Army's most successful general. He allowed the hair along his cheeks and upper lip to grow, but shaved his chin, which gave him the appearance of a man who has a pair of squirrels stapled to each side of his face. His name was inverted to give these patches of hair the name "sideburns".

promotion because he didn't think he was up to it. The Battle of Fredericksburg proved him right.

In December 1862, the Confederate Army was dug in along the heights overlooking the town of Fredericksburg. Burnside ordered a series of assaults that accomplished nothing, except the deaths of another 12,000 of his men.

The following January, Burnside was in action again when he decided to initiate a risky winter campaign. He sent his men on a long march, right at the start of a four-day deluge of freezing rain. By the end of the first day, the roads were rivers of mud, clogged with the bodies of exhausted dead horses and the artillery and wagons they were pulling. Meanwhile, as Burnside's men staggered along, soaked, freezing and starving, Confederate soldiers watched with amusement from the other side of the Rappahannock River, taunting them with signs made from bed sheets: "Burnside, stuck in the mud". Burnside abandoned the campaign, but not before hundreds of his men died of exhaustion and exposure.

He managed to top even this suicidal tactic in June 1864. At Petersburg, Burnside's men were stuck in a line of trenches. In front of them, just 100 yards away, was a rebel fort dominating a sloping ridge. One of the regiments under Burnside's command was the 46th Pennsylvanian Volunteers, a force primarily made up of miners. He ordered them to undermine the enemy defences by digging a trench and filling it with explosives. Burnside's plan was that, once the mine was detonated, his men would jump out of their trenches, run up the hill and rush the fort, taking advantage of the outright panic and confusion that would ensue in the Confederate lines.

The charge detonated, killing at least 278 Confederate soldiers and creating a crater 170 feet long, 60–80 feet wide and 30 feet deep. As the dust cleared, Burnside's men charged up the hill and jumped into the crater to take cover, only to find they couldn't climb out again. The Confederates were more than a little surprised to find the whole enemy force trapped at their feet in a big hole. As a result, 3,793 Union soldiers were killed, wounded or captured.

On hearing of this latest manoeuvre, Abraham Lincoln noted, "Only Burnside could have managed such a coup, wringing one last spectacular defeat from the jaws of victory."

## Most Embarrassing Friendly Fire Incident

On 29 March 1942, the British cruiser *Trinidad* was escorting a convoy in the Arctic when it was attacked by three German destroyers. The *Trinidad* returned fire by launching a torpedo attack. It was such a cold day that two of the three torpedoes were iced up and failed to leave their tubes; the third torpedo malfunctioned because the oil in its motor and gyroscope had frozen. When it was fired, it turned around in a wide circle and headed back the way it had come, hitting the cruiser amidships, with the loss of thirty-two men.

The ship that torpedoed herself was towed clear and limped back to Murmansk where she was partially repaired, but on her way back to Britain she was bombed and another sixty-three men died. This time, damage was such that it was decided to scuttle her and HMS *Matchless* torpedoed the unlucky ship, sending it to the bottom of the Arctic Ocean.

> *"No one will pay good money to get from Berlin to Potsdam in one hour when he can ride his horse there in one day for free."*
> King William I of Prussia on hearing of the invention of trains, 1864

## Most Disastrous Lack of Strategy

*"Hurrah, boys, we've got them!"*
George Armstrong Custer, just before
the battle of the Little Bighorn

If the last word in British military bone-headedness was Lord Cardigan's Charge of the Light Brigade, the American equivalent was George Armstrong Custer's so-called "last stand" at the Little Bighorn. At least Lord Cardigan could offer the excuse that he was following orders; Custer had no one to blame but himself.

The career of Lieutenant-Colonel George Armstrong Custer – he had "borrowed" the rank of General – got off to a flying start when he finished bottom out of a class of thirty-four at West Point Military School. He was such a useless student that Custer himself admitted that his time there should be studied by future cadets as an example to be avoided.

Normally, this would have ensured that his military career was over before it even began, or at best got him a safe posting to some far-flung outpost, but Custer was lucky to have graduated just after the start of the Civil War and the US Army was desperate for trained officers. He soon found himself reporting for duty as a Second Lieutenant in the US 2nd Cavalry.

By all accounts, he seems to have been a highly emotional man, given to grand gestures and speeches, but he also showed himself to be a brave, albeit reckless, soldier – he had only one military tactic: "Charge!" But his coolness under fire caught the eye of his superiors and he rose swiftly through the ranks. At the age of twenty-four, two years almost to the day of graduating from West Point, he was made a brigadier general and given command of a cavalry brigade from Michigan.

As the battles came and went, Custer's fame grew, thanks to his flair for self-promotion. He was as vain as he was ambitious, instantly recognizable by his non-regulation uniform of black velvet trimmed with gold lace, crimson necktie and a white hat, although he said he only wore this so that his men could easily see him in battle. After leading one successful charge, he wrote in his report in typical Custer fashion: "I challenge the annals of warfare to produce a more brilliant or successful charge of cavalry."

The press loved him. A *New York Times* reporter wrote, "Custer, young as he is, displayed judgement worthy of a Napoleon." In fact, his army record was highly erratic. Although he inspired fierce loyalty from some, he was indifferent to the welfare or safety of his men and his cavalry unit had the highest casualty rate of any in the Army.

By the end of the Civil War, Custer was a national hero, but then his star began to wane. His first post-war command ended when his Michigan Cavalry was disbanded after a mutiny, partly caused by his heavy-handed discipline. In July 1867, fifteen of his men deserted during a forced march. Custer ordered a search party "to shoot the supposed deserters down dead and to bring none in alive". Soon afterwards, he deserted his own post so he could spend a day with his sick wife. Custer was arrested, court-martialled and suspended for a year without pay, but his old Civil War mentor General Sheridan came to his rescue and called him back to active duty.

Custer spent the next few years fighting Native Americans in various "campaigns". More often than not, this amounted to nothing more than the slaughter of peaceful villages. In 1868, Custer destroyed a Cheyenne village led by Chief Black Kettle. Custer later claimed that his men killed 103 warriors. It turned out that most of the victims were old men, women and children; only eleven were fighting men including Black Kettle himself. The Cheyenne were not even at war with the Americans at this time. From that day on, the Native Americans knew Custer as "squaw-killer".

In spite of his flawed military record, by the mid-1870s Custer was still one of the most recognized celebrities of his day. He had also cultivated a new image to catch the public's imagination, wearing his reddish-blond, curly hair long and dressing in buckskin frontier clothes. Several magazine articles and a memoir – *My Life on the Plains: or, Personal Experiences with Indians* – helped acquire him an undeserved reputation as the Army's most skilled Indian fighter, although his sole plains "victory" was the massacre of 1868. But the court-martial had damaged his military career and he was desperate for a victory to re-establish his reputation and restore his flagging finances.

Custer took to the field for the last time in the spring of 1876. After the discovery of gold in the Black Hills of the Dakotas, white prospectors had flooded on to Sioux and Cheyenne land and the Army was ordered to force the natives on to reservations to make way for miners. It was presented as a defence of innocent American pioneers from Indian attack but, in truth, it was an unprovoked military invasion. After a series of bloody skirmishes in the Black Hills, the US military decided that a "severe and persistent chastisement" was required to bring the natives to submission.

In Custer's mind, the Sioux campaign might just be his big chance to make his mark on history. Which, of course, it did . . . although not perhaps in the way he had imagined.

In June, Custer and 750 men were sent out west across the Great Plains as an advance party from their base camp at Fort Lincoln to locate the villages of the Sioux and Cheyenne responsible for the Black Hills insurrections. He was under strict orders not to attack until he was joined by thousands of cavalry reinforcements. But Custer was looking for a fight. Three days later, after marching seventy-two miles, he found it on the Little Bighorn.

On 25 June, Custer stumbled on a huge camp comprising around 7,000 Sioux, Cheyenne and Arapaho bands near the Little Bighorn River. It was one of the largest groups of Native Americans ever assembled on the North American continent. Ignoring orders to wait for reinforcements and facing overwhelming superiority, Custer decided to attack.

Despite his experience of fighting Indians, he broke every rule of engagement. Warned by his Indian scouts not to light a fire because the smoke would give his position away, Custer did the opposite. He also completely underestimated his enemy. The Plains Indians were among the finest cavalrymen the world had ever seen, mostly armed with bows but many with repeat-action rifles far superior to the single-action carbines carried by the men of the 7th Cavalry.

Custer's men were far from the tough, craggy frontiersmen of the popular imagination. Nearly half were immigrants from England, Ireland, Germany and Italy. They were nervous, ill trained and, after a three-day march, desperately tired. Custer could have made it a lot easier on himself by taking with him a couple of Gatling machine-guns, which were capable of firing off 200 rounds a minute, but he didn't see the point; he said the Gatlings were too heavy and would slow him down. He is also said to have thought that the use of such a devastating weapon would cause him to lose face with the Indians. Given Custer's vanity, this isn't difficult to believe. Although he knew he was outnumbered, he didn't seem too concerned; his contempt for the Indians was well documented. He thought that the Sioux and Cheyenne would try to run away rather than fight, thus depriving him of a glorious victory that would revive his career.

His next act of stupidity, at a point where he was already hopelessly outnumbered by about ten to one, was to split his troops into three columns. Two of the three columns, led by Major Reno and Major Benteen, were instructed to ride left and right to encircle the Indian warriors. Custer would lead the third column of about 210 men, if you include packhorse drivers and native scouts, on a full frontal assault.

Dividing his force after the Indians had already spotted him was a suicidal tactical error. He never even made it to the Indian camp. Suddenly finding himself attacked from all sides by a murderous, howling mob of 4,000 well-armed warriors, his men retreated in disarray, stumbling and dying on the grassy slope above the Little Bighorn River.

Nobody really knows what happened in the final minutes. The Sioux and their allies offered very conflicting accounts and none of the white participants lived to tell the tale.[21] Judging by the remarkably small number of spent shells, there was little in the way of organized resistance and the legendary "last stand" was probably more of a panic-stricken rout. Even the most inexperienced among them had heard of the terrible tortures the Indians inflicted upon their prisoners and they all knew the old soldiers' saying: "Save the last bullet for yourself." Many of the troopers were said to have simply given up, throwing their guns away and pleading for mercy. One of the scouts was found propped up with his coffee pot and cup by his side; both were filled with his blood. His penis had been hacked off and stuffed into his mouth and his testicles staked to the ground. Some were shot by rifles, others by arrows. Several had been battered to death with stone clubs. When the body of Custer's brother Tom was found two days later, his head had been pounded to the thickness of a man's hand.

Custer himself was found stripped naked with bullet holes in his left temple and chest. His eardrums had been burst with a spiked weapon called an awl and an arrow had been lodged in his genitals. Every one of the 225 men who rode with Custer was scalped at Little Big Horn save Custer himself. Perhaps fearing the worst, he had already had his famous golden locks shorn off in favour of a close crew-cut.

The outcome might have been different had Custer received support from his subordinates Reno and Benteen. Instead, both became bogged down in defensive actions. Reno, who had been seen swigging a bottle of whisky, clearly lost his nerve. On witnessing the massacre, both men decided to make a run for it.

News of Custer's defeat, the worst military disaster in American history, reached Washington DC on 3 July, just as

---

21  From the 1870s into the 1930s, over 200 people came forward claiming to be survivors of the Little Big Horn, most as Custer's scout or a last messenger, but all were proven to be frauds. The only proven survivor was an injured US cavalry horse called Comanche. For years afterwards, he appeared in 7th Cavalry parades, rigged for riding but with an empty saddle.

people were preparing to celebrate the Centennial of the Declaration of Independence. At first the press, Army and Government were united in their condemnation of Custer for blundering into a massacre but, just like the British after the charge of the Light Brigade, America was soon doing its very best to put a gloss on it. Custer was rewarded with a hero's burial at West Point – or at least what was left of him.[22] Largely through the tireless efforts of his widow, Elizabeth, who went on speaking tours promoting her husband's legacy for the rest of her life, Custer, architect of the most astonishingly inept display of leadership in American military history, became a hero to generations of Americans; the myth of the noble US cavalry officer, battling against hopeless odds, holding off the red savages to his dying breath, would endure well into the next century. But not to the Indians, who dubbed Custer simply "a fool who rode to his death".

## Most Embarrassing Intelligence Failure

During the Second World War, the Allies were worried by the possibility that Germany might be able to build a nuclear bomb if they gained access to Norway's stocks of heavy water (deuterium oxide).

A committee was set up to investigate the possible threat with the code name "Maud". The name came after a telegram had arrived from the top Danish physicist Niels Bohr, ending with the words: "...AND TELL MAUD RAY KENT". The Allies were convinced that this could only be a coded message, possibly an anagram. Churchill's top cryptologists were set to work on decoding the message. They came up with "Radium taken..." (presumably by the Nazis?) – "U and D may react..." – indicating an atomic reaction using uranium and deuteronium – and "Make UR Day NT".

---

22  The Sioux Chief "Rain in the Face" claimed later that he had cut out Custer's heart and eaten it. He said he didn't much like the taste of human flesh, he just wanted revenge.

The mystery was finally unravelled when it turned out that Bohr was sending a message to his governess called Maud Ray who lived in Kent.

> *"Drill for oil? You mean drill into the ground*
> *to try and find oil? You're crazy."*
> Associates of Edwin L. Drake, the first man
> to drill for oil in the USA, 1859

## Most Embarrassing Intelligence Failure: Runner-Up

Since it was created in 1947, the CIA has failed to forecast almost every major political flashpoint of the last sixty-odd years, including the Iranian revolution and the fall of the Shah of Iran in 1979; the fall of the Soviet Union and the Berlin Wall in the 1980s; Indian nuclear testing in the 1990s; the attack on the World Trade Center in 2001; and the Arab Spring of 2011.

One of the CIA's earliest embarrassing failures took place in the 1950s. The Soviet Noble Prize-winning physicist Pyotr Kapitsa was an expert on low-temperature gases. In 1946, he was arrested and sent to a Gulag. Some time later, he was mysteriously released and transferred to a Soviet research institute. Naturally, the CIA wanted to know why.

Photographs taken by American U-2 spy planes of mysterious aircraft powered by hydrogen liquefaction suggested one very dangerous possibility – perhaps Kapitsa's talents had been harnessed to work on the power plant to develop a hydrogen-powered space plane.

After sinking some $6 million into trying to make their own version, the Americans realized that such a plane was not feasible. It turned out that Kapitsa had been working on an even bigger project that the CIA had somehow failed to notice – the launch of Sputnik, the world's first successfully orbited artificial satellite.

## Most Useless British General

When Britain sent an Army of 70,000 men to South Africa to fight the Boers in 1899, most people thought the war would be won within a matter of weeks. They had not reckoned on the incompetence of General Redvers Henry "Reverse" Buller.[23]

Buller was a huge man with a notorious appetite for rich food and fine wines and a speech impediment, acquired when he had received a kick in the mouth from a horse. On military campaigns, he took with him a specially made cast-iron kitchen which his men were expected to drag wherever his duties took him, along with wagons of champagne. It was rumoured that he was an alcoholic. Nevertheless, his appointment as head of the expeditionary force was hailed in the British press as a masterstroke. He had a reputation as a fearless man of action, deservedly, having served with distinction in five campaigns during the Zulu War of 1879, in which he was awarded the Victoria Cross. A contemporary noted, "There is no stronger commander in the British Army than this remote, almost grimly resolute, completely independent, utterly steadfast and always vigorous man."

Unfortunately, although Buller was a first-rate subordinate, he had never actually held a command in war and was incapable of making good decisions under pressure. His preparation before leaving for South Africa was comically inept. He returned intelligence briefings unopened on the grounds that he knew "as much about South Africa as there is to know". During training exercises, he wouldn't allow his men to dig trenches or foxholes in case they damaged the countryside or take cover in case they got their uniforms dirty. Fighting could only take place between 9 a.m. and 5 p.m. so as not to interfere

---

23   Known to his troops as "Reverse Buller" because of his record of defeats. After one spectacularly embarrassing retreat, Buller boasted to his superiors in London that he had accomplished his withdrawal without losing "a man, a flag or a cannon". When James Whistler heard about this, he added, "or a minute".

with his officers' social arrangements. Kitchener noted that Buller waged war "like a game of polo, with intervals for afternoon tea".

As far as tactics were concerned, he assumed that because the Boers were descended from Europeans, they would fight like Europeans. In other words, it was their duty to stand in the open to be shot at with British rifles. Inconveniently, the Boers however did not play by Buller's rules of war. They dressed in khaki clothes that blended into the landscape. They were also excellent marksmen and were happy to snipe at the British from concealed vantage points. This, Buller complained, was very unsporting behaviour. All the same, it simply hadn't occurred to him that there was remotest chance that his regular Army could be defeated by a group of scruffy locals.

Within days of his arrival, Buller's masterplan was in ruins. He was supposed to relieve the besieged towns of Ladysmith, Kimberley and Mafeking. Instead, his forces suffered three disastrous defeats within a week against an enemy who were mostly untrained farmers and farm boys. At the Battle of Colenso, he launched a suicidal frontal assault against well-entrenched Boer troops. At one point, his Army charged straight into a swollen river and dozens of British soldiers were drowned. The rest were dragged out by the Boers and made prisoner.

Buller sent one of his commanders, the inept General William Gatacre, known as "Backacher" to his troops, to capture a strategic railway station at Stormberg Junction. This involved sending a detachment of 2,700 men on a rapid march through the night to launch a surprise attack. It was a physically demanding plan, but Gatacre was a fitness fanatic who assumed that everyone was as fit as he was. The tactical advantage was thrown away because they forgot to take a map with them and they got lost.

When dawn broke, the confused British soldiers were surprised to find themselves at the bottom of a steep cliff. At the top of the cliff, a small unit of crack Boer riflemen was enjoying breakfast. Instead of retreating, Gatacre ordered his men to attack by climbing up the almost sheer rock face, straight into a hail of Boer bullets. Meanwhile, more Boers were arriving, attracted by the noise of the fighting. By the time Gatacre got around to calling for a retreat, twenty-eight British soldiers were dead and sixty-one were wounded. Unfortunately, Gatacre forgot to communicate his order to the 634 men who were still clinging to the cliff. They were simply left behind with no choice but to surrender. Buller telegraphed Gatacre: "Better luck next time."

Buller, meanwhile, was busy shelling a hill near Magersfontein in the belief that there was a Boer encampment at the top. The Boers were actually at the bottom of the hill enjoying the firework display. Believing that that the bombardment had softened the Boers up, Buller sent General Methuen to take the hill with 3,500 men. The Boers watched as the British troops marched confidently towards them across open ground, then opened fire; 900 British soldiers were massacred, the rest fled.

His second-in-command, General Sir Charles Warren, was somehow even more clueless than Buller. His appointment was described as "an enigma"; his previous job had been head of the Metropolitan Police while Jack the Ripper was busy killing prostitutes. He was also in the habit of bathing in public. During the battle for Hussar Hill in February 1900, Buller found Warren splashing in his bathtub when he was supposed to be directing his troops. It wasn't some kind of "bravery under fire" gesture; he was at some distance from the fighting that he was supposed to be commanding.

Buller put Warren in charge of the British forces at the critical battle for Spion Kop. For no apparent reason, both men agreed that the hill was of vital strategic importance and had to be taken. Before the battle, Warren spent twenty-six hours personally supervising the transfer of his bathtub and the rest of his personal luggage across the Tugela River, giving the Boers enough time to bolster their troops from 600 to 6,000.

Under the cover of darkness, Warren sent a team of 2,000 assault troops to climb the steep-sided hill as Buller and the rest of his Army – about 20,000 men – stood idly by and watched. Warren delegated an officer with a fractured leg to lead the climb. When his order was queried, he changed his mind and chose a disabled fifty-five-year-old to lead the assault instead.

Warren's men reached what they took to be the summit, but at first light they realized that they weren't at the summit at all. They were halfway up on an exposed plateau, roughly the size of a football pitch, surrounded by Boers on three sides. Even worse, they couldn't dig in because the terrain was rocky and they had packed only twenty shovels between them, and as someone had also forgotten to take sandbags, they had nothing to hide behind either.

The Boers opened fire and the British troops were massacred. With no means of communicating with the men on the hill, Warren could only watch. When Winston Churchill, who was there as a war correspondent, found Buller and told him that his men were being wiped out, the General had him arrested.

Buller was happy later to point an accusing finger at Warren. He wrote home to his wife: "We were fighting all last week, but old Warren is a duffer and lost me a good chance."

Warren put a different spin on it. Although 650 British soldiers lay dead with a further 554 wounded and 170 captured, he noted that "the Boers had a severe knock at Spion Kop and were ready to run on seeing British bayonets".

Buller's mistakes as a general cost him his job and his reputation. He was sacked as military commander in South Africa and placed on half pay. He returned to England disgraced, and was posted to army training at Aldershot.

Buller is often cited as an example of the Peter Principle – i.e., that people in a hierarchical organisation are promoted to their level of incompetence. As one military historian put it, "He made a superb major, a mediocre colonel and an abysmally poor general."

> *"Brains! I don't believe in brains. You haven't any, I know, Sir."*
> The Duke of Cambridge, complimenting one of his
> generals. The Duke was commander-in-chief of the
> British Army from the Crimean War until 1895. He
> did whatever he could to resist army reform and was
> particularly hostile to officers who studied warfare.

## Most Expensive Napoleonic Complex

A Napoleonic complex is a term generally used to describe short men who are driven by their perceived handicap and feelings of inferiority to overcompensate in other areas – in Napoleon's case by conquering half of Europe.[24]

The short, bandy-legged Paraguayan President Francisco Solano López (1827–70) acquired a classic Napoleonic fixation after being told, while on a trip to France in 1853, that he bore a passing resemblance to the late, great Corsican. López returned home and immediately set about redesigning Paraguay's military uniforms to look identical to those worn by the French. Meanwhile, he ordered for himself an exact replica of Napoleon's crown, then took to wearing one hand tucked inside his jacket at all times. Before long, he had several wardrobes full of fake Napoleonic military costumes worn so tight he could barely walk.

His reign alternated between extreme paranoia and brutality. Convinced of a vast conspiracy to overthrow him, López ordered hundreds of random executions, including those of two of his brothers and two brothers-in-law, plus scores of top government and military officials and several foreign diplomats.

---

24 Although, surprisingly, Napoleon wasn't particularly short for his time – about five foot six inches – but was often seen out and about with his Imperial Guard which, led to the perception of him being short because they were above-average height.

His victims were usually killed by lance thrusts to save on ammunition.

Suspicious of yet another intrigue against him, this time by Paraguay's aristocracy, López solved the problem by putting all of the sons of his country's ruling class into a single regiment, then sent them on a suicidal attack, unarmed and barefoot; all but two died. He even had his mother and sisters tortured when he suspected them of plotting against him.

In the grip of Napoleonic delusion, in 1864 López decided that his country (population 500,000) should wage war on three fronts on neighbouring countries Brazil, Argentina and Uruguay (combined population ten million). To any rational observer, Paraguay was doomed, but rational observers were in short supply, because López had long since purged anyone who disagreed with him. Hopelessly outnumbered by his enemies' armies, *el presidente* made up the numbers by drafting boys and old men. He once tried to take on the Brazilian Army by sending out a battalion of twelve-year-olds wearing false beards, and having them throw rocks when they ran out of bullets.

López trained his troops so hard and for so long that many didn't even live long enough to see a battle. Any show of dissent against the Paraguayan president's increasingly desperate military campaigns brought imprisonment, torture and lingering death.

As the military position grew ever more hopeless, López organized a spying system which encouraged every third man in his Army to rat on his comrades and to shoot anyone who showed any sign of cowardice. Many took the opportunity of shooting their officers first to avoid being shot themselves. Widespread paranoia among the ranks led to many of his men marching into battle backwards, more fearful of their own side than the enemy. When López's most senior commander found himself surrounded and facing certain defeat, he opted to blow his own brains out rather than face his president, but he missed, shooting only one eye out.

López himself always fled the battlefield at the slightest suspicion of danger and, when he ran, his generals were always
obliged to flee with him; to have shown less fear than the commander-in-chief was considered treasonable.

Meanwhile, López's mistress Eliza was doing her bit for the
war effort by touring the army camps to raise morale in a black
coach, followed by several carriage-loads of her extensive wardrobe of Parisian gowns and a grand piano. She once turned up
in the middle of a battlefield dressed in a white crinoline.

In 1870, López declared himself a Saint of the Christian
Church. When the matter was put to the bishops of Paraguay,
the twenty-three who did not agree were shot. Sainthood did
not significantly improve his military options.

At the battle of Cerro Cora, Brazilian soldiers finally caught
up with the overweight and over-decorated López and ended
his career with a bullet. By the time it was over, the War of
Triple Alliance had almost eliminated Paraguay from the map.
It is estimated that 90 per cent of the country's male population had died.

The biggest museum in Paraguay, the Museum of Military
History, has an entire room given over to their late, notorious
dictator. Highlights include a display of his pyjamas and a pair
of his giant-sized underpants.

## Most Expensive Napoleonic Complex: Runner-Up

As one of the generals who liberated his country from Spanish
rule, Antonio López de Santa Anna was a Mexican living
legend – and another leader whose head was significantly
turned by the exploits of M. Bonaparte.

When his people started calling him "the Napoleon of
Mexico", he took it to heart and took to modelling himself
upon the French emperor, right down to his hairstyle. In truth,
he couldn't have been more different from his hero, either on
or off the battlefield. Napoleon was shorting and fat; Santa
Anna was tall and skinny and only had one leg. Critically, he
rather lacked Napoleon's strategic gifts.

Apart from an early success at the Alamo, when Santa Anna struggled to defeat around 250 Texans with 2,400 Mexicans, losing nearly 600 of his men, he had the dubious distinction of losing every battle he fought in the Mexican-American War.

In one particularly inspired "surprise attack", Santa Anna dressed all of his troops in enemy uniforms. The chaos was predictable; half of Santa Anna's Army was routed by the other half and the rest were mopped up by the Americans for the loss of only twenty-six casualties.

At San Jacinto he encamped with his Army in a wood known to be full of Texan soldiers but, as it was after midday, he insisted on taking his usual siesta. While Santa Anna and his men quietly snoozed, the Texans attacked (screaming "Remember the Alamo!") and routed the entire Mexican Army in less than twenty minutes. Santa Anna himself was enjoying a nap after having pleasured a kidnapped American woman called Emily West.[25] He was later found wearing a private's uniform, hiding in a marsh.

Santa Anna was a terrible general but a born survivor. He escaped, but two years later had a leg torn off in a skirmish with the French. He recovered the severed leg and, when he eventually became the most powerful man in Mexico, he gave the limb a full State funeral. At public events, he took to riding on horseback waving his new cork leg over his head as a symbol of his sacrifices for his country.

In 1847, at the Battle of Cerro Gordo, Santa Anna was enjoying a quiet roast chicken lunch when his appetite was ruined by an uninvited regiment of Illinoisans, who stole his cork leg.

Santa Anna hopped away to fight another day but the iconic limb remained in American hands, despite many requests from the Mexican Government to return it.

---

25 The heroine celebrated in *The Yellow Rose of Texas*. There was an apocryphal story that she had been sent by Sam Houston to seduce Santa Anna to make him unprepared for the American attack.

In the 1850s, Army veterans charged a nickel or a dime for curiosity seekers to handle the leg in hotel bars. Santa Anna's prosthesis, a trophy of war, now resides in the Guard's Museum, Camp Lincoln, in Springfield, Illinois.

## Most Desperate CIA Cold War Ploy: Part 1

In the early 1950s, the CIA experimented with mind-altering drugs to see if they could find a foolproof chemical aid to assist them in interrogations. This very scientific trial mostly involved handing out LSD to Pentagon employees to see what would happen.

The CIA was forced into a rethink in November 1953 when Pentagon guinea pig Frank Olson was administered LSD by an agency representative. An internal memo explained: "On the day following the experiment, Olson began to behave in a peculiar and erratic manner and was later placed under the care of a psychiatrist."

The trials were abandoned a few days later after Olson threw himself through a New York hotel window.

---

*"If Beethoven's Seventh Symphony is not by some means abridged, it will soon fall into disuse."*

Philip Hale, Boston music critic, 1837

---

## Least Effective Attempt to Create a Good First Impression

The British Vice-Admiral Sir George Tryon (1832–93) was one of the most outstanding and highly decorated naval officers of his generation. He was also one of the most intimidating. A huge, burly man standing well over six feet tall, he had a full beard and a withering stare that was said to frighten his subordinates half to death. So when he ordered his fleet to perform a manoeuvre that would inevitably end in disaster, nobody dared question it until it was too late.

On 2 June 1893, Tryon was preparing to anchor for the night after a long day in charge of the British Mediterranean fleet on summer manoeuvres near Tripoli off the coast of Lebanon. He couldn't resist one last opportunity to show off a bit. After all, Britannia ruled the waves and it was his job to make sure that everyone knew it. Tryon wasn't usually in the habit of consulting with anyone, but on this occasion he discussed his plan with his captains in advance. The ships were to steam towards the coast in two parallel columns 1,200 yards apart; one column was to be led by Tryon on his flagship HMS *Victoria*, the other by HMS *Camperdown* under the command of Rear-Admiral Albert Markham. Each column was then to make an inwards U-turn towards each other, until they formed two new columns, sailing in the opposite direction.

There was only one problem – the warships had turning circles of 800 yards, so they would need to be at least 1,600 yards apart to avoid hitting each other. Tryon's Staff Commander, Thomas Hawkins-Smith, pointed this out. Tryon, clearly furious at having his wisdom questioned by a junior officer, brusquely overruled him. Flags were hoisted to signal the Admiral's orders to the fleet.

Rear-Admiral Markham, in charge of the other column, hesitated. It was his job as second-in-command to tell the vice-admiral that he had got his sums wrong. Tryon grew impatient, hoisting a signal flag ordering Markham to get on with it. So the doomed ships began to turn towards each other.

Now Tryon was a difficult and often dictatorial man, but he was also known to be quite brilliant at fleet handling and fond of ordering complex, unorthodox formations to keep his officers on their toes. So if any of his subordinates still had any lingering doubts, they all expected him to have a trick up his sleeve. But as the ships got closer and closer to each other, it became horribly obvious that he hadn't.

The captain of the *Victoria* asked Tryon three times for permission to put the engines into reverse. Permission was granted – too late. The ships collided and the *Victoria* sank in thirteen minutes. HMS *Camperdown* survived, but only just. The order to abandon ship came too late for many of the crew to save themselves and they went down still at their posts with the loss of 357 lives.

Tryon had somehow managed to sink one of Her Majesty's most impressive warships on a sunny day in perfect sailing conditions. Rather than face the shame of the inevitable court-martial, he chose to stay on the bridge and go down with his ship. He was heard to mutter as the waters closed in, "It's all my fault."[26]

## Most Desperate CIA Cold War Ploy: Part 2

In 1961, the CIA tried to discover Russia's Cold War secrets by installing bugging devices in a cat. They called it "Operation Acoustic Kitty".

The intention was to eavesdrop on private conversations in the vicinity of the Soviet embassy in Washington DC from window sills and park benches. Former CIA officer Victor Marchetti recalled: "They slit the cat open, put batteries in him, wired him up. The tail was used as an antenna. They made a monstrosity. They tested him and tested him. They found he would walk off the job when he got hungry, so they put another wire in to override that."

There was another design flaw they had overlooked. Acoustic Kitty was prone to wandering off in search of potential feline romance. More wires were implanted to detect and bypass his urges. After exhaustive testing, the cyborg cat was finally ready for his first assignment and was set loose in the street near the Soviet embassy followed by a CIA support truck loaded with expensive monitoring

---

26 This event inspired William McGonagall's tribute poem "The Loss of the Victoria" (see Appendix III: Selected Poems of William Topaz McGonagall).

equipment. The cat was immediately run over by a taxi cab. All the CIA had to show for their efforts was $16 million of roadkill.

It is by no means certain that this catastrophe finally killed the CIA's urge to recruit furry animals. In 2007, Iran's official Islamic Republic News Agency reported that Iranian intelligence had "detained" fourteen squirrels fitted with tiny microphones and webcams, suspected of being American spies.

To date, neither the CIA nor the Pentagon has owned up to Operation Secret Squirrel.

---

> *"The invention of aircraft will make war impossible in the future."*
>
> British novelist George Gissing, 1903

---

## Least Convincing Weapon of Mass Destruction

During the Second World War, the Allies called upon their finest scientific minds to give them a competitive edge. America turned to the Harvard chemist Dr Louis Feiser, inventor of napalm. Feiser unveiled a brand-new secret weapon he was confident would bring an early conclusion to the war with Japan – the incendiary bat.

Feiser's plan was to collect millions of bats and keep them cold, thereby inducing a state of hibernation. The slumbering bats would then be released over Japan, each carrying a tiny incendiary device containing one ounce of napalm. As the bats fell, they would warm up, settle under the eaves of buildings and set fire to them.

Feiser imagined a "surprise attack" with fires breaking out all over Tokyo at 4 a.m. Specially designed bomb casings to carry incendiary bats were manufactured for American bomber planes in a factory owned by the crooner Bing Crosby.

The plan was abandoned after trials at the Carlsbad Army Air Field in New Mexico when a number of bats, blown out of the target area by high winds, set fire to and destroyed a US army hangar and a general's car.

> *"There's no chance that the iPhone is going to get any significant market share.*
> *No chance."*
> Steve Ballmer, CEO of Microsoft, 2007

## Most Prolific Inventor of Completely Useless Military Gadgets

Britain's secret weapon during the Second World War was Geoffrey Nathaniel Pyke, civilian adviser to Combined Operations, a covert wartime think-tank headed by Lord Mountbatten. Pyke's brief was to think up new and original ideas for defeating the enemy. Within a matter of days, he was hatching the first of a series of truly eccentric plans that were to earn him the name "Professor Brainstorm".

Pyke devised a plan to avert the war by presenting the results of an opinion poll to Hitler showing that the majority of Germans wanted peace. Hitler would see the results, become discouraged and call the whole thing off. As Pyke had correctly assumed that the fascist dictator was probably dead against opinion polls *per se*, he planned to flood Germany with students, disguised as golfers, carrying clipboards in one hand and golf clubs in the other.

Although Germany had plenty of bunkers, it was not at that time known to be a nation of golf enthusiasts; however, he did persuade a few students to dress up as golfers and travel to the Third Reich. Hitler had other ideas and invaded Poland anyway. Fortunately, the students were able to flee before the Gestapo spotted them.[27]

---

27  Not all of the plans hatched by the Government's undercover "dirty tricks"

Although he enjoyed Mountbatten' support, Pyke's free-thinking visions did not go down at all well with the military brass, who were convinced that he was mad, a notion his appearance did little to dispel. Always unkempt and shabbily dressed, he wore his flies undone because it was good for his health; he once famously introduced himself in this state of undress to the Canadian Prime Minister, Mackenzie King. He mostly worked from his bed because he couldn't be bothered to get up and put clothes on and he would summon military chiefs to conferences in his Hampstead flat where they found him lying naked in bed surrounded by piles of papers, bottles, cigarette ends and other debris.

He wrote obsessively and furiously, scribbling ideas in his notebook. Periods of manic, hyperactive activity were followed by periods of depression. He would signal to his secretary that a depression was about to overcome him by humming, then shut himself away or vanish for days without explaining to anyone where he had been. In manic mode, he once phoned SO headquarters at 5 a.m. and insisted that a junior officer take dictation from him, a memo to Mountbatten. Much to the officer's fury, Pyke was still dictating an hour later.

His ideas for defeating the enemy, however, flew thick and fast. He dreamed up the "weasel", an amphibious jeep that could move easily through mud. The unique selling proposition of the weasel was that Pyke wanted it built so that it could jump sideways to avoid dive-bombers.

When he was asked to come up with a plan for the destruction of Rumania's oil fields, he suggested sending in St Bernard dogs carrying brandy, so that the Rumanian guards

---

department were quite as subtle as Pyke's. Operation Foxley was the name of a plan to kill Hitler using anthrax. Scientists pondered ways of hiding the lethal agent; they suggested the assassin could wear glasses or false teeth, or perhaps should have a "physical peculiarity such as wearing a truss or a false limb". The report noted: "Guns and hypodermic syringes disguised as fountain pens are usually not a bit convincing and are likely to lead to the death of the operator before he has had any opportunity of making his attack." After much discussion, Operation Foxley was abandoned.

would get drunk before the British attacked. He later improved on his plan by suggesting that women should carry the brandy instead of dogs; this, he explained, would more distracting for the guards.

When neither idea found much favour with the military, he came up with a better idea. British spies could start a few small fires, then British commandos could simply drive about the oilfields dressed as Romanian firemen in replica fire engines. Instead of putting out fires, the "firemen" would stoke them up by spraying them with water mixed with fused incendiary bombs.

His next project was a motorized sledge to aid travel in occupied Norway. It was controlled by a man walking behind holding reins, so that if the sledge fell into a crevasse, the driver did not – unless he forgot to let go. When the sledges were trialled, the drivers were so completely exposed to gun-fire that most preferred to ride inside and take their chances with crevasses.

A refinement to this idea was Pyke's "torpedo sledge". The sledge was to be driven slowly up a slope to tempt the Germans into giving chase. Halfway up the slope, the torpedo was to be released to roll down on to the Germans and blow them up. Just in case the equipment fell into enemy hands, it was to be marked with a sign in German warning people to keep clear: "DANGER – SECRET GESTAPO DEATH RAY". Alter-natively, Pyke suggested, the sledge was to be marked: "OFFICERS' LATRINE FOR COLONELS ONLY". The Germans, Pyke explained to his patient employees, were a very obedient race.

Just when Britain's military chiefs thought that Pyke's con-tributions couldn't possibly get any madder, he came up with his most spectacular invention of all – the *Habakkuk*. This was a huge aircraft carrier, half-a-mile long, made entirely of ice and reinforced with wood shavings – a material he called "Pykrete". This material had extraordinary properties, includ-ing remarkable strength, boasting a crush resistance greater than 300 psi – as strong as concrete but lighter. Pyke's ship was to be fitted with self-refrigerating apparatus, to keep it from melting. As the hull was thirty feet thick, it would be virtually impregnable. Pyke theorized that huge ice ships, clad in timber or cork and looking like ordinary ships but much larger, could serve as transport and aircraft carriers, while smaller ships would be adapted to attack enemy ports. The plan was for them to sail into the port and capture enemy warships by spraying them with super-cooled water, encasing them in ice and forcing them to surrender. Blocks of Pykrete would then be used to build a barrier round the port, making an impregnable fortress. From there special teams would spread out into the countryside, spraying railway tunnels with super-cooled water to seal them up and paralyse transport.

To the unscientific mind, Pyke's latest idea didn't seem at all mad. Ice is unsinkable and icebergs are known to survive for a long time even in temperate seas. Even Mountbatten warmed to Pykrete. In fact, he liked Pyke's plan so much that he interrupted Churchill's ablutions one evening by dumping a lump of Pykrete into the great man's hot bath to prove it would not melt. Churchill was also surprisingly receptive to the idea. He fired off a memo to his War Cabinet stamped "Most Secret", saying, "I attach the greatest importance to the prompt examination of these ideas. The advantages of a floating island or islands, even if only used as refuelling depots for aircraft, are so dazzling that they do not need at the moment to be discussed."

Mountbatten ordered Pyke to produce some samples of Pykrete for trials, which he did, in utmost secrecy, in a refrigerated meat locker in a Smithfield Market butcher's basement. The invention was finally unveiled at a tense secret meeting of the Allied chiefs of staff at Quebec's Château Frontenac Hotel in August 1943. Mountbatten demonstrated the strength of Pykrete in front of a group of unbelieving generals by drawing his revolver and firing at it. The bullet ricocheted off the solid lump and zipped across the trouser leg of a rather unappreciative Fleet Admiral Ernest King. Mountbatten had made his point; Churchill and Roosevelt quickly agreed that Pyke's ship should be built.

Its creator, however, was conspicuously absent from all of these high-level meetings, stunned to discover that he had been cut loose from his own project. It turns out that Pyke had sent a telegram marked "Hush Most Secret" to Mountbatten. It read simply: "CHIEF OF NAVAL CONSTRUCTION IS AN OLD WOMAN. SIGNED PYKE."

Although a prototype *Habakkuk* was actually built on a Canadian Lake and it lasted through summer without melting, the Allied invasion of Europe was already too advanced for it to be put to practical use. Pyke was later granted the rights to patent Pykrete, but he never got around to filing for them. In fact, very few projects inspired by Pyke ever got off the ground and he ended his war embittered and disillusioned.

In 1948, aged fifty-four, he said farewell to an unappreciative world by overdosing on barbiturates. On his death, *The Times* described him as "one of the most original if unrecognized figures of the present century".[28]

## Most Desperate CIA Cold War Ploy: Part 3

In 1975, the CIA hired a psychic from California to "see" details of secret military installations in the distant Soviet Union, an activity the agency described as "remote viewing".

The psychic, codenamed SG1J, was given a rough description of a suspect site in Russia and then asked to visualize it and provide details. He got a few things right, including a few squat buildings and a crane, but most of the more telling details were completely wrong. A CIA researcher reported: "One explanation of this discrepancy could be that if he mentioned

---

28  There were actually two Pykes working for the British war effort. While Geoffrey was busily alarming the top brass with his plans for ice-sculpture aircraft carriers, his cousin Magnus was attached to another think-tank working for the Ministry of Food. Magnus Pyke was one of a team of young scientists asked to come up with ideas for feeding Britain's population during a time of national food shortages. Noting blood donations were actually outstripping local storage for blood transfusions, Magnus suggested using the excess human blood to make black pudding. His idea was quietly shelved.

enough specific objects, he would surely hit on one object that is actually present."

The experiment, codenamed URDF-3, was declared unsuccessful.

---

*"No, it will make war impossible . . . "*
Hiram Maxim, inventor of the machine gun, in response
to the question: "Will this gun not make war more
terrible?" from Havelock Ellis, English scientist, 1893

---

## Most Flawed Use of Pets as Anti-Tank Devices

In the Second World War, the Nazi Blitzkrieg was a revolution in warfare. German tanks were fast and powerful and very difficult for conventional weapons to repel. They rolled over Poland with little resistance and most of Europe soon followed. The Allies were forced into a mad scramble to figure out how to slow down the onslaught. The Soviet military machine thought it had the answer.

Their plan was based on the work of a Russian, Ivan Pavlov, who won the 1904 Nobel Prize for his work studying how dogs could be conditioned to expect food. Using the example of Pavlov, the Russians starved some dogs then let them loose in a tank park. The dogs quickly learned that after being released from their pens they would find food under a tank. Once conditioned to make the connection between tanks and food, the dogs were then wired with pressure-triggered explosives. Having been denied food just before a tank attack, the dogs of war were to be unleashed into a field of oncoming German Panzers.

The plan was a partial success, but not as the Soviets had hoped. The dogs had been trained under Soviet tanks so they would run to the familiar smells and sounds of their own tanks in battle rather than the strange smells and sounds of the German tanks. With hindsight, the Soviets might have also expected that in battle a four-legged bomb would run any-where *but* towards a moving tank firing shells. At best, the dogs would spook at the rumble of a running diesel engine and run away from the battle. At worst, they became a potential threat to everyone else on the battlefield.

The anti-tank dogs were pulled from service in 1942 when several packs of hungry hounds ran amok forcing an entire Russian division into a panicked retreat.

# 5

## From Bard to Worse: Losers in Art and Entertainment

*In which a man writes poems about cheese; some theatregoers injure themselves laughing at a tragedy; an artist fails to see that less is more; and a bandage-wrapped paraplegic kicks a man dressed as a moose in the crotch.*

### Hot Doggerel: the World's Worst Poet

*"Dame Fortune has been very kind to me by endowing me with the genius of poetry."*

William McGonagall

No one followed their muse with quite the same heroic dedication as William Topaz McGonagall. His poetry was so unbelievably bad that some said his work was that of a clever hoaxer. But McGonagall's life was that of a true starving artist, a more or less tragic and continuous battle with hardship, disappointment and poverty; the only thing missing was talent.

McGonagall was one of five children born to poor Irish parents in Edinburgh in 1825. His father was a handloom weaver who travelled around Scotland to find work. The family eventually settled in Dundee where father and son became weavers in the local jute factory.

Despite a very limited education William was a prolific reader of Shakespeare and he harboured a secret ambition to become an actor. In 1858, he and his workmates clubbed together to bribe the manager of the local Theatre Royal to let him play the leading role for a remarkable two-Act version of

*Macbeth.* Determined to make the most of his big chance, in the combat scene, after being run through by the sword of Macduff, McGonagall stayed on his feet and brandished his weapon about the ears of his adversary with so much enthusiasm that the performance almost ended in actual bloodshed. The actor playing the part of Macduff repeatedly told McGonagall to "die or else" and eventually disarmed him with a well-aimed kick, but the weaponless McGonagall continued to duck and weave round Macduff like a prize fighter. Finally, Macduff threw his sword away, grabbed McGonagall by the throat and pulled him to the ground. The audience demanded seven encores of this death scene. Word of the show spread around Dundee and, at two subsequent performances, mounted police had to control the crowds. McGonagall's career as a Tragedian had begun.

In 1860, McGonagall and most of his workmates were laid off during a slump in the jute industry. This is where Australia had a very narrow escape. Most of the weavers took a ship to Queensland, but not McGonagall. He decided to take up acting full time. Travelling on foot to villages around Dundee displaying his special Shakespearean talent in halls and smithies, he scraped a living by earning sixpence here and there.

McGonagall retired from the stage at the age of forty-seven (or possibly fifty-two, he was vague about his birthdate) when in his own words, a "divine inspiration" urged him to "Write! Write!" In his autobiography, he describes how he discovered himself "to be a poet, which was in the year 1877. During the Dundee Holiday week/ in the bright and balmy month of June, when trees and flowers were in full/ bloom, while lonely and sad in my room."

He set pen to paper with his first work which was published in a local paper with the following apologia from the editor:

*W. McG of Dundee, who modestly seeks to hide his light under a bushel, has surreptitiously dropped into our letterbox an address to the Rev. George Gilfillan. Here is a sample of this worthy's powers of versification:*

*Rev George Gilfillan of Dundee,*
*There's none can you excel;*
*For you have boldly rejected the Confession of Faith,*
*And defended your cause real well.*
*The first time I heard him speak,*
*'Twas in the Kinnaird Hall,*
*Lecturing on the Garibaldi Movement,*
*As loud as he could bawl.*
*He is a liberal gentleman*
*To the poor while in distress,*
*And for his kindness unto them.*
*The Lord will surely bless.*
*My blessing on his noble form*
*And on his lofty head,*
*May all good angels guard him while living.*
*And hereafter when he's dead.*

Over the next twenty-five years, McGonagall produced more than two hundred poems, never falling below the standard set by this first epic. His choice of subject matter was eclectic and often inspired by contemporary news events. Any rhyme is a good rhyme for McGonagall, although in the whole body of his work there is not one that actually works, always striking the wrong note at every opportunity. An example of his deftness of touch is shown in these lines from his "Calamity in London; Family of Ten Burned to Death":

*Oh, Heaven! It was a frightful and pitiful sight to see*
*Seven bodies charred of the Jarvis family;*
*And Mrs Jarvis was found with her child, and both*
*    carbonised,*
*And as the searchers gazed thereon they were surprised.*

*And these were lying beside the fragments of the bed,*
*And in a chair the tenth victim was sitting dead;*
*Oh Horrible! Oh Horrible! What a sight to behold*
*The charred and burnt bodies of young and old.*

McGonagall was prolific, often at the expense of his health. In "Tribute to Dr Murison", he explains how his life was saved by a physician's advice:

> _He told me at once what was ailing me;_
> _He said I had been writing too much poetry,_
> _And from writing poetry I would have to refrain,_
> _Because I was suffering from inflammation of the brain._

He performed public recitals of his work in bars and taverns, which became enormously popular for their sheer awfulness, but McGonagall welcomed the attention and the little money it brought, despite the abuse. As he became more famous, thugs hassled him with trumpets and football rattles during his performances or showered him with dried peas.[1] He soldiered on as fruit, eggs and other missiles were thrown at him and, on one occasion, he was in mid-recital when he was felled by a brick. But nothing discouraged him. He would simply raise his voice above the uproar, determined that his inspired words should be heard.

The literary critic William Power saw McGonagall wearing full Highland dress, wielding a broadsword, oblivious to cat-calls and laughter from the audience. Power left the hall early, "saddened and disgusted".

His public readings were often halted by the police on the grounds that they constituted a breach of the peace. Most of the time, he was serenely unaffected by the reaction to his work; he put the audience's reaction down to drink. Despite the fact that most of his recitals were given in pubs, he was a staunch supporter of the Temperance movement and produced several works on the evils of strong drink (although, ironically, he attended court on at least one occasion when his daughter was "had up" for drunken brawling).

---

1   On one such occasion, he spontaneously generated the couplet:
      _"Gentlemen, please,_
      _Refrain from throwing peas!"_

McGonagall was the butt of many cruel jokes, like the time he was sent a fake invitation to meet the actor Sir Henry Irvine in London's West End. Friends raised the £1 train fare and, in June, he set off southwards on the 480-mile journey. When he finally arrived at Drury Lane Theatre and demanded to see Sir Henry, the stage door keeper chased him off. The experience gave rise to his "Descriptive Jottings of London" with its opening verse:

> *As I stood upon London Bridge and viewed the mighty throng*
> *Of thousands of people in cabs and busses rapidly whirling along,*
> *All furiously driving to and fro,*
> *Up one street and down another as quick as they could go.*

Some of his best known works were dedicated to Queen Victoria. He sent her reams of dire verse and once trudged fifty miles through the night in atrocious weather to Balmoral hoping to deliver a personal recitation of his latest poem, but didn't succeed in getting beyond the palace gates where he was threatened with arrest. Eventually, he elicited a frosty letter of acknowledgement from the Queen's private secretary, Lord Biddulph, stating that Her Majesty did not wish to receive samples of his work. This near-brush with royalty went to McGonagall's head and he had some business cards printed, on which he had restyled himself "Poet to Her Majesty".

In his lifetime, McGonagall sold just one piece of work, for which he received two guineas; a rhyme to promote Sunlight Soap:

> *Ye charwomen, where'er ye be*
> *I pray ye all be advised by me,*
> *Nay, do not think that I do joke,*
> *When I advise ye to wash with Sunlight Soap.*

> *In my time I've tried many kinds of soap,*
> *But no other soap can with it cope,*
> *Because it makes the clothes look nice and clean,*
> *That they are most beautiful to be seen.*
>
> *Ye can use it, with great pleasure and ease,*
> *Without wasting any elbow grease,*
> *And, while washing the most dirty clothes,*
> *The sweat won't be dripping off your nose.*
>
> *Therefore think of it, charwomen, one and all,*
> *And, when at any shop ye chance to call,*
> *Be sure and ask for Sunlight Soap,*
> *For, believe me, no other soap can with it cope.*
>
> *You can wash your clothes with little rubbing,*
> *And without scarcely any scrubbing,*
> *And I tell you once again without any joke,*
> *There's no soap can surpass Sunlight Soap;*
> *And believe me, charwomen, one and all,*
> *I remain, yours truly, the Poet McGonagall.*

He also wrote one praising Beecham's Pills but, as far as anyone knows, it went unsold.

In 1889, in the interests of keeping the peace, Dundee magistrates terminated his public recitals permanently and he was forced to leave the city to find work elsewhere. He gave the ungrateful people ample warning when he wrote:

> *Welcome! thrice welcome to the year 1893,*
> *For it is the year I intend to leave Dundee.*
> *Owing to the treatment I receive,*
> *Which does my heart sadly grieve.*
> *Every morning when I go out,*
> *The ignorant rabble they do shout.*
> *"There goes Mad McGonagall"*
> *In derisive shouts as loudly as they can bawl.*

Despite this threat, he stayed on until October and only left then as he and his family were evicted due to "family disturbances". After a few months in Perth, he returned to Edinburgh.[2] Despite failing health from years of working in jute dust and giving recitals in smoke-filled bars, he embarked on one final adventure in 1888 when a friend paid his steerage passage to New York so he could seek theatrical work. Three weeks later, he wired his friend for more money to return home.

William Topaz McGonagall died in poverty, unaided by the people who had paid to laugh at him, from a cerebral haemorrhage on 29 September 1902, and was buried in a pauper's grave. His final work, a poem for the coronation of King Edward VII, showed the maestro was still on form to the very end:

> *The coronation ceremony was very grand*
> *    There were countesses present, and duchesses from many a*
> *foreign land.*

The death certificate misspelled his name – "McGonigal".

## Rubbish by Royal Appointment: Worst Poet Laureate

The post of Poet Laureate has existed, with just one short gap, since 1668, when John Dryden was appointed as propagandist for the recently restored Stuart monarchy. The post has no job description to speak of and the salary is small, although in the old days there used to be a butt of best Canary wine thrown in. All the holder is expected to do is produce some verse if something important happens – a royal wedding, for example. It

---

2    His rival, the Poet Laureate Alfred Lord Tennyson, had died in the month of the McGonagalls' exodus and William hoped that he would replace him. He wrote a poem about Tennyson's death and sent a copy to the Marquis of Lorne who replied: "Sir, I thank you for your enclosure, and as a friend would advise you to keep strictly to prose for the future."

used to be a job for life until it was fixed to a term of ten years in 1999. Since Dryden, the office has been held by a handful of greats, including Wordsworth and Tennyson, several mediocre poets and two truly terrible poets. In the latter category was Henry James Pye.

Pye once said he would "rather be thought a good Englishman than the best poet or the greatest scholar that ever wrote". Which is just as well; the compiler of the *Cambridge History of English Literature* judged that Pye "was, in fact, not so much a bad poet as no poet at all". He was given the job in 1790 as a reward for his faithful support of the Prime Minister William Pitt. He specialized in rambling dirges on largely agricultural themes, including his extraordinary *The Effect of Music on Animals*. His position was also compromised by the fact that his patron, King George III, had gone completely and irretrievably mad during his laureateship. Pye did his best to avoid or to manfully circumnavigate the subject, a tricky business at the best of times, especially when it came to the obligatory annual *King's Birthday Ode*.

Another candidate for "worst ever Poet Laureate" was the eighteenth-century playwright Colley Cibber who got the job in 1730 for his support of Sir Robert Walpole rather than for his poetry – which, to be fair, even Cibber himself didn't think was up to scratch. The appointment was particularly irksome to Alexander Pope, who wrote a few scathing lines about Cibber in a couple of his poems. Cibber retaliated by pointing out that he had once stopped Pope from sleeping with a syphilitic prostitute, thereby saving Pope's life and his translations of Homer. Pope then made Cibber the "hero" of the next edition of the *Dunciad*, which has since been Cibber's main claim to fame.

The worst ever Poet Laureate was the Yorkshireman Alfred Austin, appointed after Lord Tennyson's death in 1896.[3]

---

3 When the Laureateship fell vacant in 1892, Queen Victoria expressed a preference for Algernon Charles Swinburne – "the best of my poets". It is reasonable to assume that she was unaware at the time of his reputation for

Austin trained as a barrister but, when he received a large inheritance, he left the Bar and took up writing. Law's loss was also literature's loss. He became a leader writer in the Conservative newspaper *The Standard*. He had just published his first book of prose, which sold just seventeen copies, when he was mysteriously awarded the laureateship by the Prime Minister Lord Salisbury. When asked why he had chosen such a terrible poet, Salisbury said, "I don't think anyone else applied." It has been suggested that Salisbury appointed Austin as a joke at the expense of the literary establishment because he hated intellectuals. If so, Austin didn't let him down. To celebrate the news that the Prince of Wales had fallen ill, Austin wrote:

> *Across the wires the electric message came:*
> *"He is no better. He is much the same."*

Austin was chiefly known for overblown epics and political insensitivity. One of his most infamous works, a poem celebrating the Jameson raid (a notoriously embarrassing incident for the British Government in South Africa in 1896, and a precursor to the Second Boer War a few years later) in which Austin acclaimed Jameson as a hero, was considered to be in such poor taste that it even earned a reprimand from Queen Victoria. In typical Austin fashion it began:

> *They rode across the veldt*
> *As fast as they could pelt . . .*

Austin's efforts were universally panned by the critics, who followed his career with mounting disbelief, but the poet struck a pose of lofty indifference, continuing to churn out rubbish and to lecture his public about the literary

---

cross-dressing and flagellation, not to mention the verses Swinburne had penned about Her Majesty's presumed sex life, especially the one about how she had been shagged by Wordsworth.

deficiencies of his contemporaries. When it was pointed out to him that his poems were full of basic grammatical errors, Austin replied, "I dare not alter these things. They come to me from above." Austin once complained to the judge Lord Young that he was always broke, but added, "I manage to keep the wolf from the door."

"How?" Young enquired, "By reading your poems to him?"

## Worst Poetic Tribute to a Root Vegetable

Queen Victoria had the misfortune of being pursued by two talentless but patriotic poets. The second was Joseph Gwyer, (1835–90), the "McGonagall of Penge", a potato salesman who followed his two great obsessions – poetry and potato growing – with roughly equal enthusiasm. He often combined the two, as seen in his 1875 volume *Sketches of the Life of Joseph Gwyer (Potato Salesman) With His Poems (Commended by Royalty)*.

The title was optimistic, given that at no time in his career was any of Gwyer's work ever commended by anyone, certainly not royalty, even though he had volunteered his services as unofficial Poet Laureate on several occasions over a period of twenty years. When sales of his book proved slow, Gwyer offered to throw in a sack of potatoes and a photograph of the author and his horse with every copy. A reviewer in the *New York Tribune* recommended that customers not sure whether to choose the poetry or the potatoes should choose the latter.

The potato theme looms large throughout Gwyer's work. In *Love and Matrimony*, the poet points out that the most important thing a man should look for in his choice of bride is an ability to cook and roast "POTATOES" (in Gwyer's work, the word "potatoes" was always underlined or written in capitals). Gwyer's potato theme often baffled his public but was not lost on his critics. *Punch* began a review of his work "The Alexandra Palace, Muswell Hill, Destroyed by Fire", with the observation: "We consider this work no small potatoes."

## The Ode Less Travelled

*"The quality is often vile*
*Of cheese that is made in April*
*Therefore we think for that reason*
*You should make it later in the season."*
            *Dairy Ode*, James McIntyre (1827–1906)

Love ... friendship ... death ... daffodils. These are just a few of the things that have inspired poets for centuries.

For James McIntyre, it was cheese.

McIntyre was born in Scotland and his family emigrated to Canada in 1841 when he was fourteen. He later moved to Ingersoll, Ontario, a town of 5,000 in the heart of Canadian dairy country, where he set himself up as a cabinet maker, furniture dealer and undertaker. Meanwhile, he published a couple of volumes of his poems on a variety of subjects – patriotism, Canadian authors, Ontario towns, farming, foreign wars, to name but a few. The great theme of his life's work, however, was the poetic celebration of dairy produce. His output included "Lines Read at a Dairymaids' Social", 1887; "Fertile Lands and Mammoth Cheese"; "Lines Read at a Dairymen's Supper"; "Father Ranney, the Cheese Pioneer"; and Hints to Cheese Makers". His best known work – "Ode on the Mammoth Cheese Weighing Over 7,000 Pounds" – celebrated an actual cheesy comestible produced in 1866 for an exhibition in Toronto:

*We have seen thee, queen of cheese,*
*Lying quietly at your ease,*
*Gently fanned by evening breeze,*
*Thy fair form no flies dare seize.*

*All gaily dressed soon you'll go*
*To the great Provincial show,*

> To be admired by many a beau
> In the city of Toronto.

> Cows numerous as a swarm of bees,
> Or as the leaves upon the trees,
> It did require to make thee please.
> And stand unrivalled, queen of cheese.

> May you not receive a scar as
> We have heard that Mr Harris
> Intends to send you off as far as
> The great world's show at Paris.

> Of the youth beware of these,
> For some of them might rudely squeeze
> And bite your cheek, then songs or glees
> We could not sing, oh! queen of cheese.

> Wert thou suspended from balloon,
> You'd cast a shade even at noon,
> Folks would think it was the moon
> About to fall and crush them soon.

The Toronto *Globe* and the *New York Tribune* published a few of his poems for comic relief but the general mockery did not dampen his enthusiasm and he continued to write until his death in 1906.

For the lactose intolerant, cheese was not the only challenging subject James McIntyre rose to. This is his ode to orthopaedics entitled "Wooden Leg":

> Misfortune sometimes is a prize,
> And is a blessing in disguise;
> A man with a stout wooden leg,
> Through town and country he can beg.

> And when he only has one foot,
> He needs to brush only one boot;

> *Through world he does jolly peg,*
> *So cheerful with his wooden leg.*
>
> *In mud or water he can stand*
> *With his foot on the firm dry land,*
> *For wet he doth not care a fig,*
> *It never hurts his wooden leg.*
>
> *No aches he has but on the toes*
> *Of one foot, and but one gets froze;*
> *He has many a jolly rig,*
> *And oft enjoys his wooden leg.*

McIntyre's genius was rediscovered by William Arthur Deacon, literary editor of the Toronto newspaper *Mail and Empire*, who republished some of McIntyre's work in an anthology entitled *The Four Jameses* (1927), reprinted in 1974. His art has since been perpetuated in *Oh! Queen of Cheese: James McIntyre, the Cheese Poet* (1979), edited by Roy Abrahamson, and in *Very Bad Poetry* (1997) by Kathryn and Ross Petras. An annual poetry contest is held in Ingersoll, Ontario, in his honour.

## Least Successful Attempt to Spot a Great Writing Talent

Even the greatest writers have experienced rejection. When George Orwell submitted *Animal Farm*, he was told it was "impossible to sell animal stories in the USA". H. G. Wells' book *The Time Machine* was dismissed as "not interesting enough for the general reader and not thorough enough for the scientific reader". Vladimir Nabokov was told that his *Lolita* manuscript should be "buried under a large stone". Herman Melville's *Moby Dick*, was rebuffed as "not at all suitable for the juvenile market. It is very long, rather old-fashioned."

Before it was eventually printed, the 1981 Pulitzer Prize-winning book *A Confederacy of Dunces* was rejected by two dozen publishers. Unfortunately, belated success did little good for the author, John Kennedy Toole. In despair over his repeated failures to find a publisher, he committed suicide at the age of thirty-one. The book was submitted to a publisher by his mother Thelma and published posthumously eleven years after the death of her son.

The origin of Toole's title, a quote by the author Jonathan Swift, was grimly ironic. "When a true genius appears in the world, you may know him by this sign, that the dunces are all in confederacy against him."

---

> *"Guitar bands are on the way out, Mr Epstein."*
> Decca executive Dick Rowe, explaining to Beatles manager
> Brian Epstein why his band failed their audition.

---

## Worst Published Author of Pulp Fiction

*"Keeler is to good literature as rectal cancer is to good health . . . given the choice of reading three Keeler novels back to back or being imprisoned in an Iranian jail, you'd need to think about it."*

Otto Penzler, book critic at the *New York Sun*

Between 1924 and 1967, the American author Harry Stephen Keeler churned out seventy novels and scores of short stories containing plots so nonsensical and characterization so badly written that they have been called "coincidence porn".

Harry Stephen Keeler's home town, Chicago,[4] features a lot in his writings. His childhood there was troubled. His mother, a widow several times over, ran a boarding house for theatrical performers. For reasons unknown, when Keeler was about twenty, she had him committed to a mental hospital. This was the beginning of his lifelong

---

4  "The London of the west" according to Keeler.

obsession with the insane and a deep hatred of the psychiatric profession.[5]

In 1912, he got an electrical engineering degree and for the next two years worked as an electrician in a South Chicago steel mill, writing short stories on the side. Typical of these early tales is "Victim No. 5", which he sold to *Young's Magazine* in 1914 for $10. The protagonist Ivan Kossakoff is a professional strangler of women, who ends his days locked in a vaudeville performer's theatrical trunk and is squeezed to death by the pet boa constrictor living inside it.

Between 1914 and 1924, Keeler sold dozens of short stories with titles such as "The Trepanned Skull", "The Stolen Finger" and "The Giant Moth". His first novel *The Voice of the Seven Sparrows* published in 1924[6] introduced the public to Keeler's complicated "webwork" storylines, in which several strings of outrageous coincidences and odd events would end in a surprising and completely implausible denouement. It is almost impossible to provide a plot summary of a Keeler book because they have no plot – or perhaps, more accurately, they have a hundred plots all leading nowhere. He claimed to have built his stories from randomly selected newspaper articles: he would reach into a thick file of cuttings he kept, randomly pull out a handful then try to work them into a narrative.

Here are some typical Keeler situations. In *The Man with the Magic Eardrums* (1939), a disgruntled former phone company employee calls every man in Minneapolis, informing each of them that the morning newspapers will name him as the secret husband of the convicted murderess Jemimah

---

5   One of Keeler's finest was a 135,000-word novel written in the first person whose narrator chases an escaped lunatic millionaire. The narrator uses a variety of disguises and personalities, but turns out to be the lunatic himself.

6   In which a rival Chicago newsman searches for a publisher's missing daughter and encounters Ng Chuen Li Yat, a Chinese millionaire who bet a fortune that he could walk across South America in a year and a half and Peter Zeller, a shipwreck survivor who mails 14,257 identical two-of-spades cards in order to trap one man.

Cobb, who runs a brothel specializing in women with physical abnormalities.

In *The Spectacles of Mr Cagliostro* (1929), the main character, thanks to a mysterious clause in a Will, is obliged to wear a pair of hideous blue glasses continuously for a whole year so that he will eventually be able to see a secret message that is visible only with the blue glasses.

In *The Case of the Transparent Nude* (1958), a woman's body vanishes while she taking a steam bath. Her head and toes remain, sticking out of the steam cabinet, with only her torso missing.

Woe to readers who think they might be able to guess the ending. In Keeler's crime thrillers, the character who will be revealed as the guilty party is usually introduced, for the first time, near – if not actually on – the last page of the book. In *X Jones of Scotland Yard* (1936), a man is found dead, apparently strangled, in the middle of his lawn, but there are no footprints other than his own. The police have a suspect, the "flying Strangler Baby", a homicidal midget who disguises himself as a baby and stalks victims by helicopter; in last sentence of the last page of this 448-page story, Keeler reveals that Napoleon Bonaparte is the culprit.

His special talent was not confined to surreal plot lines. His characters have names like Criorcan Mulqueeny, Screamo the Clown, Scientifico Greenlimb, Wolf Gladish and State Attorney Foxhart Cubycheck. His prose is largely indecipherable. Here is a sample passage from *The Case of the 16 Beans*:

> The door now opened, revealing, as it did so, a strange figure – a half-man, no less, seated on a "rollerskate" cart! – framed against the bit of outer hallway. But no ordinary half-man this, for he was a Chinaman; quite legless, indeed, so far as the presence of even upper leg stumps went; but amply provided with locomotion, of the gliding kind, anyway, in the matter of the unusually generous rubber-tired wheels under the platform cart.

Many of Keeler's works were colossal, including the 741-page *The Matilda Hunter Murder* (1931), which followed the exploits of Tuddleton T. Trotter, a patron of homeless cats; and *The Box from Japan* (1932), which ran to 765 pages. Not so much un-put-downable as un-pick-upable.

In the mid-1930s, Keeler briefly enjoyed cult status. His popularity peaked when his book *Sing Sing Nights* (1933) was loosely used in a low-budget B-movie, as was *The Mysterious Mr Wong* (1935), starring the screen legend Bela Lugosi. During this time, Keeler was also the editor of *Ten Story Book*, a popular pulp short-story magazine that included photos of nude and scantily clad young women. He filled the spaces between the stories with frequent plugs for his own books, as well as illustrations by his wife.

After his initial popularity, Keeler's writing style grew increasingly more baroque. In the late 1930s, he removed almost all of the action and presented it through page after page of impenetrable dialogue. For example, *The Portrait of Jirjohn Cobb* (1940), described affectionately by the Harry Keeler Appreciation Society as "one of the most astoundingly unreadable novels ever written", comprises four characters, two talking in a strange unfathomable dialect, sitting on an island in the middle of a river, talking and listening to a radio. This goes on for hundreds of pages.

By the early 1940s, even his most dogged fans had given up. After exhausting the patience of two or three English language publishers, he continued to publish in Spanish and Portuguese. When those outlets also dried up, he carried on writing anyway. The *New York Times* noted, "We are drawn to the inescapable conclusion that Mr Keeler writes his peculiar novels merely to satisfy his own undisciplined urge for creative joy."

Keeler died in his sleep on 22 January 1967, leaving a dozen books unfinished, confident that one day he'd be read again. He has been vindicated; today his spirit lives on on websites, a bi-monthly newsletter devoted to him and a small publishing house systematically issuing his complete works, including several never published in his lifetime. (See Keeler's Bibliography in Appendix I.)

## Least Perceptive Creator of Character with Superhuman Powers of Perception

You couldn't put one past Sherlock Holmes. Unfortunately, the same could not be said about his creator, Sir Arthur Conan Doyle.

Unlike his famous fictional detective, rational, deductive reasoning was not Conan Doyle's thing. In fact, he was a credulous dupe for all kinds of pseudo-science and trickery. When he wasn't writing about world's most logical detective, in his spare time he was lecturing on life after death, automatic writing, spirit photography and ectoplasm, as well as publishing books of predictions from his wife's spirit guide, Pheneas.

He also had an unlikely friendship with the American showman and escapologist Harry Houdini, who had once made a fully grown elephant vanish from the stage of the New York Hippodrome; he'd also escaped from locked boxes, wriggled out of a straitjacket while dangling from a crane and once spent an hour-and-a-half in an iron coffin submerged at the bottom of a swimming pool.

Conan Doyle devoted a whole chapter of his book *The Edge of the Unknown* to Houdini, making a detailed argument that he had genuine psychic powers, although Houdini made no such claims for himself. He once showed Conan Doyle and his wife the simple children's party trick of apparently removing the top of his thumb. Lady Conan Doyle swooned at the sight and her husband later wrote to Houdini congratulating him on his "amazing demonstration of supernatural powers".

Houdini was prepared to overlook his friend's gullibility until a bizarre incident in 1922. Conan Doyle developed an interest in spiritualism after the death of his eldest son in the First World War, and it became something of an obsession. He invited Houdini to attend a séance conducted by Lady Conan

Doyle, during which she "communicated" with Houdini's recently deceased mother. Lady Conan Doyle told Houdini that his late departed mum sent her seasonal Christmas greetings. As Houdini's mother was Jewish, her first words from the other side were unlikely to be "Merry Christmas, son". Moreover, as she spoke only Yiddish, it was even more unlikely that she and Lady Conan Doyle would have had much of a conversation. Mrs Houdini also neglected to mention the coincidence that it was her birthday. After that, Houdini's relationship with Conan Doyle turned into a full-blown public feud as he publicly denounced Lady Conan Doyle as a fraud.

In spite of the battering his reputation had taken, Conan Doyle's belief in spiritualism remained firmly intact,[7] but that was the least of it. He also believed in fairies.

In the summer of 1917, a ten-year-old girl named Frances Griffiths was on holiday in the village of Cottingley in Yorkshire. Her favourite game was messing about beside the stream at the bottom of the garden with her sixteen-year-old cousin Elsie Wright. When Frances returned home soaking wet one day, her mother demanded to know what she had been up to. "Playing with fairies," was the child's answer. To prove it, she borrowed her father's camera. The next time she came back from the stream she had pictures, taken by her cousin, of Frances in the garden with several fairies dancing in front of her. There was another with Frances and a gnome sitting on the hem of her dress. In total, there were five magical Cottingley photos.

A few weeks later Elsie's mother attended a meeting of the Theosophical Society[8] in Bradford. The lecture that evening was on "Fairy Life" and she happened to mention the

---

7   Conan Doyle was a firm believer in contact with the spirit world to the day he died, convinced that one day he would be vindicated. Although, to be fair, we haven't heard much from him since.

8   According to Wikipedia, "The theosophist seeks to understand the mysteries of the universe and the bonds that unite the universe, humanity and the divine. The goal of theosophy is to explore the origin of divinity and humanity, and the end of world, life and humanity." They also believe in fairies.

pictures. Word spread and, in 1920, Conan Doyle got to hear about them.

Coincidentally, at the time the photographs surfaced, he was writing an article about fairies for the Christmas edition of *The Strand Magazine*. He saw the fairy pictures and was very impressed. Just to be certain of their authenticity, he sought the opinion of a couple of photographic experts. First, he showed them to the photographic company Ilford, who reported unequivocally that there was "some evidence of faking". The technicians at Kodak said the pictures showed no signs of having been faked, but declined to issue a certificate of authenticity. He then sought a third opinion from the famous physicist Sir Oliver Lodge, who believed the photographs to be fake, on account of the fairies' "distinctly 'Parisienne'" hair-styles. None of this seems to have bothered Canon Doyle, who promptly declared them genuine and stuck to his guns in the face of considerable mockery.

So convinced was he that he even wrote a book – *The Coming of Fairies* – in which he lays out the story of the photo-graphs, their supposed provenance and the implications of their existence.[9] He wasn't in the least troubled by the fact that the fairy wings in the photographs never showed signs of blurred movement, even in the picture of the fairy calmly posed suspended in mid-air. Apparently, fairy wings don't work like the wings of a hummingbird.

Elsie Wright stuck to her story until 1983, when her "fair-ies" were found in a 1915 children's anthology. Only then did the 83-year-old woman admit she had copied the pictures, glued them on to a bit of cardboard and fixed them on some nearby bushes with hat-pins. The great Conan Doyle, creator of the most rational fictional character of all time, had been taken in by a 16-year-old girl with a pot of glue.

---

9  Still on sale today. According to the publishers' blurb, "This quirky and fascinating book allows us to get inside the mind of an intelligent, highly respected man who just happened to believe in fairies."

# Most Pointless Literary Hoax

In 1902, Montgomery Carmichael, a member of the British consular service in Italy and the author of a number of European travel books, went to his publishers with what seemed at first to be a proposal for a straightforward biography.

He explained that he had been left in the Will of a friend, Philip Walshe, a large and extraordinary collection of valuable manuscripts. They were the works of his father, the late Mr John William Walshe, who died on 2 July 1900, aged sixty-three, at Assisi, Umbria, where he had spent the latter half of his life. Mr Walshe, he explained, was well known to scholars as perhaps the greatest living authority on the Franciscan order of monks. It was duly published as *The Life of John William Walshe*.

It was only some time later that someone pointed out that the name of Walshe does not figure in any actual list of Franciscan scholars, living or dead. *The Life of John William Walshe* was the detailed portrait of a man who had never existed. The work was an elaborate hoax.

Librarian Edmund Lester Pearson called it "one of the most inexplicable examples of the literary hoax . . . it contained not one atom of satire, it was not a parody, and so far as I, at least, could have discovered by internal evidence, it was what it purported to be: a sober and reverent biography of an Englishman dwelling in Italy, a devout member of the Church of Rome, and in particular an enthusiastic student and pious follower of St Francis of Assisi."

Carmichael never offered an explanation for perpetrating the hoax.

---

*"My biggest fear is that we will be too successful."*
Walt Disney chairman Robert Fitzpatrick on the opening
of Disneyland Paris 1992. Over twenty years later,
it has amassed losses of €1.9 billion and, according
to financial experts, may never turn a profit.

## Worst Published Author

*"I expect I will be talked about at the end of 1,000 years."*
Amanda McKittrick Ros

Almost anyone can knock out a bad book, but to achieve fame and adulation for doing it takes a certain kind of genius.

The Irish author Amanda McKittrick Ros (or to give her adopted pen name – Amanda Malvina Fitzalan Anna Margaret McClelland McKittrick Ros) was born Anna Margaret McKittrick in 1860 to a middle-class Presbyterian family in Ballynahinch, County Down, Ireland. From 1884, she trained as a schoolteacher at Marlborough Training College, Dublin, and got her first full teaching post at Larne where she met her future husband, the local stationmaster, Andrew Ross. She dropped the second "s" of Ross to suggest a non-existent association with a noble family called de Ros from County Down.

She was in her thirties when she discovered that she had a gift for, in her own words, "disturbing the bowels" with a unique style which she attributed to never having read anything. Under the impression that authors always paid for the printing of their works, in 1897 she persuaded her husband to have her first novel *Irene Iddesleigh* produced as a wedding anniversary present. A tragic tale of an unhappy marriage and the doom that inevitably follows, it introduced to the world her unique use of language. Nothing is ever described in a straightforward way. For example, "needlework" became "the use of the finest production of steel, whose blunt edge eyed the reely covering with marked greed, and offered its sharp dart to faultless fabrics of flaxen fineness". The critic Northrop Frye described her prose as "a kind of literary diabetes". In this passage, the hero Sir John remonstrates with Irene because she is cold towards him:

> *Irene, if I may use such familiarity, I have summoned you hither, it may be to undergo a stricter examination than your*

*present condition probably permits; but knowing, as you should, my life must be miserable under this growing cloud of unfathomed dislike, I became resolved to end, if within my power, such contentious and unlady-like conduct as that practised by you towards me of late. It is now six months – yea, weary months – since I shielded you from open penury and insult, which were bound to follow you, as well as your much-loved protectors, who sheltered you from the pangs of penniless orphanage; and during these six months, which naturally should have been the pet period of nuptial harmony, it has proved the hideous period of howling dislike!*

Nobody took much notice of *Irene Iddesleigh* until, by chance, the humourist and critic Barry Pain got hold of a copy and wrote a mocking review in the magazine *Black in White* calling it "the book of the century".

When Amanda Ros read the review, she was deeply hurt. From that moment, she came to regard critics in general, and Pain in particular, as her mortal enemies – or, as she called them, "evil-minded snapshots of spleen".[10] Without Pain's review, it is likely that she would have slid into obscurity, but thanks to his efforts she established a cult following among connoisseurs of bad taste. London's literary élite threw Amanda McKittrick Ros parties at which they would take it in turns to recite favourite passages.

Meanwhile, she was hard at work on her second novel *Delina Delaney*, a larger and more ambitious effort, twice as long as *Irene Iddesleigh* and populated with a wider cast of characters, including the unforgettable Madam-de-Maine. Like her first effort, it was published privately in 1898. Much of it remains impervious to comprehension. See what you make of the opening lines:

---

10 She continued her attack on Barry Pain in the preface to her next novel *Delina Delaney* by branding Pain a "clay crab of corruption" and a "cancerous irritant wart" and suggested that he was antagonistic because he was secretly in love with her.

> *Have you ever visited that portion of Erin's plot that offers its*
> *sympathetic soil for the minute survey and scrutinous examina-*
> *tion of those in political power, whose decision has wisely been*
> *the means before now of converting the stern and prejudiced,*
> *and reaching the hand of slight aid to share its strength in aug-*
> *menting its agricultural richness?*

Parts of *Delina Delaney* were made even more inaccessible by
being written in an obscure Irish dialect known only to the
author. In this extract, Delina's mother hears of the engagement of her daughter to Lord Gifford:

> *Raising her hands above her head, Mrs Delaney first looked at*
> *her daughter, then at Lord Gifford, saying, "Father ive saints!*
> *is it thrue dthat mac poor choild has tuk lave ive hur sinses buy*
> *pramisin' ta be dthe woife ive our koind an' good landlady's*
> *son, an' hur jist dthe offspring ive poor Joe Delaney-a poor old*
> *fisherman?"*

In 1908, she inherited some property from a friend, much to
the resentment of her neighbours with whom she had fallen
out; she liked to remind them that she was a direct descendant
of King Sitric of Denmark. The Will was ambiguous in certain parts, which led to a great deal of legal wranglings.
Inevitably, lawyers joined Amanda's hate-list. Of one she
wrote:

> *Readers, did you ever hear*
> *Of Mickey Monkeyface McBlear?*
> *His snout is long with a flattish top,*
> *Lined inside with a slimy crop:*
> *His mouth like a slit in a money box,*
> *Portrays his kindred to a fox.*

Her next work, *Poems of Puncture*, was largely an invective
against lawyers and an effort intended to recoup some of the
money she had lost in legal costs.

In 1914, Ros decided to become a war poet and limited her output to patriotic gems which she had printed and distributed to soldiers and sailors billeted in Larne. "A Little Belgian Orphan" includes this description of supposed German atrocities:

> *Just then they raised the little lad and threw him on the fire*
> *   And wreathed in smiles they watched him burn until he did*
> *expire . . .*

In another she tells some soldiers:

> *We know you'll do your duty and come to little harm*
> *And if you meet the Kaiser, cut off his other arm.*

In 1917, her husband of thirty years fell ill and died. At his funeral, she snubbed various mourners by ordering the funeral hearse to move off at a trot and leave them stranded behind. She then went through the wreaths and those she didn't like were dispatched back to their donors.

For a while, she ran a couple of shops from her house, "Iddesleigh", but the business venture failed, mainly due to her local unpopularity. Fortunately, she met and married a well-off farmer and, from that time on, was financially secure and able devote herself to her writing. For the next few years, in between attacks on the English language, she issued a torrent of mostly abusive verse on her pet subjects – lawyers, fashion, the Kaiser, the abandonment of moral standards, clerics and critics, whom she called "scribblers of thick witted type". Her intense hatred on these themes found its way into nearly all her works, whether relevant to the story or not.

Ros's last novel – *Helen Huddleston* – continued the theme of tragic heroines, but was also an opportunity to vent more spleen on the subject of lawyers. She named most of the characters after fruit and vegetables, including Lord Raspberry, Sir Peter Plum, the Earl of Grape and Sir Christopher Currant, and a maid called Lily Lentil.

The author's fondness for crimes against alliteration is also given full rein. We learn that the villainous Madame Pear, a brothel keeper who secretly plans to make the virgin Helen a star attraction of her house of ill-repute, "had a swell staff of sweet-faced helpers swathed in stratagem, whose members and garments glowed with the lust of the loose, sparkled with the tears of the tortured, shone with the sunlight of bribery, dangled with the diamonds of distrust, slashed with sapphires of scandals . . ."

About halfway through the novel, she also develops the habit of interjecting random foreign words and phrases into her text, such as "capriole!" and "coup-de-main". Here is Lord Raspberry at dinner the night before he will kidnap the unsuspecting Helen Huddleston:

*In Helen Huddleston, he had seen a trunk of truism branching forth into womanhood. He was convinced that through time his desires would be directed towards every element of chastity pure and unadulterated it had not been his province yet to master.*

*As he sat meditating on the digestion of a female fowl, pebble-dashed with meagre crumbs and damped with that delicious coat of delicacy for which an empty stomach and a dry tongue craves, the room seemed to whirl round him while a silvery mist blurred his vision enveloping him in a cloak of cobwebbed frailty.*

*On his finger rested an historic ring centred with a gem of tradition that he boldly asserted was instrumental in creating evil in all its fulsome phases within the minds of its numerous possessors. Shaped like a spear in a cloud of dull white edged with delicate blue, in which could be seen a traitor's star resembling that of Rasputin when on his pinnacle of monkdom, meting out his prayers of mockery to the duped goddess of Russia.*

*Helen Huddleston* was never completed. As she worked on the final chapters, her fingers became increasingly crippled with rheumatism and she was forced to give it up.

Ros had spent her entire career in lengthy and vitriolic feuds with critics but she could give as good as she got. She once wrote a 10,000-word tirade against D. B. Wyndam Lewis who had written a sarcastic review of *Irene Iddesleigh*, judging it "a better book than *Some Reactions of Colloidal Protozoids* or *The Chartered Accountants' Year Book* for 1926."

She imagined she had a legion of literary fans who thirsted "for aught that drops from my pen" and she never quite recovered from what she took to be the massive snub of failing to secure a nomination for the Nobel Prize for Literature in 1930. But she did have fans. The heaving bosoms, trembling lips, quivering voices and clammy hands that inhabit her world won her many admirers among the literary élite. Mark Twain called *Irene Iddesleigh* "one of the greatest unintentionally humorous novels of all time". In 1928, Aldous Huxley dedicated an essay to her dazzling synonyms, which included such gems as "sanctified measures of time" (Sunday); "globes of glare" (eyes); "bony supports" (legs); "southern necessary" (pants); and "globules of liquid lava" (sweat). Shortly after the Second World War, C. S. Lewis and J. R. R. Tolkien discussed her work in their literary group, the Inklings. The task was to see who could read aloud the longest without breaking into "helpless laughter".

Her final published work was a second collection of verses, *Fumes of Formation*. She died after a fall in her home in February 1939 at the age of seventy-eight. At the time, Ros was working on her final unfinished poem "Donald Dudley, the Bastard Critic".

Although none of her books are currently still in print, a few Ros enthusiasts have kept her legend alive. A biography – *O Rare Amanda!* – was published in 1954 and a collection of her most memorable passages was published in an anthology called *Thine in Storm and Calm* in 1988. In 2008, she was also fêted at a Belfast literary festival.

One of her rarest books, *Bayonets of Bastard Sheen* (1949), compiled from letters written between 1927–39, mostly comprising attacks on critics, fetched £15,400 at auction.

## Most Pointless Work of Literature

In 1939, the world was on the brink; dark clouds were gathering as half of Europe reeled under the heel of fascism. It was a time for writers and artists to stand up and be counted. The American author Ernest Vincent Wright rushed to his typewriter – to write a 50,000-word novel without using the letter "e".

Wright spent five-and-a-half months composing his opus *Gadsby*, helpfully subtitled *A Novel of Over 50,000 Words Without Using the Letter E*. He used string to tie down the "e" key on his typewriter to make sure that it was never used accidentally. Wright failed to find a publisher and used his own money to bring out the book in 1939. Despite the magnitude of his achievement, the critics were unkind. One reviewer noted, "This book is a bit shit, frankly."[11]

This excerpt from the beginning of the book will enable you to judge for yourself:

> *If youth, throughout all history, had a champion to stand up for it; to show a doubting world that a child can think; and, possibly, do it practically; you wouldn't constantly run across folks today who claim that "a child don't know anything". A child's brain starts functioning at birth; and has, amongst its many infant convolutions, thousands of dormant atoms, into which God has put a mystic possibility for noticing an adult's act, and figuring out its purport.*

Wright died a few months after publication. He is also the author of a humorous short poem: "When Father Carves the Duck".

## Worst Science-Fiction Writer

The awful truth of bad published science-fiction writing is that it only represents the tip of the iceberg. The really atrocious stuff, it should go without saying, never gets published at

---

11  Notice what he didn't do there? Use the letter "e".

all. At least, that used to be the case before self-publishing and the Internet ensured that just about anyone can publish anything, bypassing all the traditional obstacles which have irritated writers through the centuries, such as editorial standards and censorship. So for a sci-fi work to be so memorably bad that it somehow rises above the dross that surrounds it is truly remarkable.

The genre's most beloved piece of appalling prose was tapped out on duplicator stencils by a typist who, according to sci-fi critic David Langford, "could usefully have been replaced by a infinite number of monkeys". The result was Jim Theis's legendary fantasy epic *The Eye of Argon* – the worst fiction ever to see the light of day.

Theis was a sixteen-year-old science-fiction fan living in St Louis, Missouri, when he submitted his work to a fanzine in 1970. Some time in the late 1970s, the Californian sci-fi writer Chelsea Quinn Yarbro got hold of a copy and showed it to other fans. It received a huge and incredulous reaction and was soon copied and distributed widely around science-fiction fandom. Readings quickly became a common item on science-fiction convention programmes.

*The Eye of Argon* is a sword-and-sorcery novella featuring the adventures of a wandering swordsman called Grignr. The plot is basically as follows: Grignr the Ecordian is thrown into a dungeon after a bar brawl, escapes after fashioning a makeshift knife from the pelvic bone of a dead rat, attacks a group of priests offering up a sacrifice of a prostitute to their heathen god, then steals a bauble, the Eye of Argon, which metamorphoses into a cloud of vapour and attacks our hero, Grignr. (For those unable to contain their curiosity, please see Appendix IV – Chapter 1 of *The Eye of Argon*.)

Theis's book has been made into a party game at sci-fi conventions. The challenge is to read it aloud, straight-faced, without choking and falling over. Strict rules apply, including reading all of Theis's mistakes exactly as written. Make it through a whole page without laughing and you become a "grand master".

The version which currently circulates on the Internet was painstakingly transcribed by Don Simpson from Theis's original and bears his note at the bottom:

> *No mere transcription can give the true flavour of the original printing of* The Eye of Argon. *It was mimeographed with stencils cut on an élite manual typewriter. Many letters were so faint as to be barely readable, others were overstruck, and some that were to be removed never got painted out with correction fluid. Usually, only one space separated sentences, while paragraphs were separated by a blank line and were indented ten spaces. Many words were grotesquely hyphenated. And there were illustrations — I cannot do them justice in mere words, but they were a match for the text. These are the major losses of this version (#02) of* The Eye of Argon.

Many people who have read *The Eye of Argon* find it hard to believe the story was not a collaborative effort or an intentional sci-fi satire but, in a rare 1984 radio interview, Jim Theis confessed that he was genuinely hurt by the negative reaction to his work. A copy of a 1995 reprint was sent to him, with no response. He died without addition to his literary canon in 2002.

## Most Non-PC Travel Guide

In 1850, the British explorer Francis Galton spotted a gap in the travel guide market. There was, he thought, a shortage of useful information for those who had to "rough it" in a foreign land. He followed up with his 366-page book *Art of Travel*.

Galton's guide was packed with such useful tips as: how to stay afloat by using an inflated antelope skin; how to keep your clothes dry in a rainstorm (take them off and sit on them, in case you were wondering); how to avoid blisters (break a raw egg into each boot and fill your socks with soapsuds); how to get rid of lice (make yourself a necklace out of mercury, old tea leaves and saliva); and how to prevent your teeth from falling out if you catch scurvy (spread treacle and lime juice on your gums).

Galton also offers tips on dealing with foreigners. He advises that "a skulking negro may sometimes be smelt out like a fox". In a section on "The Management of Savages", he wrote: "A sea captain generally succeeds in making an excellent impression on savages ... if a savage does mischief, look at him as you would a kicking mule, or a wild animal whose nature it is to be unruly and vicious, and keep your temper quite unruffled ... a savage cannot endure the steady labour that we Anglo-Saxons have been bred to support. His nature is adapted to alternatives of laziness and severe exertion."

*Art of Travel* is no longer in print.

---

*"If anything remains more or less unchanged,
it will be the role of women."*
David Riesman, conservative American social scientist, 1967

---

## Worst Foreign Language Phrasebook

In 1855, Pedro Carolino decided to write the first ever Portuguese-English phrase book. He wasn't about to be put off by the fact that he did not actually speak any English. Inconveniently, he also lacked a Portuguese-English dictionary. But what he did have was a Portuguese-to-French dictionary, and a French-to-English dictionary. Using both dictionaries, Carolino first translated the Portuguese expression into French, then translated the phrase from French to English. The result was the accidental classic *O Novo Guia da Conversação em Portuguez e Inglez* (*Guide to the Conversation in Portuguese and English*), now better known as *English As She Is Spoke*.

It was not the contribution to linguistics Carolino had hoped for.[12] For example, armed with Carolino's guide, a Portuguese traveller could complain about his writing implements ("This pen are good for notting"); insult a barber ("What news tell me? All hairs dresser are newsmonger"); complain about the orchestra ("It is a noise which to cleave the head"); or go hunting ("Let aim it! Let make fire him!"). They might also puzzle over what it means "to craunch a marmoset", or "he burns one's self the brains", or the lesson contained in such well-known English proverbs as "nothing some money, nothing Swiss".

In one section, Carolino lists various body parts under the heading "Of The Man":

> *The fat of the leg*
> *The ham*
> *The brain*
> *The brains*
> *The superior lip*
> *The inferior lip*
> *The reins*

In the next chapter, he takes on "Familiar Phrases":

> *Have you say that?*
> *At what O'Clock Dine him?*
> *Have you understanded?*
> *The thunderbolt is falling down*
> *No budge you there*
> *Dress your hairs*
> *Will you a bon?*
> *Do not might one's understand to speak?*
> *These apricots and these peaches make me and to come water in mouth*
> *He has spit in my coat*

---

12  It was, however, thought to have been the inspiration for Monty Python's legendary "Dirty Hungarian Phrasebook" sketch, including the notable line: "Drop your panties, Sir William – I cannot wait until lunchtime."

*I am pinking me with a pin*
*He do want to fall*
*He do the devil at four*
*Dry this wine*
*He laughs at my nose, he jest by me*

The books ends with a handy list under the heading "Idiotisms and Proverbs", including:

*The necessity don't know the low.*
*Few, few the bird make her nest.*
*He is not valuable to breat that he eat.*
*He sin in trouble water.*
*A bad arrangement is better than a process.*
*He has a good beak.*
*To build castles in Espagnish.*
*Cat scalded fear the cold water.*
*With a tongue one go to Roma.*
*Take out the live coals with the hand of the cat.*
*A horse baared don't look him the tooth.*
*Take the occasion for the hairs.*
*To do a wink to some body.*
*So many go the jar to spring, than at last rest there.*
*It want to beat the iron during it is hot.*
*He is not so devil as he is black.*
*It is better be single as a bad company.*
*The stone as roll not heap up not foam.*
*He has fond the knuckle of the business.*
*There is not better sauce who the appetite.*
*The pains come at horse and turn one's self at foot.*
*He is beggar as a church rat.*
*So much go the jar to spring that at last it break there.*
*To force to forge, becomes smith.*
*Keep the chestnut of the fire with the cat foot.*
*Friendship of a child is water into a basket.*
*Tell me whom thou frequent, I will tell you which you are.*
*After the paunch comes the dance.*

*Of the hand to mouth, one lose often the soup.*
*To buy cat in pocket.*
*To be as a fish into the water.*
*To make paps for the cats.*
*To fatten the foot.*
*To come back at their muttons.*

When the book was first published, authorship was jointly attributed to Pedro Carolino and José da Foncesca, a well-known author, almost certainly without the latter's knowledge or consent. We can only guess that Carolino hoped it would sell more copies if he put a famous name on the cover.

In 1869, Carolino brought out a new edition that he credited solely to himself. This edition was published in Peking, possibly to cash in on ignorance of proper English in the Far East. Carolino's misbegotten phrasebook was stumbled upon by a British traveller in 1860s, in the Portuguese colony of Macao, off the coast of China. He was astonished to find that it was being actually used as a textbook in the island's schools.

It has also attracted many famous fans, including Mark Twain. In 1883, he wrote an introduction for the first American edition:

> *In this world of uncertainties, there is, at any rate, one thing which may be pretty confidently set down as a certainty: and that is, that this celebrated little phrase-book will never die while the English language lasts. Its delicious unconscious ridiculousness, and its enchanting naïveté, are as supreme and unapproachable, in their way, as are Shakespeare's sublimities. Whatsoever is perfect in its kind, in literature, is imperishable: nobody can imitate it successfully, nobody can hope to produce its fellow; it is perfect, it must and will stand alone: its immortality is secure.*

*O Novo Guia da Conversação em Portuguez e Inglez* has since gone on to become a minor classic and was reprinted as recently as 2002.

# Worst Stage Actor

Robert "Romeo" Coates had them rolling in the aisles everywhere he went. The problem was he was supposed to be a serious actor. He was so very, very bad that, for a while, he was the most talked about thespian in Regency England.

He was born in Antigua in 1772, the seventh child of a wealthy sugar plantation owner, Alexander Coates. His father was so rich that he was once approached by representatives of King George III asking for a loan of £5,000 to help defend an attack on Antigua from Spanish and French raiders. Coates senior casually wrote out a cheque for £10,000 and told them to keep the change.

In spite of their wealth, the Coates family were not immune to eighteenth-century child mortality rates: eight of their children died in infancy or early childhood. Only Robert, the youngest, survived to adulthood. Alexander Coates doted on his only surviving son and, when Robert had just turned eight, took him to England for a private education. When Robert returned to Antigua at the end of his expensive schooling, he was expected to take his place beside his father as heir to the Coates plantation and fortune, but he had enjoyed his time abroad and it only made his homeland seem very dull, with little to offer in the way of amusement and entertainment. He had tasted the excitement of London's West End and had fallen completely in love with the stage. Sadly, his ardour was unrequited.

When Alexander Coates died in 1807, Robert inherited the estate and an annual income of £40,000 – around £1 million by today's reckoning. At the first opportunity, he returned to England where he took up residence in fashionable Bath. He soon became a figure of great local curiosity. He was thirty-seven years old but looked older, his skin heavily wrinkled by the Caribbean sun. He was also quite dark-skinned – a great novelty at a time when women still used arsenic to make their skin fashionably pale. It was rumoured that he was half-African.

It was his dandy-ish dress sense that attracted the most curiosity. By day, he always wore furs, even in the hottest weather, and always carried with him a cane with a huge diamond-studded handle. In the evenings, he went about in a pale-blue military overcoat covered with braids, tasselled Hessian boots and wore on his head a brightly coloured bandana underneath a large cocked hat. He was covered from head to foot with diamonds – diamond buttons on his shirts, diamond buckles on his trousers and boots – giving him the alternative nickname of Diamond Coates. He travelled around Bath in a vast, heavily gilded coach shaped like a giant scallop shell, drawn by a pair of white horses. The carriage door bore its owner's crest – a life-size cock with outspread wings below the motto: "While I live, I'll crow".

Coates put in an appearance every morning in a local coffee room for breakfast. The diarist Pryse Gordon was there one day and recorded seeing him:

> *He shortly attracted my notice by rehearsing passages from* Shakespeare *during his morning meal, with a tone and gesture extremely striking both to the eye and the ear; and, though we were strangers to each other, I could not help complimenting him on the beauty of his recitations, although he did not always stick to his author's text. On one occasion, I took the liberty of correcting a passage from* Romeo and Juliet. *"Aye," said he, "that is the reading, I know, for I have the whole play by heart; but I think I have improved upon it."*

About three months after his arrival in Bath, the local theatre manager overheard Coates reciting Shakespeare in the coffee house over breakfast. On discovering that Coates was very partial to the role of Romeo and even kept his own costume for the part (which he claimed he'd often played back in Antigua), the manager offered him the chance to perform in the play in Bath.

He made his début on 9 February 1809. A handbill advertised the event: "ROMEO, BY AN AMATEUR OF FASHION".

The show sold out. Everyone in Bath wanted to know who the mysterious, dusky stranger in their midst was. Word had also leaked out from the rehearsals that Coates's interpretation of Shakespeare was "different".

From the moment he made his entrance as Romeo, it became obvious to everyone that they were witnessing a very special talent. He bounded to the front of the stage wearing a huge grin, then took a "bow", which involved thrusting his head forward and bobbing it up and down several times. His stage costume was like nothing worn by a Romeo before or since: a sky-blue silk cloak, red pantaloons and a large cravat. On his head he wore a huge, curly Charles the Second-style wig, topped with an opera hat sprouting ostrich feathers.

The entire costume was covered from head to toe with so many diamonds that he sparkled like a disco mirror ball. It was so tightly fitted that he could barely walk and he jerked across the stage like a mannequin. He even looked awkward when he was standing still and not delivering lines. During the first Act, his pants burst, revealing a slash of white silk underwear, visible every time he turned round. At first the audience thought this might be part of the act – an intentional spoof on Romeo and Juliet. But then it slowly dawned on everyone that Coates was oblivious to the wardrobe malfunction and the reaction it was getting. There were roars of laughter from the audience, although some people in the balcony booed and threw fruit and there were cries of "Off! Off!"

During the balcony scene in the middle of Juliet's speech, Coates produced a snuffbox. Someone in the audience shouted, "Romeo, give us a pinch!" Coates strode over and offered his snuff. For the rest of the scene the spectators' roars of laughter drowned out the actors' voices.

The audience sat open-mouthed as Romeo appeared wielding a crowbar, trying to open Juliet's tomb. Then, when Romeo is supposed to carry Juliet's corpse away in sorrow and grief, according to a local theatre critic, Coates "dragged the unfortunate Juliet from the tomb, much in the same manner as a washerwoman thrusts into her cart the bag of foul linen", and dumped her on the stage.

The highlight of the show was Romeo's death scene. He produced a silk handkerchief from his top pocket with a mighty flourish and dusted the stage with it. Then he carefully laid down the handkerchief, placed his plumed hat on it and arranged himself on top of the hat. The audience roared again. Coates, bemused by the reaction, addressed them directly: "Ah, you may laugh, but I do not intend to soil my nice new velvet dress upon these dirty boards." His "death" lasted for several minutes, as he gasped and grimaced, writhing on the floor.

Even now, no one was quite sure what they were watching. Was it comic genius or the buffoonery of a talentless idiot? Fearing the worst, the theatre manager dropped the curtain. For a minute or so, the audience sat in stunned silence, then they broke into wild applause. Coates was very pleased with his stage début.

Word soon spread that "Romeo" Coates would more or less guarantee a sell-out audience. If that didn't persuade theatre managers to book him, he would simply bribe them. He toured the British Isles in what was to become his signature role, creating mayhem wherever he performed. Theatre-goers travelled great distances to see for themselves if he really was as bad as his notices.

In Cheltenham, when it got to the bit where Romeo is supposed to exit after a scene, Coates remained on stage, crawling around on all fours. "Come off, come off," hissed the prompter to no reply. After a while, Coates replied loudly that he had lost a diamond knee-buckle and would only leave the stage when he had found it.

The shows were so unpredictable that managers had the police on hand in case the spectators got out of control. If Coates thought the rowdiness was getting out of hand, he would challenge the audience directly. But nothing, not even the sound of his audience baying with laughter during a death scene, could put him off his stride, or dissuade from his belief that he was, in his own words, "the best actor in the business".

In 1811, Coates moved to London and took up residence in the Strand, where his shell-shaped carriage caused a commotion, providing him with another nickname – Curricle Coates. He became the subject of frequent newspaper gossip and his notoriety as a rich bachelor attracted a large posse of hangers-on and many begging letters. Just as he was oblivious to criticism of his acting talents, he was also a soft touch when it came to money. The more pitiful the begging letter, the more generous he was. One day, a poor widow approached him for help and he immediately offered a benefit performance. By means of rehearsal, Coates arranged a one-night stand at the Theatre Royal in Richmond. On 4 September 1811, Coates played Romeo to a packed house. This time London's rowdies – the Regency equivalent of football hooligans – came prepared with armfuls of ripe fruit, but when it came to Romeo's death several of them were so convulsed with laughter that a doctor in the audience had them removed from the theatre for first-aid treatment.

Coates appeared at the Haymarket Theatre on 9 December 1811 in the role of Lothario in Nicholas Rowe's gloomy tragedy *The Fair Penitent*. Every role was a challenge to him, but this was a particularly difficult part that he had never attempted before. The Haymarket had to turn thousands of people way and touts were offering tickets at an outrageous £5 a seat. Among those who were lucky enough to get in were some friends of the Prince Regent, including Baron Ferdinand de Géramb, who had become an ardent Coates fan. Coates came on stage and made a special bow to the Baron, which seems to have needled the crowd and there followed a cacophony of whistles and boos. Despite the hostile atmosphere in the house, Coates blundered blithely on but, by the end of the fourth Act, the heckling was so bad that the actors couldn't hear their lines. A review of the evening described how Coates amused himself during the interruptions by standing centre stage and twirling his sword, which "he did with wonderful dexterity". The other actors gave up and walked off. Coates, finding himself alone, "gave another speech, made a very fine bow, and left the stage, snapping his fingers at the audience". The curtain was brought down and, after more jeers and catcalls, the audience filed out, disappointed.

Although audiences loved Coates's fearless interpretation of the classics, the critics were less kind, especially in London. In January 1813, Coates appeared again as Lothario twice at the Haymarket. Both performances were well attended and passed without incident, apart from the usual riotous laughter, although one critic speculated later that "a baboon" or "a bear, a Newfoundland dog, or a full-sized tom cat" might have done a better job in Coates's role.

Coates performed Lothario again at the Haymarket on 24 February, to a standing-room-only crowd. The Rowdies were out in full force again and the heckling was so fierce that, before the curtain rose, three members of the cast came out to address the audience and beg for courtesy. The heckling abated briefly until Coates appeared. The actor playing Horatio left the stage in disgust.

Coates, who by this time was styling himself "the celebrated Philanthropic Amateur of Fashion", appeared again at the Haymarket in April, returning to his favourite role, Romeo, to another full house. The audience reaction veered from raucous laughter to outright abuse. The actress playing Juliet was so traumatized by the experience that she clung to the set with her arms fastened around a stage pillar until the row died down. When the duel between Romeo and Tybalt was about to start, Coates was struck by a flying bantam cock, which one of the Rowdies had smuggled into the theatre. Coates grabbed the bird and threw it off stage, then continued duelling as though nothing had happened and completed the scene. When it got to the bit where Romeo kills Paris, as Paris lay "dead" on the stage he was jarred back to life when he was hit on the nose by a flying orange. Paris got to his feet and stalked off in a huff. At the next production of *The Fair Penitent* at the Haymarket, the Rowdies again bombarded the character's corpse as they had Paris's dead body, hoping to get the same reaction.

Despite public ridicule and critical panning, Coates continued to perform on the stage until 1816, but the public had long since tired of laughing at him. The Celebrated Amateur of Fashion retired from public performing at the age of 44.

As his star faded, so did the remainder of his inheritance. In 1830, he was forced to sell his ubiquitous diamond and ruby-encrusted sword at auction. The following year, his finances were further reduced by slave revolts in his native Antigua. He got married and went to live in France, but returned to England in 1848 after reaching an arrangement with his creditors.

On 15 February, Coates was on his way home from a concert at Drury Lane when he realized he'd forgotten his opera glasses. He had barely dismounted from his famous "curricle" when he was run over by a taxi cab. He died only yards from the doors of his beloved theatre.

## "Is This a Banana Skin I See Before Me?" Most Accident-Prone Show

There are two superstitions attached to Shakespeare's *Macbeth*. The first is that it is bad luck to refer to the play by name, except during rehearsal or performance; to many, it is "the Scottish play" or simply "that play". The second is that the play itself brings bad luck to cast and crew. If the stories are to be believed, in its 400-year history it has definitely been dogged by some unnecessarily tragic events.

Beginning with its first performance in 1606, Shakespeare himself was forced to play Lady Macbeth when Hal Berridge, the boy designated to play the lady, became mysteriously feverish and died. One version has it that Shakespeare played the role so badly that he forbade his fellow actors to mention "that play", thus starting the tradition of not referring to it by name. When King James I saw the play, he was so spooked by the "realistic" witches that he banned it for five years.

When performed in Amsterdam in 1672, the actor playing Macbeth substituted a real dagger for the blunted stage version and killed Duncan with it in full view of the audience.

As Lady Macbeth, Sarah Siddons was nearly ravaged by a disapproving audience in 1775. In the same role, Dame Sybil Thorndike was almost strangled by an actor in 1926, and Diana Wynyard sleepwalked with her eyes closed off the rostrum in 1948, falling fifteen feet into the pit.

In August 1896, the London illustrated newspaper *The Sketch* reported that Mr Gordon Craig, playing the part of Macduff, got carried away and attacked his fellow actor "with such an excess of zeal that the unfortunate Macbeth suffered somewhat severely about the head". Macbeth, however, gave as good as he got and the stage fight cost Macduff both of his thumbs.[13]

In 1937, when Laurence Olivier took on the role of Macbeth, a twenty-five-pound stage weight crashed down within an inch of him, breaking his sword, which flew into the audience and hit a man who later suffered a heart attack. During the same run, Old Vic founder Lilian Baylis died on the night of the final dress rehearsal.

During the 1942 *Macbeth* production headed by John Gielgud, three actors (Duncan and two witches) died and the costume and set designer committed suicide.

In a 1953 production starring Charlton Heston, a sudden gust of wind blew flames from a realistically staged battle scene on to Heston. He was severely burned because someone had soaked his tights in kerosene.

Two fires and seven robberies plagued the 1971 version starring David Leary.

During the 1980 *Macbeth* at the Old Vic, Peter O'Toole unexpectedly exited the stage smack into a wall.

In the 1981 production at the Lincoln Centre, New York, J. Kenneth Campbell, who played Macduff, was mugged soon after the play's opening.

---

13   August 1896 was a bumper year for tragic stage accidents. At the Novelty Theatre, London, during the final moments of the first performance of *Sins of the Night*, Wildred Moritz Franks stabbed his fellow actor Temple E. Crozier to death, then with the words "Now my sister is avenged" made his exit from the stage. The audience, not realizing that a fatal blow had been struck, applauded generously. Franks said later he didn't know how he had mistaken the murder weapon for a "prop" dagger.

In 1990, at Hampstead's Pentameters Theatre, the plastic retractable dagger failed to retract and Lady Macduff (Dr Annabel Joyce) had to be rushed to hospital.

The biggest single disaster associated with *Macbeth* occurred in 1849 when two rival actors staged competing productions in New York. The British Shakespearian actor William Charles Macready was booked to perform the play at the Astor Place Opera House; meanwhile, American-born Edwin Forrest was also scheduled to perform in *Macbeth* a few blocks away. Forrest's fans, whipped up by the newspapers' anti-English sentiment, went into full riot mode. About 20,000 people amassed outside the opera house, tossing rocks through windows and attempting to set it on fire. National Guardsmen fired on the crowd, injuring rioters and innocent bystanders. By the time the riot was finally brought under control, more than twenty people had died and a further thirty-one people had been injured.

## Least Successful One-Man Show

On 7 December 1974, only one person turned up at the 225-seat Centurion Theatre, Carlisle, to see David Gooderson's solo performance of *The Castaway*, a play based on the life of the hermit/poet William Cowper.

The sole audience member outnumbered the cast – Mr Gooderson had cried off with a heavy cold.

> *"Stocks have reached what looks like*
> *a permanently high plateau."*
> Arguably the worst piece of economic analysis in history from Irving Fisher, economics professor at Yale University in 1929, days before the Wall Street Crash.

## Least Successful Opening

In the early 1980s, The Plymouth Theatre Company toured the West Country with a production of *The Golden Pathway Annual* with a company of just six actors learning twenty parts between them and their stagehands taking ten hours to erect the scenery. Before they took their play to a 200-seater theatre in Ashburton, a small market town about twenty miles from Plymouth, they blitzed the surrounding area with free tickets and posters as part of their publicity campaign.

When the curtain went up on their first performance, only a single seat was occupied, by a man in the stalls. At the end of the play, he applauded loudly and left.

The theatre's administrator, Wendy Lost, was optimistic: "Last time we went there, with *The Winslow Boy*, nobody turned up at all!"

---

*"It will be gone by June."*
    *Variety* magazine passing judgment
    on rock 'n' roll, January 1955

---

## Least Successful Audience Participation

At an open-air charity performance of *A Midsummer Night's Dream* in the grounds of Woburn Abbey, a group of theatre lovers, including the Marquis and Marchioness of Tavistock, were startled when a character dressed as Adolf Hitler ran on stage and demanded, "Vas ist going on?"

The Hitler impersonator, Ian Hinchcliffe, later told local magistrates that he had been invited to a fancy dress ball and had been wandering around for several hours trying to find it. "I thought I had found it at last," he explained.

Chairman of the bench, Mr Herbert Dell, fined him £10, warning him, "We don't stand for this sort of thing in Woburn."

> *"Democracy will be dead by 1950."*
> John Langdon-Davies, *A Short History of the Future*, 1936

## Least Successful Animal Act

America's only performing cat act, the Rock Cats Trio, features cats on guitar, piano and drums, as well as a tightrope-walker, barrel-roller and skateboarder, among other moggy performers.

Manager of the Rock Cats, Samantha Martin, admitted to the *Chicago Tribune* that the cats' music "sucks". She elaborated, "When they're playing, they're not even playing the same thing." Martin added that she had two back-up drummers because her regular drummer was prone to "walking off in a huff . . . this is why you don't see trained cat acts . . . the managers can't take the humiliation."

> *"And for the tourist who really wants to get
> away from it all, safaris in Vietnam."*
> *Newsweek*, predicting popular holidays for the late 1960s

## Most Disappointing Magic Act

The American magician William Robinson performed under the stage name Chung Ling Soo, "the marvellous Chinese conjuror". The stage persona, like his stage act, was an illusion. He didn't have a drop of Chinese blood in his body but maintained his role as an Oriental scrupulously, always performing in silence and speaking only through his personal interpreter when talking to journalists.

His final performance was at the Wood Green Empire in north London on 23 March 1918. The theatre was buzzing in anticipation as Chung Ling Soo prepared to perform his trademark trick, which involved catching two bullets fired directly at him by his assistants.

The key lay in the gun itself: it was rigged so that the bullets never left the barrel. The gun was loaded with substitute bullets, there was a flash and a bang and Chung appeared to catch the bullets in his hand or his teeth. In some versions, he pretended to be hit, then spit the bullets on to a china plate. On this particular night, however, the gun malfunctioned and the loaded bullets fired in the normal way, shooting him dead.

His last words were: "Oh my God ... Something's happened ... Lower the curtain." It was a double shock for the audience, as it was the first and last time that William "Chung Ling Soo" Robinson had spoken English in public.

> *"Four or five frigates will do the business*
> *without any military force."*
> British prime minister Lord North, on dealing
> with the rebellious American colonies, 1774

## Worst Broadway Play

In 1983, Frank Rich, theatre critic for the *New York Times* wrote: "There will always be two groups of theatregoers in this world: those who have seen *Moose Murders,* and those who have not."

Billed as a "mystery farce", *The Moose Murders*, written by Arthur Bicknell, opened at the Eugene O'Neill Theatre on 22 February 1983. The show relates the adventures of a group of characters who are pulled together on one stormy night at the Wild Moose Lodge, where several murders take place. Apparing are a nurse, a blind singer and his tone-deaf wife, some rich people, a character called Stinky who tries to sleep with his mother and a man in a moose costume who is assaulted by a mummified quadriplegic

... and, legend has it, a wild moose who hacks all his victims to pieces.

The play was beset by problems from the start when the leading lady, Eve Arden, who was supposed to be making a comeback after more than forty years away from Broadway, sensibly quit the opening night. Her role was filled at a week's notice by the veteran star Holland Taylor, who agreed to step in because she was broke. Ms Taylor later described the production as "a misshapen thing at an almost Shakespearean level ... there were things that I put my foot down about and changed. But there were things I couldn't change. Like the play."

*The Moose Murders* closed after just one performance amid some of the worst reviews recorded in theatrical history, the mood admittedly not helped by a man reeking of vomit who sat in the third row during the press preview. One critic described it as "the standard of awfulness against which all Broadway flops are judged". Dennis Cunningham, the critic at CBS in New York, advised, "If your name is Arthur Bicknell or anything like it, change it." Brendan Gill of *The New Yorker* said the play "would insult the intelligence of an audience consisting entirely of amoebas ... I won't soon forget the spectacle of watching the mummified Sidney rise from his wheelchair to kick an intruder, unaccountably dressed in a moose costume, in the groin.'[14]

Clive Barnes was more succinct: the play was "so indescribably bad that I do not intend to waste anyone's time by describing it".

## Biggest West End Flop

The writer and director Lionel Bart gave the world *Oliver!*, one of the greatest musicals of all time. Five years later, he gave the world *Twang!!*[15]

---

14  Although reviews describe a scene in which a bandage-wrapped paraplegic rises from his wheelchair to kick a man dressed as a moose in the crotch, mysteriously, this episode does not appear in the original script.

15  "One *exclamation* mark *too far*," said the critic Mark Steyn.

Based on the outlaw Robin Hood and starring Barbara Windsor as a nymphomaniac Maid Marion and Ronnie Corbett as Will Scarlett, *Twang!!* concerned the efforts of Robin and his Merrie Men to break into Nottingham Castle in a variety of disguises to prevent a marriage between the court tart Delphina and the hairy Scots laird Roger the Ugly, arranged for the purpose of securing the loan of Scottish troops for bad Prince John.

The omens were not good from the off. Behind the scenes there was constant bickering between cast and crew and endless confusing rewrites of a terrible script. At one point, the rewrites were so many and so close to performances that the new scripts were pasted on to the scenery. After a disastrous regional try-out in Manchester, the director Joan Littlewood quit just before the show opened in the West End at the Shaftesbury Theatre on 20 December 1965. Fearing the worst, the show's backers baled out at the last minute and Bart had to sink his own personal fortune into the show to keep it going.

On the opening night, the musical director, Ken Moule, collapsed from exhaustion and was too ill to orchestrate the second act. The house lights kept going up and down throughout the performance and heated backstage arguments were plainly overheard. Two songs were cut just before the curtain rose. When the line "I don't know what's going on here . . ." was spoken, a wag in the audience shouted "Neither do we!"

The show received a universal critical panning with critics asking the same question: how in the name of sanity did it ever get off the ground? Arthur Thirkell reported in the *Daily Mirror*, "The only memorable song up to the interval was the National Anthem." The *Sun* reported helpfully that "Barbara Windsor does manage to thrust her voice a little further out than her chest".

*Twang!!* closed on 29 January 1966 after just forty-three performances, playing mostly to empty houses. At one point, there were only fifteen in the audience.

The failure of *Twang!!* was a personal disaster for Lionel Bart. He lost everything and was forced to sell the music publishing rights of *Oliver!* to Max Bygraves and Jock Jacobson for £1,000; they eventually resold them for around $1 million.

The only person who came out well was Ronnie Corbett, because he was now free to make his first TV breakthrough in *The Frost Report.* Corbett said later, "In retrospect, its failure was as important to my career as any of my successes."

## Least Convincing Psychic Act

Pete Antoniou, self-styled performing "psychic detective", describes himself on his website as a "mind ninja'" with "a unique set of skills and gifts that allow him to read thoughts, pre-empt decisions people will make and influence their thought process".

On 25 November 2011, promoters were forced to cancel his appearance at the Dovehouse Theatre in Solihull when Antoniou failed to predict that only three people would buy tickets to his show.

Craig Bennett, assistant manager at the venue, noted, "Perhaps Mr Antoniou should have seen it coming," but added, "he only claims to be able to read people's minds when they are in the room with him, so I don't think it would have been fair to expect him to realize people were not interested in his act at the moment."

---

*"In all likelihood, world inflation is over."*
International Monetary Fund CEO, 1959

---

## Least Convincing Psychic Act: Runner-Up

Eduard Frenkel was one of several self-proclaimed psychic healers operating in Russia during the 1980s. He appeared on the local State-run TV several times with claims of supernatural powers, drawing huge audiences and receiving thousands of letters requesting help.

Frenkel claimed to have successfully used his psychic powers to stop moving vehicles, including bicycles and cars. In October 1989, he decided he was ready for something bigger; he stepped in front of a freight train near the southern city of Astrakhan, according to the train driver, with "his arms raised, his head lowered and his body tensed".

Associated Press reported that Mr Frenkel died from his injuries.

---

*"Remote shopping, while entirely feasible, will flop – because women like to get out of the house, like to handle merchandise, like to be able to change their minds."*
TIME magazine 1966, writing off e-commerce
before anyone had ever heard of it.

---

## Least Successful Eulogy

Rolling Stones fans were devastated in July 1969 when the band's founder member Brian Jones died in a tragic swimming pool accident. But for the Stones, the show had to go on.

During the band's tour of Denmark shortly afterwards, Mick Jagger, dressed in a white frock, announced on stage, "This one's for Brian." Then, after touching a faulty microphone stand, he was hurled backwards by an electric shock, landing on top of Bill Wyman, knocking his bass player unconscious.

---

*"Our country has deliberately undertaken a
great social and economic experiment, noble in
motive and far-reaching in purpose."*
Herbert Hoover, on Prohibition, 1928

## Least Talented Opera Singer

The singing career of Florence Foster Jenkins – known to her admirers as "the diva of din" – was the result of a lifetime of thwarted ambition.

She was born in 1868, the daughter of Charles Dorrance Foster, a rich and successful Pennsylvania banker. She had piano lessons as a child and gave her first piano recital aged eight and attended the Philadelphia Musical Academy. When she was in her teens, she hoped to travel to Europe to study opera, but her father refused to foot the bill.

At seventeen, she rebelled and eloped with a doctor, Frank Jenkins. The marriage ended in divorce and she was forced to support herself, earning a living as a teacher and a pianist but, in 1909, her father died, leaving Florence half his fortune. With her father's legacy, she was free to pursue the singing career that she felt he had denied her.

She moved to New York where she found her niche as a skilled organizer and fundraiser for assorted charity organizations. She started the Verdi Club for Ladies, which raised money for artists and musicians and sponsored the private, select playing of extracts from the composer's work. As she was personally financing these events, she also felt entitled to present herself as the featured attraction.

Florence made her début in April 1912 before a few sympathetic friends, accompanied by her pianist Cosme McMoon, singing a variety of standard opera arias, as well as a few written for her by McMoon. She billed herself as a coloratura soprano, but it was obvious from the moment she opened her mouth that she couldn't hold a tune in a bucket. She had no sense of pitch or rhythm and was incapable of sustaining a note or even of keeping time. When attempting the high note of an aria, her mouth would form the words but no sound would emerge from her throat.

Her stage costumes were almost as startling as her vocals. They were fantastic creations of silk, tinsel, tulle and feathered wings, usually at least three per recital. The highlight of her show was the Spanish waltz "Clavelitos", for which she would appear dressed as Carmen with a lace shawl, clutching castanets and a wicker basket of red roses. She would click the castanets and toss the roses into the audience one by one. When she ran out of roses, she threw the basket, then she threw the castanets.

For her grand finale, she would appear costumed as the chambermaid Adele from *Die Fledermaus* singing "Laughing Song", a good choice as it turns out, because by this point the audience would be falling about in fits of laughter. Her "fans" would invariably call for an encore of "Clavelitos", which prompted her to send Cosme McMoon into the audience to retrieve roses, basket and castanets. Props back in hand, she would sing the entire number all over again. She always finished to thunderous applause.

As news of her extraordinary talent spread by word of mouth, the curious came from miles around to see for themselves if she really was as bad as everybody claimed. For the next thirty-odd years, America's east coast upper-crust crammed handkerchiefs into their mouths to stifle their laughter as the hefty soprano murdered their favourite melodies. She paid for several recordings of her work at a New York studio with the intention of selling them to friends, although only two now remain,[16] including her rendition of the "Queen of the Night" aria from Mozart's *Magic Flute* – a demanding work by any standard. Jenkins sang the piece once, unrehearsed, and pronounced the result "too good to be improved upon". Her recordings, like her live performances, were greeted with universal critical abuse, which she attributed to professional jealousy.

In 1943, she was riding in a Manhattan taxi cab when it crashed. After the accident, she claimed that she could sing "a higher F than ever before". To express her gratitude, she sent a box of Havana cigars to the driver.

Her finest hour came on the evening of 25 October 1944,

16   A mercifully short version is available on YouTube.

when Madame Jenkins took the plunge and braved Carnegie Hall. Her charity performance was sold out weeks in advance with touts charging £20 per ticket; 2,000 people were turned away. It was an unforgettable night of opera. Reviewing her Carnegie triumph, *TIME* magazine glowed, "Mrs Jenkins' night-queenly swoops and hoots, her wild wallowings in descending trill, her repeated staccato notes like a cuckoo in its cups, are innocently uproarious to hear." The *Bulletin* advised, "Madame Jenkins' vocal art is something for which there is no known parallel." *Newsweek* observed, "In high notes, Mrs Jenkins sounds as if she were afflicted with low, nagging backache." Another critic complained of "dizziness, a headache and a ringing in the ears".

Sadly, she had shrieked her last. A few weeks after her Carnegie Hall début, she suffered a fatal heart attack in her hotel suite. Her obituary noted, "She was exceedingly happy in her work. It is a pity so few artists are."

## Most Accident-Prone Opera Singer

During a production of *Aida* at the Royal Danish Theatre in Copenhagen in 2005, opera singer David Rendall was crushed by a stage set when it collapsed on top of him midway through a performance, knocking him flat on his arias.

The singer subsequently began a £250,000 law suit, claiming his career had been ruined by the accident. The sixty-one-year-old tenor said he was unable to perform due to his injuries – his hip and knee had been shattered, and he'd sustained damage to his shoulders – and he had been forced to sell his house because work offers had dried up.

It was not his first onstage misadventure. In 1998 during a performance of *I Pagliacci* in Milwaukee, he accidentally stabbed a fellow singer in the stomach with a flick knife. The blade was supposed to be a retractable "prop" knife but, instead, he plunged a real knife three inches into the abdomen of Kim Julian, who required emergency surgery.

> *"It will be years — not in my time — before a woman will lead the Party or become Prime Minister."*
>
> Margaret Thatcher, future Prime
> Minister, 26 October, 1969

## Least Successful Stage Introduction

The actress Diana Dors was a blond bombshell known as "the British Marilyn Monroe". Her real name was Diana Fluck. The dangers posed by a missed consonant led to a rapid change of name when she was spotted at the age of fourteen by a talent scout at the London Academy of Music and Drama.

When she returned to her home town of Swindon to open a fête in 1950, a local alderman insisted upon introducing her by her real name. He stepped forward and announced, "Ladies and gentlemen, please welcome our very own Miss Diana Clunt . . ."

> *"You will be home before the leaves have fallen from the trees."*
> Kaiser Wilhelm II, to the German troops, August 1914

## Least Dignified Stage Exit

The American magician Benjamin Rucker was better known by his stage name, Black Herman. His most popular feat was his act called "Black Herman's Private Graveyard". In this, he would gather an audience a few days before his next performance to watch him fake his death. A few selected spectators would then check for a pulse and, upon verifying that he had none, the magician would climb into a coffin and allow himself to be buried near the venue of his next scheduled show. On the appointed day, the audience would witness the magician miraculously emerge from the coffin alive and well.

Black Herman performed for the last time in 1934 in Louisville, Kentucky. During his trademark performance, he collapsed and died on stage from a heart attack. The audience, assuming that it was all part of the act, followed the corpse all the way to the funeral home, anticipating the end of the "trick". It was reported that people had brought pins with them hoping to poke the body to see if he really was dead.

Black Herman's newly redundant assistant, making the best of a bad situation, charged admission to spectators to see his late employee post mortem. He explained, "It's what he would have wanted."[17]

---

> *"That virus is a pussycat."*
> Dr Peter Duesberg, molecular-biology
> professor at UC Berkeley, on HIV, 1988

---

## Most Self-Deluded Artist

Benjamin Robert Haydon was born in 1746 into a well-to-do middle-class family from Plymouth. When he was young, he hoped to join the medical profession and become a surgeon, but abandoned the idea when the sight of an amputation caused him to faint.

At school he had shown some talent for drawing, although not enough for anyone to give him any encouragement that he could make it as an artist. As soon as he was eighteen, undeterred by the objections of his parents, or the warning of a good friend who told him that he would probably starve, Haydon set off for London to become a student at the Royal Academy.

---

17   In 1988, Lemmy Chipower, a magician from Chingola, Zambia, charged his audience to watch him being buried alive. Two and a half hours later, they dug him up, finding him very dead. Hs wife noted: "Something must have gone wrong."

His career as an artist got off to a promising start when the RA agreed to exhibit one of his pictures. Haydon was delighted, until he found out that they had decided to hang his painting in a small side room instead of the main hall. He never forgot or forgave the RA, the beginnings of a lifelong feud with the art establishment.

Although short on genuine talent, Haydon was very ambitious and full of enthusiasm. He believed that it was his destiny to become one of the greats of painting in the style of Raphael, and he wasn't shy about blowing his own trumpet. He submitted anonymous articles to several art journals praising his own work. He thought that at least three of his canvases showed "indisputable evidences of genius". A couple of art critics took him at face value and described him as a promising young historical painter. Thanks in no small part to his self-publicity, he was soon rubbing shoulders with the likes of the Romantic poets Wordsworth, Shelley and Keats. These connections led to several important commissions, including a huge picture to commemorate the passing of the Reform Bill.

Not quite everyone was taken in by Haydon's self-delusion. As early as 1826, the novelist and critic Aldous Huxley wrote that Haydon "had absolutely no artistic talent", but it took the rest of the art world some time before they came around to agreeing with him.

For now, Haydon's star was on the rise. His trademark was very dull, epic historical scenes painted on enormous canvases. He believed that size was important – the bigger the better. The subjects were usually biblical, such as *The Judgment of Solomon*, *Christ's Entry into Jerusalem* and *The Raising of Lazarus*. Sticking with the biblical theme, he used to kneel in front of his canvases and pray for inspiration before every painting session.

Haydon was convinced that his massive works were much better than the smaller paintings turned out by the likes of his highly successful contemporaries Constable and Turner, because there was much more work involved in painting larger-than-life-size on a huge canvas. In keeping with his distorted and grandiose view of himself, he had a literally distorted view of his work. To begin with, Haydon had terrible problems with physical proportions. Because of his early interest in medicine, he liked to think he was an expert on human anatomy and there are accounts of him compulsively checking the proportions of his own legs as he painted. But the legs he painted were always curiously short in relation to the rest of the body. Part of the problem was that he generally worked on his huge canvases in small, dimly lit rooms, which meant he could never stand back far enough to see the overall impression. He also suffered from very poor eyesight and painted while wearing two or three pairs of spectacles, one pair over the other.

Haydon also followed the new pseudo-science of phrenology – the analysis of a person's skull shape. He thought that his own head shape was near perfect, in his words, "noble and Socratic". So rather than pay for models, he painted his own features on to his subjects, something the critics had fun with at his expense. When his painting *Curtius Leaping into the Gulf* was unveiled to terrible reviews in 1843, it was obvious that Curtius was a Haydon self-portrait, but the critics pretended not to recognize him. The art critic from the *Spectator* described Curtius as having a "florid, chubby-cheeked physiognomy".[18]

In spite of his early successes and his influential friends, Haydon was never to hit the heights he felt he deserved. Painting on an epic scale also took much longer to do and it took him about five years to complete a single canvas. His painting *Reform Banquet,* for example, contained 597 individual portraits. With a new wife and rapidly growing family to support, he had committed himself to a way of working which meant long periods with no income.

---

18   Although he was a hopeless painter, Haydon also wrote many letters, journals and diaries and, even in his lifetime, people recognized his talent as a writer and wished he had stuck to that. "Let Mr Haydon rather write than paint," wrote a *Morning Post* critic in 1841. "His pen is sometimes his friend; his brush is always his enemy."

In 1810, he started to get into serious financial difficulties when an allowance of £200 a year from his father was stopped. He temporarily maintained solvency through the generosity of friends and by borrowing heavily. For years, he toiled for sixteen hours or more a day on his canvasses, only to have his efforts panned by art critics. He spent the last twenty-five years of his life close to bankruptcy and was imprisoned five times for debt.

Haydon got into lengthy disputes with patrons over money. He was once asked by Sir Robert Peel to paint a picture, then almost as soon as he got the commission started writing to Peel demanding more money than had been agreed.

Haydon's lifelong battle with the art world, meanwhile, grew steadily more acrimonious. He published defamatory pamphlets about the Royal Academy and appeared before a select committee to complain about its incompetence and alleged corruption. It was professional suicide.

Constantly short of money and frustrated by lack of recognition, his financial situation grew steadily more dire. Meanwhile, his battle with the art establishment came to a head in 1846. He tried to win a commission to decorate the new House of Lords with six huge canvasses on historical themes. The new Fine Arts Committee overlooked him in favour of a much younger artist. Haydon retaliated by staging an exhibition of the six paintings that had just been rejected in the Egyptian Hall in Piccadilly, London. Haydon's show, put on at his own expense, was an embarrassing failure. The American dwarf entertainer General Tom Thumb was appearing next door and the public voted with its feet. In the first week of the exhibition, Haydon's pictures took £7 13s. while the dwarf took £600.

It was the most humiliating snub of his painting career. Four weeks later, on the morning of 22 June 1846, in the studio of his London home, he made a note on the final page of his journal: "God forgive me – Amen . . . Finis of BR Haydon . . . "Stretch me no longer on this tough world" – Lear . . . End."

Then, in the same way that everything else in his life had gone horribly wrong, the sixty-year-old put a pistol to his head and pulled the trigger, but somehow managed not to kill himself. He then took a razor, braced himself at the door and cut his own throat from right to left, but so badly that he had to do it again. After a second attempt, this time cutting from left to right but still missing the carotid artery, he collapsed.

His wife and daughter downstairs heard a thump as his body hit the floor, but assumed he was manhandling his final, gigantic, unfinished painting. His daughter discovered him later when she came into the room and slipped in a puddle of her father's blood.

After his death, a phrenologist felt Haydon's bumps and declared that he had artistic talent, but not very much. He also noted that, despite Haydon's alleged interest in anatomy, he hadn't even known how to cut his own throat properly.

Charles Dickens noted, "All his life he had utterly mistaken his vocation . . . he most unquestionably was a very bad painter."

## Rags to Riches . . . to Rags

In the mid-1850s, the American John Banvard was arguably the world's best-known living artist. He was adored by royalty, fêted by such great contemporaries as Charles Dickens and Henry Wadsworth Longfellow and incredibly rich – possibly the first millionaire artist in history. Thirty-five years later, he died penniless, laid to rest in a pauper's grave in a remote frontier town, his most famous works destroyed and his name all but expunged from the history books.

Banvard was born in 1815 in New York. His father Daniel was a successful builder and a dabbler in art himself. Young John showed an aptitude for sketching, writing and science. The latter interest backfired one day when he was experimenting with hydrogen and it exploded in his face, badly injuring his eyes. The family business ran into trouble in 1831 when Daniel Banvard suffered a stroke and died, then his business partner ran off with the company assets. Fifteen-year-old John watched as his family's possessions were auctioned off in a bankruptcy sale.

John Banvard decided to move to seek work. He found it in Louisville in 1833 when he was offered a job as a scene painter on a showboat called the *Floating Theatre*. The pay was so poor that it barely kept him from starvation, but it gave him lots of practice in rapid sketching and painting of very large scenery. This skill would later prove invaluable and gave Banvard the idea that he might operate his own showboats on which he would display his paintings.

The following year he disembarked at New Harmony, Ohio, and he and three or four young acquaintances built a flat boat and kitted it out for their own floating theatre company, having apparently funded the venture by swindling a gullible backer out of his life savings. Banvard served as scene painter, actor and director.

For a couple of years, he and his friends survived by displaying his landscape paintings and improvizing Shakespeare and other popular plays up and down the river for customers who bartered their way into performances with live poultry and bags of potatoes, but at least Banvard and his troupe weren't going hungry. Banvard was brought low by bouts of malaria and, when the audience stopped coming, he was reduced to begging on the docks. But he was now a hardened showman with years of experience behind him and he was still only a teenager.

Eventually, a local stage manager took pity on him and hired him as a scene painter. It was around this time that he first experimented in painting "panoramas". These were long, continuous canvases that were slowly cranked from one spool to another, so that the scene moved in front of the viewer across the stage and gave audiences the illusion of viewing moving scenery, as though from a boat or the window of a train. These 360-degree paintings were generally displayed in purpose-built circular rotundas and were usually representations of nature, battle scenes and exotic locations. The effect of total immersion in the depicted scene was enhanced by a musical accompaniment and skilful manipulation of lighting.

During the early 1800s, audiences flocked by the thousands to see the latest panoramas. It is difficult to judge the actual quality of these paintings as few in the audience would have been able to stand close enough to the moving painting to study them in detail, but there was no doubt about the effect they had on audiences: one visitor described the experience of seeing the panorama pass by as "spine-tingling".

When Banvard was a young boy in New York, he had marvelled at these gigantic rolls of painted canvas depicting seaports and "A Trip to Niagara Falls". He decided to try his hand at his own moving landscapes of Venice and Jerusalem. His biggest painting was a moving panorama that he described as "Infernal Regions". Nearly a hundred feet in length, it was completed and sold in 1841 and, to date, it was his biggest success. Meanwhile, he had his eye on a greater project: he was planning a painting so huge that it would dwarf any attempted before or since. He was going to paint a portrait of the Mississippi river.

In April 1842, he bought a skiff, filled it with provisions, pencils and sketch pads, and set off down the Mississippi to sketch the river from St Louis all the way to New Orlando, a distance of around 1,200 miles. The physical and creative challenges he faced were immense.

For the next two years, he paddled down the river filling his sketch pads with drawings, braving blistering summer heat and bouts of yellow fever. His skin became so burnt that it peeled from the backs of his hands and his face. He survived by occasionally pulling into river ports to sell cigars, household goods, anything he could lay his hands on to trade with river folk.

When he had finished sketching in 1844, Banvard built a barn on the outskirts of Louisville to house the huge bolts of canvas that he had ordered to complete his gigantic painting. His next challenge was to devise some sort of system to hold his huge canvas in place and prevent it from sagging. His solution to this problem was so ingenious that he was able to patent it and it was featured in a scientific journal a few years later.

For several months, Banvard worked furiously on his panoramic canvas, meanwhile holding down two or three part-time jobs to feed himself. Finally, he was ready to unveil his mammoth creation.

Using all of the sales techniques he had learned on the river, he worked his way through the local docks, chatting to steam-boat crews and handing out free tickets to a special afternoon matinée. The sailors who turned up were amazed by the pano-ramic painted landscape that unfurled before their eyes. As Banvard cranked the canvas past them, he would describe his travels, adding tall tales of pirates and close encounters with frontier brigands. His showmanship did the trick; news of Banvard's painting spread by word of mouth and, within the week, he found himself playing to a packed house every night.

After his successful début, Banvard went back to the studio and added more sections to his painting, then he moved to a bigger venue. Meanwhile, the crowds, and the money, contin-ued to pour in. Now Banvard was ready to take his "Three-Mile Painting"[19] to the centre of American culture – Boston. By the time Banvard installed his canvas in Boston's Armory Hall in December 1846, he had honed his narration and commis-sioned a concert pianist to accompany it, meanwhile hiding the cranking machinery from the audience's view. It was an immediate smash hit. Over the next six months, over a quarter of a million Bostonians paid 50c. a head to see his extraordi-nary synthesis of moving art, narrative and music. He made a cool profit $100,000. In less than a year, he had gone from a starving boat sign painter to the country's highest-earning artist. And there was more happy news – the young pianist he hired to accompany his presentations, Elizabeth Godman, became his wife.

---

19  A Banvard exaggeration. His painting was actually 12 feet high and 1,300 feet long and was eventually expanded to about half a mile.

Banvard was now the talk of America. The poet Henry Wadsworth Longfellow, who had never been anywhere near the Mississippi but had seen one of Banvard's Boston shows, was inspired to write his Mississippi river epic *Evangeline*.

In 1847, Banvard moved his show to New York to even bigger crowds and even greater adulation and profit. The money coming in from his show was so good that rather than count the night's takings, the banks simply weighed them.

With success also came imitation. For several years, panoramas of the American frontier dominated popular art. Samuel Stockwell, Leon Pomarede and Henry Lewis all produced Western panoramas nearly as large as Banvard's. Another artist, John Rowson Smith, produced a "Four-Mile Painting", although the title was misleading. Meanwhile, unscrupulous promoters attempted to copy Banvard's painting and show the pirated work abroad as the genuine article.

But Banvard's work remained by far the most popular and the most successful. Rather than being considered, as one modern critic has put it, a mere "folk painter of geographic newsreels", he was praised by his contemporaries as a contributor to the artistic, educational and scientific knowledge of the American wilderness.

In 1848, Banvard took his show to England, starting with a series of short exhibitions in Liverpool, Manchester and Birmingham. In November, he opened in the Egyptian Hall in Piccadilly, London, charming his audience by peppering his talk with humorous anecdotes in his novel, flat American drawl. The *London Observer* wrote: "This is truly an extraordinary work. We have never seen anything so grand in its character". The *London Morning Advertiser* agreed: "It is a great work which not only astonishes by its magnitude and grandeur, but is highly instructive and interesting."

Not everyone was impressed. A notable dissenter, the Victorian gossip columnist Henry Crabbe Robinson, called the painting an "execrable daub of a picture" and said, "the intense vulgarity of the Yankee explainer actually excited disgust." But Robinson was a minority voice. More importantly, the British public loved Banvard's show. Running for a year in London, it drew more than half a million spectators. Charles Dickens was a huge fan, and wrote Banvard an admiring note: "I was in the highest degree interested and pleased by your picture."

Meanwhile, his autobiography – *Banvard, or The Adventures of an Artist* – was flying off the bookshelves. He also experienced something he could never have dreamed of in America – the royal seal of approval. On 11 April 1849, he was summoned to Windsor Castle for a private performance for Queen Victoria. Banvard was already an extremely rich man, but this was the icing on the cake. He was no longer merely a talented showman, he was now a respectable artist. Banvard would remember this performance as his very finest hour.

Later that year, his life-size portrait was painted by the English artist Anna Mary Howitt. Appropriately, this was also a very big canvas. Banvard's height was estimated by those who knew him at between six feet four inches and six feet eight and a quarter inches.

Success brought even more imitators and, by 1850, there were at least fifty competing panoramic shows in London alone. His shows were also infiltrated by rivals, who sent "spies" – actually art students – to sit in the audience and furiously copy as his work rolled by.

Banvard eventually went back to the studio to create another epic canvas. His first painting had been a panoramic view of the eastern bank of the Mississippi. His new work would depict the western bank. While the original work was still showing in London with a stand-in narrator, Banvard took his new painting on a tour of Britain bringing in another 100,000 visitors. He then moved his show to Paris, where it was once again a sensation, running for the next two years.

During his stay in London, he had been fascinated by the collection of Egyptian artefacts in the Royal Museum. He even learned how to decipher hieroglyphics – one of only a handful of people in the world at that time to have acquired this skill – and became so adept at this that, back in America, he was able to draw large crowds as a lecturer in Egyptology.

The following year, he went to the Middle East and sailed down the Nile, filling his notebook with new sketches, the basis of the first of two new panoramas: one of the Nile, one of Palestine. Along the way, he was using his skill at deciphering hieroglyphics to snap up thousands of local artefacts at knock-down prices. He coined the phrase "Georama" to describe his latest geographic panoramas, but neither was quite as successful as his Mississippi paintings. The public was starting to grow bored with panoramic lectures and the market was flooded with imitators.

Not that this should have troubled Banvard greatly. He was now a fantastically wealthy man, the richest artist in history. In 1852, he returned to America with his growing family and bought a sixty-acre lot on Long Island, where he built a replica of Windsor Castle. He called it Glenada in honour of his daughter. The locals, unimpressed by this tacky display of ostentation, knew it as Banvard's Folly.

By the 1860s, America was in thrall to another great showman, arguably the shrewdest the world had ever seen – the great Phineas T. Barnum. His shows were a heady cocktail of freaks, circus acts, magic acts and fraud (for example, exhibiting the "161-year-old" nursemaid of George Washington). To lend some credibility to his shows, mixed in with the items of questionable provenance, Barnum had also bought up some genuine museum exhibits, including some unusual natural history artefacts.

By 1866, Barnum's ticket sales were more than thirty-five million – more than the actual population of North America.

After a few years of critical and commercial success, living quietly with his family was not enough for Banvard – he was bored and hungry for more. While sitting in his castle full of genuine Egyptian artefacts, he had a brainwave. For several years, he had been toying with the idea of showing his collection in a museum. Now he decided to take on P. T. Barnum, the greatest showman on Earth, at his own game.

For all his years of touring with his panoramic paintings, Banvard had never actually run a proper business before; at least, not a fully functioning operation with a staff to maintain. He had got by in the past with the help of a single secretary, whom he eventually fired when he suspected her of stealing a few dollars from him.

He turned to one of his old Mississippi showboat partners, William Lillienthal, for help, although Lillienthal knew nothing about running a museum either. Together they financed the new Banvard Museum by floating a stock offering with $300,000, which was bought by some of Manhattan's wealthiest families, many of them Banvard's personal friends. In lieu of cash, Banvard paid his suppliers and building workers with shares of this stock. Unfortunately, unbeknown to the backers, Banvard did not register his business, or the stock, with the state of New York. So no actual share certificates existed for the stock, rendering it worthless.

Banvard's Museum opened on 17 June 1867 in Manhattan. It was vast – a 40,000-square-foot building, housing a series of lecture rooms and displays. At the heart of the museum, in front of a 2,000-seater central auditorium, was Banvard's original Mississippi panorama. Surrounding it, in several smaller rooms, was his collection of Egyptian antiquities. In his promotional material, Banvard was very keen to stress the educational qualities of his museum, as opposed to the cheap sensationalism on offer from P. T. Barnum.

But Barnum was more than up to the challenge. Anything Banvard offered that did well with the paying public, Barnum would quickly copy, then promote with superior advertising. Banvard had his original Mississippi panting; Barnum countered with his own Nile panorama – almost certainly copied from Banvard's original. One of Banvard's most popular artefacts was The Cardiff Giant, a ten-foot-tall stone man, discovered by some workers digging a well behind the barn in Cardiff, New York.

Speculation was rife over what the giant might be. Some thought it was a petrified man, others believed it to be an ancient statue. The "petrifactionists" theorized that it was one of the giants mentioned in the Bible, from Genesis 6:4, where we are told, "There were giants in the Earth in those days." Those who promoted the statue theory followed the lead of Dr John F. Boynton, who speculated that a Jesuit missionary had carved it sometime during the seventeenth century to impress the local Indians.

The truth was more prosaic – it was actually the work of an enterprising New York tobacconist named George Hull. The idea of burying a stone giant in the ground occurred to him after he got into an argument with a Methodist Reverend about whether the Bible should be taken literally. He figured he could not only use the fake giant to poke fun at the religious establishment but also make some money. Eventually, a pale-ontologist from Yale paid it a visit and declared it to be a clumsy fake, but the public didn't seem to care and kept coming to see it anyway. Barnum offered Hull $60,000 for a three-month lease of it. When his offer was rejected, Barnum paid an artist to build an exact plaster replica of it, which he then put on display in his museum. Soon, the fake was draw-ing larger crowds than the original fake.

Throughout the summer, Banvard and Barnum battled with increasingly expensive advertising, locked in a struggle that, for one of them, would soon end in commercial death. And to add to the artist's woes, within a few weeks of Banvard's museum opening, shareholders were furious at the discovery that their stock was worthless. Creditors, meanwhile, were har-assing Banvard for payment.

With falling ticket sales, Banvard was desperate to try something new. On 1 September, he shut down his museum and had it completely refurbished, then relaunched it a month later as Banvard's Grand Opera House and Museum. Now it was offering dance productions and plays, such as adapta-tions of *Our Mutual Friend* and *Uncle Tom's Cabin*. It was a commercial disaster. With nothing working, Banvard threw in the towel.

He retreated, humiliated, to his rambling sixty-acre prop-erty, where he and his wife were now alone, except for a single servant. He tried his hand at various other enterprises, but after his terrible treatment of his museum backers no investor would touch a Banvard project.

In 1875, he turned his hand to writing a history book, *The Court and Times of George IV, King of England*. Embarrassingly, it turned out that he had plagiarized a book written forty years earlier. He didn't learn from this lesson. The following year, he wrote a play, *Corrina, A Tale of Sicily*, and performed it in his old museum, now renamed the New Broadway Theatre. The play was not only a copy of someone else's work, it was stolen from a very much alive and very angry playwright.

His business and creative integrity now in tatters, and surrounded by increasingly angry creditors, Banvard tried to sell his museum to his old enemy P. T. Barnum. The reply was swift: "No, sir. I would not take the Broadway Theatre as a gift if I had to run it." He did eventually sell it and, to his dismay, it operated under new ownership to great commercial success.

In 1883, bankruptcy forced Banvard to sell his castle. It was demolished and the contents sold off to pay creditors. The Mississippi painting alone was spared. Badly worn from forty years of use, it was considered worthless.[20] Broke and forgotten by the public, he and his wife, now in their sixties, left New York for South Dakota, where they lived in a spare room in their son's house.

In 1886, desperate for income and with failing eyesight, Banvard attempted to produce one final panoramic masterpiece, *The Burning of Columbia*. It depicted the partial destruction of the capital city of South Carolina by General Sharman's troops on 17 February 1865. According to contemporary accounts, Banvard had lost none of his skills as an artist and it was a magnificent effort, but panoramas had long since had their day. The public of South Dakota stayed away.

Banvard's wife died in 1889 and he followed soon afterwards. Unable to pay either of their funeral bills, his family fled town.

---

20   There is no record of what became of Banvard's epic panorama. According to various accounts, it was either cut up and used as stage scenery or shredded to insulate local houses.

## Most Embarrassing Oscar Nomination

The US film director Frank Capra's 1933 comedy *Lady for a Day* won him his first Academy Award nomination for Best Director and was the bookies' hot favourite to win Best Picture. He was so confident of winning an Oscar that he rented a mansion in Beverly Hills, wrote thank-you notes, rehearsed his speech and bought an expensive tuxedo for the evening.

When Oscar night arrived, the host Will Rogers got to the Best Director category and opened the envelope. "Well, well, well . . ." remarked Rogers, "What do you know! I've watched this young man for a long time. Saw him come up from the bottom, and I mean the bottom. It couldn't have happened to a nicer guy." Finally, he got to the bit Capra was anticipating, when he said, "Come on up and get it, Frank!"

Capra stood up and made his way to the podium, but when he got there he realized, to his horror, that he wasn't alone. The winner was, in fact, another Frank – *Cavalcade* director Frank Lloyd. Capra made his way back to his seat, describing it as "the longest, saddest, most shattering walk in my life".

---

*"Reagan doesn't have that presidential look."*
United Artists Executive, rejecting Reagan
as lead in 1964 film *The Best Man*

---

## Biggest Box-Office Bomb

By the time you read this it is possible that another multi-million-dollar turkey has taken pole position but, at the time of writing, 1995's *Cutthroat Island* is the biggest financial disaster in film history, a fact confirmed by the *Guinness Book of World Records*.

*Cutthroat Island* was a swashbuckling action adventure film about the efforts of a lady pirate and her slave on a quest to recover three portions of a treasure map. The director

Renny Harlin cast his wife Geena Davis as the lead after Michelle Pfeiffer pulled out. Harlin looked around for a male star and found Michael Douglas. He agreed to come on board with two conditions – first, his part had to be at least as big as that of Geena Davis; second, they had to start shooting straight away to fit in with Douglas's busy schedule. Harlin agreed and went scouting for locations, finally settling on Malta and Thailand, some 5,000 miles apart, and built two life-sized galleons.

With the budget already bloated from the scramble to get the sets ready and the logistics of co-coordinating shooting on two continents, Douglas decided he'd had enough and baled out. When Davis heard about her co-star's desertion, she, too, started having second thoughts but was bound to the project by a watertight contract, not to mention the fact that she was married to the director. Harlin searched desperately for a new male lead but had the door slammed by every available A-list actor in Hollywood. Working his way through the B-list, he settled on the young Matthew Modine.

When shooting eventually got under way, a cameraman fell off a crane and broke his leg, then some pipes burst and raw sewage spewed into the tank where the actors were supposed to be working. Harlin fired a camera operator after an argument and twelve crew walked out in support. By the time of release, the $65 million budget had leapt to $115 million. Harlin's spectacular screen effects were overshadowed by bad acting, a clichéd script and appalling continuity errors. The *New York Times* noted: "The film is too stupidly smutty for children and too cartoonish for any sane adult."

In fact, film critics everywhere agreed that everyone involved in making it should walk the plank. *Cutthroat Island* was pulled from the cinemas after a month, having cashed in $10 million in worldwide box-office gross. That was a net loss of $105 million in 1995 but, when adjusted for inflation, a net loss of $147 million, sinking the studio that made it, Carolco Pictures.

## Least Successful TV Show

The American actor Tim Conway starred in more failed TV shows than anyone in history, a fact he playfully acknowledged in his car number plate "13 WEEKS" – the length of time it took to cancel all of his solo TV projects.

He was also part of one of the most infamous network TV flops ever. On 5 February 1969, Conway hosted the first of eighteen planned episodes of a new ABC series, *Turn On*, touted as a "boundary-pushing" rival to the popular comedy *Rowan & Martin's Laugh-In*.

To offer a flavour of the sort of quality the American TV audience were treated to, among the sketches aired on the programme:

- Two policemen say, "Let us spray", before spraying cans of mace at the camera.
- A nun asks a priest, "Father, can I have the car tonight?" The priest replies, "Just as long as you don't get in the habit."
- Several gay-themed messages scrolling across the screen include "God Save the Queens", "Free Oscar Wilde" and "The Amsterdam Levee Is a Dike".
- An anxious young woman feeds coins into a broken vending machine dispensing birth control pills then shakes it.
- A puppet snake says, "Remember, folks, I could have given Eve the apple *and* the Pill!"

Before the show was halfway through, an estimated seventeen million shocked Americans had turned off and ABC's Philadelphia affiliate WFIL were forced to pull the plug on their switchboards because they couldn't handle the number of complaints.

It received such a negative reaction that several TV stations, including one in Conway's home town of Cleveland, refused to return to the programme after the first commercial break.

ABC cancelled the series on the same day it went out. Afterwards, the cast and crew held a party, simultaneously marking the show's première and cancellation.

## Worst Film Director

*"Plan 9 is my pride and joy.*
*We used Cadillac hubcaps for flying saucers in that."*

Edward D. Wood Jr

During his fifty-four years, Ed Wood produced a series of low-budget B-movies described as "among the most compelling fiascos ever committed to celluloid", including *Glen or Glenda* (1952), *Bride of the Monster* (1953), *Jail Bait* (1954), *Plan 9 from Outer Space* (1959), *Night of the Ghouls* (1960) and *Necromancy* (1972).

Wood's work was informed by a complicated private life. While happily married to the same woman until his death, he was also a transvestite. His mother, apparently disappointed that she didn't have a daughter, dressed him in skirts until he was twelve years old.

Technically, Wood was, in fact, a transvestite war hero. Six months after Pearl Harbor, he enlisted in the Marines where he earned several medals, including the Bronze Star, the Silver Star and the Purple Heart. He took part in the invasion of Tarawa, where of over 4,000 Marines only one man in ten survived. Wood was injured, losing his front teeth to a rifle butt and taking several bullets in the leg. After the battle, he confessed to a fellow Marine, "I wanted to be killed, Joe . . . I didn't want to be wounded because I could never explain my pink panties and pink bra."

Following his discharge from the Marines, Wood joined a circus freak show and played a bearded lady wearing women's clothing and prosthetic breasts. By 1948, he had written, produced, directed and performed in his first big failure, a stage play called *The Casual Company*. The play's subject matter was close to Wood's heart: a handsome man falls for a pretty woman wearing a fluffy angora sweater.

Wood tried to break into the film industry, initially without success, but finally landed the chance to direct a film based on the famous Christine Jorgensen sex-change. The result, *Glen or Glenda*, was a semi-autobiographical tribute to Wood's angora fetishism.

Wood plays the title role, while the blonde actress Dolores Fuller is his fiancée, described by the narrator as "a lovely, intelligent girl". She says things such as, "Here we are, two perfectly normal people about to be married and lead a normal life together!" not long before finding out that her husband-to-be is lusting to wear her white angora sweater. Presented as an educational documentary on the subject, *Glen or Glenda* is interrupted, from time to time, by a ranting and raving Bela Lugosi, who irrelevantly declaims: "Bevare . . . bevare . . . bevare of the big green dragon that sits on your doorstep. He eats little boys, puppy dog tails and big fat snails. Bevare . . . take care . . . bevare." The happy ending of the film was not repeated in life. According to Fuller, "Ed begged me to marry him. I loved him in a way, but I couldn't handle the transvestism."

The highlight of Wood's career was his space vampire movie, *Plan 9 from Outer Space* (1959), regularly voted the worst film ever, in which aliens try to take over the world by resurrecting the dead. The acting was terrible and the dialogue ludicrous, but the sets were even worse. The haunted cemetery was obviously built inside a studio, the floor clearly visible around the "grass" and studio floodlights remain in shot. At one point, an actor is seen tripping over a cardboard tombstone, causing it to bend.

The sudden actual death of the leading man, elderly horror star Bela Lugosi, only three days into filming might have defeated a lesser man than Wood. Enlisting his wife's chiropractor, the director had Lugosi's stand-in wear the actor's trademark Dracula cape and cover his face with it, a cunning ploy that he might have pulled off successfully had Lugosi not been a good foot shorter than his replacement.

Continuity was not one of Wood's strengths. In *Bride of the Monster*, for example, a secretary picks up a phone and answers it, then carries on a conversation, although it hasn't yet rung. The ring tone of the phone was supposed to be dubbed in afterwards, but the veteran director simply forgot to do it. Lugosi, playing a crazed scientist, delivers the line, "Don't be afraid of Lobo, he's as harmless as kitchen." The original line in the script had read, "Don't be afraid of Lobo, he's as harmless as a kitten," but Lugosi was suffering from severe drug-addiction at the time and refused to do a retake, so the line stayed in.

Wood went into alcoholic decline, directing soft and later hardcore pornography before his premature death aged fifty-four. He suffered a fatal heart attack while watching a televised football game in his bedroom. The stricken film director yelled out to his wife in the next room, "Kathy, I can't breathe!" a plea she ignored for ninety minutes before finally going in to find him dead. Apparently, he often feigned heart attacks and screamed for help as a joke. At one point, she shouted at him to shut up.

One of his movies, *Bride of the Monster*, actually made money, but not for Wood; he had already sold all his rights to it. But sixteen years after his death, a film was made about his terrible films starring Johnny Depp, called *Ed Wood*. And *that* film made a lot of money.

# 6

## Disorder in Court: Criminal Losers

*In which some burglars find crime doesn't pay; a judge turns cannibal; a gun-slinging outlaw steals a bunch of bananas; Mr Carlton is seduced by a "Staffy"; and God gets a motoring ticket.*

### Most Inept Executioner

Richard Arnett became London's hangman in 1719 after the incumbent, William Marvel, had himself been hanged for stealing ten silk handkerchiefs. Arnett turned up so late for his first appointment that, when he finally arrived, the crowd showed their displeasure by throwing him in a pond. The three condemned men were returned to Newgate Prison while Arnett received medical attention.

Arnett was once supposed to hang two felons, but turned up dead drunk and accidentally tried to hang two priests who had come to administer last rites to the prisoners. When he eventually got round to hanging the right people, the platform collapsed and Arnett and two officials fell ten feet to the ground, landing in a heap on top of the two prisoners; he had forgotten to secure the bolt that held the platform together. He also turned up late for the hanging of the gang leader Jonathan Wild at Tyburn in 1725, giving Wild's pickpockets plenty of time to relieve the spectators of their watches and wallets. Arnett received another ducking.

London's eighteenth-century chief executioner John Thrift, though, was considered the most incompetent man ever to have held that position. Thrift, a convicted murderer, set free on condition that he did the government's dirty work as an axeman, was completely unsuited to the job. He was extremely volatile, unsure with the axe and liable to bursting into tears at inappropriate moments, and couldn't stand the sight of blood.

When he was called upon to execute the Jacobite rebel Lord Balmerino at the Tower of London in 1745, he fainted, then lay on the ground sobbing while onlookers tried to persuade him to get on with it. When Thrift finally took up his axe, he took five blows to sever Balmerino's head. Although Thrift never quite got he hang of it, he somehow managed to blunder and hack his way through a seventeen-year career. His clumsiness made him such a public hate figure that, when he died in 1752, a mob pelted his funeral entourage with stones and dead cats.

---

*"There will never be a bigger plane built."*
Boeing engineer, after the first flight of the 247,
a twin-engine plane that held ten people.

---

## The Defence Rests . . . in Peace

During the Civil War era, the US Congressman Clement Vallandigham enjoyed a career as prosperous and successful lawyer until a court case in 1871. He was defending Thomas McGehan, accused of shooting another man dead in a bar room brawl. While cleverly demonstrating how the murder victim could have inadvertently shot himself, Vallandigham grabbed a pistol he thought was unloaded, re-enacted the event for the benefit of the jury . . . and shot himself dead in the process.

Having proved his point, his client was acquitted.

---

*"Space travel is utter bilge."*
Richard Van Der Riet Woolley, upon assuming
the post of Astronomer Royal in 1956.

---

## Least Accurate Sentencing by a Judge

Justice is not only blind but also hard of hearing. At Cardiff Crown Court in 1999, Alan Rashid was charged with making a death threat. After two days of evidence, his legal team were quietly confident that their client would be acquitted.

When the judge, Justice Michael Gibbon, asked the jury foreman to state their verdict, the foreman replied "not guilty" but, as he spoke, one of his fellow jurors coughed loudly, drowning out the word "not".

Judge Gibbon, mistakenly believing that the jury had just found the defendant guilty, admonished Mr Rashid for the error of his ways and sentenced him to two years' imprisonment.

The jurors were puzzled by the sentence, but assumed that perhaps Rashid was being sentenced for some other offence from an earlier hearing. On the way out of court, one of the jurors paused to ask a court usher casually why Rashid had been sent down. It was only then that the penny dropped; the bewildered defendant, who minutes earlier was facing a lengthy jail sentence, was called back to the dock and told that he was free to leave after all.

---

*"Too far-fetched to be considered."*
Editor of *Scientific American*, in a letter to Robert Goddard about his idea of a rocket-accelerated aeroplane bomb, 1940 (German V2 missiles rained down on London three years later).

---

## Most Inappropriate Summing Up

In 1997, Judge Joseph Triosi was presiding over a hearing in Pleasants County courtroom in West Virginia, at which the defendant, twenty-nine-year-old William Witten, charged with grand larceny, was refused bail.

As Witten was leaving the courtroom, he was heard to call the judge a "fucking arsehole". Triosi removed his robes, stepped down from the bench, walked up to the defendant, bit the tip off his nose, then spat it on to the courtroom floor.

The judge, who was said to have a history of erratic courtroom behaviour, resigned shortly afterwards. Attorney Steven Jones, representing Witten, noted, "I worry about what might have happened if he [Triosi] had had a gun with him at the time."

---

*"Defeat of Germany means defeat of Japan,
probably without firing a shot or losing a life."*
US President Franklin D. Roosevelt, 1942

---

## Most Inept Wild West Outlaw

Little Al Jennings always dreamed of becoming a famous outlaw, despite being inconveniently born very much on the right side of the law into a highly respectable family in Kiowa Creek, Oklahoma – his father, J. D. F. Jennings, was the local judge.

In the mid-1890s, the pint-sized cowpoke (five foot one inch with his boots on) began his career as an outlaw when he and his and brother Frank acquired some fake US marshal's badges and used them to collect "tolls" from gullible trail herders moving their cattle through Oklahoma. They were later joined by several members of the Doolin Gang – Little Dick West, and Morris and Pat O'Malley – and under Al Jennings' leadership planned to rob trains. On 16 August 1897, they stopped a southbound Santa Fe train at Edmond. After two unsuccessful attempts to dynamite the safe, they gave up and rode off, cursing their bad luck.

A few nights later, they attempted a variation on this tactic when Al Jennings tried to flag down another train by standing directly in the middle of the railroad track, holding a lantern

and waving a red flag. The engineer simply ignored him and
kept his hand on the throttle. As the train roared forward,
Jennings leaped for his life to avoid being run over. The train
raced on into the night as Jennings and the rest of his gang
stood looking on.

A few days later, Al and his brother Frank rode alongside a
fast-moving Santa Fe train, fired their six guns in the air and
instructed the engineer to stop. The engineer leaned from the
window of his cabin, gave them a cheery wave and went on his
way. The Jennings brothers chased after the train until their
horses were exhausted, then watched as their prey steamed
into the distance.

On their next job, they tried to stop a train by piling up
railroad ties across the tracks. Unfortunately, they had picked
a moonlit night and the train engineer could see the pile of ties
and the waiting horsemen from a mile away. Instead of slowing
down, the engineer set the locomotive at full throttle and
simply ploughed through the obstacle.

As train robbing was turning out to be unprofitable, they
decided to try their hand at robbing an express mail office.
The outlaws surrounded the office and peered through the
windows to see if it was manned. The express agent, seeing
faces masked with bandanas popping up at his windows,
picked up the phone and called the local sheriff. Within minutes, a posse of armed men was heading for the office. The
gang fled empty handed.

Next, they tried their hand at robbing a bank, but made the
mistake of selecting a branch near their home town and where
everyone knew them. The surprise element of the raid was also
compromised by Al Jennings' habit of shooting his mouth off
about his schemes in advance. The bank was expecting him
and, when he and his gang arrived, they were quickly
surrounded and forced to flee, again empty handed.

They went back to robbing trains. Next was a raid on a
southbound Rock Island passenger train on 1 October 1897.
Al and Frank Jennings, Little Dick West and the O'Malley
brothers found the train stopped at a water station eight miles

south of Minco. This time, Al had made sure he brought
plenty of dynamite with him. He inserted a long fuse into one
stick, lit it, and placed the dynamite next to the safe, then the
outlaws leapt from the baggage car and ran for safety. A few
seconds later, the car blew up, sending a shower of debris in
all directions. When the smoke cleared, there was no baggage
car, but the safe had remained intact. The train robbers made
off with an assortment of valuables taken from the passengers, including a jug of whisky, a pair of new boots and a
bunch of bananas.

Four weeks later, they held up the Crozier and Nutter Store
in the town of Cushing in Payne County. The robbery netted
the gang a grand total of $15. It was the last straw for Little
Dick West and the O'Malleys, who rode off in disgust.

It was, in fact, the last successful robbery for the Al Jennings
gang. A marshal in Muskogee, Oklahoma, got a tip-off that the
Jennings boys were in a covered wagon moving through his
territory. He tracked down the wagon and found Al and Frank
Jennings hiding under some blankets. They surrendered without a shot being fired. At this point, their criminal careers had
netted them less than $200 apiece.

Frank Jennings was sentenced to a five-year term in
Leavenworth. Al, the criminal mastermind of the Jennings
gang, was sent to the federal prison at Columbus, Ohio, to
serve a life term, but was freed after five years, pardoned by
President Theodore Roosevelt who happened to be an old
friend of his father, Judge Jennings. Two years later, Al married
a lady named Maude who had taken to visiting him in prison.
He always referred to her as "the little woman", although she
stood at least six inches taller than him.

Regardless of his bumbling efforts as an outlaw, in his own
mind Al Jennings was a gunslinging desperado of some repute.
In prison, he met a writer, William Sydney Porter, imprisoned
for embezzlement, who wrote under the pseudonym O. Henry.
Al regaled Porter with stories about his exploits. Whether or
not Porter was taken in by his yarns is moot, but he used them
to create a character called "The Cisco Kid".

After his release, Al Jennings headed for California and settled in Hollywood, where he continued to pose as a dangerous gunslinger who had been involved in over twenty gun fights. A typical anecdote began: "When I was fourteen, I was standing around Dodge City with Bat Masterson and the boys. An actor wearing a stovepipe hat got off the train. Bat pulled his gun and said, 'I'll plug that hat.' He fired and the man fell dead. 'Guess I shot too low,' said Bat."

Jennings claimed he robbed more trains than Jesse James and killed more men than Billy the Kid and described himself as the "the fastest gun on the range". "I always shot 'em in the throat so they couldn't talk back," he would say. His biggest claim to fame was that he was a quicker draw than James and had once outgunned him in a gunfight; in spite of the fact that James was already dead at the time Jennings claimed this contest took place. He was vague about the identities of his other shootout victims, "in case somebody might start digging that old trouble up and making something out of it again". In fact, no records exist of him ever having killed anybody.

In 1914, he ran for Governor of Oklahoma, pledging, "If elected, I promise to be honest for a year, if I can hold out for that long." He was soundly beaten, and the experience caused him to grumble, "There's more honesty among train robbers than among some public officials."

Al Jennings wrote two books about his mythical life as an outlaw which were the basis of a film biopic called *Al Jennings of Oklahoma*, and he went on to carve out a career as technical consultant, screenwriter and minor character actor in around a hundred films about the old Wild West. If only he had been as tall as his tales, he could have been a leading man.

## Least Successful Display of Impartiality by a Juror

In 1997 at Luton Crown Court, Judge Alan Wilkie QC ordered a retrial for a man accused of smuggling crack cocaine. During the original trial, a juror, Shane Smyth, had shouted at the defendant, "Why don't you plead guilty? You are fucking guilty!"

> *"Nuclear-powered vacuum cleaners will
> probably be a reality in ten years."*
> Alex Lewyt, president of vacuum cleaner company
> Lewyt Corp., in the *New York Times* in 1955

## Most Incompetent Assassin

In 1878, Max Hödel, a 31-year-old plumber and part-time anarchist from Leipzig, set out to shoot the German Emperor Wilhelm I in Berlin. It probably wasn't a good idea therefore, a few days before the attack, to book himself a photo session with a Berlin portrait photographer and to pose with his new revolver, cheerfully informing the cameraman that the photo would soon be worth a fortune because he would be world-famous within the week.

Hödel's target, the Emperor, was a sprightly if slightly eccentric eighty-one-year-old who tempted fate by being so predictable in his daily routine that Berlin tourist guidebooks could even list the exact time he could be seen looking out of his palace window. On 11 May 1878, Wilhelm was making his routine daily trip in an open carriage from his palace in Berlin along the Unter den Linden, with his daughter Louise. Hiding in the cheering crowd, armed with his pistol, Hödel struggled to get a good vantage point. As the Emperor's coach approached, he found his line of fire inconveniently blocked by a street vendor, a Mrs Hauch, who was selling drinks to the crowd from her water wagon. As Wilhelm's carriage passed by, Hödel shoved her out of the way and took aim with his gun. The woman, annoyed by Hödel's rudeness, shoved back just as he was pulling the trigger, causing his gun to fire harmlessly wide. Hödel clubbed her over the head with the butt of his revolver and pushed his way to the front of the crowd.

He fired a second time, again shooting well wide of his target, then ran into the street to get a better aim. Along the way, he fired on another bystander who tried to stop him, but again missed. Hödel dropped to his knees in the middle of the road, gripped the gun with both hands combat-style, steadied his aim then fired at the Emperor again. By this time, to everyone's astonishment, Wilhelm was standing up in the carriage to get a better view of what was going on. Hödel fired again, completely missing his target for the fourth time, then gave up and took flight, pursued by several onlookers. As he ran, he turned and fired on the chasing pack, again hitting no one. The emperor's driver and another man called Kohler cornered him in an alleyway and a violent struggle ensued in which all three men were badly hurt. Kohler died two days later from internal injuries.

At his trial, Hödel told a packed courtroom that his failed regicidal assault was in fact a suicide attempt; he'd planned to blow his own brains out in front of the Emperor to bring his attention to the plight of the poor. When confronted with the testimonies of scores of eyewitnesses, including the pistol-whipped Frau Hauch, he thought better of it and changed his plea to guilty.

The penalty for attempted regicide was beheading by axe. On 16 August 1878, Hödel faced the axeman after eating two steaks and drinking a bottle of wine. His head bounced twice before it came to rest.

Only a couple of weeks after Hödel's miss, a second unsuccessful attempt on the Emperor's life was undertaken by another incompetent gunman, Karl Nobiling. When the police moved in arrest him, Nobiling put the revolver to his own head and pulled the trigger. The bullet penetrated his skull, but incredibly did not kill him outright. As Nobiling was sped away to prison hospital in a green, open-topped police van, the driver, keen to get his passenger to his destination before he bled to death, drove his van under a low bridge, breaking the driver's neck and killing him instantly. Nature didn't take its course with Kaiser Wilhelm for nine more years.

## Least Successful Courtroom Defence

In 1985, Dennis Newton stood trial for entering a convenience store in Oklahoma City, raising a gun to the store manager's head and demanding money. The prosecuting attorney asked the chief witness, the store manager, if she could identify the culprit. When she pointed to Newton, he stood up and shouted, "Liar . . . I should have blown your fucking head off!" After a few moments of reflection, he added, ". . . if I'd been the one that was there."

Newton was jailed for thirty years.

## Least Successful Courtroom Defence: Runner-Up

In 1998, Sidney Carlton, a painter and decorator from Bradford, was tried for the offence of bestiality after he admitted having had sexual intercourse with a Staffordshire Bull Terrier called Badger.

Carlton's defence was that Badger had made the first move. He told the court, "I can't help it if the dog took a liking to me." He was sentenced to one year in prison.

---

*"The elephant's nature is such that if he tumbles down he cannot get up again. Hence it comes that he leans against a tree when he wants to go to sleep, for he has no joints in his knees. This is the reason why a hunter partly saws through a tree, so that the elephant, when he leans against it, may fall down at the same time as the tree."*

*The Book of Beasts*, twelfth century AD

---

## Most Accommodating Assassination Target

As Oscar Wilde might have put it, losing your life to a paid assassin is unfortunate; but losing your life to an assassin when you've actually paid for the murder weapon yourself looks like carelessness. This was the unusual fate which befell William "the Silent", heretic leader of the Dutch revolt against Spain.

William was one of a handful of Protestant heads of state in sixteenth-century Europe. The biggest threat to their peaceful existence at that time came in the person of the Pope's "enforcer", King Philip II of Spain, whose aim in life was to wipe out every last Protestant on Earth. To that end, the dark forces of Philip's Spanish Inquisition were employed efficiently and ruthlessly, torturing and executing heretics by the thousand.

One of the biggest pockets of nonconformism targeted by Philip was the Spanish Netherlands. William of Nassau, Prince of Orange, was known as William the Silent because of his deep, taciturn nature. William was leader of the rebel Protestant Netherlands, which from 1555 had been ruled by the King of Spain through resident governors. The Dutch people resisted Spanish attempts to impose heavy taxes on them, just as they had opposed Spain's attempts to impose their faith. In 1581, after almost twenty years of conflict with Spain, the Netherlands formally renounced allegiance to King Philip II and proclaimed William their head of state. Philip, who had long regarded assassination as a legitimate instrument of foreign policy, abandoned all pretence of diplomatic nicety and declared William the Silent an outlaw, offering a reward of 25,000 gold crowns to anyone who would silence him permanently.

William's reputation as the quiet, cautious type was misinterpreted by the Spanish as cowardice. It was suggested that even if a willing assassin could not be found, William would almost certainly die of fright anyway. The first of many attempts on his life came six months later. In December 1582, a twenty-year-old warehouse clerk, Juan Jauréguy, was able to walk up to William and level a pistol at him at point-blank range, but the gun was over-charged with gunpowder and blew up in the assailant's hand. The blast singed William's hair and set fire to his ruff and the bullet hit him in the face, lodging in his palate. Jauréguy was slain on the spot by bodyguards.

William suffered agonies from the wounds but survived the

attack, not least because of the remarkable attentions of his servants, who held the wound closed with their fingers, in relays, for seventeen days. His devoted wife Charlotte, who helped to nurse him back to health, died of exhaustion and fever in the process. Later that year, two more Catholics tried to poison him, closely followed by two unsuccessful attempts to blow up William at his palace.

In spite of the price on his head and several previous attempts on his life, William insisted on keeping open house with an almost total lack of security. On 10 July 1584, as he was talking to a group of friends in the hallway of his home in Delft, a cabinet-maker's apprentice, Balthasar Gerard, approached and shot him from close range with two pistols. The bullets passed through William's stomach into the wall beyond. The Prince of Orange died on his couch before his doctor arrived.

It was not the first time that the killer and his intended target had met, face to face. Gerard, far from being a professional assassin, didn't own a sword, let alone a gun. He didn't know how he was going to kill William without a weapon, so he approached his sponsor, King Philip, to ask for an advance on the reward so he could finance his assassination attempt. Philip refused – the terms were strictly cash on delivery. Gerard then presented himself at William's court in Delft, posing as a poor Protestant who had recently escaped persecution from the Spanish. William was so moved by Gerard's story that he gave him some money – enough for him to buy a couple of pistols – from one of William's own guards.

It was one of the most audacious assassination attempts in history; his escape plan, however, was heroically stupid. Balthasar Gerard was seized within a few minutes of the attack while trying to escape over a garden wall. He was searched and found to be carrying only a pair of deflated water wings. The assassin, a non-swimmer, hoped to escape across a nearby canal. In accordance with the law, he was mutilated, disembowelled and quartered, but King Philip honoured his promise of a reward by paying out to Gerard's family – the money, however, was taken from William of Orange's eldest son, whom Philip held hostage in Spain.

The regicidal Balthasar was hailed a heroic martyr by Dutch Catholics who preserved his head as a holy relic. William, meanwhile, earned the dubious distinction of becoming the first political leader ever to be assassinated by a handgun.

> *"Atomic energy might be as good as our present-day explosives, but it is unlikely to produce anything very much more dangerous."*
> Winston Churchill, British prime minister, 1939

## Least Successful Invocation of God's Word to Avoid a Motoring Fine

In 2001, during a routine vehicle check near Neath, South Wales, Peter David, a lay preacher, informed police that he did not need an MOT, road tax or motor insurance certificate because God was his passenger and he had divine protection. In court later, David admitted the offences but refused to enter a guilty plea, telling magistrates, "I do not recognize the authority of the court or the Parliament in England. God's word is the only law I recognize." The Crown solicitor commented later, "We get all sorts in here but we don't expect to see God in the witness box." David was ordered to pay £800 in fines, costs and back duty to the DVLA.

David was stopped again by police a few days later and found using false number plates on his Ford Sierra – DEUT 818, referring to the Bible's book of Deuteronomy, Chapter 8, Verse 18, which warns that God is the only source of power. PC Richard Coulthard, upon finding that the registration was invalid, was informed by sixty-six-year-old David, "The Lord told me I could put verses for His praise and glory."

PC Coulthard begged to differ, telling Neath magistrates, "I conducted a check on the chassis and I established that the correct vehicle index should have been A903 BUX." David said he had sold his Ford Sierra and replaced it with a Vauxhall Cavalier with the number plate JOHN 316, a reference to John 3:16. He was banned from driving for two years.

> *"Bees are generated from decomposed veal."*
>
> St Isidore of Seville, seventh century AD

## Least Perceptive Prison Guards

In July 1978, the "escape-proof" high-security Alcoentre penitentiary near Lisbon lost 124 inmates – half the prison population – in one evening. The guards had failed to notice that 220 knives and hundreds of yards of electric cable had also gone missing prior to the mass breakout, along with several spades, chisels and electric drills. Nor did they realize the significance of dozens of posters that had appeared in recent weeks hiding gaping holes in cell walls.

The guards only discovered the escape bid when one of the few remaining prisoners told them about it. Some of this may sound familiar; one of the films on the Alcoentre prison cinema schedule that week was *The Great Escape*.

> *"When [the beaver] is pursued, knowing this to be on account of the virtue of its testicles for medicinal uses, not being able to flee any farther it stops and in order to be at peace with its pursuers bites off its testicles with its sharp teeth and leaves them to its enemies."*
>
> Leonardo da Vinci

## Least Successful Prison Breakout

On 18 April 1976, seventy-five inmates of the Saltillo Prison in northern Mexico made their bid for freedom after spending six months digging a tunnel, only to find that it emerged into the nearby courtroom where most of them had been sentenced.

The surprised judges promptly returned all seventy-five to their cells.

---

> *"The so-called theories of Einstein are merely the ravings of a mind polluted with liberal, democratic nonsense which is utterly unacceptable to German men of science."*
>
> Dr Walter Gross, 1940

---

## Most Failed Attempts to Kill a Political Leader

The Cuban president Fidel Castro, according to the people who had the job of keeping him alive, survived more than six hundred attempts to assassinate him.[1] The bids to kill Castro began after the 1959 revolution that brought him to power when a CIA agent sent from Paris failed to snuff him out with a cunningly disguised pen-syringe.

There were several attempts to kill Castro using explosives. On one occasion, a barrage of shells aimed at the Cuban leader missed him by forty minutes but melted all of the traffic lights in downtown Havana. On another, three would-be assassins were apprehended while carrying a bazooka across a university campus in broad daylight. When Castro was on a visit to Panama, the CIA tried to smuggle 200 lbs of high explosives under the podium where he was due to speak. Castro's personal security team intervened and the plot was aborted.

---

1   638, according to Fabian Escalante, Castro's former head of personal security.

Some of the attempts to kill him were more fanciful. The CIA recruited one of Castro's former lovers to track him down and finish him off; she was given poisoned pills, which she hid in a jar of cold cream, but the pills dissolved. She toyed with the idea of slipping cold cream into Castro's mouth while he was snoozing, but lost her nerve. On another occasion, a poisoned chocolate milkshake was accidentally placed in a freezer; by the time it was offered to Castro, it was frozen solid and had lost its potency. There were other attempts to prepare bacterial poisons to be placed in Castro's handkerchief or in his tea and coffee, but none got off the drawing board.

In 1960, the CIA tried to dose some of his cigars with a virulent toxin, slipped into his private stash during a trip to the United Nations. They aborted similar plans to load his cigars with explosives, or with a hallucinogenic drug to give him a wild acid trip to embarrass him during a public appearance.[2]

In the most bizarre plot of all, the CIA hoped to undermine Castro's popularity by planting thallium salts – a powerful hair remover – in his shoes during a trip overseas so that his famous beard would fall out. When the CIA found out that Castro enjoyed scuba diving, they bought a diving suit and contaminated the regulator with fungus spores, hoping to give him a rare skin disease. Unfortunately, the diplomat assigned to hand over the "dirty" suit gave him a clean one instead.

Undaunted, the CIA explored the possibility of placing an exploding conch at Castro's favourite diving spot. The plan was to find a shell big enough to contain a lethal quantity of explosives, and then paint it in bright colours to attract Castro's attention when he was underwater.

The most visionary scheme to kill the Cuban leader came from General Edward Lansdale, who contemplated invoking Jesus Christ himself in the covert war against Castro. The general hoped to spark a counter-revolution by spreading the word to Cuban Catholics that Castro was the anti-Christ. At

---

2 The CIA also considered impregnating a TV studio with LSD to make Castro look "deranged" during an interview.

the imminent Second Coming, Christ was going to surface off the shores of Cuba on board a US submarine. Devout Cubans, Lansdale explained, would rise up and overthrow their evil leader.

In his autobiography *Shadow Warrior*, retired CIA operative Felix Rodriguez confessed to three trips to Cuba to assassinate Castro. In 1987, the Iran-Contra committee wanted to know if Rodriguez took part in the CIA's infamous attempt to poison Castro's cigars. "No sir, I did not," he replied. "But I did volunteer to kill that son of a bitch in 1961 with a telescopic rifle."

Unofficially, the CIA abandoned attempts to kill Castro in the 1980s, but the Cuban leader wasn't taking any chances. He moved address twenty times and gave up smoking in 1985. Jokes about Castro's apparent indestructibility were commonplace in Cuba. One told of him being presented with a Galapagos turtle; Castro declined the gift after learning that it was likely to live only 100 years. "That's the problem with pets," he grumbled, "you get attached to them and then they die on you." At the time of writing, since the Cuban revolution Castro has survived ten US presidents.

## Most Clueless Burglar

In November 1978, a burglar broke into a home in Baltimore and assaulted the lady occupant before demanding cash. When she explained that there was little money in the house, he said he would take a cheque – "Make it out to Charles A. Meriweather . . ."

He left with the cheque, warning her that if it bounced, he would be back. He was arrested a few hours later.

---

*"We need not hesitate to admit that the Sun is richly stored with inhabitants."*

Sir William Herschel

## Most Badly Planned Robbery

In 1978, police in Essex were on the look-out for three would-be Post Office raiders who had burst into a high street premises, only to discover that it had ceased to be a Post Office twelve years earlier – it was now a general store with just £6 in the till. They raided the till and left.

The seventy-six-year-old manageress commented, "I think it was a bit of a disappointment to them."

> *"You've got to call yourself 'Rock' or 'Jack' or something . . . anything as long as it's not 'Elvis Presley'."*
> Rockabilly musician Ronnie Hawkins to
> Elvis Presley, date unknown.

## Most Badly Planned Robbery: Runner-Up

In July 1997, three armed robbers planned to raid a South Shields travel agents but miscalculated and broke into the optician's next door, brandishing a knife and a replica sawn-off shotgun. Realizing their error, they beat a hasty retreat. After finally locating the travel agents, they demanded to know where the safe was but then lost their nerve. Instead of stealing £30,000 in travellers' cheques, they made off with just one large charity bottle full of unwanted foreign coins.

Their getaway car then ran out of petrol and they were forced to abandon it, leaving tell-tale clues which led to their subsequent arrest. At their trial, the judge described it as "not a very efficient robbery".

> *"These Google guys, they want to be billionaires and rock stars and go to conferences and all that. Let's see if they still want to run the business in two or three years."*
> Bill Gates, on Google magnates Sergey
> Bring and Larry Page, 2003

## Least Profitable Till Raid

In 1977, a thief from Southampton came up with an ingenious plan to steal cash from the till of a local supermarket. On the way out, he would hand the checkout girl £10 to pay for his groceries, then when she opened the till, he would grab the contents and make a run for it.

All went according to plan until she opened the till and found that it held only £4.37. He took the cash and fled the supermarket, having lost £5.63 in the raid.

---

*"The basic questions of design, material and shielding, in combining a nuclear reactor with a home boiler and cooling unit, no longer are problems . . . The system would heat and cool a home, provide unlimited household hot water, and melt the snow from sidewalks and driveways. All that could be done for six years on a single charge of fissionable material costing about $300."*

Robert Ferry, executive of the US Institute of Boiler and Radiator Manufacturers, 1955

---

## Least Successful Counterfeit Operation

In December 2011, thirty-three-year-old Michael Anthony Fuller went into his local Wal-Mart supermarket in North Carolina and tried to pass a $1 million note in exchange for a microwave, vacuum cleaner and other goods totalling $476.

Insisting that his homemade note was the real deal, Fuller demanded $999,524 in change. A suspicious checkout girl alerted the police and Fuller was arrested and charged with attempting to obtain goods by deception and "uttering a forged instrument".

Having failed to do his homework Fuller was unaware that the largest note currently in circulation in the United States is $100.

> *"Sincerity is the quality that comes through on television."*
> *The Washington Star*, on Richard Nixon, 1955

## Least Successful Unfair Dismissal Claim

In 2006, Emilee Bauer, from Iowa, USA, sought compensation for unfair dismissal after being fired by the Sheraton hotel company. Bauer, aged twenty-five, had written a 300-page journal during office hours, describing in detail her efforts to avoid work. Among her entries were: "This typing thing seems to be doing the trick. It just looks like I am hard at work on something . . ." and "Once lunch is over, I will come right back to writing to piddle away the rest of the afternoon . . ." and "Accomplishment is overrated, anyway . . ."

The tribunal ruled that Bauer did not qualify for compensation.

> *"I do not consider Hitler to be as bad as he is depicted.*
> *He is showing an ability that is amazing and he seems*
> *to be gaining his victories without much bloodshed."*
> Mohandas "Mahatma" K. Gandhi, 1940

# 7

## Quacking Up: Medical Losers

*In which a man resurrects dead chickens; a queen's bowels are mortified; a criminologist's head is pickled; an anaesthetist dies painlessly; and King Charles II enjoys a rock-salt enema.*

### The Forgotten Man of Medicine

The first great Renaissance physician was a little Swiss man called Philip Theophrastus Aureolus Bombastus von Hohenheim, otherwise known as Paracelsus.

Much of his extraordinary life is hidden in the fog of legend and myth. He was rumoured to have made a pact with the devil, to travel on a magical white horse and to have a phial containing the elixir of life in the pommel of his sword. He wrote hugely influential books on medicine and surgery while living the life of a tramp. Unfortunately, it was quite hard to tell what Paracelsus thought about anything, because he was drunk most of the time and a lot of his writings were wilfully obscure and occasionally obscene.

Paracelsus was born in Switzerland in the village of Einsiede in 1493. His mother died while he was still a boy, possibly a suicide as a result of mental illness. His father taught alchemy at the local college. At the age of fourteen, he set off on foot to seek an education at the universities of Europe, living for several years the life of a footloose, wandering scholar.

In 1517, he gained a doctorate in medicine at the university of Ferrera in Italy. After getting his degree, he hit the road again, supporting himself along the way as a doctor and occasionally as an army surgeon, treating everyone from gypsies to wealthy noblemen. Sometimes his efforts were well paid, but he was often reduced to peddling his home-made medicines by the roadside.

His bedside manner left much to be desired: obese, foul-mouthed and weather-beaten, it was said "he lived like a pig and looked like a sheep drover". Everywhere he went, he took his large broadsword with him, even to bed. He spent a large part of his life in taverns, challenging the locals to drinking contests and usually winning. On his travels, however, he picked up an amazing amount of expertise in the practical treatment of illnesses – a mixture of local remedies, common sense and old wives' tales.

In Constantinople, Paracelsus risked being thrown into the notorious Yedikule dungeons, the traditional last resting place for infidels, to learn from the local peasant women. They practised a primitive form of medicine, which protected them from a variety of diseases, including the dreaded smallpox, by cutting open a vein and inserting an infected needle. Paracelsus noted: "What makes a man ill also cures him." It was a basic understanding of inoculation 200 years ahead of its time.

Unfortunately, this good work was offset by teachings that were completely barking mad. He believed that Alpine cattle drew moisture from the air and that a man could survive without food if he planted his feet in the Earth. Many of his contributions to toxicology were based on astrological readings. He subscribed to the doctrine of signatures, that is, a plant could cure the body part it vaguely resembled. He published instructions for resurrecting a dead chicken.

Paracelsus' most bizarre claim was that he could breed homunculi – small humans who stood about a foot high – from a mixture of human sperm, hair and horseshit. According to his writings, the way to create one of these little men was to take some semen, put it in a bottle then submerge it in dung for forty days. Then, when the little man starts to form and wriggle around in the bottle, you have to feed it blood for forty

more days. His homunculi apparently ran off after turning on
their creator.

One of his more profitable discoveries, probably picked
up on his visits to Constantinople, was raw opium. He gave
it the name "Laudanum", presumably from the Latin
"*laus*", to praise. Although usually found in liquid form,
Paracelsus dispensed it in small tablets looking like mouse
droppings. Laudanum had miraculous soothing qualities
and was highly addictive. He made a fortune from wealthy
patients who inevitably came back for more; he told them
that it contained gold leaf and pearls. When he wasn't dispensing dangerous narcotics, he also liberally dosed his
patients with mercury and antimony, although he knew that
both were highly toxic.

Paracelsus did, however, challenge many of the pseudo-
scientific ideas of the day, especially the age-old belief in
bloodletting to get bid of "bad humours". It was believed that
all diseases were caused by an imbalance in the body's four
"humours" – black bile, choler, phlegm and blood. Treatment
consisted of restoring the balance, an unpleasant process of
repeated bleedings, purges and inducing vomiting. In reality,
bleeding weakened the patient by sapping the body of strength
and much needed oxygen, ruining any chance they might have
had of a normal recovery.

Paracelsus offered another solution – illnesses arose from
conditions outside the body and could be treated with chemicals. He also recognized that the body was often capable of
healing itself. While the rest of the medical profession was still
rubbing snail excrement into open wounds, Paracelsus recommended keeping the wound clean and generally leaving it
alone. Compared to snail shit, it was groundbreaking stuff.

In another novel innovation, he actually began to examine
his patients. Until then, physicians relied on urine samples for
diagnosis. Paracelsus was scornful of his colleagues' methods,
saying, "All they can do is to gaze at piss." If people knew how
they were being deceived, he said, "doctors would be stoned in
the street". The medical profession hit back by calling him a

drunk, not unreasonably, as it turns out, because Paracelsus always preferred bars to lecture theatres. He spent his entire adult life in a running battle against doctors who had learned their medicine from ancient books rather than practical experience. "All the universities and all the ancient writings put together," he wrote, "have less talent than my arse."

Paracelsus never stayed in one place for long. His routine was generally to arrive in a new town, earn accolades, enjoy accolades . . . and then self-destruct. In 1527, he pitched up at Basel, where a local luminary called Johan Frobenius was resigned to amputation of his right leg. The local barber-surgeon was on the verge of removing it when, out of desperation, Frobenius invited Paracelsus to take a look. To everyone's astonishment, Paracelsus cured him and the leg was saved. It was an amazing stroke of good fortune for Paracelsus, too, because Frobenius would become a very important and influential ally. He was a personal friend of the great Dutch scholar Erasmus, no less, who was at the time staying with him as a houseguest. Erasmus asked Paracelsus if he could treat him for gout and a painful kidney condition; Paracelsus found a cure. Erasmus was so impressed that he secured for him, at the age of thirty-three, the post of lecturer at the University of Basel.

Paracelsus had it made, or so it seemed. To begin with, he impressed everyone with his medical skills. One day, he offered to give the faculty a lecture, promising to uncover the "greatest of medical secrets". The event was widely advertised and attracted not just members of the faculty but also local barber-surgeons and civic dignitaries from all over Basel. The "secret" turned out to be the workings of the digestive system, which Paracelsus illustrated by holding aloft a pan full of steaming human excrement. As the audience retreated from the hall in disgust, he shouted obscenities after them; they were not fit to call themselves physicians. After a few more run-ins with the authorities, he had to flee Basel. It wasn't the first or the last town he had had to leave in a hurry. In Salzburg, he almost got himself hanged.

After several similar career-limiting moves, Paracelsus resumed his life as a wanderer, lodging at public inns, getting drunk, but still performing amazing cures. In 1530, while staying at Nuremberg, the local faculty denounced him as an impostor, but he won round his critics by apparently restoring to full health, in just a few days, several people with "incurable" elephantiasis.

Paracelsus died prematurely after years of endless travelling and alcohol abuse after a brief illness at the age of forty-eight, in the back room of a public inn. His death was hastened, it was said, after a scuffle with some hired thugs in the pay of the local medical faculty. His written works, mostly published posthumously, although full of insults and bluster, were full of genuine insights. Giordano Bruno marvelled years later: "Just think what he might have discovered had he been sober."

## Least Successful Amputation of a Limb

In the pre-anaesthetic era, the key qualification for a good surgeon was quick hands. Operations had to be finished quickly so the patient didn't bleed to death or die from the pain or the shock of a prolonged procedure. Queen Caroline's personal surgeon William Chiselden armed his assistant with a watch to try to keep his operations down to less than three minutes; Napoleon's famous chief surgeon Dominique Lorrey could amputate a leg in less than fifteen seconds.

The nineteenth-century Scottish surgeon Robert Liston was described as the finest surgeon in Europe and "the fastest knife in the West End". Liston had a personal best for a leg amputation at twenty-eight seconds, although while achieving this record he accidentally cut off his patient's left testicle and two of his assistant's fingers. Both patient and assistant died afterwards in the ward from gangrene, making it the only amputation in history with a 200 per cent mortality rate.

---

*"The actual building of roads devoted to motor cars is not for the near future, in spite of many rumours to that effect."*
*Harper's Weekly*, 1902

## Worst Contribution to Medical Science

The third-century Greek anatomist Galen, personal physician to the Roman Emperor Marcus Aurelius, was for several centuries recognized by the Catholic Church as the world's only authority on human anatomy. Galen's word on the inner workings of the human body was absolute; even to question his word was an act of heresy punishable by death. The Church was not in the least concerned by the minor fact that the Imperial doctor had never actually seen the inside of the human body and that his one hundred or so medical text books were wild guesswork based on his observations of dead pigs and dogs.

Although Galen managed to get a few things right, his mistakes had terrible consequences for centuries to come. Thanks to Galen, generations of medical students learned that the brain was a large clot of phlegm; that the best way to cure a headache was to cut holes in the skull; that the quickest way to cure a cough was to amputate the uvula at the back of the patient's palate; and that post-operative wounds should be dressed with pigeon's excrement.

The ban on human anatomical dissection remained long after Galen's death; only a Pope could grant permission for the odd criminal to be exhumed and cut open, albeit under the severest of restrictions. The dissection had to be performed by a servant, while a doctor stood and solemnly read from the works of Galen and pointed to the parts described. When it became obvious, as it nearly always did, that Galen was a fraud, his errors were always excused by the official line that the corpse was a criminal and therefore abnormal.

---

*"The only thing different is the hair, as far as I can see. I give them a year."*
Musical director of *The Ed Sullivan Show*, predicting the death of the Beatles, 1964

# Least Credible 'Ology

In 1796, a Viennese doctor specializing in mental illness, Franz-Josef Gall, had a peculiar insight. Patients with big eyes tended also to have very good memories. Excited by his "discovery", Gall spent the next four years dissecting the heads of mental patients to see if there was a link between skull shape and personality.

By the time he had finished, he had mapped out a total thirty-five human attributes – including emotions such as wonder and veneration, and actions such as murder and larceny – which, he believed, caused corresponding bulges on the surface of the skull. He worked that out by using a chart of the human skull and, by examining the bumps and crevices on the head of the subject, he claimed he could "read" the subject's personality. He called it "craniology", although it soon became known as phrenology – the study of the shape and size of the cranium. More popularly, it was known as "having your bumps felt".

It is now widely recognized that, if anyone needed their head examining, it was Gall himself. To begin with, brain tissue is far too soft to produce changes as significant as a bulge in the bone of a human skull. If brain tissue was dense enough to change the shape of your skull, your head would be too heavy for you ever to get out of bed.

However, at the time, his ideas really took off and in some very unexpected directions. His supporters, including Johann Spurzheim in America and George Combe in Britain, sold hundreds of thousands of books, claiming to have identified more "bumps" such as those for wit, colouring and weight. Two New York farmer brothers, Orson and Lorenzo Fowler, made a business out of phrenology, examining millions of Americans' heads and building such a booming business empire that it continued well into the twentieth century. Gall's phrenological theories were particularly popular in England, where the ruling class used it to justify the "inferiority" of its colonial subjects. At the other end of the scale. thousands of charlatans offered to "read" heads for money and offered to massage away unwanted bumps.

Another sinister legacy was the work of an Italian criminologist, Cesare Lombroso, who thought he could identify potentially dangerous villains by the shape of their skull (unless, of course, they wore a hat) so that they could be "treated" before they transgressed. Common characteristics of "the criminal type", according to Lombroso, were "facial asymmetry, enormous jaws, developed frontal sinus and protruding ears".

Although his ludicrous theory died with him, Lombroso's own pickled head is still preserved for all to see in the Museum of Criminal Anthropology in Turin.

> *"If your eyes are set wide apart, you should be*
> *a vegetarian, because you inherit the digestive*
> *characteristics of bovine or equine ancestry."*
> Dr Linard Williams, Medical Officer to the
> Insurance Institute of London, 1932

## Least Successful Attempt to Find a Cure for VD

The thirst for medical knowledge inspired the great eighteenth-century Scottish surgeon and anatomist John Hunter to follow a line of research with life-changing results. To find out how venereal disease was transmitted, Hunter injected pus from the weeping sores of a gonorrhoea-infected prostitute into the glans of his own penis. Unfortunately for Hunter, the prostitute he chose to take his sample from also suffered from syphilis. It was a rare combination and a mistake that delayed Hunter's marriage for three years and from which he never completely recovered.

It was also bad news for venereology, because Hunter mistakenly concluded that syphilis and gonorrhoea were stages of the same infection, setting back the study of both diseases for many years. Hunter's heroism inspired several medical students to follow his example and inject their own penises with pus, but it was another fifty years before proof of venereal transmission was finally discovered when a German bacteriologist, Ernst von Bumm, injected a perfectly healthy woman with gonorrhoea.

> *"Approximately 80 per cent of our air pollution stems from hydrocarbons released by vegetation. So let's not go overboard in setting and enforcing tough emissions standards for man-made sources."*
> US president Ronald Reagan, 1980

## Worst Royal Doctor

On Monday, 2 February 1685, while King Charles II was being prepared for his morning shave, he suffered a stroke and fell to the floor, crying out in pain. Six royal physicians rushed to his aid. Over the next few days they bled him, purged him, shaved his head and applied blister-raising cantharides plasters to his scalp. They pressed red-hot irons against his skin, administered twice-hourly enemas of rock salt and syrup of buckthorn, and orange infusion of metals in white wine.

Having shown no sign of improvement, he was then made to swallow therapeutic potions of oriental bezoar stone from the stomach of a goat and boiled spirits from a human skull. On 7 February, after five days of being tortured, as the historian Thomas Babington Macaulay put it, "like a red Indian at the stake", his body red raw with burns and blisters, the king succumbed and lapsed into a merciful coma, dying the following day. The cause – death by injuries caused by a doctor.

King Charles was not the first or the last monarch to have "died of the doctor". This was a subject that King Louis XIII of France knew a thing or two about. His physician Boulevard, an enthusiastic "bleeder" even by the standards of the day, ordered his royal patient 47 bleedings, 215 emetics or purgatives and 312 clysters (enemas) during the period of one year alone. When he was lying on his deathbed in 1643, the forty-one-year-old king told Bouvard, with a touch of bitter understatement, you might think, "I would have lived much longer if not for you."[1]

Dr Fagon, the eighteenth-century resident French court physician at Versailles, was known as "the killer of princes". Within a fortnight, in 1715 he wiped out almost the entire French royal family while treating a measles epidemic with a tough regime of purges, emetics and prolonged bleedings. The infant Louis XV only escaped the ministrations of the deadly physician because his nurse hid him. Sixty years later, the Russian Empress Catherine "the Great" observed that anyone delivered into the hands of her Scottish physician Dr John Rogerson was "as good as dead". When the Empress fell off her toilet seat with a fatal stroke, the able Dr Rogerson responded by applying plasters of Spanish fly to her feet.

No monarch in history suffered quite so horribly from the ignorance of contemporary medicine as Queen Caroline, wife of King George II. Ironically, Caroline was known to have been an incredibly enlightened Queen, medically speaking. Unlike some of her predecessors who claimed to cure through some kind of magic – "the royal touch" – she put her faith in science and had been a very strong supporter of the new and deeply controversial practice of inoculation against smallpox. She even gave it the ultimate seal of royal approval by having her own children inoculated. If it hadn't been for Caroline's example, the treatment may not have caught on in England for many more years.

The public and the press, then as now, had an apparently insatiable appetite for gossip about their royal family. The king's mood, even his bowel movements, were considered

---

1   King Louis XIII, not a fan of seventeenth-century medicine, once remarked, "I have had the misfortune of all great men – which is to be put into the hands of doctors."

topics of great interest, but royal health was usually surrounded by great secrecy. The king was obliged to maintain what the court favourite John Hervey called "a ridiculous farce of health", because if any sign of royal illness leaked out, it could, in Hervey's words, "disquiet the minds of his subjects, hurt public credit, and diminish the regard and duty which they owe him".

George II, like his father before him, suffered terribly from piles and eventually had to endure a primitive and very painful operation to have them removed. Both Georges, however, tried to keep their illness a secret from everyone, including their servants. Queen Caroline was similarly expected to show a brave public face, although her health was poor. Worn out by repeated pregnancies, she had grown so fat that she had to be wheeled around in an armchair. She was nevertheless expected to be present and correct at her husband's side for court occasions even when she felt ill. At one of these events, she was "close to swooning" but the king made her stand until 11 p.m.

In November 1737, the fifty-four-year-old Caroline collapsed to the floor of her library with a severe pain in her stomach, accompanied by violent vomiting. At first, her doctors explained her illness as "gout in the stomach", a mysterious complaint they attempted to cure with a dose of Sir Walter Raleigh's "Cordial", a powerful sedative made from alcohol and a compound of forty different roots and herbs. In fact, Caroline had a strangulated abdominal hernia, caused by the last of her nine pregnancies, a condition she had hidden for many years. As she grew older and her stomach muscles got weaker, a painful hernia, or hole, appeared and a large loop of her bowel was now poking through the wall of her stomach. The Queen's doctors should have simply pushed the bowel back inside and sewn her up. Instead, they decided to cut it off, thereby destroying her digestive system and all hope of recovery.

Her surgeon, Dr John Ranby, enjoyed considerable status within his profession and was something of a celebrity. He had published an account of some of the medical oddities he had encountered, including a man whose swollen testicle contained four ounces of water; a boy with an abnormally large spleen weighing four pounds; and a bladder containing sixty gallstones. Ranby was assisted by Dr Bussier, a former doctor of George I, and now nearly ninety. Unfortunately, neither of them had read a contemporary book published by the Royal Society entitled *New Discoveries and Improvements in the Most Considerable Branches of Anatomy and Surgery*, including the section on "Ruptures of All Kinds Without Cutting". They didn't really have a clue what they were doing and assumed that they were dealing with some sort of abscess that would grow unless removed.

It was reported that Caroline endured the surgery heroically, without the benefit of opium. She even laughed when the doddering old Dr Bussier stood too close to a candle and set fire to his wig. A few days after the operation, as the Queen lay in bed surrounded by courtiers, her bowel practically exploded, showering a torrent of excrement all over the bed and the floor. After an embarrassed silence, one of her ladies-in-waiting said that she hoped the relief would do Her Majesty some good. The Queen replied that she hoped so, too, because that was the last evacuation she would ever have.

Caroline selflessly begged her husband to remarry. George spoiled the moment by declining her offer, adding that he'd rather stick to his mistresses. Although there was a complete news blackout, the gruesome details of the Queen's final hours somehow reached the poet Alexander Pope, who was moved to write:

> *Here lies wrapt in forty thousand towels*
> *The only proof that Caroline had bowels*

Later, when it was confirmed that the Queen had died of what was officially classified as "a mortification of ye bowels", Dr Ranby tried to blame his patient for her predicament claiming that if only she hadn't tried to hide her condition and he had known about it a couple of days earlier, her life would have been saved. Of course, this was complete nonsense: he would have simply killed her a couple of days earlier.

---

> *"The abdomen, the chest and the brain will forever be shut from the intrusion of the wise and humane surgeon."*
> Sir John Eric Erichsen, Surgeon Extraordinary
> to Queen Victoria, in 1873

---

## Briefest Career in Dentistry

In 1844, the young American dentist Horace Wells was at a travelling circus in his home town of Connecticut when a saw a demonstration of nitrous oxide – laughing gas – being performed on a member of the audience. He noticed that when the man was returning to his seat, he gashed his shin on a row of chairs but didn't register any feeling of pain. Wells immediately spotted the potential of nitrous oxide as an aid to tooth extraction.

Afterwards, he invited the laughing-gas showman, Gardner Colton, to meet him at his surgery the next day to administer nitrous oxide to him while another dentist extracted one of Wells's teeth. The extraction, Wells was relieved to find, was painless. Wells then began experimenting with nitrous oxide and extracting teeth on his own patients, who also suffered no pain whatsoever. Wells was elated, hailing nitrous oxide as "a new era in dentistry and tooth pulling . . . the greatest discovery ever made". In fact, Wells's discovery of anaesthesia was one of the greatest advances in the history of medicine.

Unfortunately, he didn't live long enough to enjoy the fruits of his discovery. Although he used the gas successfully on his own patients, the medical profession remained unconvinced. A public demonstration in January 1845 backfired badly when he began his extraction before the gas had taken effect and the patient screamed in pain. The audience booed and Wells was dismissed as a charlatan in the Boston press. Haunted by public ridicule, he began sniffing chloroform and ether. One day, in a chloroform-induced delirium, he ran into the street and doused two passing prostitutes with acid.

Wells killed himself before his case came to trial; he smuggled a can of chloroform into his cell, opened a main artery in his leg and bled painlessly to death.

# 8

## Slower, Lower, Weaker: Great Sporting Losers

*In which a marathon runner coats himself in beeswax; Miss Fick takes
out her tennis partner with a forehand smash; some Olympians swim
through raw sewage; a Brit finds he's useless in snow; and a racehorse
has a terrible horoscope.*

### The Phantom of the Open

Maurice Flitcroft, a chain-smoking shipyard crane operator
from Barrow-in-Furness, didn't take up golf until his mid-
forties, just after acquiring his first colour TV. Inspired by the
BBC golf theme at the beginning of coverage of the 1974
World Matchplay Championship, and buoyed by dreams of
becoming the next Jack Nicklaus, he sent off for a mail-order
half-set of golf clubs. After honing his skills in a local field,
Flitcroft set his sights high – a place in the 1976 British Open
Championship at St Andrews.

Although he had never actually played a round of golf in his
life, and therefore did not have an official handicap, he gained
entry to the Open by registering as the only other option on
the form – "professional".[1] Confirmation duly arrived by post
that the forty-five-year-old virgin professional golfer had been

---

1 Flitcroft also took inspiration from the Milwaukee postal sorter called Walter
Danecki, who wanted to become a professional golfer but was thwarted by the
USPGA and their insistence on evidence of playing ability. Danecki announced
himself to the R&A as a professional and entered the 1965 Open, shooting a two-
round total in qualifying of 221 – 70 too many to earn him a place in the
championship field.

chosen to play at Formby Golf Club, near Liverpool, in one of the five qualifying tournaments for the Open on Friday, 2 July 1976.

In the weeks leading up to his qualifying round, Flitcroft prepared by studying a Peter Allis golf manual borrowed from the local library and practised his swing on the local beach, meanwhile dodging random objects rained on him by a gang of schoolchildren. He was able to practise for only two hours a day, after which the tide came in (and on several occasions nearly drowned him), but it was the one place where he could be guaranteed not to hit anyone accidentally with club or ball.

On the big day, he got lost on the way to the course and arrived with no time to practise, then put in a performance described by Ian Wooldridge of the *Daily Mail* as a "blizzard of triple and quadruple bogeys ruined by a solitary par". His playing partner Jim Howard had suspicions from the start: "After gripping the club like he was intent on murdering someone, Flitcroft hoisted it straight up, it came down vertically and the ball travelled precisely four feet. We put that one down to nerves, but after he shanked a second one we called the R&A officials."

After 121 shots and an argument with an official about slow play, Flitcroft's Open dream was in tatters, but he had made his mark. His forty-nine over par was the worst score recorded in the tournament's 141-year history. This was only a rough estimate – his marker had lost count on a couple of holes. After calculating that he would need to shoot twenty-three the next day to qualify, he decided to bow out gracefully and go home. Flitcroft was upbeat, blaming his poor performance on lumbago and fibrositis, and the fact that he had left his driver in the car. The club, he insisted, would have ensured a very different outcome. "I was an expert with the four-wood – deadly accurate."

Flitcroft's round dominated the sports pages and he was interviewed endlessly. A journalist tracked down his mother; when asked what she thought about her son's record-breaking performance, she replied, "Does that mean he's won?" When gently informed that her son was the worst golfer in Open history, she said, "Well, he's got to start somewhere, hasn't he?"[2]

The Royal & Ancient decided to tighten its entry rules, but it didn't stop Flitcroft trying again the following year. After prolonged and heated correspondence with the R&A, during which he challenged their secretary Keith Mackenzie to a match at the Old Course to settle the argument about his golfing talents or lack thereof, Flitcroft was banned for life from R&A tournaments.

Refusing to acknowledge defeat, Flitcroft somehow passed under the radar again and blagged his way into the qualifying round in 1978 under an assumed identity as Gene Paceki, but was rumbled after a couple of holes and forcibly ejected from the course.

In 1980, he was ready to compete again in the qualifying round at Gullane Golf Club, near Edinburgh, but on arriving the day before, Flitcroft got lost and pitched his tent in the dark on an open stretch of land. The next morning, when he popped out in his Y-fronts to do his stretches, he was surprised to find himself surrounded by Open officials with walkie-talkies. He had pitched his tent on the golf course.

He tried again in 1983 masquerading as Gerald Hoppy, this time cunningly disguised with dyed hair and a false moustache. He did better, getting through nine holes, until the tell-tale little signs – running off numerous triple bogeys – gave him away and he was evicted.

Back in Barrow-in-Furness, his employers, who had been following his adventure at the Open in the newspapers with surprise since he was supposed to be off sick with a heavy cold, sacked him. Flitcroft immediately saw the silver lining – more time to practise. Every day he sneaked into the cricket

---

2  The 1976 Open was eventually won by the American Johnny Miller with a young Seve Ballesteros coming second.

field of a local school, tearing up divots and enraging the school janitor. He was fined £50 in the Barrow Magistrates' Court for playing on school property. By now, Flitcroft was writing to car manufacturers to ask for sponsorship, but Ford, Rover, Volkswagen, Talbot, Renault and Peugeot all politely declined to have their brand associated with the world's worst golfer.

In 1990, he entered the Open qualifier at Ormskirk as an American golf professional called James Beau Jolley (a pun on Beaujolais). He hit a double bogey at the first hole and a bogey at the second. Flitcroft's progress at the third was rudely interrupted by a golf buggy which screeched to a halt in front of him. He remonstrated with the driver for ruining his chances of "looking at a par", not realizing that it was another R&A official. It was the usual dénouement, with Flitcroft being chased from the course.

Although his persistent attempts to gatecrash the British Open golf championship produced a sense of humour failure among members of the golfing establishment, Flitcroft became a minor celebrity and received fan-mail for many years. On reaching retirement age, he devoted his life to his beloved golf but was eventually banned from all his local clubs for playing courses without paying. He died in March 2007 but the legacy lives on. The Blythefield Country Club in Michigan, Ohio, has a tournament named in his honour.

## Least Successful Attempt to Play a Water Hazard

In 1938, Californian golf pro Ray Ainsley was in with a chance of winning the US Open at Cherry Hills until he dunked his approach shot into a stream fronting the par-four sixteenth hole. The ball was completely submerged but, despite the fast-moving current, Ainsley was determined not to take a penalty drop shot and gambled on trying to chip the ball out of the water.

According to a newspaper report, he attacked the ball "like a wild man" for a full thirty minutes. As the ball drifted,

Ainsley slashed and slashed and slashed again. At one point, the scorekeeper was laughing so hard he fell to the ground. By that time, Ainsley had taken nine swings at the waterlogged ball. Several times the ball made it to the bank, only to roll back in the water. Spectators were yelling, "There it is! There it is!" when the ball appeared above water. But it wouldn't stick.

By the time Ainsley finally hit the ball out of the creek on his seventeenth stroke, he was seventy-five yards downstream – and further away from the green – from his original position. He eventually got down in nineteen, setting a record for the highest ever score on a single hole in professional golf. Not surprisingly, Ainsley missed the cut, although, he quipped, he did kill a lot of fish.

---

*"Shakespeare's name, you may depend on it, stands absurdly too high and will go down. He had no invention as to stories, none whatever."*

Lord Byron, poet, 1814

---

## Most Expensive Caddie Error

At the age of forty-three, it looked as though Welsh golfer Ian Woosnam's best years were behind him. It had been ten years since his last major win in the US Masters and seven years since his last grand slam top-ten finish. But then, dramatically, he promised an astonishing comeback at the 2001 Open at Royal Lytham & St Anne's.

Going into the final eighteen holes, Woosnam was tied for the lead alongside Alex Cejka, David Duval and Bernhard Langer.

The Welshman might have guessed it wasn't going to be his day when he and his caddy Miles Byrne made a mistake over their tee-time and they barely made it to the first with a couple of minutes to spare. Woosnam was clearly flustered, but he soon found his groove. By now just one shot off the lead, he nearly hit a hole in one at the par-three opening hole and tapped in for a splendid birdie, regaining a share of top spot. Spectators cheered wildly, the momentum now clearly with the home favourite. As the diminutive Welshman strode to the second tee, he could be forgiven for thinking that his first Open was there for the taking. And that was when the wheels came off.

Players are only permitted to carry fourteen clubs. As the pair were standing on the second tee, Byrne realized that, in the rush, an extra test driver had found its way into Woosnam's bag. "You're going to go ballistic about this . . . I left that spare driver in the bag. We've got fifteen clubs," Byrne whispered to his man. Woosnam, notorious for his short fuse, snatched the rogue club from the bag and tossed it into a bush. As millions of TV viewers around the world looked on, the Welshman was clearly seen to mouth, "The one fucking thing you had to do!"

His Open was doomed. Handed a two-shot penalty, his game went to pieces, although he rallied and eventually carded a one-over-par seventy-two – just four shots behind winner David Duval. It cost Woosnam a potential £220,000 and a place in Europe's Ryder Cup team.

He wasn't the only one affected by Byrne's error. Woosnam's playing partner, the German Alex Cejka, went to pieces, almost bursting into tears on the tee. He dropped five shots through the first five holes, ending the tournament in thirteenth place.

Even so, Woosnam was magnanimous in defeat. "It was the biggest mistake he [Byrne] will make in his life. He won't do it again. He's a good caddie. He will have a severe bollocking when I get in but I'm not going to sack him." Woosnam was as good as his word and stood by his man . . . for a couple of weeks anyway. Two weeks later they were at the Scandinavian Masters. Woosnam's caddie was required for the final round but, after a heavy night out, Byrne overslept. With his caddie still in bed with a sore head, Woosnam had to break into his locker to get to his golf shoes. This time there was no way back for Byrne – he was sacked.

"All I want to say is that Ian Woosnam treated me well throughout everything. He's an absolute gentleman," the caddie noted later. He was last seen working on a building site in Ireland.[3]

## Worst Choke in Open Golf

In the final round of the 1928 US Open at Olympia Fields, Roland Hancock, an unknown twenty-one-year-old pro from South Carolina, was poised to complete one of the biggest shocks in golfing history. Finding himself in the unlikely position of leading the field with just two to play, he could afford to bogey both holes and still win.

Word spread around the course that golf history was about to be made and spectators flocked to watch Hancock's final two holes. At that time, there were no gallery ropes to hold spectators back and fans were allowed to wander alongside the players on the fairway. By the time Hancock and his playing partner Willie Hunter arrived at the seventeenth tee, there was total chaos. A crowd of around 10,000 people streamed across the hole, refusing to heed the pleas of marshals to clear a path to the green. A spectator yelled, "Stand back! Make way for the next US Open Champion!"

After a ten-minute delay, the seventeenth fairway was finally cleared and Hancock sliced his drive into the rough directly behind a tree. The ball was also now resting in mud. The crowd swarmed around him, making it difficult for him to judge the distance to the green. Eventually, marshals cleared a path, but Hancock half-topped the ball and it stayed down. Again, the marshals had to clear a path to give Hancock enough room to

---

3  The mistake of carrying more than the fourteen clubs allowed is not unique to Byrne. When Glenn Ralph's female caddie discovered a child's putter in the bag, she tried to explain away her lapse by saying, "It's only a small putter . . . does it matter?"

swing his club. He pitched over the green and then chipped back, taking two putts for a double-bogey six.

But all was not lost. A par on the last hole would still put him in a playoff against golf legends Bobby Jones and Johnny Farrell. Five should have been an easy score on the par-five hole but, because of the delays, the light was fading fast and, amid the din and congestion from the crowd, Hancock pulled his drive left into the rough, forcing him to chip back out on to the fairway. Then Hunter hit his second shot and it struck the head of a spectator who walked out in front of him. People rushed over to aid the injured man and play was held up for a quarter of an hour as the unconscious man was carried off the fairway.

Hancock, rattled by the latest delay, hacked at his shot, coming up short of the green. He pitched up, but from twenty feet missed his par putt. From a seemingly insurmountable lead, he had lost the US Open by a single stroke.

The final-round collapse was devastating for Roland Hancock and he never again found anything like the form he enjoyed over seventy holes at Olympia Fields. He played the US Open six more times without making the cut, then completely vanished from the pro circuit.

## Worst Golf Jinx

The golf legend Sam Snead, once said to have "the sweetest shot in golf", won more PGA events than anyone in history, but incredibly he never won a US Open despite twelve top-ten finishes.

In 1937, he lost by a single stroke and, in 1947, he tied for first place and lost in a play-off, but his greatest disappointment came at the US Open in Spring Hill in 1939. Convinced that he needed a birdie on the par-five final hole, Snead tried to reach the green in two strokes. Everything went to plan until Snead hit his second shot into a bunker, finishing with a triple-bogey eight, losing the tournament by two strokes. He only learned later that he had miscalculated and had not needed a birdie after all; par on the hole would have won him the title. Electronic leader boards were not introduced until several years later. At St Louis, Missouri, in 1947, he missed a two-footer in the closing stages of a play-off and eventually lost by a stroke.

In 2002, Snead, aged eighty-nine, was invited to sign off on an illustrious career by opening the US Masters by hitting the ceremonial tee shot, marking his sixty-second and final Masters appearance. The ball travelled 100 yards before hitting a spectator directly in the face.

> *"Before man reaches the moon, your mail will be delivered within hours from New York to California, to England, to India or to Australia by guided missiles . . . We stand on the threshold of rocket mail."*
> Arthur E. Summerfield, US Postmaster General, 1959

## Least Successful Attempt to Organize a Title Fight

Bare-knuckle boxing was illegal in nineteenth-century America, but it flourished underground with fight locations kept under wraps until the last minute. The decision to host the 1887 middleweight title fight between Johnny Reagan and Jack Dempsey on New York's Long Island beach, however, left boxers and spectators alike at sea.

Dempsey and Reagan were supposed to have met in the ring before, but both of those scheduled fights had been postponed, the first due to a police raid and the second because of fog. The third effort to match the fighters was set for 13 December 1887, in Huntington, New York, off Long Island, but they hadn't allowed for the incoming tide. By the fifth round, the Atlantic was lapping the canvas and, by the eighth, both boxers were knee-deep in sea water. Dempsey and Reagan, along with a small audience, agreed to board a tug-boat and travel twenty-five miles in search of drier ground.

When they found a place to their liking, they docked and resumed their battle. This time, hail and snow disrupted the bout, but the champion Dempsey wasn't to be denied. Reagan finally threw in the towel in the forty-fifth round and Dempsey retained the title. A grand total of twenty-five spectators had watched the entertainment on offer.

---

*"My dynamite will sooner lead to peace than a thousand world conventions . . . As soon as men will find that, it one instant, whole armies can be utterly destroyed, they surely will abide by golden peace."*

Alfred Nobel, 1833–96

---

## Unluckiest Boxer

When Thomas Hamilton-Brown of South Africa lost his opening-round boxing match at the 1936 Berlin Olympics by a split decision, the disappointed lightweight consoled himself by going on an eating binge.

It was only several days later that it was discovered there had been a scoring error. One of the judges had accidentally reversed his scores and the South African had actually won the fight – he was through to the second round. By this time, Hamilton-Brown had already put on five pounds. Unable to make the scales for his next bout, he was disqualified for being too heavy for his weight class.

---

*"The dangers of atomic war are overrated. It would be hard on little, concentrated countries like England. In the United States, we have lots of space."*

Colonel Robert McCormick, publisher of the *Chicago Tribune*, 1950

## Most Controversial Boxing Defeat

Olympic boxing has a long and murky history. One of the most unusual controversies took place at the Paris Games in 1924 when the defending middleweight champion, Britain's Harry Mallin, lost a split decision to France's Roger Brousse in the quarter-finals. Mallin complained of foul play, offering bite marks on his chest and shoulder as proof. After an appeal, the home fighter was disqualified, clearing the way for Mallin to go on to win his second home medal. It emerged later that Brousse's first-round opponent had also complained of being repeatedly bitten. The press later suggested that Brousse had been "sampling the unroasted beef of Old England".

Four years later in Amsterdam, there were unscheduled ringside fisticuffs after some brazenly biased home decisions and, at the Rome Games in 1960, judges were sacked for "getting the score wrong".

At the 1984 Los Angeles Olympics, a number of controversial decisions went the Americans' way. Of the thirty-eight boxing matches involving Americans that went the full three rounds, thirty-seven ended up being judged as home victories. One of several South Korean officials sent to the Los Angeles Olympics as observers noted, "We came here to learn a lot about the Olympic Games, because we are the hosts in 1988, and we've decided there's nothing to learn." Except, it seems, how to get revenge.

Four years later at the 1988 Seoul Olympics in the light-middleweight class, America's nineteen-year-old boxing sensation Roy Jones Jr was the hot favourite to win gold. It had taken him just two minutes to dispose of his opening opponent M'tendere Makalamba. His second-round opponent managed to stay on his feet, but lost by a unanimous 5-0 decision. In the quarter-final, he pummelled his opponent Yevgeni Zaytsev to win by a similar margin. In the semi-final, Britain's Richie Woodhall fought bravely but lost to another unanimous decision by the judges.

Jones's opponent, South Korea's Park Si-hun, had been far less impressive on his way to the final. In fact, some commentators felt he should have lost all four of his fights. Some of his opponents certainly felt that way. In the quarter-final, the Italian Vincenzo Nardiello was so upset when the 3-2 split decision went to the South Korean that he had to be dragged away from the ring.

The final, as expected, was an utterly one-sided affair. Jones was barely troubled, landing eighty-six punches to Park's thirty-two. The Korean took two standing eight counts and was twice warned by the referee. NBC ringside pundits scored the rounds a massive and convincing 20-3, 30-15 and 36-14 in Jones's favour.

The three judges didn't see it that way. Uganda's Bob Kasule, Uruguay's Alberto Durán and Hiouad Larbi of Morocco gave Park the fight, two others giving it to Jones. When the referee, Aldo Leoni, raised Park's hand in victory, the Korean fighter looked embarrassed. Even the referee was shocked by the decision. "I can't believe they're doing this to you," he whispered to the American.

In the aftermath, the Moroccan ringside judge, Larbi, told the angry American press, "The American won easily; so easily, in fact, that I was positive my four fellow judges would score the fight for the American by a wide margin. So I voted for the Korean to make the score only 4-1 for the American and not embarrass the host country."

The three judges who awarded Park the win were later suspended and an IOC investigation in 1997 proved that they had been bribed by South Korean Olympic officials. However, Park was allowed to keep his medal and the injustice suffered by Jones was never put right.

## Least Successful Professional Boxer

In November 2000, light-middleweight Des Sowden from Plymouth was knocked out four seconds into his bout at the Leisure Centre, Ebbw Vale, Wales.

Spectators were still taking their seats when Sowden was KO'd by a single right hook to the jaw from his opponent Russell Rees. Sowden's previous record over eleven fights was one win and ten losses.

His only victory came when Irishman Martin "The Dancing Leprechaun" Moore was disqualified during the second round at the Leisure Centre, Bracknell, in May 1999 for continuing to hit Sowden as he lay on the canvas.

---

*"The wireless music box has no imaginable commercial value. Who would pay for a message sent to no one in particular?"*
Associates of David Sarnoff responding to his call for investment in the radio in 1921.

---

## Most Successful Attempt to Shorten a Test Career

The Yorkshire slow left-arm bowler Bobby Peel, who played cricket for England from 1884–96, was frequently drunk during matches, a condition tactfully interpreted by the cricketing bible Wisden as "unwell" or "gone away". After one county game, the Yorkshire captain Hawke suspended Peel for "running the wrong way" and "bowling at the pavilion in the belief that it was the batsman".

He was sacked from the Yorkshire team after his performance against Warwickshire at Edgbaston in May 1896. During an unbeaten partnership of 367 with Hawke, Peel was caught short and urinated on the wicket. He never played for England again.

---

*"That is the biggest fool thing we have ever done. The bomb will never go off, and I speak as an expert in explosives."*
Admiral William D. Leahy, US Admiral working on the US Atomic Bomb Project, advising President Truman on atomic weaponry, 1944

## Most Easily Dismissed Batsman

James Southerton spent most of his first-class cricket career playing for Sussex, and represented his country in the two first ever Test matches against Australia. He was almost fifty when he made his Test début, making him the oldest ever Test débutant, a record unlikely ever to be beaten.

In 1870, he was the tail-ender for Surrey against Marylebone and the great W. G. Grace at the Kennington Oval. Southerton hit the ball to Grace who picked it up on the rebound. Nobody but Southerton thought he was out, but he walked anyway. When the umpire called him back, he refused. It went into the scorebook as "J. Southerton retired thinking he was out."

The easy dismissal of Yorkshire's Ludd when he faced the Nottinghamshire fast bowler John "Foghorn" Jackson was more excusable. Jackson was a formidable figure at well over six foot tall, weighed over fifteen stones and was credited by some cricket historians as the true inventor of "bodyline" bowling. Ludd, after being struck on the foot by a particularly hostile delivery from Jackson, was given "not out".

"Maybe not, but I'm going anyway," said Ludd as he was leaving the field.

---

*"The French people are incapable of regicide."*
King Louis XVI of France, 1789

---

## Worst Bowling Figures

The Australian left-arm spinner "Chuck" Fleetwood-Smith had a very rarely seen bowling action known as left-arm wrist spin or a "Chinaman". He was also famous for several other eccentricities on the field: he would sing, whistle, practice his golf swing, imitate kookaburras, pretend to catch imaginary butterflies and chat to spectators with his back to the play. This attitude was a constant source of irritation to his teammates.

He once said, "If you can't be the best batsman in the world, you might as well be the worst." Taking a leaf out of his own book, he achieved the worst bowling figures in Test match history. Playing against England at the Oval in 1938, England declared at 903 for 7. Leading the Aussie attack, Fleetwood-Smith pitched in with 1 for 298.

## Most Boring Batsman

The batting figures of Nottinghamshire and England left-handed batsman William "Stonewall" Scotton (1856-93) read like binary code. In the 1886 Oval Test, he hit 34 runs in 225 minutes including a spell of over one hour without hitting a single. He once carried his bat through a first-class innings and scored 9 not out, and in another innings he took 155 minutes to hit 17. Following another soporific display in 1890 when Scotton took two hours to hit six runs, the magazine *Punch* paid tribute with a piece of verse, a parody on Tennyson called *Wail of the Weary*.

But Scotton was no Geoffrey Boycott. He was, by all accounts, an extraordinarily sensitive man who took criticism of his style of play badly. According to a teammate, he was prone to bursting into tears at the least provocation. It all got a bit too much for him on 9 July 1893 when he was dropped by Nottingham. He retired to his lodgings in St John's Wood and killed himself.

> *"If God had wanted a Panama Canal,*
> *he would have put one here."*
>
> King Philip II of Spain, c. 1552

## Worst Loss of an Unassailable Lead

The year was 1956; the place, Aintree; the event, the world's greatest steeplechase – the Grand National. An enthusiastic crowd was looking forward to witnessing the first royal victory in the famous race for more than fifty years when nine-year-old Devon Loch, owned by the Queen Mother, took up the running three fences from home.

Devon Loch was not the bookies' favourite that day because a couple of past winners were in the race, but the horse was a hugely popular choice thanks to his royal connections. He had already won twice that year and ran a good third at Cheltenham that season; all was looking good for a crack at the title. His prospects looked even better when two of the favourites, Must and Early Mist fell at the first, leaving M'as-tu-vu in the lead and Devon Loch still going well.

Devon Loch's jockey Dick Francis was impressed with the ease with which his horse was jumping. Clearing the last and going on to the long run-in, Francis recalled in his autobiography, "Never had I felt such power in reserve, such confidence in my mount, such calm in my mind. It was clear that there was only going to be one winner." He accelerated away from the field in search of his place in Grand National legend. Men in the stand were already throwing their hats into the air to salute a great win for Devon Loch, Francis and the Queen Mum.

Then just fifty yards from the line, with a huge lead and the race apparently sewn up, Devon Loch pricked up his ears, appeared to jump a phantom obstacle and belly-flopped to the turf with his four legs splayed out. As the horse slithered along the turf to an embarrassing halt, his nearest pursuer, ESB, galloped past to win.

Numerous theories abounded as to what had caused Devon Loch to fail when failure seemed impossible. The horse was checked at the stable afterwards and was found to be in good health with no sign of abnormality. In fact, it went on to win more races. Dick Francis believed that the roar of the crowd frightened his horse. A police officer on duty that day reported seeing "a dark wet patch on the course and that caused the horse to stumble". It was also suggested that the horse had been spooked by a shadow causing it to think there was a fence. It remains to this day one of sport's greatest mysteries.

There was probably no one more disappointed than the stricken Devon Loch's owner, the Queen Mother, but she was remarkably sanguine in defeat, merely noting, "That's racing." After the race, she even congratulated the winning jockey Dave Dick, who had profited so unexpectedly from Devon Loch's inexplicable dive.

"What did you think when my horse fell down?" she enquired.

Replied Dick, tactlessly, "I was absolutely delighted, Ma'am."

## Slowest Racehorse

On paper, the brown gelding Zippy Chippy should have been a contender in the ultra-competitive world of US thorough-bred racing. It had a decent enough pedigree, including several famous winners. Sadly, of course, it didn't work out that way.

His racing career began in 1994 in New York State where he was never placed better than third in eleven races. Fearing the winless horse could end up in the meat market, owner and trainer Felix Monserrate took pity and acquired Zippy Chippy in 1995 in a straight swap for an eight-year-old Ford truck.

Racing glory, however, proved elusive. By 1998, Zippy Chippy's reluctance even to leave the starting gate saw him receive a ban from every track in the area except one. On 6 September 1999, he lost his eighty-sixth consecutive race, setting the record for lost races among US thoroughbreds. The following year, Zippy Chippy lost a forty-yard dash with a baseball player in a publicity stunt.

Winless in his ninety-nine starts, Zippy Chippy's final loss came in September 2004 at the Three County Fairgrounds, Northampton, Massachusetts. He was sent off as the 7-2 second favourite with a huge party of fans there cheering him on. Despite the support, he finished last. Tom Gilcoyne, historian for the National Museum of Racing and Hall of Fame, noted optimistically that the horse "hasn't done anything to harm the sport. But it's a little bit like looking at the recorded performances of all horse races through the wrong end of the telescope."

Zippy Chippy's career as a four-legged flop is only bettered by Britain's Quixall Crossett, the first thoroughbred in racing history to lose 100 consecutive races.

The eleven-year career of the "equine turtle" took in 103 starts over jumps, giving his owner Ted Caine a grand total of no victories, two second-place and six third-place finishes, although this was usually when most of its rivals fell. Even in races with a field as small as five, Quixall Crossett regularly started with odds of 500-1, and sometimes went off at odds of 1,500-1. The *Racing Post* once noted of the horse's efforts: "Ran a cracker by his standards when he was second of two finishers in May."

As his hundredth race loomed in 2001, an astrologer brought in to help try to avoid a century of disasters found "planetary transits which could cause nervous tension and lead to him being hyped up. His chart shows he can have problems channelling his energies in the right area, and also a tendency to be impulsive and a touch accident prone. Thankfully, Mars is due to start moving in the right direction two days before Quixall's race . . . and he will be less likely to get hurt." Quixall Crossett managed to complete a circuit before being pulled up.

He quit the racing game for good in 2002 after unseating his rider on his 103rd defeat.

## Least Successful Race Fix

The English multi-millionaire newspaper baron and fraudster Horatio Bottomley owned several racehorses but never achieved success in the Derby or the Grand National, even though he spent a fortune trying to achieve this ambition. He was also famous for losing a great deal of money on failed betting coups.

In 1914, Bottomley thought he had organized the perfect swindle. He found an out-of-the-way racecourse at Blank-enberge on the Belgian coast and bought all six horses entered for one of the races, hired six English jockeys and paid them to finish in a specified order. Then he put a huge amount of money on the outcome. What could possibly go wrong?

Sadly, Bottomley had overlooked just one key factor – you can never bet on the weather. A sea mist came in and covered the entire course. The jockeys couldn't see each other or work out who had won. Bottomley lost a fortune.

> *"Video won't be able to hold on to any market it captures after the first six months. People will soon get tired of staring at a plywood box every night."*
> Darryl F. Zanuck, Head of Twentieth
> Century-Fox Studios, 1946

## Least Successful Horse Race

A global TV audience of 250 million people tuned in to watch the 1993 Grand National, "the race that never was".

The sequence of events that brought about the most embarrassing race in steeplechase history began when fifteen animal rights demonstrators ran on to the Aintree course seconds before the race was due to start. The horses had arrived at the start at least ten minutes ahead of schedule and, after several

minutes walking around in the rain that was lashing relent-
lessly on to the runners and riders, patience was wearing thin.
The starter, Keith Brown, who was officiating at his last Grand
National before retirement, finally called the horses into line
and was just about to pull the lever and shout "Come on!"
when several of the thirty-nine riders spotted the protestors
ahead and stood up in their saddles, pointing. After a delay
while the course was cleared, the tape failed to rise properly,
half-strangling champion jockey Richard Dunwoody. Brown
raised his red flag to declare a false start, but it didn't unfurl
and half of the field continued unchecked.

The crowd shouted frantically at the jockeys to stop as race
officials tried desperately to flag them down from the side of
the track. Nine horses did pull up before the first fence but the
rest of the field charged on. When they reached The Chair, a
couple of Aintree officials tried to attract their attention again
but the jockeys mistook them for protesters. Ten runners
stopped after the first circuit but seven horses raced on to the
finish line in the four-and-a-half-mile race. Esha Ness, a 50-1
outsider ridden by John White, crossed the line first and was
devastated when he found out the race had been declared null
and void. Keith Brown, wearing his bowler hat and a terrified
expression, was given a police escort through a gauntlet of
irate race goers.

Bookmakers had to repay £75 million in bets placed on the
race. Not least among the disgruntled punters was Judy Higby,
a housewife from St Albans, Hertfordshire. She had tried to
place a bet with her local bookie that the 1993 Grand National
would not be run after she had had a premonition. Her bookie
told her that he would do her a favour by not taking her money
because it could never happen.

## Worst Jockey

The Spanish aristocrat Beltran de Osorio y Diez de Rivera, the
"Iron" Duke of Albuquerque, decided to take up horse-racing
after receiving a film of the Grand National as a gift for his

eighth birthday. He set his sight on winning England's greatest steeplechase and almost died trying.

The Duke entered the National seven times from 1952. The outcome was nearly always the same. He would usually start with the rest of the field, jump a few fences and then wake up in hospital.[4] On his first attempt, he fell from his horse at the sixth fence and was hospitalized after almost breaking his neck. He tried to win again in 1963 and was unseated again, this time at the fourth fence, much to the delight of bookies who were offering odds of 66-1 against him finishing. Two years later, he fell and broke a leg after his horse collapsed beneath him. Over the course of his painful career he managed to finish only one race.

In 1974, just after having sixteen screws removed from his leg after another nasty fall in another race, he fell again while training for the National, breaking his collarbone. He competed in a plaster cast, finishing the race for the only time in his career in eighth (and last) place, a very long way behind the winner Red Rum. The Duke was delighted, but noted after the race, "I sat like a sack of potatoes and gave the horse no help."

At one point, his horse collided with Ron Barry at the second Canal Turn. Barry said, "What the fuck are you doing?" to which the Duke replied, "My dear chap, I haven't a clue. I've never got this far before!"

In 1976, he sustained his worst injuries yet after falling in a race and being trampled by several horses – seven broken ribs, several fractured vertebrae, a broken wrist and thigh and major concussion, as a result of which he spent two days in a coma. After recovering, he announced, at the age of fifty-seven, that he planned to race yet again. Grand National officials had other ideas and revoked his licence "for his own safety", although the brave Duke continued to ride competitively in Spain up until 1985 – at the age of sixty-seven.

---

4  The Royal Liverpool, where he always took the precaution of booking a private room before the race.

Although the Iron Duke never achieved his childhood dream of a Grand National title, he did break a record – he sustained more fractures than any other jockey in the race's history.

## Least Successful Racehorse Owner/Breeder

Despite owning the largest stable in the UK, the wealthy aristocrat James Carr-Boyle, Fifth Earl of Glasgow (1792–1869) was the worst racehorse owner and breeder in the history of the sport.

Part of the problem was the Earl's refusal to give any of his horses names until they had proved themselves by actually winning a race. He was oblivious to the general confusion that this caused, especially when came to identifying which horses came from the best or worst bloodlines. One evening before a race, his trainer persuaded him to break his lifetime habit, so three of his horses ran with the names "Give-Him-a-Name", "He-Hasn't-Got-a-Name", and "He-Isn't-Worth-a-Name".

The Earl's notoriously bad temper also got in the way. If a horse failed to show promise, he had it shot on the spot. After his daily gallop, he thought nothing of executing half-a-dozen horses; as most of them did not have names, it was anybody's guess if the right ones ended up at the knacker's yard.

One that got away was the great Carbine, sensational winner of the Melbourne Cup, carrying a record weight of 10 st 5 lbs, setting a new race record time. In his career, Carbine won 33 races out of 43 starts, with six seconds and three thirds, failing to place only once due to a badly split hoof. The Earl had intended to have him shot at the age of two, despite his trainer's pleas, but fate intervened when his lordship dropped dead himself.

---

*"Pish! A woman might piss it out."*
Sir Thomas Bloodworth, Lord Mayor of
London, on being informed of what would
become the Great Fire of London, 1666

## Least Successful Investment in a Racehorse

In 1983, Sheikh Mohammed paid a world record $10.2 million for the racehorse Snaafi Dancer. Sired by 1964 Kentucky Derby winner Northern Dancer, as yearlings go he was the nearest to a sure thing that had ever stepped into an auction ring.

Snaafi Dancer never made it to the racetrack. It was reported that he was so slow in training that it would have been embarrassing to run him in public. He was retired to stud duty where he was discovered to have fertility problems. From two years of breeding, he sired only four foals, three of which raced with very limited success and none sired good runners. Retired, Snaafi Dancer was last reported as living somewhere in Florida.

> *"You ain't goin' nowhere, son. You ought to go back to drivin' a truck."*
>
> Jim Denny, Manager of "Grand Ole Opry", to Elvis Presley, 1954

## Worst Tennis Player

No sporting title drought was as painfully felt and as endlessly debated as Britain's seventy-six-year wait for a men's Grand Slam tennis champion.[5] But fear not, the Great British Tennis Loser is still alive and kicking.

Robert Dee from Bexley, Kent, didn't win a single match during his first three years on the international professional circuit, touring at an estimated cost of £200,000 and a record fifty-four defeats in a row. But when he found himself being described in the press as "the worst professional tennis player

---

5    Before Andy Murray won the US Open in 2–2, the last male Brit to win was Fred Perry, who won same event in 1936.

in the world", he decided he wasn't going to take it lying down. Attacking with a single-mindedness he had never quite managed on the tennis court, he took legal action against dozens of newspapers and websites to defend his name and reputation.

At last, Dee had some trophies to boast about on his personal website. But these trophies were not from international tennis tournaments, they were the apologies of thirty news organizations in response to threatened libel claims. Every one had backed down and settled up – all except the *Daily Telegraph*, who refused to give way over two articles, which it ran on the front page and in the sports section on 23 April 2008. Despite the threat of a libel trial that could have cost the paper £500,000, the headlines were unequivocal: "WORLD'S WORST TENNIS PRO WINS AT LAST" and "A BRITISH SENSATION – THE WORLD'S WORST" . The stories said Dee had finally ended this "dismal run" by beating an unranked seventeen-year-old in the first round of a tournament in Barcelona in April 2008,[6] and compared him to the ski jumper Eddie "the Eagle" Edwards (see later entry, Where Eagles Daren't).

Dee was outraged and sued for defamation, arguing the piece exposed him to ridicule and could damage his ability to work in the tennis world in the future. In court, his barrister pointed out that Dee wasn't quite as bad as everyone said, because he had won games on a Spanish domestic circuit during his fifty-four-match losing streak on the international circuit.

But the *Daily Telegraph* stuck by its story – his wins on the Spanish national circuit did not alter the fact that he held the longest record for consecutive defeats based on the official world ranking system.

The judge upheld the comments made by the newspaper – and Dee had to face up to yet another defeat.

---

6  He lost in the second round.

## Least Successful Interpretation of "Non-Contact Sport"

At the 1912 Olympics in Stockholm, Sigrid Fick and Gunnar Setterwall of Sweden were favourites to win gold in the outdoor mixed-doubles tennis. They were on top until Fick accidentally took out her partner with a forehand smash to the face with her racquet during the very first set.

According to the Official Report of the 1912 Games, "This little accident put Setterwall off his game, for his play fell off tremendously." They went on to lose 6-4, 6-0 to Heinrich Schomburgk and Dorothea Koring of Germany.

---

*"I'm sorry, Mr Kipling, but you just don't know how to use the English language."*
Editor of the *San Francisco Examiner*,
to Rudyard Kipling, 1889

---

## Slowest Out of the Blocks

It isn't the winning that counts, it's the taking part . . . or sometimes the just turning up. At the 1960 Games in Rome, Wim Essajas was the toast of Suriname, the first ever athlete from his country to qualify for the Olympics.

He was scheduled to compete in the 800 metres on the track, but was accidentally given the wrong starting time. Thinking that the event was later that evening, he decided to take a nap and ended up sleeping through the race.

Poor Essajas lost his only chance at glory and Suriname had to wait another eight years to field another Olympian.

---

*"An orgy of vulgar noise."*
Louis Spohr, on Beethoven's Fifth Symphony, 1808

---

## Chariots of Dire:
## Worst Olympic Marathons

For pure farce, the early modern Olympic marathons were hard to beat. The first was run in 1896 in Greece from the city of Marathon to Athens. Twenty-five athletes put their names forward for the race but only seventeen started. The American team turned up too late to compete because they had forgotten that Greece still used the old Julian calendar and was eleven days ahead of them.

The Italian Carlo Airoldi was favourite to win. He couldn't afford to pay for transport to the event so he walked almost 1,000 miles from his home in Milan to Athens, only to be turned away when he got there. Airoldi had received prize money for winning a race and, as a professional athlete, was not eligible to compete. There was a strong suspicion that the Greeks had only blocked his application because they wanted their own man, a shepherd called Spyiridon Louis, to win – which he eventually did.

On the way to victory, Louis overtook the leader Edwin Flack, a London-based Australian. Flack had no experience of running a marathon and, suffering from dehydration, became delirious, attacking a Greek spectator who tried to help keep him on his feet. The third-placed finisher Spyridon Belokas was disqualified for travelling part of the course by carriage.

In Paris four years later, the pre-race favourite Georges Touquet-Daunis stopped for refreshments a few miles into the race. After a beer or two at a local hostelry, he decided it was much too hot to continue and stayed put. The course markings were so poor that several athletes got lost and could be seen running confused through central Paris. The American Arthur Newton finished fifth but insisted that nobody had overtaken him all day. Meanwhile, his fellow countryman Richard Grant claimed he had been deliberately run over by a cyclist as he was about to catch up with the leaders. It was widely suspected that the winner, local lad Michel

Theato, had used his knowledge as a baker's boy to take short-cuts.[7]

The third Olympiad held in St Louis in 1904 was such a badly organized and shambolic affair that it threatened to kill off the modern Olympic movement altogether. Spread out over five months, the event was held alongside the much more popular and established World's Fair and was reduced to little more than a sideshow. Suspecting it was going to be a disaster, Olympics founder Baron de Coubertin didn't even bother to show up. He wasn't alone: tensions caused by the ongoing Russo-Japanese War and the problem of getting to St Louis kept most of Europe's top athletes away and only twelve countries were represented. Of the 625 competitors who turned up, 533 were American and in several events, including boxing, wrestling, tennis and gymnastics, they were virtually the only competitors. Unsurprisingly, the United States did rather well, winning 80 of the 100 gold medals and 238 of the 300 total medals.

The 1904 marathon was run in energy-sapping conditions and over brutal terrain, starting in mid-afternoon in scorching August heat over badly rutted dirt roads with only one water stop. The course was described by the trainer of the eventual champion, Thomas J. Hicks, as "the most difficult a human being was ever asked to run over".

Exactly half of the starters failed to finish and there were a number of serious injuries, including American Bill Garcia who collapsed with a stomach haemorrhage. Of the eighteen who did complete the course, South Africa's Len Tau still managed to finish ninth despite running barefoot and, at one stage, being chased a mile off course by an angry dog.

First home, with a time of three hours thirteen minutes, was New Yorker Fred Lorz. The race officials were not overly concerned that Lorz looked a little too sprightly for someone who

---

7  An athlete called Champion came second and one named Fast finished third.

had just covered twenty-six miles in ninety-degree heat, nor were their suspicions raised when the second-placed runner, Tom Hicks, turned up looking half dead.

They were just about to hang the gold medal around Lorz's neck when word got out that he had covered the last eleven miles in a car. When confronted, Lorz owned up; suffering from cramps early in the race, he had hopped into his manager's car at the thirteen-mile mark. They only managed eleven miles before the car broke down, so Lorz jumped out and decided to complete the race, claiming he did it as a joke. The Olympic officials handed him a lifetime ban.[8] Second-placed Hicks, an English-born American, was awarded the gold. Hicks had crossed the finish line after three hours, twenty-eight minutes and fifty-three seconds, the worst marathon time in Olympic history, with more than a bit of help. What the officials hadn't spotted was that his coach had assisted him – if that is the appropriate word – with strychnine (used as rat poison) and egg whites in brandy to keep him going. It was the first known incident of a drug-enhanced performance at the Olympics. Even then, Hicks was practically carried across the line.

Arguably the biggest loser of the day was Felix Carvajal, a postman from Cuba. Carvajal qualified for the Olympic marathon, but almost penniless and with no Olympic Committee to sponsor him, he decided to pay his own way to the Games. Carvajal walked, ran and hitch-hiked up the Mississippi River to St Louis, where he lined up for the marathon wearing the clothes he had travelled in – woollen trousers, a linen shirt, street shoes and a felt beret. The race was delayed while a friendly American discus thrower cut Carvajal's trousers down to fashion a pair of running shorts.

He had no trouble at all keeping pace with the leaders and, despite the brutal conditions, appeared to be thoroughly enjoying himself, laughing, joking, running backwards and practising his broken English on bystanders. He looked the

---

8   Lorz was later reinstated and won the Boston Marathon in 1905.

freshest in the field by far and would undoubtedly have finished among the medals (and probably would have won) if he hadn't decided to take a detour through an orchard to eat some unripe apples – the organizers hadn't bothered to lay on any refreshments for the runners. Badly afflicted by stomach cramps, Carvajal could only finish fourth. He did not appear in international competition again and it was seventy-two years before Cuba had another entrant in the Olympic marathon.

The London 1908 Olympic marathon was originally supposed to start from a street outside Windsor Castle, but Queen Alexandra wanted her children to watch, so the start was moved by a few hundred yards to inside the castle grounds, just outside the nursery window. Those extra 385 yards, as it turned out, were very important.

The race favourite, Canadian Tom Longboat, collapsed after nineteen miles, possibly because his helpers had been plying him with champagne during the race. The Canadian team later claimed he had been drugged.

The first half of the race was dominated by two Englishmen, Thomas Jack – then Jack Price – then in the later stages by a South African, Charles Hefferon. He was still leading at the twenty-four-mile post, but fading fast and with just two miles to go he was passed by the Italian Dorando Pietri,[9] a twenty-two-year old pastry chef. Sir Arthur Conan Doyle, who was doing a spot of freelance journalism for the *Daily Mail* because it got him a free ticket into the stadium, described him as "a tiny boy-like creature".

A hundred thousand people had crammed into the stadium at White City in London to witness the finish of the marathon, with an estimated one million locked outside. If the amount of interest in viewing just the last 400 yards might seem a little strange, it was fully justified. Pietri staggered into the stadium first and was poised to win but was clearly in some distress,

---

9  The organizers even managed to get his name wrong in the official programme: it was listed back-to-front as "Pietri Dorando".

suffering badly from dehydration and exhaustion. In his diso-
riented, confused state, he started to run the wrong way round
the track. When the officials redirected him, he fell down.
Some officials helped him up and, after several more falls, they
could bear to watch no longer and they carried Pietri across
the finish line, thereby destroying his chance of gold.

In second place, the American Johnny Hayes, a sales assistant in Bloomingdale's department store in New York,
completed the final circuit and his team promptly lodged a
protest (at this point the Americans had been averaging at
least one official protest a day). The appeal was upheld; Pietri
was disqualified and Hayes claimed the gold medal. Pietri
was thought to have taken some mid-race strychnine, but he
blamed his diet; his failure to complete the race, he said later,
was because he had eaten too much steak for breakfast.[10]

He might have been all right if the race hadn't been length-
ened by 385 yards at the behest of Queen Alexandra. In placing
the finish line directly in front of the queen, the organizers
extended the length of the marathon, which had previously
been randomly set at between 25 and 26 miles, to 26 miles and
385 yards, which remains the official distance to this day.

The Olympic marathon took inspiration from the legend of
Pheidippides in ancient Greece, where the victor fell at the
finishing line and, with a wave of triumph, collapsed and died.
The modern Olympic event had to wait until 1912 for its first
death. Portugal's very first involvement at the Olympics came
to a sticky end during the marathon in Stockholm. They were
represented by twenty-one-year-old Francisco Lazaro, who
prepared for the race by covering most of his body with
beeswax to keep him cool and prevent sunburn. It had

---

10   Joseph Forshaw, who won the bronze medal having marinated his socks in
beef fat to aid comfort, noted later, "We followed the plan adopted at previous
marathon races, eating a good breakfast of steak, following this with two raw eggs,
some tea and toast ... on the way, we took nothing but water, except four miles
from the finish, having a stitch in the side, I took a drop of brandy. Ordinarily, I
don't believe in drinking spirits, but I had to do something as the side was giving
me trouble."

completely the opposite effect because his body couldn't cool down. He collapsed and died at the eighteen-mile mark with a body temperature of 41°C.

## Longest Time Taken to Complete an Olympic Marathon

Hailed in his homeland for his prowess in track events and known as "father of the marathon", the Japanese long-distance runner Shizo Kanakuri qualified for the marathon in the 1912 Olympics by setting a new world record, making him the favourite for the event in Stockholm.

After a gruelling eighteen-day journey to the Games involving sea travel and a trip on the Trans-Siberian Railway, Shizo was not at his best when he lined up for the event. Early in the race, he was overcome by heat exhaustion and passed out. He managed to drag himself into a family garden party near the marathon course and was given orange juice and a chance to recover. Deeply ashamed at his failure to complete the race, Kanakuri hung around the party for an hour or so and then returned directly to his hotel and departed for Japan the next day without notifying anybody. As far as the Swedish authorities were concerned, he was a missing person for the next fifty years before discovering that he was living in Japan.[11]

In 1966, he was contacted by Swedish television and offered the chance to complete his run. He accepted and completed the marathon in a time of fifty-four years, eight months, six days, eight hours, thirty-two minutes and twenty seconds.

> *"People are becoming too intelligent ever to have another war. Statesmen have not anything like the prestige they had years ago, and what is educating the*

---

11  Kanakuri also competed in the 1924 Olympics, where he failed to complete the race again.

> *ordinary people against war is that they are mixing*
> *so much. The motorcar, radio and such things are the*
> *great 'mixers'. I believe the last war was too much an*
> *educator for there ever to be another on a large scale."*
>
> Henry Ford, 1928

## Worst Olympic Team Performance

The Tunisian team competing in the 1960 Olympic Modern Pentathlon finished a historic last in every single event and, in some cases, failed to score a single point.

First up was the show-jumping section, during which the entire team of three fell off their horses. In the next event, swimming, one of their competitors came very close to drowning.

The third event was the shooting; one of the team nearly shot an official and they were ordered from the shooting range for fear that they were endangering lives. When it came to the fencing, they were handicapped by the fact that only one member of their team could actually fence. Hoping nobody would notice, they sent the same team member up three times with his mask on. One of his opponents recognized him as the man he had just fought and the Tunisian was disqualified. The final event was the cross-country run, in which they scored their highest tally of 1,758 points, but still finished in last place.

The total score for Team Tunisia was 5,126, a massive 10,000 points behind the next to last, marking the worst performance by a team in Olympic history.

> *"If excessive smoking actually plays a role in the*
> *production of lung cancer, it seems to be a minor one."*
>
> Dr W. C. Heuper, National Cancer Institute, 1954

## Worst Olympic Track-and-Field Team

Olmeus Charles was one of several Haitian athletes sent to the Olympic Games by the "Baby Doc" Duvalier regime during the 1970s–80s, mostly picked from among Duvalier's personal friends, who gained notoriety by setting record worst times, many of which are still held.

Charles set an Olympic record at the Montreal Games in 1976 by finishing last in the 10,000 metres by the biggest margin ever recorded. He was so far behind the rest of the field that, as he was completing his solo run of the last six laps, an argument broke out among the track officials as to whether he should be allowed to finish the course because he was holding up the other track events. He eventually completed the course in the slow-motion time of forty-two minutes eleven seconds, fourteen minutes behind the heat winner Carlos Lopes of Portugal. He was lapped by everyone in the race at least three times, including the next to last, Canadian Chris McCubbins.

Other notable Haitian under-performers include Anilus Joseph who started his 1972 10,000 metres qualifying heat in a sprint, then dropped out when he was already a mile behind the leaders and Dieudonne Lamothe who completed a unique double by finishing last in both the 5,000 metres in 1976 and the 1984 marathon. Lamothe revealed later that he'd only found out about his selection for the event a couple of weeks before the finals: Baby Doc's Olympic selection committee had offered to kill him if he didn't take part.

> *"There is not the slightest indication that nuclear energy will ever be obtainable. It would mean that the atom would have to be shattered at will."*
>
> Albert Einstein, 1932

## Least Harmonious Display of Sporting Unity

The Summer Olympics are supposed to embody the very essence of fair play and sporting brotherhood. The Games of 1908 would test this theory to destruction. The event was originally to have been held in Rome but, in 1906, Mount Vesuvius erupted, causing widespread devastation in Naples. Italy pulled out, blaming the cost of reconstruction work, although everyone suspected that this was an excuse, a suspicion that the Italian Prime Minister Giovanni Gioletti did little to dispel when he said that the Olympic Games were "a complete waste of money".

The IOC had to find another venue quickly. Luckily, an Anglo-French exhibition was being planned at Shepherd's Bush, London. The organizers agreed to incorporate a sports stadium into their arrangements in return for a cut of the takings, so the IOC was able to announce that London would now host the games.

Right from the opening ceremony, the 1908 Games lurched from one disaster to another.[12] Unlike the three previous Olympics, it had been decided that athletes would compete in national teams rather than as individuals, so flags of all the competing nations were posted around the new White City stadium. Unfortunately, someone forgot to fly the Swedish and American flags. The Swedes stormed out of the stadium in protest while the Americans refused to dip their flag when they walked past the Royal Box. The Finns, who had been told to carry a Russian flag, marched without one. Some of the Irish competitors, who had been told to parade under a British flag, refused to march at all.

The actual sport kicked off with the tennis event at Queen's Club in West London. Every single Olympic entry was British. The final between E. B. Noel and H. M. Leaf

---

12  At least there weren't any problems with the Olympic torch relay, for the simple reason that there wasn't one. It was a ritual invented by the Nazis for the 1936 Berlin Olympics.

was cancelled when Leaf injured his hand. Noel won gold without hitting a ball.

The motor-boating was literally a washout. Gales blasted the Solent course, which attracted five British boats and one French. In the first heat, a race between the Duke of Westminster and Lord Howard de Walden, both boats had to withdraw for fear of sinking.

The rugby was similarly farcical. Only one team, Australia, turned up to contest the gold medal, only to find that Britain's top rugby players had actually set off for a tour of Australia.

On the plus side, there was the first purpose-built Olympic swimming pool. Unfortunately, the fishing competition was also in the same Olympic pool and the water was not changed. The pool became so murky that competitors complained that they couldn't see more than six inches in front of them. This at least was an improvement on the Paris Olympics of 1900 where the competitors had had to race through sewage in the River Seine. The night before the three-mile race, the French favourite Jean Bouin was arrested for brawling in a London pub and failed to show for the event.

Almost as soon as the athletics event started, a distracted judge walked into the path of a flying javelin, necessitating urgent medical attention. In the shot-put, an American contestant was accused of nobbling his British opponent by dropping the shot on his foot.

Bad feelings between the American and British teams marred proceedings to the extent that the Games were dubbed the "Battle of Shepherd's Bush". Right from the opening ceremony, the American team made daily protests about the British, including a complaint about the boots worn by the British tug-of-war team, but their biggest complaint was about the officials. In 1908, as at all previous Games, they were provided by the host nation. The US team manager James E. Sullivan was incensed by "biased and snobbish" British refereeing. He may have had a point: Johnny Douglas, Britain's gold medallist in the middleweight boxing division, was awarded a split decision by the contest's referee, who happened to be Douglas's father.

It all came to a head in a highly controversial men's 400-metre race. The event was not yet run in lanes, so the race could often be a rough and tumble affair. In the USA, interference with another runner by pushing, blocking or jostling was considered fair game. In England, however, the organizers had a different idea of what constituted fair play.

The Americans were confident of success, having won all the sprint events in the previous Games. When it came to the final, three Americans – John Taylor, William Robbins and John Carpenter – lined up against a solitary British runner, Wyndham Halswelle. On the final bend, just as Halswelle was making his move for the finish line, the American trio appeared to block him, forcing him off the track. On the run-in, just before Carpenter and Robbins were set to finish first and second, two British judges rushed on to the track and cut the tape. After some confusion, the British judges disqualified Carpenter for "blocking" and ordered a re-run.

The Americans refused to run again in protest, so the British runner Halswelle ran the race alone to win the gold, the only walkover in Olympic history. Beneath the headline "BAD LOSERS", the *New York Press* reported sourly, "Our uncousinly competitors have to learn how to win from American athletes, and they still more need to learn how to lose."

The gold medal winner Halswelle was equally disgusted by the whole affair and gave up running. On 31 March 1915, while serving in France during the First World War, he was killed by a sniper's bullet.

## Least Harmonious Display of Sporting Unity: Runner-Up

The Islamic Solidarity Games were founded in 2005 to strengthen ties among fifty-seven Islamic countries, a "Muslem Olympics" to be held every four years. The second games were due to be held in Tehran in 2009. The event ran into trouble when the host nation Iran insisted on calling the section of the Indian Ocean separating it from Arabia the "Persian Gulf" on all its medals. Fellow Arab countries begged to differ and insisted it was called the "Arabian Gulf". In the end, no one could agree what to call it so the whole event was cancelled.

> *"The Americans have need of the telephone, but we do not. We have plenty of messenger boys."*
> Sir William Preece, engineer-in-chief for the British Post Office, 1876

## Most Generous Use of the Term "Sprinter"

In 2001, the American Samoan shot-putter Trevor Misipeka arrived in Edmonton, Canada, to take part in the World Championships, only to find that a rule change to limit numbers had forced him out of his event.

Undeterred, the tattooed twenty-one-stone giant signed up for the 100-metre sprint, taking on the best in Olympic champion speedsters, Maurice Greene, Ato Boldon and Donovan Bailey.

Wearing a black sleeveless T-shirt bought from a street market and ordinary street trainers, he grunted and spluttered through the finish line in 14.28 seconds, a full four seconds behind the winner – the slowest ever seen at a World Championships.

"Trevor the tortoise" said he was delighted with his performance, a personal best. It would be: he had never run the distance before. "I was the biggest guy out there by 150 lbs," Eric noted after the race. "If I was the same weight as them, I'd have been a contender."

## Worst Professional Football Team

As every football fan knows, you win some, you lose some. But not if you support the Belgian fourth-division side SSA Antwerpen – you lose some then you lose more. They had the worst season in football history in 1995/96, ending their thirty-game campaign with this record: played 30, won 0, drew 0, lost 30, goals for 12, goals against 271, points 0.

Relegated without a single point, SSA Antwerpen conceded a goal every ten minutes during league play. At least they managed to score four away from home.

---

*"The cinema is little more than a fad. It's canned drama. What audiences really want to see is flesh and blood on the stage."*
Charlie Chaplin, actor, producer, director, and studio founder, 1916

---

## Least Successful Attempt to Treat an Injured Player

The first ever FIFA World Cup finals were staged in Uruguay in 1930. During the semi-final game between the USA and Argentina, the American physio Jack Coll ran on to the pitch to tend to an injured player. Tossing his first aid bag on the ground, he accidentally broke a bottle of chloroform and while stooping to pick it up, inhaled the fumes and knocked himself out.

While the physio had to be stretchered off the pitch by his teammates, the injured player recovered without any treatment. Argentina went on to trounce their opponents 6-1.

---

*"Who the hell wants to hear actors talk?"*
H. M. Warner, co-founder of Warner Brothers, 1927

## Worst Goalkeeping Début

Crewe Alexandra goalkeeper Dennis Murray hoped to make a good impression on his professional début in 1951. It didn't go entirely to plan; he let in nine goals and made only one further appearance for the club.

At least he fared better than Halifax Town goalkeeper Steve Milton, who got his professional début on 6 January 1934 against Stockport County. He let in thirteen goals, setting an all-time league record. The final scoreline was 13-0, still a club record defeat for Halifax Town and a club record victory for Stockport County. There is no word on what became of Steve Milton.

> *"This 'telephone' has too many shortcomings to be*
> *seriously considered as a means of communication.*
> *The device is inherently of no value to us."*
> A memo at Western Union, late 1870s

## Most Embarrassing Tournament Exit

In October 2011, there were scenes of wild jubilation as the South African football team celebrated a 0-0 draw with Sierra Leone, earning them the point they needed to qualify for the 2012 Nations Cup in Equatorial Guinea. Or so they thought. Sadly, someone hadn't read the small print.

South Africa had played for a draw from the kick-off. At the final whistle, players celebrated on the pitch for several minutes with a lap of honour while the state-run African Broadcasting Corporation proclaimed qualification. The country's president went on air to congratulate the team. Seemingly, no one in South Africa realized that goal difference was not the deciding factor for qualification to AFCON 2012; it was head-to-head results between the top three teams in the group. Which meant that South Africa had had to win – and had failed to qualify.

When the penny finally dropped, coach Pitso Mosimane told a press conference, "I'm confused. Just have a look at the table of the group now and see who is top of the group." This didn't inspire confidence. South Africa Football Association president Kirsten Nematandani sacked him and then apologized to his country for Bafana Bafana's failure to qualify, promising that it wouldn't happen again.

As someone posted under footage of the game on YouTube, if the team had spent as much time acquainting themselves with the rules as they did choreographing their "victory" celebrations they would have qualified.

---

*"While theoretically and technically television may be feasible, commercially and financially it is an impossibility, a development of which we need waste little time dreaming."*
Lee DeForest, American radio pioneer and inventor of the vacuum tube, 1926

---

### We're Kicking Which Way?

Middlesbrough left-back Bobby Stuart holds the record for the most own-goals in a single season in English football history. During the 1934/35 season, he netted five times against his own team.

During a total of 247 league appearances for the Teesside club, Stuart only managed two goals at the right end.

---

*"I must confess that my imagination refuses to see any sort of submarine doing anything but suffocating its crew and floundering at sea."*
H. G. Wells, British novelist, in 1901

# Least Successful Attempt to Organize a Fixture List

In the 1930s, Charles Sutcliffe was one the most powerful men in football. He was also one of the sport's Little Englanders. Sutcliffe believed that British football was vastly superior to that played elsewhere and voted to pull England out of FIFA, meanwhile referring to Germany, France and Austria as "midgets". Six years later, he described the World Cup (played without England, of course) as "a joke".

His antipathy towards foreigners extended to English clubs who attempted to sign them. When Arsenal tried to sign Rudy Hiden from Wiener AC in 1930, Sutcliffe wrote, "The idea of bringing foreigners to play in league football is repulsive to the clubs, offensive to British players and a terrible confession of weakness in the management of a club." The FA agreed with him and brought in a rule the following year which effectively banned foreign players from playing in England. Thanks to Sutcliffe, England followed a policy of "splendid isolation", insulating themselves from advances in the world game from which their national team has arguably never fully recovered.

As a referee, Sutcliffe didn't shy from controversy either. In a game between Blackburn Rovers and Liverpool in the 1890s, he managed the heroic feat of disallowing a record six goals. After provoking the displeasure of the crowd in a match at Sunderland, he had to sneak out of the ground disguised as a policeman.

But it is for his disastrous attempt to ban gambling in football, however, that Sutcliffe is chiefly famous.

In 1936, he became England Football League President, which made him personally responsible for devising the schedule of fixtures for all Football League matches. Sutcliffe had an additional vested interest: he didn't just work out the fixtures, he literally owned the copyright on the fixtures list and was paid 150 guineas a season by the League for doing it on their behalf, with the aid of a complex system of charts.[13]

He was also a staunch Methodist and believed that gambling on football was evil. At the time, advertisements for "the Pools" – the traditional working man's flutter on predicting the outcome of matches – were banned from football grounds, but Sutcliffe wanted to go further. He wanted to stamp out all football gambling, sparking what became known as the "Pools War". As Charles Sutcliffe saw it, the solution to the "evil" of football gambling was very simple – if the Pools companies such as Littlewoods didn't know in advance which matches were to be played, they wouldn't have time to produce the coupons, so no one could do the Pools and the companies who ran them would be put out of business. So, in February 1936, Sutcliffe completely cancelled the entire football league programme, announcing fixtures for the weekend with just forty-eight hours' notice.

Pandemonium ensued. Clubs that would have the farthest to travel didn't have enough time to make the necessary arrangements. It was also impossible to keep the fixtures a secret: they were leaked to the newspapers, who published them anyway every Friday, giving the pools companies just enough time to operate as normal.

The biggest loser was football: the late publication of fixtures caused so much confusion amongst the fans that attendances around the country fell sharply (although Sutcliffe tried to blame the bad weather). George Orwell commented later that Hitler's re-occupation of the Rhineland was greeted "with hardly a flutter", but the decision to withhold the football fixture lists to stop the Pools companies "flung all Yorkshire into a storm of fury". The plan was scrapped after just two weeks.

---

13  Sutcliffe's method for working out fixtures involved a chequerboard of 924 red and white squares, each club being allocated a different number each season. Apparently, the only mistake he ever made was once to mix up Sheffield Wednesday with Sheffield United. His method, which was a closely guarded secret, was taken on by his son and continued to provide fixtures until 1967, when the process was computerized.

The Pools War had ended in humiliating defeat for Charles Sutcliffe, but his malign influence over the English game lingered on long after his death. Incredibly, his ban on foreign players remained in place until 1978.

## Most Sensitive Referee

If you are a football referee, it helps to be thick-skinned. Ask the man who officiated at the 1878 FA Cup final between Wanderers and Royal Engineers, Mr Bastard.

Similarly unfortunate was Eric Braamhaar, who made his début as a referee officiating at the 2001 Dutch First Division game between Fortuna Sittard and NEC Nijmegen. His surname rhymes with Dutch slang for female private parts. It wasn't long before the crowd picked up on the coincidence and began to incorporate it into their banter. Mr Braamhaar was so upset that he stopped the game and refused to continue until the crowd apologized. Eventually, after they had finally milked the humour out of the situation, they began chanting, "We are sorry . . ." and play continued.

There's no record of how much "insult-and-injury time" was added at the end of the match.

---

*"Very interesting Whittle, my boy, but it will never work."*
Cambridge Aeronautics Professor, when shown
Frank Whittle's plan for the jet engine

---

## Five Most Pathetic Excuses for Losing a Game of Football

1. England's goalkeeper David James made a few high-profile gaffes during his career, earning him the nickname "Calamity James", but the 'keeper had an excuse for his irregular form. He said he was addicted to playing his

PlayStation and was not getting enough sleep. It was the sort of excuse a twelve-year-old might offer for not doing their homework.

2. Bulgaria are one of the great under-achievers of the World Cup, but not when it comes to creative excuses for failure. Following their 1993 defeat in qualification against Austria, manager Dimitar Penev blamed the loss on: (a) the flag raised by their hosts ("nothing like the Bulgarian one"); and (b) the Bulgarian national anthem ("the band played a dreadful version"). As a result of both, Penev explained to the press afterwards, "the team's composure and concentration disappeared and that's why we lost."

3. In terms of talent, the Scotland-Uruguay fixture at Switzerland in the 1954 World Cup finals should have been evenly matched, but it ended in a 7-0 rout for the Uruguayans. Scotland seemed to be caught out by the summer weather in Basel which reached temperatures of over 100°F. They were wearing old-fashioned, thick woollen jerseys with long sleeves and buttoned collars. Scottish midfielder and former Manchester United manager Tommy Docherty explained, "The Scottish FA assumed Switzerland was cold because it had mountains. You'd have thought we were going on an expedition to the Antarctic. The Uruguayans wore light V-necked shirts with short sleeves. No wonder we lost 7-0."

4. After their 4-0 drubbing at the hands of Spain in 2006, Ukraine's defender Vladislav Vashchuk said the humiliating defeat was not the fault of the players – he blamed the frogs. They were croaking outside the team's hotel all night before the game, leaving the team tired and out of sorts. A spokeswoman for the hotel denied that they had a frog problem. "Obviously, there are

frogs in the lake. But there are also birds as well. In the morning, they wake up and start going 'cheep'. It's logical really."

5. Anything can derail a team's preparations – a hamstring, a metatarsal, a flu bug. In North Korea's case, it was a bolt from the blue. After they slipped to a 2-0 defeat in their opening women's World Cup game against the United States in 2011, their coach, Kim Kwang-min, said his team lost because they were struck by lightning – not while they were at the tournament, mind, but a month earlier in Pyongyang. He wasn't specific as to how many players from his squad had been hospitalized with electrocution – "probably more than five". FIFA officials were sceptical about the claim.

## Worst Losing Streak as a Football Manager

Results are not the only way to judge a football manager. Actually, many believe they are, in which case Dumbarton's Jim Fallon is your man.

In 1995, two games into the new season, Fallon was appointed manager of Scottish First Division team Dumbarton. He lost his first game 4-0 and it sort of went downhill from there. His first season record makes horrific reading: played thirty-six, won three, drawn two, lost thirty-one. It gets worse: two of the wins came in the opening two games, before they appointed Fallon. Dumbarton finished bottom with twenty-five points fewer than the next worst team. A record of 0.147 points per match convinced the Dumbarton board that they needed to act decisively – Fallon was promptly given a new contract.

His team opened the following campaign in determined fashion with two more draws and a defeat. Fallon's run of thirty-one league games without a win finally came to an end with a 1-0 victory away to Clyde on 7 September 1996. He promptly set off on another winless run, drawing one and losing seven of the next eight games before finally leaving the club in November.

Dumbarton promptly won three of their next four games.

> *"I see no good reasons why the views given in this volume should shock the religious sensibilities of anyone."*
> Charles Darwin, *On the Origin of Species*, 1869

## Most Expensive Own Goal

Colombia had been tipped as a dark horse for the 1994 FIFA World Cup finals, but their dream ended almost as soon as it had begun when defender Andreas Escobar put through his own goal in a group match against hosts USA at the Rose Bowl, Pasadena. His mistake helped the USA to a 2-1 victory and condemned Colombia to bottom place in the group and elimination from the competition.

A few days later on his return home, he told newspapers that his team's exit was "not the end of the world". Sadly, it was for Escobar, who was found dead in a car park shortly afterwards, shot by a gangster vexed at having lost a bet on his national team to beat the USA.

> *"The idea that cavalry will be replaced by these iron coaches is absurd. It is little short of treasonous."*
> Aide-de-camp to Field Marshal Haig,
> at tank demonstration, 1916

## Least Successful Attempt at Keeping Discipline

The record for accruing the most red cards by one player in a football match belongs to Hawick United striker Paul Cooper. During a Borders Amateur League match in 2009, the thirty-nine-year-old lost the plot when referee Andy Lyon gave him his marching orders after picking up a second booking for dissent.

Instead of leaving the pitch, Cooper launched into a lengthy, foul-mouthed rant at Mr Lyon, who felt obliged to brandish the red card five more times.

When banned for two years, Cooper said, "I'm gutted because I love my football."

---

*"Caterpillar landships are idiotic and useless. Those officers and men are wasting their time and are not pulling their proper weight in the war."*

Fourth Lord of the British Admiralty, 1915

---

## Least Successful Impact Substitution

On 6 September 1992, Derby County's Andy Comyn was brought off the bench during a game against Bristol City at the Baseball Ground.

A free kick had been awarded near the halfway line. As the ball was floated into the area, Comyn rose majestically to head the ball into the net, straight past his own 'keeper Paul Williams. It was his first touch and he had been on the field less than ten seconds. His team lost 4-3.

---

*"What, sir, would you make a ship sail against the wind and currents by lighting a bonfire under her deck? I pray you, excuse me, I have not the time to listen to such nonsense."*

Napoleon Bonaparte, when told of Robert
Fulton's steamboat, 1800s

---

## Sore Losers: Football's Top Five

### 1. El Salvador (1969)

Some wars begin with a surprise attack, others with a massacre. The "100-Hour War" began with a high tackle. El Salvador were paired with Honduras for the second North American qualifying round of the 1970 World Cup. Before the first game, held in the Honduran capital Tegucigalpa on 8 June 1969, the El Salvadorian side were kept up all night by riotous fans outside their hotel. They went on to lose 1-0.

A female El Salvadorian supporter watching on TV back home reportedly shot herself through the heart just after her team went behind. She was given a televised State funeral, designed to whip up nationalist fervour before the return fixture a week later.

Back on home territory, the El Salvadorians took the chance to repay Honduras's inhospitality by welcoming their star player Enrique "the Rabbit" Cardona at the airport with posters of him being sexually assaulted by a large rabbit. Other posters depicted various black players from the Honduran side with a bone through their nostrils. On the Friday before the game, two people were murdered outside the visiting team's hotel.

El Salvador went on to give the Hondurans a 3-0 drubbing. The results left both countries' hopes of qualifying for the World Cup hinging on a deciding third match to be played in Mexico City. An estimated five thousand Salvadorians travelled to the game, many doing the 770-mile journey on motorbikes. El Salvador twice took the lead, but Honduras drew level, thanks to their star player Cardona, but the threat was blunted by a series of vicious two-footed lunges, one connecting with Cardona's throat.

The game went into extra time then, right at the death, Rodríguez headed El Salvador's winner. Afterwards, their coach put the victory down to the small details: not eating in the hotel for fear of food poisoning and ensuring that his players all touched their testicles before the game "so they didn't leave them in the dressing room".

El Salvador dissolved all ties with Honduras, which led to border clashes between the two nations. Tensions rose until, on 14 June, the El Salvadoran Army launched an attack on Honduras. By the time a ceasefire was put into effect on 20 June, just 100 hours after the first shots were fired, there were 3,000 dead on both sides.

## 2. Kuwait (1982)

Kuwait's only appearance in the World Cup made football history for the wrong reasons in the 1982 finals in Spain. After an opening 1-1 draw with Czechoslovakia, Kuwait saw their hopes of reaching the second round fade when, with ten minutes to play in their second game against France, French midfielder Alain Giresse ran through a static defence and slammed the ball into the net to give his team an unassailable 4-1 lead.

The Kuwaiti players surrounded Russian referee Miroslav Stupar protesting furiously that they had all stopped after hearing a whistle in the crowd during the build-up. Despite the referee's best efforts to persuade them otherwise, Kuwait refused to re-start the game. The match looked set to be abandoned until Kuwaiti FA president Prince Fahid entered the field of play from the stands to give the referee a piece of his mind and threatened to call off his team.

Unbelievably, referee Stupar overturned his decision and gave a drop ball, much to the disgust of the French. Incensed at the referee's U-turn, France's coach Michel Hidalgo had to be restrained by police and, amid ugly scenes, his players refused to play on, but the game eventually resumed and France finished 4-1 winners courtesy of an eighty-ninth-minute goal by Maxime Bossis.

Although they had lost the game by three clear goals (four, if you include the one they had successfully overturned),

Kuwait went into full-on conspiracy theory mode. Prince Fahid described FIFA as "worse than the mafia ... everyone knows FIFA wants certain teams to qualify for the second round. The minute they appoint USSR referee and Yugoslav linesman, we know we lose. If they would not let us beat France, they will not let us beat England."

Meanwhile, Kuwaiti defender Abdullah Mayouf pitched in: "There is no doubt in my mind that the referees in this World Cup are looking to help the top teams and are against the smaller countries like Kuwait. Every match, we have in our mind that we are playing against twelve players." FIFA fined Kuwait and cautioned Prince Fahid for unsporting behaviour. The referee was never seen on the international stage again.

## 3. Chile (1989)

Brazil were leading Chile 1-0 in Rio and just twenty-one minutes away from a place at Italia '90 when the Chilean goalkeeper Roberto Rojas went down, blood streaming from his face, having apparently been struck by a stray firecracker. The crowd looked on as Rojas rolled around on the ground in a pool of his own blood, before being stretchered from the field, followed quickly by the Chilean team as the game was abandoned. FIFA awarded Brazil a 2-0 win, but the Chilean FA, citing a similar incident between Holland and Cyprus in 1987, demanded a replay in a neutral country.

A riot ensued outside the Brazilian embassy in Chile, as 4,000 people burned the Brazilian flag and smashed windows. Meanwhile, Brazil's team doctor had said that he was "absolutely certain" that Rojas was not hit as "the flare that fell is for signalling and not explosive" and called for a FIFA investigation. They found that the Chilean 'keeper, under instruction from his coach, hid a razor blade in his glove and used it to cut himself in a bid to get the game abandoned. Video evidence confirmed that Rojas had not been touched by the firecracker.

Chile were thrown out of the 1994 World Cup, while Rojas, the coach and the team doctor were all given life bans (overturned in 2002).

## 4. *Iraqi Team Manager (1996–2001)*

Saddam Hussein appointed his son Uday as head of the Iraqi soccer federation, an inspired choice designed to give his nation's top footballers an extra incentive to do well. Underperformance was rewarded with beatings with iron bars or canings on the soles of the feet, followed by dunkings in raw sewage to ensure the wounds became infected. Motivational team talks included threats to cut off players' legs and throw them to ravenous dogs; a missed training session was punishable by imprisonment; a loss or a draw brought flogging with electric cable, or a bath in raw sewage; a penalty miss carried the certainty of imprisonment and torture.

During a World Cup qualifying match in Jordan, Iraq drew 3-3 with the United Arab Emirates, calling for a penalty shootout, which Iraq lost. Two days after the team's return to Baghdad, the captain Zair was summoned to Uday's headquarters, then blindfolded and taken away to a prison camp for three weeks.

A red card was particularly dangerous. Yasser Abdul Latif, accused of thumping the referee during a heated club match in Baghdad, was confined to a prison cell two metres square, stripped to the waist, then ordered to perform press-ups for two hours while guards flogged him with lengths of electric cable. When Iraq lost 4-1 to Japan in the Asian Cup, goalkeeper Hashim Hassan, defender Abdul Jaber and striker Qahtan Chither were fingered as the main culprits and were tortured for three days by Uday's bodyguards. When Iraq failed to reach the 1994 World Cup finals, Uday recalled the squad for extra training – with a concrete ball.

## 5. Esperance (2000)

The 2000 African Champions League showpiece final between Tunisia's Esperance and Ghana's Hearts of Oak was beamed live around the continent, complete with rioting, missile-throwing and another bizarre, self-inflicted wound by a desperate goalkeeper.

Hearts had won the first leg in Tunisia 2-1 and Esperance were winning the second leg 1-0 in Ghana when the home fans started to pelt match officials and police with missiles. The police responded with tear gas, sparking a pitch invasion. Amid the confusion, one of the away fans ran on to the pitch and handed Esperance 'keeper Chokri El Ouaer a sharp object. As Simon Kuper wrote in the *Guardian* at the time: "In full sight of the stadium, he bravely cut himself in the face. Bleeding like a pig, he tottered to the halfway line, where he fell over. El Ouaer was presumably trying to get the match called off, but as he'd disregarded the most elementary precepts of secrecy, he simply looked silly."

After an eighteen-minute delay, El Ouaer was bizarrely substituted for an outfield player while the Esperance players began fighting with policemen. Esperance's Walid Azaiez was then sent off for a headbutt, but refused to leave the field and punched a policeman on his way out. Hearts won 3-1 and become continental champions.

### Worst Bullfighter

The Spanish bullfighter Rafael Gómez Ortega, known to his fans as El Gallo (the Chicken) came from a family of matadors. He was chiefly famous for his unique fighting technique known the "*espantada*" – or "the bolt". This involved him fleeing and jumping over the barrier as soon as the bull entered the ring. Crowds loved this so much that he was brought out of retirement seven times.

In his last fight, in October 1918, he claimed he spared the bull because it "winked" at him. The audience again felt this was hilarious, but Ortega's brother, José (also known as "Joselito El Gallo"), concerned for the family honour, hopped into the ring and killed the bull.

> *"If the motion of the earth were circular, it would be violent and contrary to nature, and could not be eternal, since nothing violent is eternal. It follows, therefore, that the earth is not moved with a circular motion."*
>
> St Thomas Aquinas, 1270

## Briefest International Rugby Career

French rugby player Gaston Vareilles missed his international début against Scotland in 1910 thanks to a baguette.

When the French team train stopped at Lyon, Vareilles hopped off to sample the station snack bar. But the queue was so long that by the time he returned to the platform his train was disappearing into the distance. He was never picked for his country again.

> *"Animals, which move, have limbs and muscles; the earth has no limbs and muscles, hence it does not move."*
>
> Scipio Chiaramonti, Professor of Philosophy and Mathematics, University of Pisa, 1633

## Worst Sailor

The sea has been a more dangerous place since Stuart Hill, a retired metalwork designer from Suffolk, took up sailing in 2001.

The first of several quixotic attempts to circumnavigate the British Isles in a homemade boat began in June that year. He suffered a setback when he experienced an allergic reaction to the resin he was using on the hull of his boat *Maximum Exposure*, a modified fifteen-foot rowing boat, propelled by a windsurfing sail. After a month's delay while waiting to recover, he launched his boat into the River Stour, hitting another boat within minutes. Six days later and a hundred miles into his journey, he fell asleep from exhaustion and, drifting off the coast of East Anglia, had to be towed ashore by lifeguards. Over a period of several weeks, he was the cause of five lifeboat call-outs and two air-sea rescue helicopter scrambles.

After abandoning his attempt, Hill was defensive. None of the rescue attempts had been initiated by him, he said; they were the result of well-meaning but mistaken members of the public who took his vessel for a windsurfer in trouble. A spokesman for the RNLI begged to differ, noting that Hill's attempted voyage was "like putting someone blindfolded in the middle of the M1 and telling everyone to avoid him".

Six months later, despite being advised by experts of his vessel's unsuitability for the journey, and overlooking the fact that the costs incurred by the rescue services on Hill's behalf were counterproductive to his fundraising for charity, he made a second attempt at the anti-clockwise circumnavigation of the British Isles using the same vessel, this time launching from Southwold in Suffolk. Hill optimistically declared his boat "unsinkable", claiming receipt of a gold safety award from the RNLI.

His ordeal came to an end a few weeks later when he was found clinging to the hull of his boat fifty miles west of Shetland. Coastguards described him as "very lucky to be alive" – it turned out that his boat had been leaking from the start and the water caused his radio to fail.

In 2008, the sixty-five-year-old Hill was rescued yet again in heavy seas off Shetland after his latest self-built boat – resembling an oversized punt and described as "about as seaworthy as a Welsh dresser" – was swamped by large waves. According to his rescuers, he had no life-jacket or radio and was equipped with a flare he didn't know how to use.

In 2010, Stuart Hill told the *Shetland Times* newspaper that he was hoping to try again and that his reputation as a calamitous mariner was one thing he would "like to put to bed . . . it seems to follow me around".

## Worst Chess Player

Finding themselves desperately short of foreign players, the organizers of the 1965 Baku International Chess Tournament invited Geoffrey Hosking, an Englishman studying at Moscow University, to take part.

Hosking was completely unprepared, but manfully accepted the challenge. He only found out later that a Russian friend had put his name forward on the basis of his performance in a vodka-fuelled friendly chess game. Hosking lost all twelve games and performed so badly that officials were too embarrassed to publish any of the results.

---

*"All the ills from which America suffers can be traced back to the teaching of evolution. It would be better to destroy every other book ever written, and save just the first three verses of Genesis."*
William Jennings Bryan, Democrat US presidential candidate

---

## Worst Wrestler

During a 1930s wrestling match in Rhode Island, the American grappler Stanley Pinto was facing "Count George" Zaryoff. While trying to work himself into a winning position, Pinto became entangled in the ringside ropes. As he struggled to extricate himself, while his bemused opponent stood and watched, Pinto's shoulders touched the mat for a three-second count. He had succeeded in pinning himself and Zaryoff was declared the winner.

> *"Negro equality! Fudge! How long, in the Government of a God great enough to make and rule the universe, shall there continue knaves to vend, and fools to quip, so low a piece of demagogism as this?"*
>
> Abraham Lincoln, 1859

## When Fighting Nicknames Go Bad

When Quinton "Rampage" Johnson lost his mixed martial arts light-heavyweight title in July 2012, he was so upset that he literally went on a rampage through the streets of California in his one-tonne monster truck, driving on the pavement, shredding a tyre and injuring a pregnant woman.

After a brief chase, Jackson was apprehended by the police. He was identified by the life-size portrait of himself on the side of his vehicle, next to the word "Rampage".

> *"Rembrandt is not to be compared in the painting of character with our extraordinarily gifted English artist, Mr Rippingille."*
>
> Nineteenth-century art critic John Hunt, date unknown

## Least Successful Medal Ceremony

The triumph of Luxembourg's Joseph Barthel in the 1,500 metres at the 1952 Helsinki Olympics was greeted with embarrassed silence. A surprise winner of the middle-distance event, nobody had anticipated a gold-medal winner from the tiny European duchy, so when it came to the medal ceremony, there was no sign anywhere of the score to the Luxembourg national anthem. After an awkward delay, the band struck up a hastily improvised version.

Not nearly as awkward, however, as the situation faced by

Maria Dmitrienko from Kazakhstan in March 2012. She had just won the gold medal at a shooting tournament in Kuwait and was standing proudly on the podium waiting for the opening words of the Kazakh national anthem – "*Sky of golden sun/ Steppe of golden seed/ Legend of courage/ Take a look at my country!*"

Instead, the first notes were followed by the words, "*All other countries are run by little girls . . .*" and "*Kazakhstan's prostitutes are the cleanest in the region . . .*" and "*We invented toffee and the trouser belt!*" This was followed by an invitation to "*come grasp the mighty penis of our leader*".

Dmitrienko stuck grimly to her task, reacting only with a bemused smile, as the song went on to boast that her country was the "*number-one exporter of potassium*" and its Tinshein swimming pool was endowed with a "*filtration system a marvel to behold . . . It removes 80 per cent of solid human waste.*"

Someone had switched the tapes and they were playing the spoof version of the Kazakh national anthem written by Sacha Baron Cohen for the 2005 film *Borat: Cultural Learnings of America for Make Benefit Glorious Nation of Kazakhstan*. Kuwaiti officials kept the tape playing, unaware of the mistake.

The Kazakh team manager denounced the error as "a gross insult to our nation", although, to be fair, they should have been used to medal ceremony cock-ups by then. Earlier that year, at the opening of a skiing event, the Kazakh national anthem was accidentally replaced by Ricky Martin's 1999 hit "Livin' la Vida Loca".

## Worst Olympic Swimmer

For most swimmers, posting a personal best and a national record at the Olympic Games would give you a decent shout at contesting a medal. It was sadly not the case for twenty-two-year-old Eric 'the Eel' Moussambani, the 100-metre freestyle swimmer from Equatorial Guinea.

Twelve months before he took part in the first qualifying heat of the men's 100-metre freestyle at Sydney 2000, Eric couldn't even swim and had never seen – let alone dipped his toe into – an Olympic-sized fifty-metre pool, having taught himself to swim in a twenty-metre pool in a hotel in his home town of Malabo. Training alone without a coach, he had nobody to help him clock his efforts. He also thought he would be swimming only fifty metres at the Olympics. So it came as some surprise when he lined up at the start in the first qualifying heat of the men's 100-metre freestyle, twice the distance he'd been expecting and had "trained" for, a test of endurance he had never once attempted.

Confusion reigned when two of the three nervous participants, Niger's Karim Bare and Tajikistan's Farkhod Oripov, jumped the gun, vaulting into the Olympic pool before the starter even had a chance to finish saying, "Get set!" With two out of three contestants now disqualified for false starts, and only one competitor left, it was presumed the heat would be abandoned and Moussambani would get a "bye" to the next round but, after conferring, the judges ruled that he would have to swim alone against the clock in front of 17,000 spectators in a bid to make the Olympic qualifying time of one minute ten seconds.

After a dive that looked suspiciously inept, it quickly became apparent to even the untrained eye that Eric wasn't much of a swimmer. As he approached the halfway turn in 40.97 seconds, it was painfully obvious that he was quite literally out of his depth. BBC commentator Adrian Moorhouse thought that Eric was going to drown. "This guy doesn't look like he's going to make it . . . I am convinced this guy is going to have to get hold of the lane rope in a moment!"

At one point, Eric appeared to be treading water, but with the 17,000 crowd now roaring their support, he splashed and grunted his way to the finish, "winning" the heat in a time of 1 minute 52.72 seconds, the slowest time in Olympic history, as well as being forty-three seconds outside the qualifying time and seven seconds longer than it had taken the Australian swimmer Ian Thorpe to swim exactly twice the distance in the same pool the previous day.

But Eric did get a lot better. By 2004, his personal best for the 100 metres was down to less than fifty-seven seconds and he hoped to qualify for the Olympics and win a medal, but due to a visa problem his dream was to remain unfullfilled. Eric was so disappointed he retired from international swimming.

Remarkably, Eddie the Eel wasn't the only aquatic under-achiever from Equatorial Guinea to grace the Olympic pool at the 2000 Games. Eddie's exploits guaranteed a media circus around his female compatriot, Paula "the Crawler" Barila Bolopa. Her last-placed time of 1 minute 3.09 seconds in the fifty-metre freestyle was double that of the next worst competitor and the slowest in Olympic history, completing a unique double for Equatorial Guinea. Her team manager, Enrique Roca Nguba, blamed the high starting blocks, which she had never seen before she arrived in Sydney. "It was a long way down to the water . . . she wasn't used to that."

## Least Successful Channel Swimmers

Since merchant seaman Captain Matthew Webb first swam the Channel coated in porpoise fat in 1875, at the time of writing only another 810 people have made it to the French coast. That leaves at least another 6,000 people who have tried and failed.

There are good reasons for this high failure rate. Powerful tides, the geography of the French coast, unpredictable weather, tankers, oil slicks, the risk of hypothermia (the water rarely gets above 15°C), not to mention the horrors of jellyfish and raw sewage, make it an incredibly dangerous swim. Not for nothing is the crossing known as "the Everest of open-water swimming".

Jabez Wolfe reputedly tried to swim the Channel twenty-two times, starting in 1906 and never making it despite getting within a mile of France on three separate occasions – his 1911 attempt ended just 100 yards short. A Glaswegian, Wolfe relied on a bagpiper in the support boat to help keep his swimming stroke steady.

Another of the most persistently unsuccessful Channel swimmers was Lord Freyberg, Governor-General of New Zealand from 1946–52. As a young man, Freyberg made numerous futile attempts to swim the Channel. On his closest attempt, he got within 200 yards of the French coast where he paused to rest before one last push. Seeing his exhaustion, his wife leant over the side of his support boat and gave him a "fortifying slug" of brandy – and that was the end of the attempt. It knocked him out and he had to be pulled out of the water.

At least he lived to tell the tale. To date, at least seven people have died trying. Ueli Staub, a Swiss extreme sports enthusiast, spent sixteen hours in the water in August 2001 before disappearing under a seven-foot wave in the dark just off Calais. His body was found a week later off the Belgian port of Ostend. He was presumed to have suffered a heart attack, very likely brought on by his caffeine-heavy diet of strong coffee and flat Coca-Cola.

The most controversial death was that of Renata Agondi in August 1988. The twenty-five-year-old Brazilian lady died from exhaustion after her coach allegedly refused to let her leave the water.

The very first Channel casualty was a Briton, Ted May. As a teenager in Dartford, Ted was renowned as a strong long-distance swimmer who enjoyed tackling rough water. On stormy nights, he would swim the Thames to visit his girlfriend Florence. "One of these days," he told her, "I'm going to swim right down this river and clear across to France." Eventually, they became married and the responsibility of raising nine children got in the way of Ted's teenage ambition. He was forty-four years old, six foot two inches and close to 250 lbs when he finally got round to attempting it in 1954. By this time, none of the organized long-distance swimming competitions would take him seriously or give him the necessary back-up support, so May decided to go it alone. Unable to afford a support boat, he swam towing an inner tube with his food and drinks inside.

Despite one failed attempt, which ended in rescue, he tried again a few days later. The Calais police, suspecting that the overweight, middle-aged Englishman was inviting certain death, seized his passport, but May didn't care. On the morning of 7 September 1954, he was once more on the beach. The last sighting of him was by a tanker. He was in a churning sea, waving his arms wildly and shouting. The chief officer threw a lifebelt, which fell short by twenty feet. It took the tanker eight minutes to turn around, by which time May was gone. The rubber ring was found floating in the Channel the next day, and his body washed up on a Dutch beach shortly afterwards.

## Where Eagles Daren't

Michael "Eddie the Eagle' Edwards was one of the very few athletes who have been able to work their way into sporting folklore with headline-grabbing mediocrity.

In the early 1980s, he was an ordinary twenty-four-year-old plasterer from Cheltenham. He had learned to ski on a school trip and ever since had dreamed of going to the Winter Olympics as a downhill skier. Having failed to make the cut for the GB team for the 1984 Olympics, he decided to switch disciplines and aim for the 1988 Games as his country's first ever competitor in the ski jump. He got the nod from the British Ski Federation because nobody else applied.

To prepare for the Games, Eddie joined the World Cup circuit, but with little money or sponsorship he was forced to improvise. He trained by running up and down stairs and learned to jump in borrowed boots so big he had to wear six pairs of socks and a borrowed helmet tied on with string. To keep costs down, he roughed it in a spare bed in a Finnish mental hospital and, at one point, he was eating scraps from rubbish bins. He had a lucky break when he went to Switzerland and got some free training advice from sympathetic Austrian and French ski-jumping coaches. Unfortunately, he didn't understand a word they were saying because he couldn't speak French or German.

His first major competition was the 1987 World Championships, finishing ninety-eighth in a field of ninety-eight. His thick glasses, worn for his extreme far-sightedness, tended to steam up on the runway as he sped towards possible death. However, despite several injuries, he qualified for the 1988 Winter Olympics.

By the time he arrived at Calgary for the 1988 Games, he had been given the ironic nickname "Eddie the Eagle" when critics suggested that the Briton, who was twenty pounds heavier than his nearest competitor, would fly like a brick and was more likely to end up in traction rather than on the medallists' podium.

But first he had to negotiate his way through the airport without injury. His bags burst on the carousel and he had to jump on and chase after his underwear. On his way to the arrivals lounge, he saw a large banner saying: "Welcome to Calgary, Eddie the Eagle". He made a bee-line for the sign without realizing that it was 2 a.m. and the automatic doors had been turned off – he walked straight into the glass. That's when he acquired the nickname "Mr Magoo". When he finally reached his accommodation, he found that his ski bindings had been damaged and, while he was repairing them, he missed the first practice session for the opening seventy-metre event. He then got himself locked out of his room at the athletes' village. It all went downhill from there.

When Eddie completed his final jump in the seventy-metre event in last place (one Italian journalist dubbed him a "ski dropper"), Olympic officials advised him for his own safety not to jump in the ninety-metre competition. One observed caustically that "in such near-perfect conditions, an eleven-year-old child could jump further".

Eddie persisted and completed the ninety-metre event, trailing in a predictable last place with his best jump of 73.5 metres. Matti Nykänen, the double-gold-winning Finn, recorded 118.5m with his first jump. But Eddie had still set a British record which stood for six years.

After the Olympics, the rules were changed. The so-called "Eddie the Eagle rule" required Olympic hopefuls to compete in international events and place in the top 30 per cent of competitors. He was now, officially, the benchmark of Olympic failure. Of course, this didn't stop him from trying to qualify for the 1992, 1994 and 1998 Games, without success.

The Eagle soared, briefly, during the 1989 World Cup in Lake Placid when he finished ahead of Dutchman Gerrit Koninenberg on "style". A jubilant Eddie said afterwards, "I kicked some butt!" A week later, he fell and broke his collarbone. "The jump was so good, and I was in such a good position that I started to panic," he explained ruefully.

Back at home, Eddie enjoyed his fifteen minutes of fame. He wrote an autobiography – *On the Piste* – in 1990 and had a stab at a pop career with the song "Fly, Eddie, Fly" – less heroic than his jumping but every bit as amateurish and reaching number two in Finland. But then, sadly, the money dried up, bankrupting Edwards and forcing him to return to the day job.

Eddie has no regrets about his career. The one thing that still annoys him, though, is that in his *annus mirabilis* he was pipped by the world's most boring snooker player Steve "Interesting" Davis as BBC Sports Personality of the Year.

## Ten Gambling Losers

1. The Nebraska businessman Terry Watanabe spent over twenty years building up his family business, selling party goods and novelty toys. Then he blew the lot in a losing streak at the gambling tables at Caesar's Palace and Rio Casinos. Watanabe lost over $120 million in just one year in 2007 and an eye-watering $205 million in total – to date the biggest loss by an individual in Las

Vegas history. Tourists came from miles around just to watch him lose on the blackjack table where he would sit playing three hands simultaneously, often hitting even when he was on twenty, hoping for an ace. To add insult to injury, Caesar's Palace sued him for $15 million in unpaid debts, despite having already taken over $100 million from him.

2. Most Britons remember the media tycoon Kerry Packer as the man who shook up cricket. In Australia, he was known as the richest man in the country. In 2004, his net fortune was estimated at $6.5 billion – even after his lavish gambling habit put a massive dent in it. In 1999, Packer is believed to have lost up to $40 million in ten months, including almost $28 million during a three-week losing streak at a casino in London. One night he walked into a Mayfair casino on his own, lost £15 million on four roulette wheels in a matter of minutes, then nonchalantly walked out again, apparently untroubled by his loss. Then again, he did survive eight heart attacks.

3. Omar Siddiqui wasn't a tycoon; he was an executive at an electronics company. In his spare time, he was also operating a huge fraud, siphoning off millions of dollars in kick-backs; the money went mostly on blackjack. At one point, he was averaging a loss of $8 million a day, with total losses of at least £65 million. Even though he amassed huge IOUs, casinos continued to lend him millions more because he was good business. He was jailed for fraud and sued by casinos right across America for unpaid gambling debts.

4. The Japanese property developer Akio Kashiwagi was known in 1992 as "the world's biggest gambler" thanks to his addiction to baccarat. He still holds the record for the biggest baccarat loss in history when he

blew $10 million in one session at the Trump Casino. It doesn't get much worse, although for Kashiwagi it did – he was stabbed to death outside his home shortly afterwards.

5. In gambling circles, the Syrian businessman Fouad-al-Zayat was known as "The Fat Man". He acquired a taste for fat losses at London's Aspinall's casino on his favourite game, roulette. That's the one where you can quickly get panicked into chasing losses and doubling up every bet, and the quickest way to lose money in a casino. He had visited Aspinall's more than 600 times in twelve years, losing a whopping £23 million. One night, he opened his account with £500,000 in chips and lost the lot in a mad opening fifteen minutes of play. He promptly bought another £500k in chips and lost it all again. That night, he lost £2.25 million in total. He was now £4 million in the red – then his cheque bounced. A UK court subsequently froze all his assets, including his 747 jumbo jet and his Rolls-Royce.

6. Zhenli Ye Gon is known in Las Vegas as "Mr Ye". He has reportedly lost $125 million at a number of Vegas casinos over a number of years. Apparently, this isn't a huge deal for Gon, who was a pharmaceuticals importer based in Mexico City (or a drugs baron, to you and me). When police raided his home, they uncovered $200 million in cash. Now he's in a place where there are no roulette wheels. Gon says he was framed and most Mexicans buy his story. Bumper stickers reading "I believe the Chinaman" are now on sale.

7. The Czech-born British media proprietor and over-sized crook Robert Maxwell reputedly made one of the quickest and biggest casino losses of all time while playing at the Ambassadeurs casino in London. While playing three roulette wheels at the same time, he managed to

lose £1.5 million in under three minutes. That works out at about £8,000 a second of someone else's pension money.

8. The Greek-American Archie Karas became known as the greatest gambler of all time after the largest and longest documented winning streak in gambling history when he turned $50 in December 1992 into over $40 million by the beginning of 1995, simply known as "The Run". In true Greek financial spirit, he then lost the whole lot again in just three weeks playing dice and baccarat, which war known as "The Loss". Karas himself claims to have gambled with more money than anyone else in history.

9. The legendary Stu Ungar, three-time World Series of Poker main event winner, is called the greatest Texas Hold 'Em and Gin Rummy player of all time. Unfortunately, he didn't stick to what he did well. Most of his winnings at the poker table were lost betting on sports. After one of his WSOP wins he lost $1.5 million in a weekend betting on sports and even lost $80,000 the first time he ever played golf. Ungar didn't even make it to the first tee and lost the $80k on the putting green; the rest he spent on drugs. Despite having won an estimated $30 million during his poker career, he died in his forties of a heart condition with no assets to his name. Friends had to have a whip-round at Ungar's funeral to raise funds to pay for the service.

10. In 2008, the Austrian casino player Josef Reiner lost thousands on the roulette table at his local casino in Vienna. He was so scared of facing his wife that he faked an assault on himself and claimed that he had been the victim of a robbery. To be fair, he did such a great job that he was admitted to hospital, having used an iron bar to smash his own face in, breaking his nose

and jaw and finally his arm. Doctors called police after he confessed.

## Ten Most Creative Excuses for Failing a Dope Test

1. When the US Anti-Doping Agency asked the cyclist Tyler Hamilton to explain the presence of someone else's red blood cells in his veins, the road racer claimed that the cells belonged to a "vanishing twin" who'd died in his mother's womb. Medical experts agreed that this was theoretically possible but unlikely. Sporting authorities were more sceptical but Hamilton was allowed to keep his 2004 Olympic medal because his second sample had been accidentally damaged in the laboratory and couldn't be tested. Hamilton was banned for two years in 2005 after a second positive test.

2. When the Cuban high-jumper Javier Sotomayor protested his innocence after testing positive for cocaine at the 1999 Pan American Games, he had support from high places – his country's president, no less. In a tele-vised address, Fidel Castro insisted that Sotomayor was set up by "professionals of counter-revolution" – namely the "Cuban-American mafia". Sotomayor was allowed to compete in the 2000 Olympics after his ban was shortened, but decided to call it a day and opted for early retirement after failing yet another drugs test in 2001.

3. The conspiracy route was also tried by World and Olympic 100-metre champion Justin Gatlin. He claimed that he was the victim of sabotage by a vindictive mas-seur who rubbed a cream containing the banned substance testosterone into his legs. Gatlin received a four-year ban. And in another claim of "tampering", seven years after winning the 1992 Olympic

5,000-metre title, the German distance runner Dieter Baumann claimed that somebody had maliciously spiked his toothpaste with a performance enhancing drug. But without a suspect and seeing as how, unlike Prince Charles, he is able to squeeze his own toothpaste tube, the authorities decided that this was just another steroid tall tale.

4. In 1994, British shot-putter Paul Edwards blamed his positive test for steroids on accidentally drinking an entire bottle of shampoo. Why did the bronze-medal winner ingest his hair product? He wouldn't say. Fortunately, he didn't follow it up with a conditioner chaser.

5. In 2007, baseball's Glenallen Hill acknowledged that a shipment of steroids had indeed shown up at his house, but he swore he had never used them. So why had he ordered them? Hill's explanation: "marital stress".

6. When the Spanish discus thrower David Martínez tested positive for nandrolone, he blamed it on eating infected pork. In an attempt to prove his innocence, the 1992 Olympic finalist went to the trouble of injecting his pet pig with the steroid before slaughtering and eating it. Sadly, his experiment did not leave traces of the drug in his system and the authorities decided he was telling porkies.

7. When Olympic gold-medal-winning race walker Daniel Plaza crossed the finish line in first place in the 20-km walk at the 1992 Olympics, he was celebrated as the first Spanish track-and-field athlete to win an Olympic gold medal. He fell from grace four years later at the Spanish championships when he tested positive for nandrolone. He claimed that the steroid had got into his system while performing oral sex on his pregnant wife. Pregnant women do produce nandrolone naturally, and

Plaza did eventually clear his name, but it took him ten years, by which time he was long retired.

8. In 2007, the Genoa FC striker Marco Borriello went down a similar route. He was suspended for nearly three months when banned steroids turned up in his urine sample. Borriello blamed the test results on a cream he was rubbing into his penis to treat an STD acquired from his then-girlfriend, Argentine model Belén Rodríguez. When doctors pointed out that the quantity in his system was too high for absorption, Borriello said he must have swallowed some as well because his girl-friend was using the cream on herself.

9. The Czech left-hander Petr Korda was once ranked number-two tennis player in the world. Korda's explana-tion as to how the banned steroid nandrolone came to be found in his system during the 1998 Wimbledon tourna-ment was his fondness for veal. Young calves are fattened on the steroid, but Korda would have to have eaten forty veal calves a day for twenty years to have built up the levels found in his body. An easy mistake to make. But the authorities didn't believe him and he received a one-year ban, which, at his age, effectively brought his professional career to a close.

10. Finally, we salute the most creative way of actually admitting having taken drugs, provided by Californian baseball pitcher Chuck Finley. When his ex-wife accused him of smoking marijuana, alcohol abuse and of injecting steroids during their five-year marriage, Finley said, "I can't believe she left out the cross-dressing."

# 9

## Close, but No Cigar: A Litany of Losers

*In which the Antichrist fails to win a seat in Parliament; Madame Steinhal gets lockjaw; the Loch Ness monster loses an election; and Captain Cook finds himself the main course in a Hawaiian buffet.*

### Most Failed Election Candidate

Commander Bill Boaks (1921–86), war hero and road safety campaigner, was the most unsuccessful parliamentary candidate in British election history.

His first candidacy was in the 1951 general election when he fought Walthamstow East as an independent candidate for the Association of Democratic Monarchists Representing All Women. He had intended to stand against Prime Minister Clement Attlee in Walthamstow West, but accidentally put his name down for the wrong seat. In the event, Boaks received 174 votes out of 40,001 cast.

His political label changed several times over the years, but it was the issue of road safety that engaged him most, if not exclusively; he also stood for a ban on fireworks and the removal of homosexuals from public office. In one election, he stood as the Trains and Boats and Planes candidate, a cunning plan to sway floating voters by adopting the title of a contemporary pop song, but eventually settled for Public Safety Democratic Monarchist White Resident. He justified the name on the grounds of "that's exactly what I am". After securing the nomination for a seat, he claimed that he would often approach a "black", give him £1 and invite him to find another

149 people willing to do the same so that he could stand as a "Black Immigrant" but there were no takers.

Boaks cycled around the target constituency wearing a large cardboard box daubed with various slogans, mostly about road safety. Later, he traded his bike in for a white van painted with black stripes and a large mast and sail on the top. He championed the cause of pedestrians to have the right of way at all times, reinforcing his point by deliberately holding up traffic at zebra crossings. He once stopped his van outside Wembley Stadium just before the start of an England-Scotland match and refused to move until all 100,000 football fans had crossed the road in front of him. Even more recklessly, he sat in a deckchair in the fast lane of the Westway, the raised section of the A40 dual carriageway in London. He was subsequently convicted of two counts of obstructing the highway, although he appealed against both convictions on the grounds that it was his right to stop his car at any time "to offer courtesy to any road user". His appeal was dismissed.

Frustrated at his general lack of success as a defendant, Boaks decided to try his luck as a prosecutor. In the 1950s, he launched a series of private prosecutions against public figures who had been involved in road accidents, including the wife of Prime Minister Clement Attlee. Lady Attlee was a notoriously accident-prone driver and the survivor of nine car crashes in thirteen years, prompting nine Boaks prosecutions.

When Prince Philip, the Duke of Edinburgh, drove his Rover into a Ford Prefect owned by a Mr Cooper of Holyport, Berkshire, Boaks issued a summons against the Queen, as Prince Philip's passenger, for aiding and abetting. In these, as in his electoral campaigns, Boaks was unsuccessful. The litigant was unfazed: "Cars kill impartially," he noted. "I don't care whether the driver is a duke or a bloody dustman." Subsequent attempts by Boaks to prosecute the Conservative Deputy Prime Minister Rab Butler and Princess Anne for road traffic offences also came to nothing.[1]

---

1 As far as Mrs Attlee was concerned, Boaks may have had a point. *TIME*

In 1958, he applied for the vacant post of Chief Constable of Berkshire and was disappointed not to get an interview; at the time he was simultaneously attempting to prosecute the Home Secretary as the accomplice of a police officer who was driving him to the House of Commons and, according to Boaks, had committed six traffic offences in Parliament Square.

As well as his strongly held views on road safety, Boaks had radical views about transport in general, which he vented under the guise of the British National Airways National Heliport Network and Central London Airport and Aerodrome Association. Specifically, he wanted to get rid of planes and replace them with helicopters. In February 1961, he applied for planning permission to build a heliport in his garden, despite the fact that he was completely broke and didn't own a helicopter or a garden big enough to house one.

The low point of his political career came in 1982 when he contested the Glasgow Hillhead by-election and gained five votes, the fewest ever recorded in a modern British Parliamentary election. What made this defeat even more remarkable was that he needed the support of at least ten voters to get his name on the ballot paper in the first place. Boaks remained optimistic in defeat. "Had I been elected," he said, "I think I would have become the next prime minister."

Over a period of thirty years, Bill Boaks contested twenty-one general elections and by-elections without coming close to winning a seat. Ironically, he died as a result of head injuries sustained in a traffic accident.

## Least Perceptive Electorate

In November 2000, Missouri governor John Ashcroft lost his bid for re-election to the US Senate when his opponent Mel Carnahan clinched victory by about 49,000 votes out of more

---

magazine once described her as "a terrible driver who should never have been allowed on a public highway ... [it was] almost as certain as fog that she would have a traffic accident every so often."

than 2.3 million ballots cast. Missouri voters hadn't spotted
that their man Carnahan had died in a plane crash thirty-eight
days earlier.

In 2009, the voters of Missouri were at it again. When the
town of Winfield went to the polls, they gave their recently
deceased mayor Harry Stonebraker a fourth term with a land-
slide 90 per cent of the vote. According to the *New York Daily
News*, Stonebraker's death from a heart attack had made him
considerably more popular.

---

> "*Forget it, Louis, no Civil War picture ever made a nickel.*"
> Irving Thalberg's warning to Louis B. Mayer
> regarding *Gone with the Wind*

---

## Least Successful Diplomatic Mission

In 1842, a British envoy, Lieutenant Colonel Charles Stoddart,
was sent to Bukhara in Central Asia (modern-day Uzbekistan)
to negotiate with the ruling Emir Nasrullah Khan. Stoddart's
mission was to convert the Emir to the benefits of Christianity
and British-made goods.

The Emir, known throughout Asia as "The Butcher",
was not a man to be messed with, having assassinated his
own father and four brothers for the throne. Unfortunately,
Stoddart was unschooled in the subtleties of Eastern diplomacy. Contrary to local custom, he rode into the Emir's
castle on horseback rather than walking, then floored an
attendant instead of offering the customary sign of submission. Worse, he was not bearing gifts or letters from Queen
Victoria, only a note from the governor-general of India.
The Emir made the Englishman wait half an hour. Stoddart was so annoyed that, when finally introduced, he
refused to bow; instead, he drew his sword and told the
Emir to "eat shit".

The Emir had the Englishman thrown into a thirty-foot-deep,

vermin-infested hole called "the Bug Pit", accessible only by a rope lowered down through a hole in the centre of the ceiling. Into this hole the prison guards daily poured doses of scorpions, sheep ticks, rodents and raw offal. Stoddart was left to languish in this pit alone for a year. His nerve cracked only once, when the executioner climbed down a rope into the pit with orders to behead him unless he converted to the Islamic faith. Stoddart became a Muslim on the spot. Unfortunately, this did not signal any improvement in his living conditions.

In September 1840, a would-be rescue mission rode into town in the shape of a young British officer, Captain Arthur Connolly of the Sixth Bengal Tiger Cavalry. Connolly was a graduate of Rugby School, immortalized in *Tom Brown's Schooldays*. Cultural sensitivity was not Connolly's strong point, either. When he complained about the treatment afforded to his countryman, the amused Emir had him thrown into the pit to keep Stoddart company.

For two long, horrific years, the two men were slowly eaten alive by bugs, until, in the jailer's own words, "masses of their flesh had been gnawed off their bones". Their only break was when they were occasionally brought to the surface for a series of mock executions. Finally, the sadistic Emir got tired of this mind game and, on 24 June 1842, the two lice-ridden men were dragged from the spit, forced to dig their own graves in the public square and were then beheaded, before a cheering crowd, on charges of spying for the British Empire.

Their fate remained a mystery for some time until friends of Stoddart and Connolly had a whip-round and funded an expedition to look for them, in the form of a Jewish-born Christian missionary Rev. Joseph Wolff. He reached Bukhara in 1845 only to discover that the two men had long since been executed.

At least Wolff did not repeat Stoddart's mistakes. He prostrated himself before the Emir, crying "*Allah Akbar*" about thirty times instead of the proscribed three, then presented his gifts – three dozen copies of *Robinson Crusoe* in Arabic and several cheap watches. He was only spared the same fate as Connolly and Stoddart because the Emir couldn't stop laughing.

## Worst Inaugural Speech

Some American presidents are remembered for delivering brilliantly memorable inaugural addresses. Franklin Roosevelt's in 1933, during the depths of the Great Depression, proclaimed, "the only thing we have to fear is fear itself". John F. Kennedy in 1961 challenged fellow citizens with the words: "Ask not what your country can do for you; ask what you can do for your country."

William Henry Harrison's inaugural address, delivered on 4 March 1841, was the longest ever at more than 8,000 words. It took more than two hours to deliver, in the middle of a snowstorm. Much of the speech dealt, inexplicably, with ancient Roman history. It bored the freezing crowd but, for the new president, it was fatal. As a show of bravado, the sixty-eight-year-old Harrison didn't wear a hat or coat while delivering his seemingly endless oration. A month later he died of pneumonia, setting a new record as the first American president to die in office.

---

*"We know, on the authority of Moses, that longer ago than 6,000 years the world did not exist."*
Martin Luther, German leader of Protestant Reformation

---

## Least Successful Prediction of an Election Outcome

In 1948, according to the overwhelming predictions of pollsters across the nation, the "unstoppable" Republican candidate Thomas Dewey stood poised to defeat the incumbent Harry

Truman to become the thirty-fourth President of the United States of America.

The *New York Times* announced: "THOMAS E. DEWEY'S ELECTION AS PRESIDENT IS A FOREGONE CONCLUSION". *LIFE* magazine ran a cover photo of Dewey beneath the headline: "THE NEXT PRESIDENT OF THE UNITED STATES". On election eve, Dewey asked his wife, "How will it be to sleep with the President of the United States?"

"A high honour," she replied, "and quite frankly, darling, I'm looking forward to it."

The next morning, the news arrived that Truman had won. His victory was such a surprise that the *Chicago Daily Tribune* had already printed a premature "DEWEY DEFEATS TRUMAN" headline. When the Deweys sat down for breakfast, Mrs Dewey said, "Tell me, Tom – am I going to Washington or is Harry coming here?"

---

> *"There will be no C, X or Q in our everyday alphabet.*
> *They will be abandoned because unnecessary."*
> *Ladies Home Journal* article, "What May
> Happen in the Next 100 Years?" (1900)

---

## Least Successful Election Campaign

In 1995, thirty-six-year-old David Griffiths was expelled from the Twickenham branch of the Conservative Association after telling a meeting of its members that he favoured the death penalty for all crimes, that homosexuals should be encouraged to commit suicide and that people who claim social security should gun each other down in the street.

Griffiths returned to politics a year later when he ran for the Twickenham seat in the 1996 General Election as "the Antichrist". He said that he had been aware that he was the Antichrist for some time, but had kept quiet about it in case it damaged his career in the Conservative Party.

> *"The Macintosh uses an experimental pointing*
> *device called a 'mouse'. There is no evidence*
> *that people want to use these things."*
> John C. Dvorak, technology writer for the
> *San Francisco Examiner*, 1984

## Least Dignified Exit from Office
## by a French President

In 1899, Felix Fauré, 58-year-old President of France, died suddenly and unexpectedly at the Presidential residence the Elysée Palace in the arms of Marguerite Steinheil, his mistress of two years.

It wasn't her arms he was in, exactly. It was widely reported that Fauré's aides heard screams and broke down the door to find him seated on a sofa while his mistress was fellating him. Madame Steinheil went into in a state of trauma-induced lockjaw when she realized that her blowjob had just killed *le président*. After freeing the hysterical mistress, the fallen leader was placed back in his bed with his hands folded over a crucifix.[2]

> *"[They] might as well try to light London*
> *with a slice from the moon."*
> English chemist William H. Wollaston,
> on gas lighting, date unknown

---

2   Or so it was widely rumoured. Fauré's supporters later claimed that his political opponents made the bit up about the blowjob.

## Least Dignified Exit from Office by a French President: Runner-Up

When Paul Deschanel was elected President of the French Third Republic in January 1920, his aides couldn't help noticing that his approach to protocol veered far from the traditional. When a delegation of schoolgirls presented him with a bouquet, he tossed the flowers back at them one by one. Later, he received the British Ambassador to France stark naked apart from the ceremonial decorations of his office.

On 23 May, the French president was travelling by train near Montargis when he fell through the window of his train after having taken some sleeping pills. He was found, wandering in his pyjamas and covered in blood, by a rail worker, who took him to the nearest level-crossing keeper's cottage. Deschenel struggled for some time to convince them that he was the President of France. The stationmaster's wife told news reporters, "I knew he was a gentleman because he had clean feet." It was several hours before the president's staff realized that he was missing.

As if falling from a moving train wasn't quite embarrassing enough, a few weeks later Deschanel walked out of an important meeting straight into a lake, fully clothed.

His resignation offer was accepted on 21 September 1920, seven months after he took office, and he was subsequently hospitalized in a nursing home.

---

*"It's a bad joke that won't last. Not with winter coming."*
Coco Chanel, designer, on the miniskirt, 1966

---

## Most Creative Excuse for Losing an Election

David James, Conservative MP for the constituency of Brighton Kemptown, lost his seat in the 1964 general election after a record seven recounts, by just seven votes, to Labour's Dennis Hobden, the first ever Labour MP for a Sussex constituency.

James, who was also the founder of the Loch Ness Monster Information Bureau, had spent most of the three-week election campaign in Scotland on his annual hunt for "Nessie". He was blamed for his party's defeat because Labour went on to win the election with a two-seat majority that was soon whittled down to one in a by-election.

This is thought to be the only occasion *Nessiteras rhombopteryx* has been blamed for losing a British general election.

> *"Whatever happens, the US Navy is not*
> *going to be caught napping."*
> Frank Knox, US Secretary of the Navy, three days
> before Pearl Harbor was attacked, 1941

## Shortest Time in Office

1. Pope Urban VII was the shortest-serving Pope in the history of the Catholic church, only managing to hang on to his job for thirteen days in 1590 before dying from malaria before his official instalment. But in that time, he was still able to pass the world's first smoking ban, threatening to excommunicate anyone who "took tobacco in the porchway of or inside a church, whether it be by chewing it, smoking it with a pipe or sniffing it in powdered form through the nose".

2. Sweyn Forkbeard was King of England for just five weeks until he fell off his horse in 1014, to be succeeded by his son Cnut.

3. In 1998, the Russian president Boris Yeltsin sacked his prime minister and cabinet and declared that he was going to be prime minister from now on. A few hours later, he changed his mind.

4. William Pulteney, the First Earl of Bath, became prime minister on 10 February 1746. He resigned two days later because nobody wanted to join his cabinet.

5. On 1 February 1908, the Portuguese royal family were riding in an open carriage through Lisbon when thirty-year-old Manuel Buica shot at them at point-blank range, killing King Carlos. His two sons, Crown Princes Luis and Manuel, drew their own pistols and returned fire. Buica turned his gun on twenty-one-year-old Luis and discharged several more bullets. Manuel was saved by his mother Queen Amelie, who shoved a bouquet of flowers into Buica's face just as he was taking aim. Crown Prince Luis Filipe had the shortest reign of any monarch, surviving his dead father by just twenty minutes.

## Dead as a *"Didus Ineptus"*

Everyone was rude about the poor old dodo. The name may have originated from the Portuguese *"doudo"* which means foolish or simple; or maybe it was the Dutch when they colonized the island where it was discovered in 1644. Their word *"dodaars"* means either "fat-arse" or "knot-arse", referring to the bird's ungainly appearance. Linnaeus, the father of taxonomy, mockingly called it *"Didus ineptus"*.

The dodo was living quite happily on the Indian ocean island of Mauritius until the start of the sixteenth century when a storm blew some Portuguese sailors in its direction. Things started to go badly for the species from then on. For the next 200 years, the ungainly but friendly bird that had never known a predator was an easy target, and not just for insults. Apart from ridiculing the dodo's appearance, or its rolling gait, people were also rude about the taste of its flesh – not that it stopped them from clubbing the bird to death for fun. Then the cats, dogs and pigs they brought to the island with them found that dodo eggs were also easy meat, lying vulnerable in grassy nests on the forest floor. Soon after the forest itself began to disappear as people began to plant sugar cane where the bird liked to nest.

By 1693, the dodo was extinct; only a handful of stuffed specimens was left. One was donated to the Ashmolean Museum in Oxford, but was burned in 1755 by curators under orders to get rid of old and tatty artefacts. It was only when they looked for a replacement that they realized they had destroyed the last specimen in existence.

> *"Hitler will end his career as an old man in some Bavarian village who, in the biergarten in the evening, tells his intimates how he nearly overturned the German Reich . . . The old man, they will think, is entitled to his pipe dreams."*
> Harold Laski, *London Daily Herald*, 1932

## Least Convincing Display of Supernatural Powers

Empedocles, a Greek philosopher who lived in Sicily during the fifth century BC, was one of the most renowned geniuses in history and is attributed with a number of "firsts". Some considered him the inventor of rhetoric, the art of public debate; others regarded him as the founder of the science of medicine in Italy. He was also the first person to realize that the Moon shines by reflected light from the Sun. He also came up with the first ever theory of evolution by which man and animals evolved from some ancient, monstrous forms. He is probably best known as the world's first chemist because of his important insight into the nature of matter – he said that all things are composed of four primal elements: Earth, air, fire and water.

In another insight, Empedocles came to believe that he was a god. In 433 BC, while seeking to prove his immortality to his supporters, he jumped into the crater of Mount Etna. The volcano spewed out one of his bronze sandals but there has been no sign of the owner since.[3]

---

*"We are probably nearing the limit of all
we can know about astronomy."*
Simon Newcomb, Canadian-born
American astronomer, 1888

---

## Least Successful Declaration of Independence

On 15 March 1939, the Republic of Carpatho-Ukraine declared its independence from Czechoslovakia with a former teacher, Augustin Voloshyn, as their new head of state.

Boasting an armed force of just 12,500 men, it was annexed by Hungary the very next day, having enjoyed self-rule for twenty-four hours.

---

*"Louis Pasteur's theory of germs is ridiculous fiction."*
Pierre Pachet, British surgeon and Professor
of Physiology at Toulouse, 1872

---

3  Inspiring the poet Richard Osborne to write:
   *"Great Empedocles, that ardent soul;*
   *Leapt into Etna, and was roasted whole."*

## Least Successful Cult

The great Greek philosopher and mathematician Pythagoras was the first person to insist that natural phenomena could be explained mathematically, paving the way for the study of Physics.

Five hundred years before the birth of Christ, he also started up his own religion, which, at its peak, had around 300 followers living in a commune in Italy. Pythagoras' new religion had three central tenets: (1) Do not kill; (2) Souls are reincarnated; (3) Beans are evil. He issued a long list of pithy precepts to his disciples, including "Don't pick anything up that has fallen over"; "Never step over a pole"; "Don't shake hands too eagerly"; "Refrain from handling white cockerels"; "Don't look into a mirror by the light of a taper"; and, sensibly, "Never eat your own dog". His followers were also forbidden from having sex during the summer (it was only permitted in winter). And, of course, they were forbidden to eat beans.

Just after Pythagoras discovered his famous mathematical theorem, he celebrated by feasting on a roasted ox. This came as something of a surprise to his followers, who were also required to be strictly vegetarian. After a brief but wind-free existence, the cult disbanded after the commune was attacked and destroyed by a mob from the neighbouring town. Pythagoras himself died in a fight, which was also bad press for a pacifist.

*"The abolishment of pain in surgery is a chimera. It is absurd to go on seeking it . . . knife and pain are two words in surgery that must forever be associated in the consciousness of the patient."*
Dr Alfred Velpeau, French surgeon, 1839

## Briefest Career as a Deity

By an extraordinary coincidence, Captain James Cook's arrival in Hawaii[4] in 1779 came just in time for the local celebration of Makahiki, a festival dedicated to the god Lono. Not only did Cook's ship, the *Resolution*, bear sails that looked very much like the large cloth banners that hung from the cross-bar standard of the Hawaiian god, but Cook had arrived directly from Kahiki (Tahiti) – according to legend, the home of Lono. Many Hawaiians believed that the mysterious, pale-skinned, strangely clothed visitor, equipped with wonderful objects brought from beyond the horizon, actually was Lono.

Although the presence of Cook and his men put a great strain on their subsistence economy, the Hawaiians were understandably generous to the strangers. After all, they didn't want to offend Lono and his earthly helpers. After a couple of weeks, Cook was ready to leave. His departure, fortuitously, also synchronized with the Lono legend and the Hawaiian sacred calendar.

Soon after setting sail, however, disaster struck and the *Resolution* broke its foremast, forcing Cook to return to the island a week later. This time, the reception was distinctly cooler. According to legend, the god Lono was not supposed to come back quite so soon. And he had sailed the wrong way around the island. The Hawaiians became suspicious; perhaps the hospitality they had shown this stranger had been a waste of resources after all.

The Hawaiians took to stealing from the seamen to restore the balance. Having been treated like a god the first time around, the grumpy Cook reacted harshly. When the *Resolution*'s cutter was stolen, he assembled a large landing party and took the Hawaiian High Chief hostage until it was returned. The chief, who knew nothing about the theft, was

---

4   Or, ironically as it turned out, the Sandwich Islands, as he preferred to call it after his patron the Earl of Sandwich.

happy to go with Cook, but a number of his wives were not and they began to make a scene. In the ensuing commotion, a couple of thousand natives surrounded the landing party as they retreated to their boats. One of then clubbed Cook from behind and he fell to his knees in the surf, where he was stabbed to death.

Hawaiian tradition says that he was killed by a chief named Kalanimanokahoowaha. That night, Cook returned the favour of all the feasts he had enjoyed as a god, when he was eaten himself. His heart was shared between the four most powerful chiefs on the island and his bones were distributed around the island as mementoes. Only the skull, hands and thighbones of the former god remained and were placed in a small coffin, which, after a brief service, was tossed into the Pacific Ocean.

## Least Successful Attempt to Spot a News Scoop

In 1979, the *Washington Post* offered the *San Francisco Chronicle* the opportunity to syndicate a series of news stories two reporters named Bob Woodward and Carl Bernstein were writing about a break-in at the Watergate Hotel, the Democratic headquarters in Washington, D. C. *Chronicle* owner Charles Thieriot turned them down. "There will be no West Coast interest in the story," he explained.

His rival, the *San Francisco Examiner,* stepped in and bought the rights to the hottest political news story of the century for $500.

---

*"Television? The word is half Latin and half Greek. No good can come of it."*
C. P. Scott, editor of the *Manchester Guardian* (1872–1939)

---

## Worst Call by an Academic Expert

Sir Hugh Trevor-Roper – Lord Dacre – had an enviable career. He was a best-selling author, Regius Professor of Modern History at Oxford, a director of Times Newspapers and a peer of the realm. A glittering career history, undoubtedly, but when judged against the only benchmark that everyone remembers him for, he is seen by history as an abject loser, to put it mildly.

In 1983, the German magazine *Stern* paid £2.3 million (about £50 a word) for "the publishing scoop of the century", sixty-two volumes of Adolf Hitler's diaries dated from 1932–45, covering the entire period of the Third Reich. The remarkable volumes, *Stern* reported, had been found by farmers in a plane crash at the end of the war and had eventually made their way into the hands of *Stern*'s investigative reporter, Gerd "the Detective" Heidemann. Suspiciously, the diaries shed little light on the momentous events of the age and were mostly a collection of banal personal musings.

A typical excerpt dated June 1935, read: "Eva now has two dogs, so she won't get bored." An entry from December 1938 stated: "Now a year is nearly over. Have I achieved my goals for the Reich? Save for a few small details, yes!" Another during the 1936 Berlin Olympics revealed: "Eva wants to come to the Games in Berlin, have had tickets delivered to her and her girlfriends. Hope my flatulence doesn't return during the Games."

Voices of scepticism were raised. Hitler, it was pointed out, could never be bothered to take notes, so he was an unlikely diarist. The diary covers were also decorated with the brass Gothic initials "F. H.", the author having apparently mistaken the Gothic capital "A" for an "F" when he bought the type.

Enter Lord Dacre. The great and much respected English historian examined the diaries and declared them genuine. He said, "I'm staking my reputation on it." A few months later, they were exposed as a clumsy modern forgery, written in the back room of a Stuttgart shop by Konrad Kujau, a small-time dealer in Nazi memorabilia.

On Saturday, 23 April 1983, the night before the *Sunday Times* was due to serialize the dairies as the genuine article, Sir Hugh changed his mind and decided they were a fake. *Sunday Times* owner Rupert Murdoch, who had just paid a fortune for serialization rights, was informed. But the newspaper had already been printed – so what was to be done? Murdoch instructed his editor, "Fuck Dacre. Publish."

Despite the short-term embarrassment, sales of the *Sunday Times* shot up, but Lord Dacre's reputation, meanwhile, was heading in the opposite direction. Despite a lifetime of high achievement, when he died in 2003, *The Times* headline ran: "HITLER DIARIES HOAX VICTIM . . . DIES AT 89".

Herr Kujau's more ambitious creations included a sequel to *Mein Kampf,* poems by Adolf Hitler and the beginnings of an opera penned by the Führer entitled *Wieland der Schmied* ("Wieland the Blacksmith").

## Least Successful Missionary

Preparation is the key for any successful missionary. Among David Livingstone's provisions when he started his famous trek across Africa were seventy-three books weighing a total of 180 lbs. He eventually agreed to discard some of his portable library, but only after his weary porters had carried them for 300 miles. As the journey continued, his library grew progressively smaller until only his trusty Bible remained.[5]

Livingstone died in Africa in 1873, after braving illness and years of paddling up and down snake-infested rivers, none of them, alas, leading to the source of the Nile. Along the way, he only ever converted a single African, who later lapsed.

---

5 Still not quite in the same league as the French explorer Alexander Debaize, who reached the African town Ujiji in 1878 packing twenty-four umbrellas, two suits of armour and a portable organ.

> *"X-rays will prove to be a hoax."*
> Lord Kelvin, President of the Royal Society, 1883

## Strangest Losing Bet

The most extraordinary wager in history was made over a hundred years ago in a London club. One evening, in 1907, an American businessman, John Pierpoint Morgan, bet a British aristocrat, the Fifth Earl of Lonsdale, the then extravagant sum of £21,000 that it was not possible for a man to walk around the world without being recognized.

The conversation was overheard by a certain Harry Bensley, a notorious gambler who had lost heavily to the two men and was desperate to find some way of repaying them. Bensley agreed to take up the challenge.

There were certain conditions: he had to wear an iron mask for the whole trip and pay his way by selling pictures of himself. While travelling, he also had to find a woman who would marry him, he had to push a pram and carry only one change of underwear.

Bensley set off from Trafalgar Square in London in January 1908 and was arrested a few miles down the road for selling postcards without a licence. No one knows for certain to what extent Bensley actually complied with the terms of the wager. There is no proof that he travelled far outside the British Isles but the legend claimed that he got as far as China and Japan. He was said to have received 200 marriage offers but accepted none of them and a newspaper was said to have promised £1,000 reward to anyone who could reveal his identity.

Bensley supposedly got most of the way round the world and was in Italy on his way home in 1914 when the First World War broke out and he had to call the whole thing off.

> *"For some years now, there has been promise of
> a large flat TV screen which would hang on the
> wall like a picture . . . [but it's likely] we shall
> never see such a system in operation."*
> Science writer and BBC broadcaster Arthur Garratt, 1978

## Least Successful Picnic

In 1982, Larry Walters, a truck driver and amateur aviation enthusiast from California, decided to build his own flying machine. One sunny summer's afternoon, in his backyard in San Pedro, with the help of a few friends, he strapped forty-five helium-filled weather balloons to his favourite patio chair and armed himself with a pellet gun, a CB radio, a camera and a cooler full of sandwiches and beer.

His plan was to cut the cord tethering him to the ground, rise to a height of thirty feet or so and have a little picnic. Then he'd just shoot out a couple of balloons with his pellet gun and float gently back to Earth.

The maiden flight of Larry's flying lawn chair far exceeded his expectations, or his basic grasp of physics. According to some reports, he didn't shoot out the balloons for fear that the chair would tip. Instead of a gentle ascent to 200–300 feet he shot up to a height of 16,000 feet (about three miles), much to the surprise of a couple of passing airline pilots, who quickly alerted the Federal Aviation Authority that a drunken man with a gun was drifting in US airspace. Eventually, he touched down in the Long Beach area, but not before getting tangled in some power lines and knocking out power in the entire neighbourhood.

Larry was arrested and eventually fined $1,500 by the FAA for violating airspace. When asked by a news reporter why he did it, he replied, "A man can't just sit around."

Larry gave up his job as a truck driver to try a new career as a motivational speaker, with even less success than he'd enjoyed as an aeronaut. He took his own life in 1993 at the age of forty-four by shooting himself in the heart.

## Least Successful Reward Claim

In 2012, a Taliban commander was captured after walking up to a US army checkpoint in Afghanistan brandishing a wanted poster featuring his own face and demanding the $100 reward money for his own arrest.

Mohammad Ashan was wanted for organizing attacks on Afghan troops. A US soldier told the *Washington Post*, "We asked him, 'Is this you?' Mohammad Ashan replied, 'Yes, yes, that's me! Can I get my award now?'" US forces confirmed his identity using a biometric scan.

"Clearly, the man is an imbecile," a US official added.

> *"We can close the books on infectious diseases."*
> Surgeon General of the United States
> William H. Stewart, 1969

## Egrets, I've Had a Few: Shortest Career as a Celebrity Chef

The Victorian naturalist Francis Buckland was a popular author of natural history books, especially books on fishing. In 1859, he decided to branch out and try his hand as a latter-day Jamie Oliver by educating the British public on how they could ease food shortages by eating new types of meat.

As a boy, he had experimented with squirrel pie, mice cooked in batter, hedgehog and garden snails, but he had his eye on more exotic items. In 1859, he set up the Society for the Acclimatisation of Animals in the United Kingdom after coming to an arrangement with London Zoo whereby he would receive a cut of any animal that died. It was an excuse for Buckland and his friends to sample boiled elephant's trunk (which he described as too rubbery, but OK in a soup); rhinoceros (like very tough beef); steamed and boiled kangaroo; wild boar; roasted parrot; garden snails; and earwigs.

Some culinary experiments were more successful than others. His favourites were giraffe and boa constrictor, both apparently tasting like veal. Stewed Japanese sea slug were "like the contents of a glue pot", while the boiled and fried head of a long-dead porpoise tasted like "broiled lamp wick". He once ate a panther, after one was sent to him by the zoo. He noted, "It had been buried for two days, but I got them to dig it up. It was not very good."

In 1868, Buckland took part in an all-horse banquet, served to 160 people, to encourage the increased use of horses as a source of nutrition. After working his way through the entire eight courses, he conceded, "In my humble opinion, hippophagy has not the slightest chance of success in this country."

## The End of the World Isn't Nigh: Ten Failed Apocalyptic Predictions

1. In the sixteenth century, an apocalyptic sect emerged in northern Europe called the Anabaptists. In 1534, a young Dutch Anabaptist called Jan Bockelson announced himself to the inhabitants of the German town of Munster by running naked through the streets before collapsing into a three-day trance. Upon emerging from his stupor, he claimed that he had received messages from God, on the basis of which he was setting up a New Jerusalem in Munster ahead of Christ's imminent Second Coming.

In the meantime, Bockelson told his followers that God had told him that men could now take multiple wives and that women must, under penalty of death, submit to whichever men chose them. Leading by example, Bockelson took sixteen wives and used a pegboard system to keep track of which one he was supposed to be sleeping with each night. He tore down church steeples, communized all property, issued coins bearing his likeness and generally made life in his new Christian state a living hell for everyone except for himself and a few fellow Anabaptists, who lived very lavishly. Bockelson's reign in Munster ended in a bloody siege in 1535 when troops nailed his genitals to the city gates.

2. According to Christian tradition, the number 666 is the "mark of the beast" in the Bible's Book of Revelation.[6] So it was no surprise that many Europeans approached the beastly-numbered year 1666 with some trepidation. Of course, it didn't help when, the preceding year, a plague wiped out about a fifth of London's population. Then, on 2 September 1666, a fire broke out in a bakery on London's Pudding Lane. As the fire spread for three days, London looked literally hellish, as more than 13,000 buildings and tens of thousands of homes burned. In total, fewer than ten people died in the blaze, which was bad news for the families concerned but not the end of the world. In fact, the year 1666 later become known as the "*annus mirabilis*" – year of miracles – because some people chose to interpret the absence of even greater disaster as a miraculous intervention by God. So God wins either way.

3. After several years of careful study of the Bible, in 1831 an American farmer, William Miller, announced that Jesus Christ would return for the long-awaited

---

6 In Revelation 13:18 it is written: "Here is wisdom. Let him that hath understanding count the number of the beast: for it is the number of a man; and his number is six hundred threescore and six." Anything associated with that number was known to be pure evil. A devout Puritan in London would have been shitting himself.

Second Coming and that Earth would be engulfed in fire sometime between 21 March 1843 and 21 March 1844. As Judgment Day drew nearer, Miller steadily gained followers and, by 1840, the United States was firmly in the grip of Millerism. Over the next four years, around 100,000 people sold their belongings and took to the mountains to wait for the end.

When 21 March 1844 came and went, Miller revised the date to 18 April 1844. When the world survived this date unscathed as well, he admitted he had made a mistake, but the end of the world was definitely nigh – he just wasn't sure how nigh exactly. Then one of his loyal followers, Samuel S. Snow, double-checked Miller's numbers and arrived at a different date: it was not March or April but 22 October 1844. When the fateful day came and went without any supernatural incident, 22 October became known to Millerites as "The Great Disappointment of 1844", although it was slightly better news for the rest us, the world not having ended. The Millerites disbanded but a few of them went and formed the Seventh-Day Adventist movement.

4. The appearance of Halley's comet, which is seen from Earth every seventy-six years, has been causing panic throughout history. The comet's impending arrival in 1910 caused the biggest reaction of all. Initially, thanks to extensive newspaper coverage, it was eagerly awaited by the general public, but while most reporters turned to astronomers to get their facts straight, the tabloid press stirred apocalyptic hysteria by claiming that there was danger of a celestial collision with Earth; and even if we escaped a direct hit, it was reported that the comet's tail contained poisonous cyanide gases that would impregnate the atmosphere and snuff out all life on the planet.

During the evening of 18 May 1910, some people took precautions by sealing the chimneys, windows and doors of their houses; others confessed to crimes they had committed because they did not expect to survive the night; and a few panic-stricken people actually committed suicide. In the event, the Earth's orbit carried it through the end of the comet's twenty-four-million-mile-long tail, unscathed, for six hours on 19 May. Some people did quite well from the panic: sales of masks and "comet pills" rocketed, as did oxygen supplies, as people hoped to keep themselves alive on bottled air until Earth passed through the danger.

5. The onset of the First World War was a scary time for most people, but it was especially significant for the Zion's Watch Tower Tract Society – or, as we know them, Jehovah's Witnesses. The society's founder, Charles Taze Russell, had previously predicted the end of the world in 1873. When nothing happened on the appointed day, he postponed it to 1874. When the new deadline passed with little sign of an apocalypse, Russell announced that the Second Coming had actually taken place as planned – it was just that Christ was here, but invisible. The actual end of the world – that is, the one we would all be able to see for ourselves – would come in 1914. This gave Russell and his followers a full forty-year breather to carry on with their mission of saving lost souls without being further embarrassed by their own predictions.

When the First World War broke out that year, Russell interpreted it as a sign of Armageddon and the upcoming end of days or, as he called it, the end of "Gentile times". The war was bad enough, but people couldn't help noticing that the world had not yet ended. After Russell's death in 1916, his followers continued to push back the fateful day, first to 1917, then 1925. From the mid-1930s to early 1940s, pamphlets said it was "months away". Later, another delay was effected until 5 September 1975. Ever since then, the cult's followers have been predicting that the world will end "shortly".

6. The American media mogul and TV evangelist Pat Robertson has had little success with his apocalyptic predictions. In late 1976, Robertson predicted that the end of the world was coming in October or November 1982. In a May 1980 TV broadcast, he repeated his prediction: "I guarantee you, by the end of 1982, there is going to be a judgment on the world."

In May 2006, after receiving another revelation from God, Robertson declared that a tsunami would hit America's coastline sometime later that year. The following January, Robertson said that God had told him to expect "mass killings" in 2007 by way of a terrorist attack on the United States. He elaborated, "The Lord didn't say nuclear. But I do believe it will be something like that."

When the terrorist attack failed to materialize, Robertson explained, "All I can think is that somehow the people of God prayed and God in his mercy spared us." In 2011, Robertson incorrectly predicted several more dates for the end of world and was jointly awarded an "Ig Nobel Prize" for "teaching the world to be careful when making mathematical assumptions and calculations". Robertson countered, "I have a relatively good track record. Sometimes I miss."

7. The Christian writer Hal Lindsey did more than just predict the end the world; he popularized a whole new literary genre. His book, *Late Great Planet Earth*, the best-selling non-fiction book of the 1970s, predicted that the world would end sometime before 31 December 1988. Lindsey cited a host of world events as proof, including nuclear war, the communist threat and the restoration of Israel.

His follow-up book, *The 1980s: Countdown to Armageddon*, was less specific, implying that the battle of Armageddon would take place in the not-too-distant future and "the decade of the 1980s could very well be the last decade of history as we know it" adding that the US could be "destroyed by a surprise Soviet nuclear attack". The book was taken out of print in the early 1990s.

His next effort, *Planet Earth – 2000 AD*, stated that Christians should not plan to still be on Earth by the year 2000. Lindsey's apocalyptic vision did not come to pass, but he still has much to answer for. Edgar Whisenant published a book in 1988 called *88 Reasons Why the Rapture Will Be in 1988* which sold 4.5 million copies. Whisenant was quietly confident, saying, "Only if the Bible is in error am I wrong."

When 1989 rolled around, Whisenant published another book claiming that the Rapture would occur that year instead. It didn't sell as well, and neither did later titles that predicted the world would end in 1993 and again in 1994.

8. Edgar Cayce was known as the "American Nostradamus" or "the sleeping prophet" after his habit of going into a trance to predict the future or heal the sick. Although Cayce's track record on the predictions front was generally so erratic that he was obliged to keep up his day job selling photographic supplies, he had one notable success just before the 1929 Wall Street Crash when he advised a client against investing in the stock market because he saw "a downward movement of long duration".

Cayce is also said to have foreseen the First and Second World Wars, the independence of India, the state of Israel and the assassination of President Kennedy. He also predicted the fall of Communism in China, California's collapse into the Pacific Ocean in

1969 and the return of Christ after a Third World War in 1999 and the Earth's and mankind's total destruction by flooding and earthquakes in 2000. His hopeful followers, the Association for Research and Enlightenment, keep his memory alive from their base at his former home in Virginia.

9. In 2011, Christian radio host and serial alarmist Harold Camping picked 21 May as the date of the Rapture. "Beyond the shadow of a doubt," he said. Confirming his reputation for moving in mysterious ways, God refused to stick to this itinerary. Camping recalculated and shifted his prediction to 21 October.

It wasn't the first time Camping had had trouble with his maths. In 1992, he published a book called *1994?*, which proclaimed that Christ would return and the world would end in mid-September 1994. He based his calculations on numbers and dates found in the Bible and was "99.9 per cent certain" that he was correct. But the world did not end in 1994, not even on 31 March 1995, another date Camping provided when September 1994 passed without incident.

In 2012, Camping announced his retirement from end-of-the-world predictions. "I'm like the boy who cried wolf again and again, and the wolf didn't come," he told the press, "but this doesn't bother me in the slightest."

10. By the standards of ancient peoples, the Maya of pre-Columbian America were technologically backward. They lacked the wheel, the arch, the plough and domesticated animals. They did, however, build mightily impressive temples and monuments and made astronomical observations. They were also totally obsessed with measuring time. The Maya had several calendars, including one known as the Long Count, counting forwards from the date of the creation of the world – 8

September 3114 BC, according to the Maya. Their biggest unit of time was not a year or a century but the 144,000-day B'ak'tun.

Although Mayan glyphs and hieroglyphs aren't very clear about what the mysterious calendar means, it has become of enormous interest to astrologers/Internet rumour-mongers who believe that the Maya could predict the future, including the date when the world will end. Because the number thirteen was significant for the Maya, many believed that the thirteenth B'ak'tun – on the 21 or 23 December 2012 – would herald the end of the world. Scenarios suggested for the apocalyptic moment included the arrival of a huge solar flare, or Earth's collision with a black hole or a passing asteroid, or with a planet called "Nibiru". But while the Mayan prophets were busy predicting what would happen in the far distant future, did they foresee their own collapse in the ninth century? Or the coming of Cortéz and the imminent cataclysmic Spanish invasion?

No, they didn't.

# Appendix I

## Harry Stephen Keeler Bibliography

*The Voice of the Seven Sparrows* (London: Hutchinson & Co., 1924); (New York: E. P. Dutton, 1928)

*Find the Clock: A Detective Mystery of Newspaper Life* (London: Hutchinson & Co., 1925); (New York: E. P. Dutton, 1927)

*The Spectacles of Mr Cagliostro* (London: Hutchinson & Co., 1926); (New York: E. P. Dutton, 1929)

*Sing Sing Nights* (London: Hutchinson & Co., 1927); (New York: E. P. Dutton, 1928)

*The Amazing Web* (London: Ward, Lock & Co., 1929); (New York: E. P. Dutton, 1930)

*Thieves' Nights: The Chronicles of Delancey, King of Thieves* (New York: E. P. Dutton, 1929); (London: Ward, Lock & Co., 1930)

*The Fourth King* (London: Ward, Lock & Co., 1929); (New York: E. P. Dutton, 1930)

*The Green Jade Hand* (New York: E. P. Dutton, 1930); (London: Ward, Lock & Co., 1930)

*The Riddle of the Yellow Zuri* (New York: E. P. Dutton, 1930); (London: Ward, Lock & Co., 1931)

*The Matilda Hunter Murder* (New York: E. P. Dutton, 1931); (London: Ward, Lock & Co., 1931)

*The Box from Japan* (New York: E. P. Dutton, 1932); (London: Ward, Lock & Co., 1933)

*The Washington Square Enigma* (New York: E. P. Dutton, 1933); (London: Ward, Lock & Co., 1933)

*The Crilly Court Mystery* (London: Ward, Lock & Co., 1933); (New York: E. P. Dutton, 1933)

*Behind That Mask* (London: Ward, Lock & Co., 1933); (New York: E. P. Dutton, 1938)

*The Fiddling Cracksman* (London: Ward, Lock & Co., 1934); (New York: E. P. Dutton, 1934)

*The Riddle of the Traveling Skull* (New York: E. P. Dutton, 1934); (London: Ward, Lock & Co., 1934)

*Ten Hours* (London: Ward, Lock & Co., 1934); (New York: E. P. Dutton, 1935)

*The Five Silver Buddhas* (New York: E. P. Dutton, 1935); (London: Ward, Lock & Co., 1935)

*The Marceau Case* (New York: E. P. Dutton, 1936); (London: Ward, Lock & Co., 1936)

*X. Jones of Scotland Yard* (New York: E. P. Dutton, 1936); (London: Ward, Lock & Co., 1936)

*The Wonderful Scheme of Christopher Thorne* (New York: E. P. Dutton, 1937); (London: Ward, Lock & Co., 1937)

*The Defrauded Yeggman* (New York: E. P. Dutton, 1937)

*The Mysterious Mr I* (London: Ward, Lock & Co., 1937); (New York: E. P. Dutton, 1938)

*10 Hours* (New York: E. P. Dutton, 1937)

*When Thief Meets Thief* (London: Ward, Lock & Co., 1938)

*Finger! Finger!* (New York: E. P. Dutton, 1938)

*Cheung, Detective* (London: Ward, Lock & Co., 1938); (New York: E. P. Dutton, 1939)

*The Chameleon* (New York: E. P. Dutton, 1939)

*Find Actor Hart* (London: Ward, Lock & Co., 1939); (New York: E. P. Dutton, 1940)

*The Man with the Magic Eardrums* (New York: E. P. Dutton, 1939); (London: Ward, Lock & Co., 1939)

*The Crimson Box* (London: Ward, Lock & Co., 1940); (New York: E. P. Dutton, 1940)

*Cleopatra's Tears* (London: Ward, Lock & Co., 1940); (New York: E. P. Dutton, 1940)

*The Wooden Spectacles* (London: Ward, Lock & Co., 1941); (New York: E. P. Dutton, 1941)

*The Peacock Fan* (New York: E. P. Dutton, 1941); (London: Ward, Lock & Co., 1942)

*The Sharkskin Book* (New York: E. P. Dutton, 1941); (London: Ward, Lock & Co., 1948 – as *By Third Degree*)

*The Vanishing Gold Truck* (New York: E. P. Dutton, 1941); (London: Ward, Lock & Co., 1942)

*The Lavender Gripsack* (London: Ward, Lock & Co., 1941); (New York: Phoenix Press, 1944)

*The Bottle with the Green Wax Seal* (New York: E. P. Dutton, 1942)

*The Book with the Orange Leaves* (New York: E. P. Dutton, 1942); (London: Ward, Lock & Co., 1943)

*The Case of the Two Strange Ladies* (New York: Phoenix Press, 1943); (London: Ward, Lock & Co., 1945)

*The Search for X-Y-Z* (London: Ward, Lock & Co., 1943); (New York: Phoenix Press, 1945)

*The Iron Ring* (London: Ward, Lock & Co., 1944); (New York: Phoenix Press, 1945)

*The Case of the 16 Beans* (New York: Phoenix Press, 1944); (London: Ward, Lock & Co., 1945)

*The Case of the Canny Killer* (New York: Phoenix Press, 1946); (London: Ward, Lock & Co., 1946 – as *Murder in the Mills*)

*The Monocled Monster* (London: Ward, Lock & Co., 1947); (Madrid: Instituto Editorial Reus, 1955 – as *El caso Jaarvik*)

*El caso del reloj ladrador: Mezcla de novela policiaca y narración misteriosa* [*The Case of the Barking Clock*] (Madrid: Instituto Editorial Reus, 1947)

*The Case of the Barking Clock* (New York: Phoenix Press, 1947); (London: Ward, Lock & Co., 1951)

*The Case of the Transposed Legs* by Harry Stephen Keeler and Hazel Goodwin; (New York: Phoenix Press, 1948, (London: Ward, Lock & Co., 1951)

*The Case of the Jeweled Ragpicker* (New York: Phoenix Press,

1948); (London: Ward, Lock & Co., 1948 – as *The Ace-of-Spades Murder*)

*The Murdered Mathematician* (London: Ward, Lock & Co., 1949)

*The Strange Will* by Harry Stephen and Hazel Goodwin Keeler (London: Ward, Lock & Co., 1949)

*The Steeltown Strangler* (London: Ward, Lock & Co., 1950); (Madrid: Instituto Editorial Reus, 1958)

*The Murder of London Lew* (London: Ward, Lock & Co., 1952)

*Stand By – London Calling!* by Harry Stephen and Hazel Goodwin Keeler (London: Ward, Lock & Co., 1953)

*Noches de verdugo* [*Hangman's Nights*] (Madrid: Instituto Editorial Reus, 1957)

*O caso do cadáver endiabrado* [*The Case of the Crazy Corpse*] (Lisbon: Editorial Século, 1958)

*Ladrones de circos* [*The Circus Stealers*] by Harry Stephen Keeler and Hazel Goodwin Keeler (Madrid: Instituto Editorial Reus, 1958)

*El cubo carmesí* [*The Crimson Cube*] (Madrid: Instituto Editorial Reus, 1959)

*Una versión del Beowulf: Novela de aventuras y romance de amor del circo* [*A Copy of Beowulf: A Circus Novel of Romance and Adventure*] by Harry Stephen and Hazel Goodwin Keeler (Madrid: Instituto Editorial Reus, 1960)

*La misteriosa bola de marfil de Wong Shing Li* [*The Mysterious Ivory Ball of Wong Shing Li*] (Madrid: Instituto Editorial Reus, 1961)

*El caso de la mujer transparente* [*The Case of the Transparent Woman*] by Harry Stephen and Hazel Goodwin Keeler (Madrid: Instituto Editorial Reus, 1963)

*Yo maté a Lincoln a las 10:13* [*I Killed Lincoln at 10:13*] (Madrid: Instituto Editorial Reus, 1964)

*El círculo blanco* [*The White Circle*] (Madrid: Instituto Editorial Reus, 1965)

*La calle de los mil ojos* [*The Street of a Thousand Eyes*] by

Harry Stephen and Hazel Goodwin Keeler (Madrid: Instituto Editorial Reus, 1966)

*El hombre que cambió de piel* [*The Man Who Changed His Skin*] (Madrid: Instituto Editorial Reus, 1967)

# Appendix II

## Selected Poems of Amanda McKittrick Ros

### "The Lawyer" from *Poems of Puncture*

*Beneath me here in stinking clumps*
*Lies Lawyer Largebones, all in lumps;*
*A rotten mass of clockholed clay,*
*Which grown more honeycombed each day.*
*See how the rats have scratched his face?*
*Now so unlike the human race;*
*I very much regret I can't assist them in their eager 'bent'*

### "The Old Home" from *Fumes of Formation*

*Don't I see the old home over there at the base*
*Of a triangle not overcrowded with space:*
*'Twas there I first breathed on the eighth of December,*
*In the year of Our Lord the month after November.*

*I've been told it was snowy and blowy and wild*
*When I entered the home as a newly-born child,*
*There wasn't much fuss, nor was there much joy*
*For sorrow was poignant I wasn't a boy.*

*I felt quite contented as years flitted on*
*That I to the coarser sex did not belong*
*Little dreaming that ever the time would arrive*
*That of female attire I would be deprived.*

By a freak of the lustful that spreads like disease
Which demanded that females wear pants if you please,
But I stuck to the decentest style of attire
And to alter my "gender" I'll never aspire.

During that hallowed century now dead and gone
In which good Queen Victoria claimed to be born
From childhood her modesty ever was seen
Her exalted position demanded when Queen.

She set an example of decency rare,
That no English Queen before her you'd compare
Neither nude knee nor ankle, nude bosom nor arm
Dare be seen in her presence this Queen to alarm.

She believed in her sex being loving and kind,
And modesty never to march out of line
By exposing those members unrest to achieve,
Which pointed to morals immorally grave.

But sad to relate when she bade "Adieu"
To earth and its vanities tainted with "rue",
That centre of fashion, so French in its style,
Did its utmost to vilify decency's smile

And mock at these garments which proved in their day,
At a glance – who was who – and wherein gender lay,
But alas! Since the death of our great and good Queen
That attribute "Modesty"'s ne'er to be seen.

It wasn't long after till modesty grew
A thing of the past for me and for you;
Last century's fashions were blown quite aside,
The ill-advised folk of this age now deride.

The petticoat faded away as we do
In circumference it covered not one leg but two,

*Its successor exposes the arms, breasts and necks,*
*Legs, knees and thighs and too often – the —.*


## "On Visiting Westminster Abbey"

> *Holy Moses! Have a look!*
> *Flesh decayed in every nook!*
> *Some rare bits of brain lie here,*
> *Mortal loads of beef and beer,*
> *Some of whom are turned to dust,*
> *Every one bids lost to lust;*
> *Royal flesh so tinged with "blue"*
> *Undergoes the same as you . . .*
> *Famous some were—yet they died;*
> *Poets – Statesmen – Rogues beside,*
> *Kings – Queens, all of them do rot,*
> *What about them? Now – they're not!*

# Appendix III

## Selected Poems of William Topaz McGonagall

In 1882, Queen Victoria was attacked by Roderick Maclean, giving rise to this poem:

### "Attempted Assassination of the Queen"

*God prosper long our noble Queen*
*And long may she reign!*
*Maclean he tried to shoot her*
*But it was all in vain.*
*For God He turned the ball aside*
*Maclean aimed at her head;*
*And he felt very angry*
*Because he didn't shoot her dead.*

*There's a divinity that hedges a king,*
*And so it does seem,*
*And my opinion is, it has hedged*
*Our most gracious Queen.*
*Maclean must be a madman*
*Which is obvious to be seen,*
*Or else he wouldn't have tried to shoot*
*Our most beloved Queen.*

*Victoria is a good Queen*
*Which all her subjects know,*
*And for that God has protected her*

*From all her deadly foes.*
*She is noble and generous*
*Her subjects must confess;*
*There hasn't been her equal*
*Since the days of good Queen Bess.*

*Long may she be spared to roam*
*Among the bonnie Highland floral,*
*And spend many a happy day*
*In the palace of Balmoral.*
*Because she is very kind*
*To the old women there,*
*And allows them bread, tea, and sugar*
*And each one gets a share.*

*And when they know of her coming*
*Their hearts feel overjoy'd,*
*Because, in general, she finds work*
*For men that's unemploy'd.*
*And she also gives the gipsies money*
*While at Balmoral, I've been told,*
*And, mind ye, seldom silver*
*But very often gold.*

*I hope God will protect her*
*By night and by day,*
*At home and abroad*
*When she's far away.*
*May He be as a hedge around her*
*As he's been all along,*
*And let her live and die in peace*
*Is the end of my song.*

On 28 December 1879, the Tay Bridge – a 3.5 km long railway bridge in Scotland – collapsed in fierce winds just as a train was passing over it. All seventy-five passengers on board the train were killed. The event prompted McGonagall to pen his most famous poem:

## "The Tay Bridge Disaster"

*Beautiful Railway Bridge of the Silv'ry Tay!*
*Alas! I am very sorry to say*
*That ninety[1] lives have been taken away*
*On the last Sabbath day of 1879,*
*Which will be remember'd for a very long time.*

*'Twas about seven o'clock at night,*
*And the wind it blew with all its might,*
*And the rain came pouring down,*
*And the dark clouds seem'd to frown,*
*And the Demon of the air seem'd to say -*
*"I'll blow down the Bridge of Tay."*

*When the train left Edinburgh*
*The passengers' hearts were light and felt no sorrow,*
*But Boreas blew a terrific gale,*
*Which made their hearts for to quail,*
*And many of the passengers with fear did say -*
*"I hope God will send us safe across the Bridge of Tay."*

*But when the train came near to Wormit Bay,*
*Boreas he did loud and angry bray,*
*And shook the central girders of the Bridge of Tay*
*On the last Sabbath day of 1879,*
*Which will be remember'd for a very long time.*

---

1  *The death toll was in fact seventy-five, not ninety, as reported by McGonagall. Facts were not his strong point.*

*So the train sped on with all its might,*
*And Bonnie Dundee soon hove in sight,*
*And the passengers' hearts felt light,*
*Thinking they would enjoy themselves on the New Year,*
*With their friends at home they lov'd most dear,*
*And wish them all a happy New Year.*

*So the train mov'd slowly along the Bridge of Tay,*
*Until it was about midway,*
*Then the central girders with a crash gave way,*
*And down went the train and passengers into the Tay!*
*The Storm Fiend did loudly bray,*
*Because ninety lives had been taken away,*
*On the last Sabbath day of 1879,*
*Which will be remember'd for a very long time.*

*As soon as the catastrophe came to be known*
*The alarm from mouth to mouth was blown,*
*And the cry rang out all o'er the town,*
*Good Heavens! The Tay Bridge is blown down,*
*And a passenger train from Edinburgh,*
*Which fill'd all the people's hearts with sorrow,*
*And made them for to turn pale,*
*Because none of the passengers were sav'd to tell the tale*
*How the disaster happen'd on the last Sabbath day of 1879,*
*Which will be remember'd for a very long time.*

*It must have been an awful sight,*
*To witness in the dusky moonlight,*
*While the Storm Fiend did laugh, and angry did bray,*
*Along the Railway Bridge of the Silv'ry Tay,*
*Oh! Ill-fated Bridge of the Silv'ry Tay,*
*I must now conclude my lay*
*By telling the world fearlessly without the least dismay,*
*That your central girders would not have given way,*
*At least many sensible men do say,*
*Had they been supported on each side with buttresses,*

> *At least many sensible men confesses,*
> *For the stronger we our houses do build,*
> *The less chance we have of being killed.*

On 2 June 1893, HMS *Victoria* sank on naval manoeuvres (see Least Effective Attempt to Create a Good First Impression).

## "The Loss of the *Victoria*"

> *Alas! Now o'er Britannia there hangs a gloom,*
> *Because over 400 British Tars have met with a watery tomb;*
> *Who served aboard the "Victoria", the biggest ship in the*
>   *navy,*
> *And one of the finest battleships that ever sailed the sea.*
>
> *And commanded by Sir George Tyron, a noble hero bold,*
> *And his name on his tombstone should be written in letters of*
>   *gold;*
> *For he was skilful in naval tactics, few men could with him*
>   *cope,*
> *And he was considered to be the nation's hope.*
>
> *'Twas on Thursday, the twenty-second of June,*
> *And off the coast of Syria, and in the afternoon,*
> *And in the year of our Lord eighteen ninety-three,*
> *That the ill-fated "Victoria" sank to the bottom of the sea.*
>
> *The "Victoria" sank in fifteen minutes after she was rammed,*
> *In eighty fathoms of water, which was smoothly calmed;*
> *The monster war vessel capsized bottom uppermost,*
> *And, alas, lies buried in the sea totally lost.*
>
> *The "Victoria" was the flagship of the Mediterranean Fleet,*
> *And was struck by the "Camperdown" when too close they did*
>   *meet,*
> *While practising the naval and useful art of war,*
> *How to wheel and discharge their shot at the enemy afar.*

Oh, Heaven ! Methinks I see some men lying in their beds,
And some skylarking, no doubt, and not a soul dreads
The coming avalanche that was to seal their doom,
Until down came the mighty fabric of the engine room.

Then death leaped on them from all quarters in a moment,
And there were explosions of magazines and boilers rent;
And the fire and steam and water beat out all life,
But I hope the drowned ones are in the better world free from
    strife.

Sir George Tyron was on the bridge at the moment of the
    accident
With folded arms, seemingly quite content;
And seeing the vessel couldn't be saved he remained till the
    last,
And went down with the "Victoria" when all succour was
    past.

Methinks I see him on the bridge like a hero brave,
And the ship slowly sinking into the briny wave;
And when the men cried, "Save yourselves without delay,"
He told them to save themselves, he felt no dismay.

'Twas only those that leaped from the vessel at the first alarm,
Luckily so, that were saved from any harm
By leaping into the boats o'er the vessel's side,
Thanking God they had escaped as o'er the smooth water they
    did glide.

At Whitehall, London, mothers and fathers did call,
And the pitiful scene did the spectators' hearts appal;
But the most painful case was the mother of J. P. Scarlet,
Who cried, "Oh, Heaven, the loss of my son I'll never forget."

Oh, Heaven! Befriend the bereaved ones, hard is their fate,
Which I am sorry at heart to relate;

But I hope God in His goodness will provide for them,
Especially the widows, for the loss of their men.

Alas! Britannia now will mourn the loss of her naval
    commander,
Who was as brave as the great Alexander;
And to his honour be it fearlessly told,
Few men would excel this hero bold.

Alas! 'Tis sad to be buried in eighty fathoms of Syrian sea,
Which will hide the secret of the "Victoria" to all eternity;
Which causes Britannia's sorrow to be profound
For the brave British Tars that have been drowned.

## "A Tribute to Henry M. Stanley"

Welcome, thrice welcome, to the city of Dundee,
The great African explorer Henry M. Stanley,
Who went out to Africa its wild regions to explore,
And travelled o'er wild and lonely deserts, fatigued and
    footsore.
And what he and his little band suffered will never be forgot,
Especially one in particular, Major Edmund Barttelot,
Alas! the brave heroic Officer by a savage was shot,
The commandant of the rear column – O hard has been his
    lot!

O think of the noble Stanley and his gallant little band,
While travelling through gloomy forests and devastated land,
And suffering from all kinds of hardships under a burning
    sun!
But the brave hero has been successful and the victory's won.

While in Africa he saw many wonderful sights,
And was engaged, no doubt, in many savage fights,
But the wise Creator was with him all along
And now he's home again to us, I hope quite strong.

*And during his travels in Africa he made strange discoveries,*
*He discovered a dwarfish race of people called pigmies,*
*Who are said to be the original natives of Africa,*
*And when Stanley discovered them he was struck with awe.*

*One event in particular is most worthy to relate,*
*How God preserved him from a very cruel fate:*
*He and his Officers were attacked, while sailing their boat,*
*By the savages of Bumbireh, all eager to cut his throat.*
*They seized him by the hair and tugged it without fear,*
*While one of his men received a poke in the ribs with a spear;*
*But Stanley, having presence of mind, instantly contrives*
*To cry to his men, Shove off the boat, and save your lives!*

*Then savages swarmed into three canoes very close by,*
*And every bow was drawn, while they savagely did cry;*
*But the heroic Stanley quickly shot two of them dead,*
*Then the savages were baffled and immediately fled.*

*This incident is startling, but nevertheless true,*
*And in midst of all dangers the Lord brought him through*
*Then, welcome him, thrice welcome him, right cheerfully,*
*Shouting, "Long live the great African explorer, Henry M.*
     *Stanley!"*

*Therefore throw open the gates of the city of Dundee,*
*And receive him with loud cheers, three times three,*
*And sound your trumpets and beat your drums,*
*And play up, See the Conquering Hero Comes!*

## "An Address to the New Tay Bridge"

*Beautiful new railway bridge of the Silvery Tay,*
*With your strong brick piers and buttresses in so grand array,*
*And your thirteen central girders, which seem to my eye*
*Strong enough all windy storms to defy.*
*And as I gaze upon thee my heart feels gay,*

*Because thou are the greatest railway bridge of the present*
    *day,*
*And can be seen for miles away*
*From North, South, East or West of the Tay*
*On a beautiful and clear sunshiny day,*
*And ought to make the hearts of the "Mars" boys feel gay,*
*Because thine equal nowhere can be seen,*
*Only near by Dundee and the bonnie Magdalen Green.*

*Beautiful new railway bridge of the Silvery Tay,*
*With thy beautiful side-screens along your railway,*
*Which will be a great protection on a windy day,*
*So as the railway carriages won't be blown away,*
*And ought to cheer the hearts of the passengers night and day*
*As they are conveyed along thy beautiful railway,*
*And towering above the Silvery Tay,*
*Spanning the beautiful river shore to shore*
*Upwards of two miles and more,*
*Which is most beautiful to be seen*
*Near by Dundee and the bonnie Magdalen Green,*

*Thy structure to my eye seems strong and grand,*
*And the workmanship most skilfully planned;*
*And I hope the designers, Messrs Barlow and Arrol, will*
    *prosper for many a day*
*For erecting thee across the beautiful Tay.*
*And I think nobody need have the least dismay*
*To cross o'er thee by night or by day,*
*Because thy strength is visible to be seen*
*Near by Dundee and the bonnie Magdalen Green.*

*Beautiful new railway bridge of the Silvery Tay,*
*I wish you success for many a year and a day,*
*And I hope thousands of people will come from faraway,*
*Both high and low without delay,*
*From the North, South, East and West,*
*Because as a railway bridge thou art the best;*

*Thou standest unequalled to be seen*
*Near by Dundee and bonnie Magdalen Green.*

*And for beauty thou art most lovely to be seen*
*As the train crosses o'er thee with her cloud of steam;*
*And you look well, painted the colour of marone,*
*And to find thy equal there is none,*
*Which, without fear of contradiction, I venture to say,*
*Because you are the longest railway bridge of the present day*
*That now crosses o'er a tidal river stream,*
*And the most handsome to be seen*
*Near by Dundee and the bonnie Magdalen Green.*

*The New Yorkers boast about their Brooklyn Bridge,*
*But in comparison to thee it seems like a midge,*
*Because thou spannest the Silvery Tay*
*A mile and more longer I venture to say;*
*Besides the railway carriages are pulled across by a rope,*
*Therefore Brooklyn Bridge cannot with thee cope;*
*And as you have been opened on the 20th day of June,*
*I hope Her Majesty Queen Victoria will visit thee very soon,*
*Because thou art worthy of a visit from Duke, Lord or Queen,*
*And strong and securely built, which is most worthy to be seen*
*Near by Dundee and the bonnie Magdalen Green.*

## "McGonagall's Ode to the King"

*Oh! God, I thank Thee for restoring King Edward the*
    *Seventh's health again,*
*And let all his subjects throughout the Empire say Amen;*
*May God guard him by night and day,*
*At home and abroad, when he's far away.*
*May angels guard his bed at night when he lies down,*
*And may his subjects revere him, and on him do not frown;*
*May he be honoured by them at home and abroad,*
*And may he always be protected by the Eternal God.*
*My blessing on his noble form, and on his lofty head,*

May all good angels guard him while living and when dead;
And when the final hour shall come to summon him away,
May his soul be wafted to the realms of bliss I do pray.
Long may he reign, happy and serene,
Also his Queen most beautiful to be seen;
And may God guard his family by night and day,
That they may tread in the paths of virtue and not go astray.
May God prosper King Edward the Seventh wherever he goes,
May he always reign victorious over his foes;
Long may he be spared to wear the British Crown,
And may God be as a hedge around him at night when be lies
  down;
May God inspire him with wisdom, and long may he reign
As Emperor of India and King Edward the VII.
Amen.


## "The Death of Prince Leopold"

Alas! noble Prince Leopold, he is dead!
Who often has his lustre shed:
Especially by singing for the benefit of Esher School,
Which proves he was a wise prince, and no conceited fool.
Methinks I see him on the platform singing the Sands o' Dee,
The generous-hearted Leopold, the good and the free,
Who was manly in his actions, and beloved by his mother;
And in all the family she hasn't got such another.
He was of a delicate constitution all his life,
And he was his mother's favourite, and very kind to his wife,
And he had also a particular liking for his child,
And in his behaviour he was very mild.
Oh! noble-hearted Leopold, most beautiful to see,
Who was wont to fill your audience's hearts with glee,
With your charming songs, and lectures against strong drink:
Britain had nothing else to fear, as far as you could think
A wise prince you were, and well worthy of the name,
And to write in praise of thee I cannot refrain;
Because you were ever ready to defend that which is right,

*Both pleasing and righteous in God's eye-sight.*
*And for the loss of such a prince the people will mourn,*
*But, alas! unto them he can never more return,*
*Because sorrow never could revive the dead again,*
*Therefore to weep for him is all in vain.*
*'Twas on Saturday the 12th of April, in the year 1884,*
*He was buried in the royal vault, never to rise more*
*Until the great and fearful judgment-day,*
*When the last trump shall sound to summon him away.*
*When the Duchess of Albany arrived she drove through the*
    *Royal Arch,*
*A little before the Seaforth Highlanders set out on the funeral*
    *march;*
*And she was received with every sympathetic respect,*
*Which none of the people present seem'd to neglect.*
*Then she entered the memorial chapel and stayed a short time,*
*And as she viewed her husband's remains it was really*
    *sublime,*
*While her tears fell fast on the coffin lid without delay,*
*Then she took one last fond look, and hurried away.*
*At half-past ten o'clock the Seaforth Highlanders did appear,*
*And every man in the detachment his medals did wear;*
*And they carried their side-arms by their side,*
*With mournful looks, but full of love and pride.*
*Then came the Coldstream Guards headed by their band,*
*Which made the scene appear imposing and grand;*
*Then the musicians drew up in front of the guardroom*
*And waited patiently to see the prince laid in the royal tomb.*
*First in the procession were the servants of His late Royal*
    *Highness,*
*And next came the servants of the Queen in deep mourning*
    *dress,*
*And the gentlemen of his household in deep distress,*
*Also General Du Pla, who accompanied the remains from*
    *Cannes.*
*The coffin was borne by eight Highlanders of his own*
    *regiment,*

*And the fellows seemed to be rather discontent*
*For the loss of the prince they loved most dear,*
*While adown their cheeks stole many a silent tear*
*Then behind the corpse came the Prince of Wales in field*
    *marshal uniform,*
*Looking very pale, dejected, careworn, and forlorn;*
*Then followed great magnates, all dressed in uniform,*
*And last, but not least, the noble Marquis of Lorne.*
*The scene in George's Chapel was most magnificent to behold,*
*The banners of the knights of the garter embroidered with gold;*
*Then again it was most touching and lovely to see*
*The Seaforth Highlanders' inscription to the Prince's memory:*
*It was wrought in violets, upon a background of white flowers,*
*And as they gazed upon it their tears fell in showers;*
*But the whole assembly were hushed when Her Majesty did*
    *appear,*
*Attired in her deepest mourning, and from her eye there fell a*
    *tear.*
*Her Majesty was unable to stand long, she was overcome with*
    *grief,*
*And when the Highlanders lowered the coffin into the tomb she*
    *felt relief;*
*Then the ceremony closed with singing "Lead, Kindly Light",*
*Then the Queen withdrew in haste from the mournful sight.*
*Then the Seaforth Highlanders' band played "Lochaber No*
    *More",*
*While the brave soldiers' hearts felt depressed and sore;*
*And as homeward they marched they let fall many a tear*
*For the loss of the virtuous Prince Leopold they loved so dear.*

# Appendix IV

## The Eye of Argon by Jim Theis

### Chapter One

The weather-beaten trail wound ahead into the dust-racked climes of the barren land which dominates large portions of the Norgolian empire. Age-worn hoof prints smothered by the sifting sands of time shone dully against the dust-splattered crust of Earth. The tireless Sun cast its parching rays of incandescence from overhead, half way through its daily revolution. Small rodents scampered about, occupying themselves in the daily accomplishments of their dismal lives. Dust sprayed over three heaving mounts in blinding clouds, while they bore the burdonsome cargoes of their struggling overseers.

"Prepare to embrace your creators in the Stygian haunts of hell, barbarian," gasped the first soldier.

"Only after you have kissed the fleeting stead of death, wretch!" returned Grignr.

A sweeping blade of flashing steel riveted from the massive barbarian's hide enamelled shield as his rippling right arm thrust forth, sending a steel-shod blade to the hilt into the soldier's vital organs. The disembowelled mercenary crumpled from his saddle and sank to the clouded sward, sprinkling the parched dust with crimson droplets of escaping life fluid.

The enthused barbarian swivelled about, his shock of fiery

red hair tossing robustly in the humid air currents as he faced the attack of the defeated soldier's fellow in arms.

"Damn you, barbarian," shrieked the soldier as he observed his comrade in death.

A gleaming scimitar smote a heavy blow against the renegade's spiked helmet, bringing a heavy cloud over the Ecordian's misting brain. Shaking off the effects of the pounding blow to his head, Grignr brought down his scarlet-streaked edge against the soldier's crudely forged hauberk, clanging harmlessly to the left side of his opponent. The soldier's stead whinnied as he directed the horse back from the driving blade of the barbarian. Grignr leashed his mount forward as the hoarsely piercing battle cry of his wilderness-bred race resounded from his grinding lungs. A twirling blade bounced harmlessly from the mighty thief's buckler as his rolling right arm cleft upward, sending a foot of blinding steel ripping through the Simarian's exposed gullet. A gasping gurgle from the soldier's writhing mouth as he tumbled to the golden sand at his feet, and wormed agonizingly in his death bed.

Grignr's emerald green orbs glared lustfully at the wallowing soldier struggling before his chestnut-swirled mount. His scowling voice reverberated over the dying form in a tone of mocking mirth. "You city bred dogs should learn not to antagonize your betters." Reining his weary mount ahead, Grignr resumed his journey to the Noregolian city of Gorzam, hoping to discover wine, women and adventure to boil the wild blood coarsing through his savage veins.

The trek to Gorzom was forced upon Grignr when the soldiers of Crin were leashed upon him by a faithless concubine he had wooed. His scandalous activities throughout the Simarian city had unleashed throngs of havoc and uproar among its refined patricians, leading them to tack a heavy reward over his head.

He had barely managed to escape through the back entrance of the inn he had been guzzling in, as a squad of soldiers tounced upon him. After spilling a spout of blood from the leader of the mercenaries as he dismembered one of the officer's arms, he retreated to his mount to make his way towards Gorzom, rumoured to contain hoards of plunder, and many young wenches for any man who has the backbone to wrest them away.

# Further Reading

Anthony Brandt, *The Man Who Ate His Boots: Sir John Franklin and the Tragic History of the Northwest Passage* (2011)

Bill Bryson, *A Short History of Nearly Everything* (2004)

John Carter, *Sex and Rockets: The Occult World of Jack Parsons* (2005)

R. M. Crawford, *Australia: A Biography of a Nation* (2001)

Graeme Donals, *Loose Cannons: 101 Things They Never Told You About Military History* (2009)

Tim Flannery, *The Explorers: Stories of Discovery and Adventure from the Australian Frontier* (2000)

Fergus Fleming, *Barrow's Boys* (1998)

Cris Freddi, *The Guinness Book of Sporting Blunders* (1994)

Ken Geiger, *Frozen in Time: The Fate of the Franklin Expedition* (2004)

David Grann, *The Lost City of Z: A Legendary British Explorer's Deadly Quest to Uncover the Secrets of the Amazon* (2010)

John Gribben, *Fitzroy: The Remarkable Story of Darwin's Captain and the Invention of the Weather Forecast* (2003)

Robert Hughes, *The Fatal Shore* (2003)

Roland Huntford, *Scott and Amundsen: The Last Place on Earth* (2000)

Lisa Jardine, *The Curious Life of Robert Hooke: The Man who Measured London* (2004)

Frank T. Kryza, *The Race for Timbuktu: In Search of Africa's City of Gold* (2006)

Ken McGoogan, *Fatal Passage* (2002)

David Miller, *Athens to Athens: The Official History of the Olympic Games and the IOC, 1896–2004* (2004)

Sarah Murgatroyd, *The Dig Tree: The Extraordinary Story of the Ill-fated Burke and Wills 1860 Expedition* (2003)

Paul O'Keeffe, *A Genius for Failure: The Life of Benjamin Robert Haydon* (2009)

Nick Page, *In Search of the World's Worst Writers* (2000)

Geoffrey Regan, *The Guinness Book of Military Blunders* (1991)

Geoffrey Regan, *The Guinness Book of Naval Blunders* (1997)

Doron Swade, *The Cogwheel Brain* (2001)

Christine Taylor-Butler, *Explorers of North America* (2008)

Michael White & John Gribbin, *Darwin: A Life in Science* (2009)

Michael White, *Isaac Newton: The Last Sorcerer* (1998)

Glyn Williams, *Voyages of Delusion: The Search for the North West Passage in the Age of Reason* (2010)

Andrea Wulf, *The Brother Gardeners: Botany, Empire and the Birth of an Obsession* (2009)

R. M. Youngson and Ian Schott, *Medical Blunders* (1996)